The Gender Line

Negrophobia and Reasonable Racism:
The Hidden Costs of Being Black in America
JODY DAVID ARMOUR

Black and Brown in America:
The Case for Cooperation
BILL PIATT

Black Rage Confronts the Law
PAUL HARRIS

Selling Words:
Free Speech in a Commercial Culture
R. GEORGE WRIGHT

The Color of Crime: Racial Hoaxes, White Fear,
Black Protectionism, Police Harassment, and Other Macroaggressions
KATHERYN K. RUSSELL

The Smart Culture:
Society, Intelligence, and Law
ROBERT L. HAYMAN, JR.

Was Blind, but Now I See:
White Race Consciousness and the Law
BARBARA J. FLAGG

American Law in the Age of Hypercapitalism:
The Worker, the Family, and the State
RUTH COLKER

The Gender Line:
Men, Women, and the Law
NANCY LEVIT

The Gender Line

Men, Women, and the Law

Nancy Levit

NEW YORK UNIVERSITY PRESS

New York and London

NEW YORK UNIVERSITY PRESS
New York and London

The University of California at Los Angeles Law Review graciously gave
permission to adapt my article, *Feminism for Men: Legal Ideology and the
Construction of Maleness*, that first appeared at 43 UCLA L. Rev. 1037
(1996), for this book.

Robert Bly kindly granted copyright permission to reprint in Chapter 6
an excerpt of the poem, "For My Son Noah, Ten Years Old," from his book,
Selected Poems (1986).

Library of Congress Cataloging-in-Publication Data
Levit, Nancy.
The gender line : men, women, and the law / Nancy Levit.
p.   cm. — (Critical America)
Includes index.
ISBN 0-8147-5121-0
Contents: Gender separatism — How courts enforce gender separatism —
Making men : the socio-legal construct of masculinity — The "f" word :
feminism and its detractors — Feminist legal theory and the treatment of
men — Reconstructing images of gender in theory — Remaking gender in
practice : looking forward.
1. Men—Legal status, laws, etc.—United States. 2. Women—Legal status,
laws, etc.—United States. 3. Sex role—United States. 4. Sex and law—
United States. 5. Sex discrimination in justice administration—Law and
legislation—United States. 6. Feminist jurisprudence—United States.
7. Feminist theory—United States.
I. Title. II. Series.
KF475.L48   1998
305.3—DC21   97-45398
                                 CIP

New York University Press books are printed on acid-free paper,
and their binding materials are chosen for strength and durability.

Manufactured in the United States of America

10   9   8   7   6   5   4   3   2   1

Contents

Acknowledgments

Bob Hayman's contributions and influence were immeasurable, and I thank him for the intellectual partnership.

My colleagues and friends David Achtenberg, Bob Chang, Julie Cheslik, Bob Downs, Barbara Glesner-Fines, Kris Kobach, Doug Linder, Joan Mahoney, Sam Marcosson, Michael Mello, Doris Mendel, Ed Richards, Ellen Suni, and Ray Warner were extraordinarily generous with their time, advice, and comments about various ideas in the book. Rob Verchick, in particular, tolerated frequent work interruptions with considerable good humor and supplied very helpful ideas.

I wish to thank Toby Egan, Todd Jacobs, Jolie Justus, Amy Maloney, Eric Moss, and Shannon O'Brien for their superb research assistance. Debra Banister and Brooks Best provided efficient and precise administrative support.

I am grateful to Richard Delgado and Jean Stefancic for the inspiration of their work, as well as their endless patience and sheer brilliance in editing successive drafts of chapters, and to my editor, Niko Pfund, who provoked, cheered, and offered excellent advice.

This book would not have been possible without the love, support, and encouragement of Tim Geary, Aaron Geary, and Dylan Geary. It is dedicated to Marty Levit, for fathering, mothering, and living the ideals of a pro-feminist man before there were words to describe them.

1

Introduction

Our first child, Aaron, loves books and likes to draw, cook, and play any game involving a ball.

Our second child, Dylan, is also a sports fanatic. When Dylan entered toddlerhood we stationed two Little Tykes basketball goals at opposite ends of the living room so that we could play "full court."

People meeting our second child are often surprised to find out that Dylan is a girl.

Names have a gender.

When Dylan wears her brother's hand-me-down overalls, strangers are uncomfortable with the gender bending. There seem to be expectations of fair advertising with respect to one of society's most visible means of classification.

Clothes have a gender.

Among the gifts Dylan received for her second birthday are mini-cooking utensils, a vacuum cleaner that lights up as it sweeps the floor, and a Cabbage Patch doll that came with an adoption certificate identifying her as Belinda Doreen. No one outside the family gave her cars or trucks or tools.

Toys have a gender.

One night Aaron and Dylan were helping prepare dinner. Dylan had taken over Aaron's old job of setting the table, while Aaron had graduated to substantive food preparation and was pouring milk. Dylan carefully put two spoons at one place. The next place setting was a neatly positioned fork and knife. I complimented her on the third effort: "That's right, sweetie. One knife, one fork, and one spoon for each person."

"Good girl!" I added. It's a phrase that trips pretty easily off the tongue. But it's one that I never seem to use when she's fielding grounders or shooting hoops.

Parents reinforce gender daily. Unthinkingly. Unnecessarily. Even when they know better.

We still live in a world in which the sexes are sharply segregated: early in life, in names, clothing, and possessions; later, in occupations, civic associations, social groupings, and domestic roles. This gender separation is so pervasive it is almost invisible. Gender is constructed in everyday social routines. Traditional gender practices are embedded in social institutions, where they guide what we think proper about the relationship of sex and gender.

People generally believe that men and women are fundamentally different in interests, inclinations, and abilities. We accept that boys excel at math, girls at verbal skills, that women exhibit nurturing behaviors while men are less capable in that realm. The images and messages sent through the cultural portrayal of gender end up limiting the visions and options of boys and girls.

The first aim of this book is to expose the ways gendered behaviors are carefully cultivated. Chapter 2 traces the pink and blue tracking that begins in infancy. Beginning with the first few moments and months of life, countless social practices reinforce gender differences and keep the sexes separate: toys, sports, songs, books, advertisements, fashions, schooling, and peer and parental habits, expectations, and pressures. Different gendering of the sexes occurs within the spheres of home and school, media, church, and work. It takes place in everyday language. Girls and boys grow up to be women and men who live in different cultures of gender.

One persistent theme resonates throughout these spheres of socialization. Masculinity is tied to the strict separation of the genders and the avoidance of characteristics and behaviors perceived as feminine. Boys are trained to distance themselves from girls and not to identify with women: "In the hierarchical and rigorously competitive society of other boys, one categorical imperative outranks all others: don't be a girl."[1]

The social segregation of the sexes is often justified by the idea that inherent biological differences create the different cultural worlds that men and women inhabit. Chapter 2 reviews the empirical evidence regarding the biological basis of sex differences. Cumulatively, the physical, neurophysiological, and psychological evidence, as well as measures of academic performance and achievement, shows few purely biological sex differences. Given these findings, the question is how to explain the popular perceptions of extensive differences between the sexes?

Differences in mental abilities and emotional responses of men and women are far more intriguing than similarities. People are more interested in reading about differences. *Men Are from Mars, Women Are from Venus* is a best-seller; it has a great deal more pizzazz than would a book about gender similarities, entitled perhaps *Men and Women Are from Earth*. An emphasis on the politics of difference rather than sameness encourages attention to differences. Differences are emphasized in many ways, from research biases to media reporting to popular interpretations of scientific research.

Media reports on gender highlight differences, putting the spotlight on ones that are found. For political reasons, researchers too may be more interested in exploring gender differences than similarities, if only because research results showing differences command publication opportunities. This information is then received by the public in accordance with preexisting stereotypes about sex role differences. Finally, in popular opinion, tendencies and probabilities may be remembered simply as differences, with the visible correlations between gender and behavior converted into "obvious" causal relations. Politicized research and reporting thus combine with resilient stereotypes and social practices to create cultural feedback loops that replay conventional images of gender.

To the extent that they are mistaken or exaggerated, these beliefs about the biological bases of gender have frightening consequences. History is replete with examples of the use of biological characteristics to classify certain groups not just as different but as cognitively or socially inferior. Even to the extent that they are accurate—sex differences may have biological or cultural bases, and often some of both—the fact of sex differences is relatively uninteresting. The cultural construction—the *significance* that we give to those differences that do exist—is what, in Martha Minow's words, "makes all the difference."[2]

Law collaborates with other institutions in the creation and maintenance of gender differences, constructing and legitimizing both the separation of the sexes and the conception of gender in naturalistic terms. In chapter 3 we see that sex in law is bipolar. Assumptions about the importance of biological distinctions between males and females have driven legal theory. The idea of a natural order is embedded in legal analysis, making gender differences seem natural and inevitable. Constitutional doctrine, for example, perpetuates the idea that gender is a biological phenomenon by looking for "real" or "immutable" differences.

The images of gender contained in Supreme Court and lower federal court decisions show that "separate but equal" remains very much alive in constitutional gender cases. The decisions in the Citadel and Virginia Military Institute (VMI) cases, which concerned women seeking admission to the two remaining male-only public military colleges, illustrate the point.

The analysis in this chapter will not concentrate on the schools' insistent rejection of women, their attempts to rationalize these all-male preserves as providing a "diversity" of educational experiences, or, in Virginia's case, the proposed construction of a parallel, all-female military academy, woefully underfunded, with an expected enrollment of twenty-five students and no barracks life, uniforms, or military training (which the Supreme Court later called a "pale shadow" of VMI). Instead, the focus will be on what the images of gender tacitly accepted by the lower federal courts and some members of the Supreme Court say about the constitutional construction of gender and the significance of those legal images in the minds, hearts, and behaviors of men and women.

In the VMI litigation, the trial court accepted, and the appellate court approved, the idea that the creation of good "citizen-soldiers" required the exclusion of women. Despite the wealth of empirical evidence to the contrary, the lower courts adopted the school's position that single-sex education was beneficial for men. Not only was masculinity shaped by the compulsory separation of men from women, but "adversative training"—which subjected freshmen (called "rats") to rigorous physical exercise, spartan barracks living, a complete lack of privacy, random stresses, unrelenting control of daily life, and constant harassment—was deemed essential to character formation. Boys, through this process that induced terror-bonding, endurance of pain, and disconnection from their feelings, would become men and soldiers. The images of gender in the Citadel and VMI litigation are not the anachronisms they seem, but instead represent the conventional constructions of masculinity that are still embodied in our dominant social and legal traditions. Stereotypes about women are becoming more visible to us, but stereotypes about men and implicit discrimination against men, the unthinking acceptance of traditional expectations of males, remain largely imperceptible because we have not been looking for them.

In many other areas, courts have staunchly supported the rigid separation of the sexes. We will look at cases dealing with defiance of dress and grooming codes in schools and employment situations, objections to Ladies' Night and other practices of gender-based pricing at dry cleaners, gas stations, and hair salons, and challenges to sex-segregated voluntary associations, such as the Jaycees, Rotary, Elks, and Boy Scouts. In controlling cross-dressing, condoning gender separatism, and promoting traditional images of the sexes, courts endorse the gender line and help keep it firmly in place.

*

The second objective of this book, an inquiry that begins in chapter 3 and continues in chapter 4, is to explore the ways men are harmed by gender stereotypes. These chapters apply insights from feminist thought to situations in which gender role stereotypes operate to the detriment of men. Chapter 3 looks at two recent, celebrated Supreme Court decisions, the VMI case and another concerning a manufacturer's "fetal protection policy" that excluded fertile women, but not fertile men, from positions threatening hazardous lead exposure. In each of these cases, the Court disregarded actual physical harms to men and, at a deeper level, reinforced separation from women and cultural expectations that men defy risks and suffer harms in stoic silence.

Chapter 4 considers the ways legal constructs and methods of analysis have helped to shape masculinity. Maleness has been constructed in a number of ways by statutes, judicial decisions, and legal reasoning. One component of male aggression has been legal doctrines that shape concepts of personhood by dictating who society's criminals and warriors are. The image of masculinity is also formed by legal responses to areas in which men suffer injuries. Laws preventing male plaintiffs from suing for same-sex sexual harassment, as well as analysts' lack of interest in male rape and spousal battery of men, contribute to a climate in which men are taught to suffer in silence. In the areas of parental leave and child custody, men are socially and legally excluded from caring and nurturing roles.

Various legal doctrines thus send distinct messages about what it means to be male. But this cumulative ideology of masculinity—the package of cultural myths and symbols, constructed in part by law, that dictates appropriate male behavior—is underexplored. Some of the damaging stereotypes and harms suffered by men have been invisible to public consciousness because they are particular to men, while the feminist project has so clearly concentrated on women.

The remaining chapters explore the relations between feminism and men. Part of the focus of feminist legal theory needs to shift. The project of cataloging the omission of men from feminist theory should not be seen as an attempt to diminish the centuries of horrors experienced by women. The argument is that a key part of the problem remains to be explored. In what ways have men systematically been harmed by gender stereotypes? How does this harm redound to the disadvantage of women and society generally?

It may seem odd to suggest that feminist theory has overlooked men. In varying ways, liberal feminism, difference theory, dominance theory, and postmodern feminism have analyzed, objectified, vilified, and deconstructed men as a population, maleness as a gender and constellation of role expectations and typical behaviors, and men as historical crafters of doctrine, theory, and language. Yet in several important respects, men have been largely omitted from feminism, except for their crucial role as culprits.

Feminist legal theorists have paid mild attention to whether men could embrace feminist objectives—the "Can men be feminists?" question. This issue is treated as a relatively unimportant one, usually relegated to footnotes.[3] Legal literature has given relatively modest and incidental attention to how a wide variety of gender role stereotypes harm men, and how legal constructs perpetuate these stereotypes.[4] The injurious effect gender role stereotypes have on men is typically subsidiary to the main focus of feminist legal literature, documenting patterns of subordination of women.

Theorists in disciplines other than law have demonstrated significantly more interest in constructs of masculinity.[5] Perhaps most importantly, though, men have been omitted as participants in the reconstructive project. This may have been a necessary omission during the formative years of the second wave of feminism, or at least it seemed so at the time, but is it one that has outlived its usefulness? Australian sociologist R. W. Connell frames the dilemma:

> Men who do undertake action in support of feminism are not in for an easy ride. They are likely to be met with antagonism and derision from other men, picturing them as eunuchs, queers or sell-outs to "political correctness." They will not necessarily get warm support from feminists—some of whom are deeply suspicious of all men, most of whom are wary of men's power, and all of whom make a primary commitment to solidarity with women.[6]

Chapter 5 unpacks the popular image of feminism: it examines the reasons feminism has acquired such a bad name. In doing so, it looks at those strands of the feminist movement that have alienated potential supporters (racial exclusivity, the failure to include men, a politics of anger, and an uneasy alliance between feminism and lesbianism), questions the necessity of the factionalism within feminism, and points to the need for coalition-building (intergenerational, international, and inter-issue) among feminists.

Intrafeminist controversy has the power to spark useful debate, encourage thoughtful reflection, and mobilize political action. In its recent guises, it has done little of that. The chapter touches on the schisms and personal hostilities of pop culture feminists who adopt splashy labels (such as "gender feminism" and "victim feminism") and hurl insults at one another. The chapter also reviews the deeper theoretical battles in which feminists have fractured over issues such as pregnancy accommodation, pornography, and abortion. It is important to situate events in their historically appropriate time frame. This requires recognition that the exclusionary rhetoric a few fringe feminist thinkers mouthed several decades ago may be replayed misleadingly as representative of modern feminism.

While chapter 5 will explore the ways some feminists have alienated potential supporters and discouraged adherents, it is intended as a sympathetic critique, since many, if not most, misunderstandings of feminism are caused by its opponents, not its supporters. This chapter considers public opinion surveys about feminism and explores the construction of the popular ideology of feminism. How did we arrive at a place where "feminist" translates into "feminazi" in the popular mind, where the label itself is dangerous, as Marc Lepine proved when he burst into Montreal University's engineering school in 1989 armed with a semiautomatic rifle and slaughtered fourteen women whom he called "a bunch of feminists"?

Some of the misunderstandings come from an unskilled or unsympathetic treatment of feminist issues by reporters. Most of the attacks on feminism do not originate from objective, unbiased sources, but from people who have deep-seated reasons to try to undermine it. The images and labels attached to feminism are used as forms of denigration by people who have a vested interest in continuing the subjugation of women. The label "feminism" feels accusatory because it is used as an accusation of a panoply of evils. It is a technique of silencing that feminists are likely to understand, whether they accept the label or not. The incessant warring among feminist camps and media glee over these battles accentuate the lack of popular acceptance of feminism. With respect to many specific events and ideas in the feminist story, the cultural reactions to them often define the phenomena in the popular mind. I thus try to separate some of the strands of academic feminism from their popular culture incarnations. The various incarnations of feminism are not fundamentally misguided, but they are plagued by unnecessary factionalism and unwarranted bad publicity.

The third purpose of this book is to suggest that feminist legal theory needs to turn its attention to issues of relational justice: avoiding gender role stereotyping in both directions. The legal academy has not been much interested in theorizing about majority group masculinities. Racial and sexual outsiders were rightly concerned with their exclusion from dialogue, and with subordination based on ethnicity, skin color, or sexual orientation. Gays and scholars of color raised their voices collectively in queer theory and critical race theory. For feminist scholars, the urgencies lay elsewhere.

Chapter 6 evaluates how the different strands of feminist legal theory have approached men. Equal treatment theorists view men as objects of analysis, secondary to their principal project of attaining equal rights for women. Cultural feminists or difference theorists treat men as "other": in highlighting differences between men and women, some cultural feminists have celebrated women's differences to the exclusion of men. Radical feminists or dominance theorists see men as oppressors, literally the bad guys. Postmodern feminist theories have, for the most part, simply omitted men.

In significant part, this inattention to men was understandable, a necessary stage. In the early years, feminist theory may have needed to be exclusionary to carve out its own space. But in law and even in the social sciences, gender colonization persists: just as women's studies are often divorced from theories about masculinity, legal theory has devoted little attention to the situations of men.

Feminism has cast men principally as malefactors or dupes, and has not explored the manner in which gender role stereotypes harm men or the ways legal decisions perpetuate that stereotyping. Throughout the women's movement, one side of the picture has remained in the shadows—the ways patriarchy affects men. Feminists want those embracing patriarchy, a significant portion of whom are men, to change. To that end, we need to concentrate on the situations of men.

Maleness is both a privileged and victimized status. Men hold the balance of power in America. Men—particularly white, heterosexual, nondisabled men—generally have superior economic and political standing. Comparing the average wages of all working men and women, the Bureau of Labor Statistics found that for every dollar earned by white men, white women earn 75 cents, black women 63 cents, and Latina women 56 cents.[7] Women are generally in the workforce a shorter amount of time and thus accrue lower pension and Social Security benefits. After studying work patterns and wage differentials, Elizabeth Toth concluded that "during a 40-year career, a woman will lose $1 million on gender alone."[8] In 1995 the Federal Glass Ceiling Commission reported that in Fortune 1500 companies, between 95 and 97 percent of senior managerial positions were held by men.[9] In 1997 women account for only nine of the one hundred U.S. senators, two of the country's fifty governors, and 12 percent of U.S. congressional representatives, numbers almost double those five years previously. The numbers at the state level are slightly more encouraging, although only 21 percent of state legislators are women.[10]

As a culture, we have gone from the 1950s single-earner households (kept in place with rigid stereotypes and lots of sexism) to the 1990s with many single-parent households or households in which both parents work outside the home. At the same time, we have bid up the prices of homes, cars, and colleges, and the dual-career household is now entrenched. We cannot and would not want to go back to the nostalgia of the 1950s. We don't want to socially, and can't economically. What happens now is that women have the worst of both worlds: full-time jobs both inside and outside the home. To the extent that things get done domestically, stereotypes usually persist, unless they have been renegotiated on the individual level. The default rule in society is that women do the indoor domestic work and child care, while men haul out the garbage, shovel the snow, and take care of cars and yards.

But men have the worst of both worlds as well. The past decade has witnessed some transition away from historical roles of masculinity; yet cultural expectations of men remain tied to traditional definitions. Men are still expected to be the family's breadwinners and society's risk-takers. They are still judged according to a set of stereotypically masculine expectations, including rugged individualism, independence, competitiveness, physical prowess, and emotional toughness. Men are trained to be emotionally restricted and reluctant to seek help. Research shows that until about six months of age, baby boys are "more emotionally reactive and expressive" than baby girls, exhibiting more voluble crying and greater anxiety, and shedding more tears.[11] Parents teach boys to suppress these feelings by explicitly or subtly steering them away from exhibiting vulnerable emotions.

Perhaps most important, masculinity continues to be constructed in opposition to femininity: "A man should avoid the stigma of anything feminine, especially emotions that make him appear vulnerable."[12] What it means to be male is created by the distancing of boys from female things. This was, and still is, one of patriarchy's chief methods of reproduction. Most religions have a masculinized idea of males (but not females) as stewards, icons, and leaders. Male cultural archetypes of the 1950s, like John Wayne and Gary Cooper, did not mix with women, and the influence of their images persists today. This vision was promoted by psychoanalytic theory, which tied male identity formation to separation from domineering mothers. Sex-segregated institutions historically were used to keep females out of influential inner circles—and to shape the consciousness of developing males. In many arenas, boys were, and still are, encouraged to engage in activities that are defined, at least in part, by the absence of women: the Boy Scouts, organized sports, fraternities, the military.

In some ways, male power is diminishing and being challenged. Despite the concentrations of women in lower-wage clerical and service jobs and underrepresentations of women in managerial, professional, and technical occupations, women constitute 46 percent of the workforce. In the two decades between 1970 and 1990, the percentage of female physicians doubled from 8 to 17; during roughly the same period, the proportion of female lawyers and judges more than tripled, from 6 percent to 23 percent. In cities with populations over 30,000 the percentage of women mayors increased from 5 (35 mayors) in 1975 to 18 (177 mayors) in 1995.[13] Among dual-earner couples, 48 percent of women provide half or more of the family's income.[14] "[M]ore women than men have been enrolled in college every year since 1979, with commensurate growth in their economic clout."[15] Society is beginning to take notice of men's health and social disadvantages. Men's life expectancy (72 years, compared to 78.8 for women), suicide rates (four times those of women), as well as consumption of alcohol and cigarettes are telling of the relative life stresses.[16] A homicide victim is 400 percent more likely to be male.[17]

Power dynamics within relationships are changing in more ways than simply an increase in female breadwinners. The women's movement represents a systematic challenge to entrenched male political, social, and economic domination. Some men have become increasingly resentful of and threatened by women's political empowerment. Betty Friedan speaks of the "'angry white male' backlash," significant among college-educated white men, who "have been the real targets of job downsizing. Their frustration is building—and talk-radio hosts, the religious right and the new leaders in Congress are manipulating that economic insecurity into rage against women and minorities. Increased violence against women, the political war on welfare mothers and children, and the new attack on affirmative action may be symptoms of that rage."[18]

The crisis of male identity stems not only from men's loss of privileged status, but also from mixed social messages about what it means to be a good man. "Guys are in trouble these days," Garrison Keillor writes in *The Book of Guys*. "Years ago, manhood was an opportunity for achievement and now it's just a problem to overcome." Men worry that their role as breadwinner is undermined by social and economic forces and that their role as father will be limited to that of "sperm donor." Feminism demonstrated that many of the traditional images of masculinity, images on which most men were raised, were flawed. But the new images include warring expectations of "an almost feminine softness and . . . a traditionally masculine toughness."[19]

Not surprisingly, men are confused. What are they supposed to do and how can they possibly do it? Hold doors for women? Work seventy-hour weeks and still be available for child care? Be emotionally open and communicate their inner feelings, risking subtle forms of public censure for doing so? Psychologists Ronald Levant and William Pollack explain the turbulence: "These new pressures—to commit to relationships, to communicate one's innermost feelings, to nurture children, to share in housework, to integrate sexuality with love, and to curb aggression and violence—have shaken traditional masculinity ideology."[20] These conflicting role demands will continue as long as social segregation of the sexes and traditional constructs of masculinity influence the emotional training of men.

Chapters 7 and 8 discuss ways of reconstructing images of gender, in theory and in practice. On the theoretical level, we need to turn feminist attention to the situations of men and masculinity. I argue that feminism is ready to take the next step and concentrate on the ways social institutions, including law, can reshape traditional masculinity, invite men into the discourse, and include men as political allies.

Some feminists may resist integration: Do we really need men to validate feminist theory? Must we do *everything*—the housework, the child care, and now their political theorizing—for them? Or consider the much simpler claim, made by Christine Littleton, that feminism is about women: "I am not making a claim that it is 'wrong' to try to help anyone (although, if we are going to spend our energy helping men, it might make sense to help nonprivileged men before privileged ones). The claim is merely that, even though many feminists do sincerely care about men, caring about men is not what feminism is about."[21] Even those writing to urge feminists toward inclusivity imply that feminism is exclusive to women. Naomi Wolf, for example, writes, "On one level all women should be able to own the word 'feminism' as describing a theory of self-worth, and the worth of other women. On this level saying, 'I am a feminist,' should be like saying, 'I am a human being.'"[22]

Feminists have raised a number of arguments against being more inclusive of men. The powerful rhetoric of the feminist movement was often inseparable from anger, much of it targeted at men. Some concede that men may be oppressed too, but point out that the oppression is of their making, and thus, for these writers, male oppression can be readily dismissed. For others, the resource issue is most important: with limited time and personal resources, feminism should focus on the most egregious wrongs, and those, they argue, are harms to women.

At the turn of the twenty-first century, feminism needs to find a new rhetoric, explore new subjects, and begin a new dialogue that affirmatively includes men. It is not simply that feminist discourse can be powerful without being a conversation of exclusion, but that for feminist objectives to become widely accepted, they must become more all-encompassing. I argue that it is not only possible for men to become feminists, but imperative that they do. Social movements do not work if they are wedded to theoretical frameworks that omit necessary people or issues. It is difficult to imagine the triumph of a theory that neglects half of the human race.

Laws and legal theory need to remove barriers for men and encourage possibilities. The feminist practices that enabled people to reflect on the situations of women should also make possible compassionate yet critical assessments of the situations of men. These include recognizing men's experiences, acknowledging intersectional oppressions (the confluences of masculinities, race, and sexual orientation), minimizing the significance of the biological construct, and encouraging the crossing of traditional gender lines.

This book is about legal ideology, but it is not a conventional jurisprudence or legal philosophy book, because the conversation it contemplates can neither begin nor end with law. While laws send messages—statutes and decisions are powerful symbols of appropriate social relations—many of the most important messages about gender are already in place by the time issues arise in legal cases. Those messages are sent at a much earlier point in time through social relations, families, schools, churches, and the media. Professor Mark Fajer succinctly explains why the social learning must begin early: "To be blunt, we can hardly expect that boys who learn that their peers who cry or play with dolls are sissies and faggots will grow into men interested in displaying sensitivity or in taking on child-care responsibilities."[23] The final chapter thus suggests ways men and women can reconstruct a social world in which traditional gender roles diminish in importance.

Transformations in gender roles will not occur in any given generation. Changes in people's roles and expectations come only slowly and over time. So the possibilities offered in chapter 8 are not a panacea; they are some suggested theoretical and practical approaches to the problem. In the hopes of making available the analytical tools to draw men to feminism, chapter 8 considers empirical research regarding the development of sympathetic feminist consciousness. It also offers thoughts on ways to remake legal images of masculinity, and urges movement away from legal strategies that are captive to a zero-sum game.

Reconstructing gender requires addressing consciously and collectively the social processes we engage in, and critically evaluating assumptions we accept, when we create gender differences. To that end, I offer some suggestions on ways we can make gendering visible: in spheres ranging from consumer product differentiation to language and child-rearing practices. Chapter 8 also anticipates possible hazards of dismantling the gender line: the specters of, on the one hand, gender identity disorder, and, on the other, a unisex universe.

If we are to move beyond gender wars, it is absolutely crucial to recognize that *the oppressions of men and women are intertwined*: men are excluded from nurturing and caregiving roles, while the responsibility for child and family care is a significant factor in the oppression of women; conventional concepts of masculinity promote aggressive, individualistic behaviors, which translate into disrespect for and violence against women. Feminism has been a viable theory of liberation for women; why not feminism for men?

This book is intended for people who have at least some interest in gender issues. In part, this is an appeal to feminist women that there is a huge group of natural—and, I make the stronger argument, necessary—allies. As well, it is an invitation to men, whether self-describing as feminists or not, to explore the ways gender stereotypes have defined and, in many ways, trapped or cabined them. By demonstrating some of the ways conventional gender roles harm men, I hope to encourage men to care about, and to work toward, the dismantling of patriarchy. The book also broaches a dialogue about the label "feminism" itself. So, nestled in the book is a hope that nonfeminists who have the intellectual curiosity to explore their positions will do so.

This book advocates radical feminism for the sensible middle. The radical prescription urges that we move away from traditional gender roles: in domestic tasks, occupations, social roles, and perhaps even in the clothing and paraphernalia of life. The conservatism in the proposal is a call for reason, civility, action, and unification. It may seem harsh to criticize feminist theory for succeeding, for doing what it set out to do: to thoroughly document the persistence of patriarchy across time and cultures. But the nature of my critique is different. I argue that feminism has stalled in an important way by not reaching far enough. The hope is to advance the cause of feminism by pointing out the more universal harms of gender role stereotyping of men. This book was largely impelled by the lessons of feminist theory itself—not to allow issues to remain silenced and to "question everything."[24]

2

Gender Separatism

Can you imagine elevating one half of a population and denigrating the other half and producing a population in which everyone is the same?   —Catharine A. MacKinnon *Feminism Unmodified*

In this chapter we will look at the institutions that construct gender. Some are sharply gender divisive; others are more or less harmful to both men and women. Society constructs two separate gender cultures, and the beliefs, social practices, and institutions that separate the sexes disadvantage both females and males. While specific beliefs vary according to a range of factors—ethnicity, race, religion, socioeconomic stratum, and the gendering practices of individuals—the ways culture makes basic divisions between males and females often transcend race, class, and other axes of identity, and cut across most of American society.

The Feedback Loops

One way to test whether separation of the sexes is, in any sense, good or necessary is to ask whether inherent differences exist between them warranting differences in treatment. Recent explorations have probed the biological bases of sex differences. Yet the reporting of much of that research has overlooked the politics of biology. One of the feedback loops in the construction of gender deals with the politicization of biological research. Data concerning the biological basis of sex differences can be steered in important ways: tests can be constructed, often unwittingly, to lead to results that comport with the political philosophy of the researcher, and data about sex differences can be put to use in ways that support particular ideological positions about gender.

The research loop is tilted sharply toward discovering the existence of gender differences. A vast amount of the recent neurological, psychological, and sociological research and theorizing on biological and cognitive sex differences unsurprisingly emphasizes the differences that do exist between the sexes. Differences research attracts researchers; findings that sex differences exist attract media attention. The first feedback loop is completed: not only does differences research command media attention, it gets published, which fuels the research, which provides the media fodder.

In a second feedback loop, these findings and attention amplify existing stereotypes about gender differences. The empirical research, filtered back to popular audiences through the media, helps construct the ways people think about gender. People begin with preexisting suppositions that sex differences abound and are innate. When new information is received, those perceptions of gendered behavior are exaggerated in ways consistent with sex role stereotypes. The combination of research that is politicized toward finding gender differences and media presentations skewed toward headlining any differences that are found tends to magnify gender differences in popular consciousness.

These feedback loops create a dissonance between the perceptions and the realities or possibilities of gender. This chapter focuses on those disparities. It begins with the highlights of physiological, neurophysiological, academic performance, and psychological research on gender differences. Few true, biologically anchored gender differences exist. Perceptions of innate gender differences far outstrip the testable realities. Thus, the second part of this chapter tries to account for continued perceptions of gender differences, despite the research showing only weak or modest biological correlations. It explores the research and reporting biases that slant interpretations of the data on differences, and thus distort popular perceptions. We will also examine the social backdrop of testing, the cultural milieu in which the tests take place and the tested behaviors are constructed. The third and fourth sections look at why the myths of sharp gender differences persist: the resilience of stereotypes and the relentless cultural practices of gendering that promote the stereotypes.

Gender Differences: What the Research Shows

Physiology

Of course men and women differ in some aspects of physical makeup: in reproductive functions and, on average, in size, strength, cardiovascular and lung capacity, hemoglobin concentration, balance, flexibility, and percentage of body fat. Physical characteristics, though, are enormously variable. Initial differences between the genders in physical attributes, such as strength or body fat, are magnified by cultural factors, such as differences in diet and patterns of exercise. For instance, men generally find more time for physical exercise than women.[1]

The significance of the biological differences between the sexes is diminishing. An example of the narrowing gap can be seen in athletics. In several events, such as ultramarathoning, skeet shooting, marathon swimming, and dog sledding, women have surpassed men in recent years.[2] A 1992 comparison of men's and women's running speeds since the turn of the century in middle- to longer-distance running events showed that women's rates of improvement were double those of men. Exercise physiologists Brian J. Whipp and Susan A. Ward concluded that if these performance trends continue, "these events will be no different for men and women within the first half of the 21st century."[3] Other experts are highly skeptical of this prediction,[4] but many researchers believe that performance differences would further diminish if cultural variables, such as coaching and resource devotion, were equalized.[5]

Neurophysiology

Few purely structural differences separate men's and women's brains. Men's brains are approximately 10 percent larger than women's, but men's body weight is, on average, at least this much more. The frontal lobe in men's brains, but not women's, begins to shrink when men are in their twenties. In women, one part of the corpus callosum—the region that functions as a bridge between the left and right hemispheres—is thicker. And since women have more neurons in the portion of the cerebral cortex responsible for language, this could account for greater verbal abilities in some women.

With increasingly sophisticated tools for exploration and measurement, a number of recent studies have centered on innate differences between the sexes in brain composition and function. In 1995 brain researchers reported on their use of magnetic resonance imaging, which measures blood flow, to watch brains of men and women while they performed rhyming tasks and while they rested. A team of Yale University School of Medicine scientists concluded that men and women use different portions of their brains while sorting nonsense words. Women used areas related to language on both the right and left sides of their brains, while men principally used an area of cortex in the left hemisphere.[6]

Other researchers have found evidence that men's and women's brains differ in the uses of the limbic center, the portion of the brain associated with emotional behavior. Men demonstrated greater brain activity in the lower region, while women had greater activity in the more highly evolved areas associated with symbolic expression. Researchers at the University of Pennsylvania suggest that this may explain why many women are better able to recognize emotions in others, while many men are inclined toward physically aggressive responses.[7]

In contrast to these findings, a study conducted at Washington University School of Medicine shows that men and women use the same areas of the brain to produce language. Using positron emission tomography to measure cerebral blood flow, neurologists observed test subjects performing word association tasks. Their tests showed that women and men activate the same areas of the prefrontal cortex during speech production.[8]

It is relatively uncontroversial that there are small structural and functional differences between male and female brains, perhaps contributing to some performance differences on tests of spatial and verbal abilities. Of paramount importance, but usually overlooked, is that similarities between the sexes far outweigh differences: differences between men and women are not as large as differences among members of the same sex.[9] Even those scientists who have discovered functional performance differences between the brains of males and females are careful to point out that their research is tentative and suggestive, and that while their research attends to differences, similarities abound: "Fundamentally, the brains of men and women are more similar than different."[10]

Academic Performance and Achievement

Popular wisdom has it that males are far better at math than females while females excel at verbal skills. Recent studies challenge this generalization. A 1995 large-scale survey of research regarding sex differences in cognitive abilities shows minor differences in a few indicators. Larry Hedges and Amy Nowell performed secondary analyses on six sets of data collected on national populations between 1960 and 1992. They reviewed the performance of a sample of over seventy-three thousand fifteen-year-olds who took twenty-three different cognitive tests. In another set of data, they looked at the performance of close to twenty-five thousand eighth-grade students who were resurveyed in twelfth grade in a National Educational Longitudinal Study.

Hedges and Nowell observed that "[o]n average, females exhibited a slight tendency to perform better on tests of reading comprehension, perceptual speed, and associative memory, and males exhibited a slight tendency to perform better on tests of mathematics and social studies."[11] Males demonstrated more variability in scoring—larger numbers of males performed at the top and bottom of the distribution on most tests. They did find two more significant differences based on sex: "males are, on average, at a rather profound disadvantage in the performance of [basic writing skills]" and "substantially fewer females than males . . . score in the upper tails of the mathematics and science ability distributions and hence are poised to succeed in the sciences." Ultimately, however, they concluded that "these data suggest that average sex differences are generally rather small."

Modern research challenges the popular belief that sweeping differences in abilities exist between the sexes. The broad conclusion that females are verbally superior while males excel mathematically is misleading. "Gender differences appear to account for no more than 1%–5% of the population variance" in verbal, quantitative, and spatial abilities.[12] Janet Shibley Hyde and Marcia Linn conducted statistical analyses of the results of 165 prior studies of sex differences in verbal ability, representing the testing of over 1.4 million subjects. They determined that studies finding no statistically significant differences in gender abilities far outweighed those finding that differences exist: "44 (27%) of the 165 studies found females to perform significantly better than males, 109 (66%) found no significant gender difference, and 12 (7%) found males performing significantly better than females."[13]

With respect to mathematical abilities, an assembly of data from a hundred different assessments, representing the testing of over 3.9 million subjects, yielded the conclusion that sex differences in performance on tests of quantitative or mathematical abilities were statistically minuscule. In elementary and middle school, girls slightly outperformed boys on computational exercises, and no sex-based differences existed in comprehension of mathematical concepts; "gender differences favoring males in problem solving do not emerge until the high school years."[14]

Finally, men and women overall score equally on intelligence tests—"the mean IQ of both [sexes] is 100."[15] Men, however, are overrepresented at both the top and the bottom of the IQ spectrum. Of those scoring in the top 1 percent on IQ tests, seven out of eight are men. Men also represent an almost equally large percentage of the mentally deficient.[16]

Psychology

Observable behavioral differences between the sexes are more pervasive than measurable physiological differences. Consider a few facts regarding two traits perceived as representative of the gender axes: aggression and nurturing behavior. Boys are approximately seven times more likely to be the perpetrators of violent crime.[17] They are also three times more likely to be its victims.[18] Studies of girls at play show that they consistently demonstrate more nurturant and cooperative behavior than boys.[19] These social facts paint pictures of the gendered lives of boys and girls; they are facts that many people think are explained by biological imperatives.

The belief, supported by some early research in the behavioral sciences, is that boys are hormonally "hardwired" for aggression and physical risk taking because boys have less serotonin and more testosterone than girls. Initial studies in the 1960s and 1970s pointed to a hormonal influence on behavior: that testosterone makes boys aggressive, while estrogen has a calming effect on girls. Several studies have showed that those convicted of violent crimes had higher levels of testosterone than nonviolent offenders.[20]

Modern research questions the causal influence of testosterone in human aggression. A study of 4,462 men from the armed forces showed that while a statistically strong relationship existed between testosterone levels and adult deviance, the relationship was not strong enough to operate as a major determinant of adult deviance.[21] One eleven-year longitudinal study of 178 schoolboys (drawn from an original sample of over 1,100 subjects) in Canada traced their behavior and testosterone levels from kindergarten onward. The study found that socially successful but nonaggressive boys had higher levels of testosterone than their peers who were more physically aggressive. The boys with lower levels of testosterone exhibited more impulsive and fighting behavior; in other words, higher measures on the physical aggression scales were correlated with lower levels of testosterone.[22] This study confirms others that showed that socially successful or winning behavior is associated with a rise in the level of testosterone. Researchers at UCLA studied a group of hypogonadal men who were low in testosterone. They found that testosterone deficiency leads to aggressive behavior, and that after treatment with testosterone replacement therapy, the subjects displayed *less* anger, irritability, and aggression.[23]

Despite mixed empirical evidence on the relationship between hormones and behavior, the popular perception is that much of the social behavior of the sexes is genetically determined. When any evidence of biological impulses is found, it is often talked about both as determinative—that the behavior is hardwired—and as existing prior to or apart from cultural practices of gendering. Social theorists and even legal philosophers seize on folk wisdom to maintain that women are biologically more suited to nurturing and caregiving.[24] In our culture, little girls are given dolls with which to practice caretaking behaviors. Parents also distribute a greater share of child care responsibilities to girls. Cross-cultural studies suggest that both boys and girls who are given caregiving roles as young children develop stronger nurturant abilities.[25]

Stereotypes hold that the innate abilities of men and women differ dramatically, despite a wealth of psychological, sociological, and industrial data that the performance capabilities of women and men, on the whole, are equivalent. Although psychological illnesses afflict genders somewhat differently—women are more likely to suffer from depression than men, while more men are afflicted with schizophrenia, for example—men and women are more similar than different with respect to attitudes toward work, helping behaviors, empathy, general reactions to stress and joy, and other basic behavioral reactions.[26] Regarding "behavior at and attitudes toward work . . . when compared to men, women have been reported to evidence much the same task and interpersonally oriented leadership behaviors, career motivation, need for achievement and need for power, career commitment, and job attitudes."[27]

Summary

Men and women exhibit some small physiological differences, on average, across populations, but much greater variability when individuals are compared. The statistical correlation between gender and performance on standardized tests and other measures of academic performance and achievement is fairly weak. And, as the next section shows, measurable disparities between boys and girls in academic and standardized test performance have declined over time.

Neurological differences between the sexes may contribute modestly to observed differences in linguistic abilities and aggressive tendencies. Men and women exhibit some fairly stark differences in behaviors, but those behavioral differences have not been empirically linked directly to biological causes. One factor complicating the sex differences discussion is the confusion of correlation for causation. At times the observed behavioral differences of the sexes are mistaken for causal explanations. When boys and girls are observed to act differently—in choice of toys, affinity for physical roughhousing, or displays of nurturant behavior—it is easy to assume that the explanation lies in biology.

At a minimum, the emerging picture is much more complicated than a direct causal link between basic biological or hormonal differences and behaviors. The evidence of strong biological or physiological influences on behavior is increasingly challenged by modern research. Given the modest empirically demonstrable correlations between biological, physiological, and neurological sex differences and behavior, the question becomes how we should account for observed gender differences.

Accounting for Difference

Research and Testing Biases

Some feminist psychologists and sociologists have a political agenda that causes them to ignore empirical research demonstrating statistically significant social and behavioral differences between women and men.[28] Others have biases toward an overemphasis on differences.[29] What is clear is that the issue of empirical research into sex differences is highly politicized.

The research on gender differences may be slanted in ways not immediately visible. Theories about the importance of mother-child interactions in early child development, for example, may have encouraged cultural anthropologists to conduct field studies during times when father-child interactions are less often observed, such as evening hours.[30] The parameters of statistical proof make it much easier to demonstrate differences. As neurologist Steven Petersen says, "It is much more difficult to statistically show similarity, than it is to statistically show a difference. In most cases, this is used to keep investigators intellectually honest, but when adjudicating between questions of difference and similarity, [it] produces a scientific asymmetry." Bias creeps in at the publication level as well. "[S]ocial science research tends to be about looking for differences. Gender researchers nearly always start out by looking for gender differences. . . . When they find similarities, the social science world considers these non-findings. They are not publishable because they are not considered newsworthy; they are not sexy; they are not interesting and nobody really cares."[31] Negative conclusions simply are not news. One study of publication policies showed that psychology journals "accept more readily reports in which statistically significant differences have been recorded, and so it is difficult to publish results in which no significant differences have been found."[32] A selection bias exists for new things, and against proving the null hypothesis.

In science and social science, both submission and publication biases incline researchers toward positive findings and an underreporting of negative results. One study of submission and publication rates of papers in psychotherapy found that "82 percent of studies with positive outcomes led to submission of papers to a journal, while only 43 percent of negative outcomes provoked an attempt at publication. Of papers submitted, 80 percent reporting positive outcomes were accepted for publication, but only 50 percent of papers claiming negative results."[33] In another less empirical assessment of publication and attention bias, Anne Fausto-Sterling surveyed the reported literature regarding physiological and hormonal influences on gender behavior. While she "does not deny that genuine differences often exist, and in the direction conventionally reported," she then conducted a different sort of survey: looking at "her colleagues' file drawers for studies not published, or for negative results published and then ignored." What she found was that "a great majority report either a smaller and insignificant disparity between sexes, or find no difference at all. When all studies, rather than only those published, are collated, the much-vaunted differences often dissolve into triviality."[34]

Reporting Biases

The role of the media in shaping gender is both subtle and powerful. Reporters highlight differences that are not supported by real evidence, and seize upon and magnify weak evidence of real difference. The media spin ignores similarities and overplays differences.

Magnetic imaging research by the scientists at Yale and the University of Pennsylvania that showed biological differences relating to gender was given seemingly unlimited airplay in the media. The Yale University study commanded forty-four articles in the popular press, while the University of Pennsylvania results were trumpeted in thirty-five articles. The conclusions of the Washington University neurologists—that men and women use the same areas of the brain to produce speech—were largely ignored. The Washington University study results were reported in only two articles, one in the *Fresno Bee*, the other in the *Sacramento Bee*. As Petersen explains, "A study like ours, that points out that basically men and women are pretty damn similar, it's just not interesting."[35]

Differences are not just overattended, they may also be overblown. Tendencies and probabilities may be misrepresented or misinterpreted as determined behaviors. "Social scientists present results on the basis of statistics and chance and discuss the 'significance' of their findings. When these significant differences, often based on small numbers, are reported and repeatedly cited, they get exaggerated and lead to gross generalizations."[36] In short, biological explanations are interpreted as more significant than they are, while general tendencies are treated as virtual certainties.

The interpretation of results of biological experiments is thus politicized and given a media headline spin. Headlines announce "Men and Women Truly Don't Think Alike," "Could Women Be the Weaker, Fairer, Cleverer Sex?" and "Battle of the Sexes Gets New Weapon." Many of the stories overgeneralize not only the significance and possible implications of the research, but also the scientific findings themselves. For instance, the summary of a wire story proclaims, "A study of brain use patterns shows what people have long suspected: men are better at math and women are nonviolent."[37] The headline implies conclusions very different from those suggested by the text of the article, such as the views of neuropsychologist Ruben Gur, the principal author of the brain scan study: "Our findings do not answer the question of whether the differences are genetic or cultural in origin. . . . After all, culture shapes the brain just as the brain shapes culture."

The manner of journalistic presentation may amplify the misleading results. Fault resides with "a media eager to trumpet breakthrough discoveries in genetic research and unwilling or unable to be skeptical of the ambitious claims sometimes constructed on quite shaky scientific foundations."[38] Newspapers and magazines often report results of scientific research in staccato bursts of new information. In addition to overemphasizing individual studies, reporters often focus on singular, positive findings. These may be newsworthy, but not representative of the work in a field. Most media squibs are not think pieces detailing the history of research into sex differences and exploring the larger picture that has evolved over time: "the media tend to report each new study in isolation, as a new breakthrough."[39]

Maybe the sensationalism can be dismissed, since magazines are just trying to sell issues, journalists are just trying to sell stories, and newspapers are just trying to sell papers. But they also sell "truth": the reported information becomes popular "knowledge," and this is how people remember the data. The effect of the headline reporting approach may be that significant numbers of Americans come to believe the deterministic version of events, such as claims that obesity or the employment prospects for girls or the nurturing capacities or aggressive nature of boys is decided at birth.

Even when reports about sex differences are stripped of overgeneralization and exaggeration, the translation of scientific data into news for popular consumption inevitably involves some reductionism. Reporters must compress pages of scientific research into thirty-second sound bites or seven hundred words of copy. What may be lost is the complexity of causal influences on behavior. The reporting of complex phenomena as the product of single, simple, biologically based mechanisms overlooks the myriad cultural and social influences on personality and behavior and the individual choices people make.

Socialization

Gender does not exist outside culture. Even those modest correlations between sex and neurophysiology or sex and academic performance have no existence independent of their social milieu. Culture is continually manufacturing behaviors. More important, culture denominates behaviors as having genders and assigns values to those behaviors.

Again, the definitional problem intrudes. In discussions of sex-linked behavioral differences, nurturing, caregiving, and mothering often are equated with the biological capacities to become pregnant, give birth, and breastfeed. If nurturing and caregiving behaviors are thought of more broadly as the impulses to be affectionate, protect, educate, be patient, offer security, and solve problems for others, then men suddenly qualify as compassionate caregivers.

Let's revisit for a moment our paradigm examples of gendered traits: aggression and nurturing behavior. Women are thought to be society's natural nurturers and caregivers. Some also maintain that men are inherently less capable of nurturing. A confluence of economic and social factors has led to a scarcity of male role models with principal caregiving responsibilities, which perpetuates both the perception and the reality of males as the less nurturing sex. Abundant evidence shows that men are constrained in choosing caregiving occupations and nurturing behaviors as opposed to other jobs and tasks.

Some of the social forces are changing, however. Men increasingly are assuming more caregiving roles. While the sheer number of single fathers remains low relative to that of single mothers—3.2 million compared to 12.2 million—the number has grown 163 percent in the past quarter century.[40]

The psychosociological research regarding the nurturing potential of men is only of recent vintage. Primate studies and human research testing the "maternal instinct" hypothesis find "no significant differences between males and females in their capacity to nurture."[41]

Cross-cultural studies tend to confirm that fathering behaviors are culturally and socially contingent, and that in cultures in which mothers and fathers have equal responsibilities as providers and both parents have comparable access to their infants during the day, they share equally in caregiving responsibilities. For example, a study of the Aka Pygmy tribe of hunter-gatherers in Africa involved the observation of a culture in which "men's and women's subsistence activities take place in the same geographic locations" and in which each parent was responsible for providing half of the family's daily nutrition. Researchers concluded that "Aka fathers do more infant caregiving than do fathers in any other human society. Forty-seven percent of the father's (24 hr) day is spent either holding the infant, or within arm's reach of the infant."[42] Of course, in industrialized societies, many fathers may not have the luxury of close infant contact that the Aka father has. But research suggests how crucial nurturing paternal involvement is in child development. "In a study of pre-school-aged youngsters, children whose fathers were responsible for 40–45% of the child-care responsibilities exhibited higher cognitive competence and higher empathy toward their peers."[43]

Just as nurturing behavior is not a trait belonging exclusively to women, aggression is not solely the province of men. Social evidence indicates that females are becoming more aggressive. A Justice Department study measuring juvenile arrests for 1995 showed that one in four juvenile arrests were of females, which represented a rate for girls growing more than twice as fast as that for boys.[44] While this is not a social fact to applaud, it is indicative of growing societal acceptance of girls and women demonstrating aggressive behaviors. Women are becoming more aggressive as drivers[45] and investors,[46] more socially and financially independent, more ambitious in fighting for equal treatment and better working conditions, more competitive in sports, and more assertive at work, home, sexual relations, recreation, and public speaking. Aggressive behavior on the part of women is gradually ceasing to appear unnatural.

The social explanation for equating maleness and aggression is also abundantly clear. Society considers male aggression natural. Male aggression is promoted when parents are tolerant of little boys working out their differences with physical violence. Violent images are emblazoned on little boys' clothes, cartoons, video games, and television, and in their minds. Conversely, the American cultural taboos against female expression of anger are enormous. Boys learn to use aggression as a problem-solving technique, while girls are taught to cooperate.

Consider a comparative study of 160 Israeli and American preschoolers, aged eighteen months to four years. The data showed that preschool girls in Israel are much more likely than American girls to use physical aggression when fighting.[47] The Israeli girls are even more likely, in many instances, than American boys to participate in aggressive encounters. Anthropology professor Carol Lauer says that the cultural message to children in Israel, a country that has been at war with its neighbors for half a century, is that aggression is an acceptable method of handling interactions.

Part of the study concerned an assessment of the different lessons teachers taught boys and girls about the usefulness of aggression: "When interviewed, the Israeli metapelot [house parents] said they did not consider girls to be less aggressive than boys. In one group a metapelet was frequently seen encouraging an 18-month-old girl to assert herself in agonistic encounters. In contrast, in several American groups teachers were seen telling girls that 'girls do not fight.'"[48] The expectation in America is that little girls will demonstrate caring and nurturant behaviors, and so they do: consistent with socialization patterns, American girls demonstrate less agonistic behavior. Other cross-cultural studies confirm the learned nature of aggressive behaviors.[49]

Consider another example of how the stark numbers seeming to locate behavioral differences in biology may mask competing social explanations. The results of standardized test performance seem to demonstrate that girls have less aptitude for math than boys. Here again, it is easy to mistake the correlation of gender and performance for a causal relationship.

On the SAT (formerly Scholastic Aptitude Test, then Scholastic Assessment Test), girls' scores, particularly in mathematics, have lagged behind boys' scores for decades. Based on the new scoring scale used since 1995, out of a possible eight hundred points, girls scored roughly forty-two points lower than boys on math and eleven points lower on verbal between 1980 and 1990.[50] Popular wisdom has it that the first of these performance discrepancies is evidence of boys' innate superiority in mathematical reasoning abilities.

But in the early 1990s the picture began changing. First, the gender gap in SAT performance narrowed. According to the 1995 and 1996 scores, girls were thirty-five points behind boys on math and four points behind on verbal. The decrease over time in differentials between the sexes on standardized tests implies that socialization experiences may account for some of the performance differences.

Then the picture gained a social backdrop. Attention began to be paid to the ulterior motives of test designers. The designer of the first version of the SAT in 1925, Carl Brigham, a psychometrician and eugenicist, believed in using intelligence tests to demonstrate the innate intellectual inferiority of blacks and immigrants.[51]

Even the modern incarnations of the SAT and its younger sibling, the PSAT, are skewed in gender impact. While men's SAT test scores, on average, are higher than women's, women generally receive higher college grades than men. A prospective regression analysis study conducted by two staff members of the Educational Testing Service showed that the SAT consistently underpredicted the performance of women in college math courses.[52] What at first may appear to be a gender differential may actually be the result of other demographic variables: "more females than males take the test; the females are disproportionately members of racial and ethnic minority groups; and the females are disproportionately from families with lower incomes and levels of parental education."[53] Finally, on the feedback end of the loop, middle and high school girls may be self-excluding from math classes due to stereotypes they have internalized.

In 1994 the National Center for Fair and Open Testing (FairTest), a nonprofit organization devoted to fairness and accuracy in standardized tests, filed a complaint with the Department of Education's Office of Civil Rights. The complaint argued that the Educational Testing Service and the College Board violated Title IX by using the PSAT as the sole screening device for National Merit Scholarships. While girls constitute more than half of the test takers, they receive only 36 percent of the scholarships. According to FairTest, the PSAT systematically underpredicts girls' performance in college math courses. In late 1996 ETS and the College Board agreed to a settlement with FairTest in which the testing service would attempt to weed out gender bias by adding a multiple-choice section designed to measure writing skills to the PSAT.[54] A federal district court in New York similarly invalidated the use of SAT scores alone in the award of college scholarships.[55]

The educational testing furor highlights the controversy over measuring differences. When sex differences appear, are they really a function of genetics or something else (prior education, class, income)? When boys and girls repeatedly received differential scores on seemingly objective tests, are the tests gender-free from the start? And what do the tests measure: mathematical abilities, prior proficiency in signing up for math classes, or aptitude in taking multiple-choice tests? What may appear to be hardwired differences in abilities between the sexes may in fact be an assemblage of embedded biases.

The recognition that culture is *teaching* differences may go a long way toward explaining observed differences between the sexes on standardized tests. Developmental geneticist Anne Fausto-Sterling cautions that the results of sex differences research should not be understood to imply innate differences. Fausto-Sterling lists some of the exogenous variables that may influence the results: parental attitudes may steer boys toward and girls away from mathematics; boys may be socialized in ways that give them more informal mathematics experiences than girls; and teachers' attitudes in the classroom may gender the learning of reading and mathematics. She reports on an observational study of teachers' behaviors toward second-graders: "The boys received less direct instruction in reading and more in math. In other words, boys and girls learning together in the same classroom did not receive the same instruction."[56]

Popular beliefs in—and overgeneralizations about—the biological bases of sex differences may result in differences in treatment of the sexes. This, in turn, may affect performance on standardized tests, such as tests measuring abilities to manipulate objects in three-dimensional space. "Study after study shows people are more physical with baby boys than with baby girls. They throw them in the air, they dangle keys in front of their faces, meanwhile being more protective of baby girls. So why should we be surprised when boys and girls end up behaving differently in response to these gender-specific experiences?"[57]

The Biological Gestalt

The available evidence suggests that there may be some gender-specific biological impulses toward behavior. Of course, biology itself is not fixed; biology is never distinct from social development. Any biological cause is developmentally dependent on external conditions, including nutrition, stimulus, and other aspects of the environment. Cognitive abilities are continually sculpted by the environment. Research finding biological differences between the sexes cannot be disaggregated from the conclusion that environmental influences may shape those biological differences. Evidence regarding biological or social origins of differences is difficult to sort out because gendered cultural programming begins so early.

Yet even if gendered biological differences exist, we cannot meaningfully separate those differences from our perceptual, research, and reporting biases. Even measurable neurophysiological differences between men and women do not exist independently of testing and journalistic biases. Biology, in one sense, can never be the independent variable, because it is never outside culture. To the extent that differences exist, what do they mean? Biological differences cannot be separated from the cultural process of assigning meaning to the differences.

Research into differences—between genders, races, or populations on any basis—is a politically sensitive area. Overaggressive claims about structural or performance differences may be used to make unjustified arguments about innate intelligence. Just as *The Bell Curve* attempted to resurrect myths that people of color are less intelligent, so have differences in brain size been used to argue that men are smarter than women. Of course, beliefs in differences do not necessarily lead to claims of genetic determinism or imply racism or the superiority of any population. But the extreme version of the argument is one that demands reckoning. The danger is that a focus on differences can lead to a reification of differences and to beliefs that qualities that may result from some degree of biological influence are socially inalterable.

Across time and cultures, people in power have used biological measures to devalue the worth of disempowered groups. History offers countless examples. Beliefs in black inferiority provided a major justification for slavery in the United States and for British colonization of Africa. After World War I, intelligence testing led to the labeling of Jewish and Italian immigrants at Ellis Island as "feebleminded." Eugenics movements resulted in compulsory sterilizations in the United States and unspeakable horrors in Germany.

In 1861 French anthropologist Paul Broca conducted a study in which he weighed the brains of 292 male and 140 female cadavers, and calculated that the males' brains weighed, on average, 1,325 grams, while the females' brains averaged 1,144 grams. Broca concluded, "[W]e must not forget that women are, on the average, a little less intelligent than men, a difference which we should not exaggerate but which is, nonetheless, real. We are therefore permitted to suppose that the relatively small size of the female brain depends in part upon her physical inferiority and in part upon her intellectual inferiority."[58]

Little more than a century ago, influential social psychologist Gustave Le Bon used Broca's data to argue against allowing women access to higher education, remarking that women's "brains are closer in size to those of gorillas than to the most developed male brains.... [Women] represent the most inferior forms of human evolution and ... are closer to children and savages than to an adult, civilized man. They excel in fickleness, inconstancy, absence of thought and logic, and incapacity to reason."[59]

These resurgent patterns of locating explanations for class or race or gender differences in the biological exhibit a search for constants, for fixed differences. They also reflect a very broad cultural belief in simple, ultimate causes. The first part of the message is that differences are inevitable. The second part is that biology plays an enormous role in determining human behavior. It is easy to commit a heuristic error when interpreting evidence of biological and environmental influences: "[o]ne of the major ... ideological weapons used to convince people that their position in society is fixed and unchangeable and, indeed, fair is the constant confusion between inherited and unchangeable."[60] People may assume that if differences are even partly innate in origin, behaviors relating to those differences are not changeable.

The confusion of biological origins with inevitable social consequences is more than an academic error. Implications for public policy often follow insidiously from the location of differences in biological causes. A focus on biological causes may implicitly dismiss the need to search for cultural or institutional causes of disadvantage. At the extreme, the theory of biological origins may be transformed into arguments about biological necessity. The danger, of course, is that biological explanations can be used to justify discriminatory practices.

A friend of mine, Bob, tells a story of how he and his wife shared a common driveway with their next-door neighbors, a family of four. The father, Tom, was a truck driver. Bob and Tom would talk about Tom's work pretty regularly. Bob once asked Tom why there weren't more women truck drivers. Tom thought about it for a minute, then said, with great assurance, "They couldn't shift gears." "They're not strong enough?" Bob asked. "No, not tall enough; you have to be pretty decent-sized to reach the pedals." That might have been the end of it, Bob said, if he hadn't been reading about feminist theory. But he had, so he asked the question, "But Tom, do they have to build the cabs that way? Couldn't they build 'em so shorter folks could reach the pedals?" "Yeah," Tom shrugged, "I guess they could." He thought for a second. "But I'll tell you what; no woman would ever want to use a truck stop." It is indeed a challenging project: trying to imagine a feminized truck stop. (But not impossible.)

Beliefs in biological determinism may be used to structure social practices that reinforce the traditional division of labor between the sexes. Law professor Richard Epstein argues that biological constraints on behavior are "quite strong." From this, he encourages a "specialization of roles within marriage that allow both husbands and wives to use their talents to the fullest." Epstein concludes flatly that "[a]n insistence on identity of roles within marriage would require each party to do tasks that the other can do better."[61] While Epstein does not spell out what these biologically imbued talents are, presumably he means that men are innately "better" at fixing cars, while women are innately "better" at cooking or housecleaning.

The notion of biologically determined roles has undergirded legal arguments about allowing women to fight in combat, and echoes older custody decisions recognizing a maternal preference. And the idea of genetic determinism is used as an argument against affirmative action. According to this view, affirmative action will never achieve its desired results because of the biological inferiority of women.[62]

The idea of biological determinism has tremendous ideological appeal. It can reassure men and women that the entrenched inequalities of power, child care responsibilities, and wages are appropriate. If behavior originates with biological differences between the sexes, people will tend to believe that the traditional social roles are natural, right, and unchangeable. We simply have not escaped the notion that both men and women possess immutable biological characteristics that determine their appropriateness for certain roles and inappropriateness for others.

The Persistence of Stereotypes

Even with what we know about the biological basis for differences, we perpetuate stereotypes of typically masculine and feminine behaviors, and those stereotypes become self-fulfilling. The statistical support for pure biological differences is weak, since every measure of biology implicates culture—in construction, testing, and interpretation. Given that, it is remarkable that stereotypes about masculine and feminine instincts, traits, and natures persist. This section uses research from cognitive psychology to explain why the stereotypes continue even though they have little empirical support. The following section demonstrates the persistence of cultural practices of gendering despite what we know about real differences. Together, they show how the cognitive errors are reinforced daily through prevailing practices of thought and social interaction.

Popular Beliefs about Gender Differences

National and international public opinion polls indicate substantial acceptance of gender stereotypes. A 1996 international Gallup poll revealed that "[i]n every country surveyed, respondents—whether male or female—were more likely to describe women as emotional, as talkative and as affectionate."[63] According to this poll, only 6 percent of respondents thought that being affectionate was a male trait. Cultural ideas about appropriate gender roles are readily internalized. In a 1995 study designed by the Families and Work Institute and conducted by Louis Harris and Associates, 88 percent of the women surveyed believed it was their primary responsibility to take care of their family.

Traditional gender roles come with a hierarchy. The customary practices of gender are embedded with notions of female inferiority: "According to recent public opinion polls, a majority of Americans believe that most men think they are 'better' than women. . . . About half of surveyed women also consider women inferior for certain occupations ranging from airline pilot to combat soldier."[64] These popular beliefs about appropriate roles are unmistakably influenced by perceptions of gender characteristics as innate in origin: "About a third of surveyed adults view masculine and feminine characteristics as biologically based, and an equal percentage of women express support for traditional male breadwinner/female homemaker roles."[65]

Gender research, popularized by the media, ultimately finds a home in the public consciousness. The public mind readily acknowledges the idea that gendered behavior is biological in origin and unthinkingly accepts that biological attributes are tantamount to social destiny.

Are the Stereotypes Accurate?

An important question is whether gender stereotypes correctly reflect modern realities. Some psychologists have demonstrated that gender stereotypes are generally accurate reflections of observed male and female behaviors.[66] Others who have compared actual behaviors with self-reports suggest that "people are not very accurate in stating the differences between the genders: they often overestimate differences and sometimes underestimate them."[67] While the evidence is mixed, a variety of researchers believe that public perceptions overstate gender differences and that gender stereotypes, while reflecting reality, exaggerate differences in important ways.[68]

Stereotypes possess a self-reinforcing quality. They help construct a world in which people think both in generalities and in fixed ways. First, stereotypes themselves perpetuate archaic ideas about the competencies of women and men, and in so doing, they limit gender possibilities. When stereotypic notions of gender abilities and roles persist despite evidence to the contrary, decisions in important arenas such as education, employment, politics, and the home may be based on outmoded concepts of appropriate roles. Stereotypes also depersonalize by encouraging class-based generalizations that may have little to do with the qualities or aptitudes of a particular individual. When stereotypic thinking about gender occurs, the culture accepts a standard mental picture, repeated without modification and admitting of no individual variations. Finally, stereotypes may be transmitted generationally. When children start forming their own identities and attitudes about gender, they look to peers, the media, and their parents. A study at Tel Aviv University discovered that the "traditionality of the mother's occupations correlated significantly with the traditionality of the interests of both boys and girls."[69] If stereotypes are inaccurate and outdated, it is not only the treatment of people in the present that suffers, but also the process of shaping the gender of future generations.

Why Stereotypes Outlive Their Usefulness

Research regarding social stereotypes indicates why they persist in the face of information to the contrary. People routinely utilize cognitive schema to process information: "We tend to view all of those within a social category as the same—their perceived similarities are exaggerated and their differences and variability are downplayed or ignored altogether."[70] We tend to generalize about sex-based behavior, if only as a simplifying device or heuristic. People use cognitive shortcuts to efficiently process a complex amount and variety of information. And sex is one of a few personal characteristics that are visually determinable in an instant with a reasonable degree of accuracy.

When people process information—including data about the role played by genetics in shaping behavior—they tend to distort risks and probabilities, through use of common sense reasoning and an overreliance on personal experiences. Individuals may weigh their own experiences ("My son mowed down the Cabbage Patch dolls to reach the trucks") as heavily representative of an issue. Others may give undue emphasis to available information or to a particularly vivid example they recollect—such as a single article probing genetic causes of behavior.[71]

Biases in perception, memory, and interpretation all tend to reinforce stereotypes as against data that would upset the stereotype:

> Once stereotypes take hold, other information inconsistent with the stereotype is ignored or excluded from consideration or is interpreted in a way that is consistent with the stereotype. . . . Stereotypes are also maintained by the way in which individual actions are interpreted. When the same behavior is performed by members of different social groups, its implications are seen differently. Thus, the same critical remark was found to be abrasive coming from a woman, but incisive and direct coming from a man.[72]

In addition, many of the studies regarding gender differences feed into prejudices and insecurities we all have. Of course this could be an example of weighing one's own experiences too heavily, but during the time I was researching the material for this chapter, I came across an article in *Science* suggesting that consistency in hand preference over time in twelve- to forty-two-month-old children was indicative of precocious intellectual development for females but not males. Having an eighteen-month-old daughter at home who has exhibited a distinct left hand preference for half of her little life, I was pleased at the prospect of future intelligence. Despite all the cautionary facts about which I was writing—regarding the correlation of any single variable with sex-specific performance—and despite the relatively small sample size in the study, I could not help experiencing the warm glow of parental pride. In short, for a host of varying reasons, people may want to believe in differences.

The great weight of tradition favors the difference view; culture has been built around it for centuries. To believe otherwise might require change, and people typically lean heavily in favor of the status quo; the inertial impulse is huge. Our society also focuses on differences other than sex differences, and this general attention to differences may feed the acceptance of sex differences. We are preoccupied with biological causes in realms other than sex differences. Researchers and the American public are continually searching for genetic markers of alcoholism, insanity, Alzheimer's, aggression, risk taking, and many other diseases and behaviors. The discovery of genetic causal links in other areas probably disposes us to accept the fixity of sex differences. The search for biological origins of behavior is undoubtedly part of the general—and useful—exploration of causal relations, but it can take a dangerously myopic turn. The search for first (and final) causes can easily become reductionist. Oddly, the complexities of genetics in explaining sex differences seem simpler and more "scientific" than the murkier amalgam of historical, anthropological, sociological, and psychological explanations for gender differences.

We tend to think of differences in an all or nothing way: differences must be either innate or learned. The process of scientific research may tend to downplay the interdependence between internal and external causes. Each study is a search for similarities or differences, often the latter. And each research venture looks at a piece of the whole biosocial gender puzzle. The isolated nature of research inquiries, therefore, structurally shifts attention from the macro level of interplay between biological and social causes to the micro level of individual causes.

Biological information—whether dealing with genetic markers, insanity tests, medical tests, DNA fingerprinting, or polygraphs—has extraordinary social consequences. Scientific testing has the power to label behavior functional or dysfunctional, and to attribute those behaviors to biological causes. The public also accords an exalted place to the results of scientific experiments, particularly when those tests speak in measurable, quantifiable terms. In turn, popular beliefs in the biological origins of behavior can have dramatic consequences on social arrangements. If people think that roles and distinctions in life are based on biologically occurring sex-related differences, they may accept sex-based distinctions as correct and perhaps inevitable.

Contemporary Cultural Practices

How many of the toddler boys on television snuggle in bed with a pink blanket? As you drive around town, have you seen many "Father's Day Out" signs in church yards? The reflections of culturally enforced notions of gender are not difficult to find; their sources are somewhat more problematic. As these brief examples indicate, so often gender stereotypes are deeply embedded and thus hidden, appearing *as stereotypes* only when the gender manifestation jars with traditional expectations.

An array of cultural influences concretizes the separation of the genders. Masculinity and femininity are cultural constructs, and children are socialized to conform to cultural expectations of gender. Some of these practices also promote the stereotypic attribution of certain qualities to each of the genders. Observed gender differences can be traced to differential socialization of male and female children. As we track the gendering process from infancy through adulthood, we will see that experiences in the sociocultural context are extremely important in the formation of gender identity.

Infancy and Early Childhood

In America we gender children from birth. While the determination of a child's sex is a biological event, the formation of gender identity is a cultural process. Sex differentiation begins with birth announcements proclaiming the baby's sex, color-coded baby blankets, and gender-appropriate infant gifts. Schooling, parenting, social relations, and play activities all construct gender identity. Studies repeatedly confirm that parents, grandparents, teachers, and strangers treat male and female children, from infancy onward, differently based on their sex. The message is unmistakable: girls and boys belong in separate categories and follow wholly different sets of rules.

At a young age, children understand the concept of sex-group membership. By two years of age, children can correctly identify whether they are boys or girls. Toddlers have already begun to mimic and incorporate gendered mannerisms of their same-sex parent. Certainly some behavioral differences of toddlers have biological influences. Studies have demonstrated that even at very early ages, boys are more aggressive, active, and exploratory than girls. The muscles of two-year-old boys may be better developed than those of two-year-old girls, which may facilitate more active or aggressive play. It is impossible, though, to separate the biological and social influences, when the genetic differences that do exist are instantly and strongly reinforced.

For many years, behavioral differences of infants and toddlers were perceived as rooted in biology. More recent research, though, has exposed the early cultural influences to which baby girls and boys are subjected. The evidence is overwhelming that parents respond differentially, and with gender-stereotypic expectations, to very young children. Physically, parents treat their newborns in gender-specific ways. Parents swaddle infant girls and handle them more delicately, while bouncing baby boys and permitting them greater freedom to explore. A group of researchers reviewing the literature regarding gendered play differences concluded, "Mothers seem to be more emotionally warm and responsive with girls, and more encouraging of independence with boys. Fathers often spend more time with their sons and engage in more physical play with sons than with daughters."[73] Parents are even likely to perceive the behavior of newborn infants as conforming to gender stereotypes, and respond in ways that guide children toward gender-stereotypic behavior.[74] In one study, parents of newborns who scored equally on a number of indicators (such as weight, height, and muscle tone) were asked to describe their child. The parents rated their boys as larger, more muscular, and more coordinated, while describing their girls as softer, less coordinated, and more fragile.[75]

Most parents relentlessly tutor their boys to develop athletic skills, indulge boys' interests in cars, trucks, and tools, and encourage boys to be brave when they are hurt. Many parents also try to diminish their girls' rough play and promote nurturant doll play and cooperative social behaviors instead. In short, what parents think of as the "car and truck gene" may be the result of more physical play with baby boys, a greater provision of typically masculine toys, the decoration of the infant's room with male-toy motifs, and other gendering behaviors on the part of the parents. Studies show that the vast majority of parents—even parents committed to egalitarianism—abide by society's gender role expectations.

Discouraging Gender Deviance

Parents typically provide their children, from infancy on, with gender-"appropriate" toys. Little boys in particular are discouraged from cross-gender play activities. Most children request sex-typed toys, and most parents comply with those requests. One study of eighty-six children, however, revealed an interesting pattern for nonrequested toys. In that study, "[n]ot one boy received a toy judged to be cross-sexed, and although only 8% of the total nonrequested toys the girls received were cross-sexed, one third of the girls received at least one cross-sexed toy."[76] Parents thus demonstrated a specific reluctance to give their children, particularly their boys, toys deemed appropriate for the opposite sex. In another study comparing children's Christmas wish lists with the toys they received, parents were much less likely to purchase requested but gender-atypical toys from the children's lists.[77] Parents generally reward gender-typical play and punish gender-atypical activities. Researchers have found that even parents who report that they did not encourage sex-stereotyped play with toys subtly did so with questions, suggestions, and nonverbal reinforcement.[78]

When little girls cross the gender divide and play with action figures, cars, and sporting equipment, they are labeled "tomboys." Being called a tomboy is mildly prestigious in some circles; nowhere in the country is being called a "sissy" a compliment. Even parents who describe themselves as nonsexist flinch when their eight-year-old son wants to play "beanie babies" with the girl across the street. They fear that identification with typically feminine activities will result in effeminate behavior and will guarantee that their son will grow up to be homosexual.

> Although a girl can now wear almost any item of clothing and play with almost any toy without so much as an eyebrow being raised by her social community, let a boy even once have the urge to try on a princess costume in the dress-up corner of his nursery school, and his parents and teachers will instantly schedule a conference to discuss the adequacy of his gender identity.[79]

Gender separatism is intricately tied to homophobia. "Much of the psychological literature examining homophobia has concluded that support for the traditional gender-role structure is a primary cause of homophobia."[80] One result of treating women as "inferior" is the creation of homophobia, especially toward gay males, since they are perceived as "acting" like women. Gays and lesbians are a threat to the prevailing ideology of gender separatism: their existence demonstrates one of the flaws in society's binary construction of gender.

Children, the Media, and Gender: Image Indoctrination

Gender stereotypes are embedded in the images children see in literature and on television. While some of the literary stereotypes about girls seem to be diminishing, many of the stereotypes about boys persist with the same force. Studies comparing characters in Caldecott Medal books and Coretta Scott King award-winning books in the past decade with Caldecott winners in the 1970s have shown a greater visibility of female characters in children's storybooks, and less stereotypic behavior of female characters.[81] Girls and women in children's books written in the mid- to late 1980s are more adventurous, aggressive, competitive, and independent. Male characters, however, are depicted in traditional gender roles. Boys are rarely portrayed as passive, dependent, or nurturing beings; they are expected to be the problem solvers. They are unlikely to be shown caring for a pet or a sibling.[82] While it is becoming increasingly acceptable culturally for girls to engage in what society has traditionally viewed as masculine behaviors, boys still cannot cross the gender divide and engage in traditionally feminine ways.

Consider the illustration of "boy behavior" in several prominent children's books. Mercer Mayer's Little Critter series for preschoolers depicts conventional gender role behavior. In *Just Me and My Mom,* Little Critter and his mother spend the day together going shopping, while in *Just Me and My Dad,* Little Critter's father takes him camping for their special time together. In Maurice Sendak's *Where the Wild Things Are* and Crockett Johnson's *Harold and the Purple Crayon,* "[s]mall boys are characterized by naughtiness, anger, oppositional feelings, and desires for nighttime adventure."[83] In the modern classic *Willy the Wimp,* by Anthony Browne, the protagonist is a small, sweet-natured but unhappy gorilla, who worries about stepping on insects and apologizes for things that are not his fault. Willy, dressed in a patchwork vest, tie, and rainbow-striped socks, is bullied by a suburban gorilla gang. (He apologizes when they hit him.) Embarking on a mail-order Charles Atlas program of diet, exercises, jogging, aerobics, boxing, and weight lifting, he transforms himself into a larger physical specimen. The ending is thuddingly predictable: Willy now feels good about himself and wins the heart of the girl gorilla whom he rescues from the gang.

On the preteen reading shelf, the extraordinarily popular Baby-sitters Club books, which portray adolescent girls in training for caring and nurturing roles, have no parallel for boys. And the club itself is an exclusive one, with no boy members. The club does have one male "associate member"— a boyfriend of the principal character—who has been featured in two of the series' hundred-plus books . . . at the request of readers. The "special edition" book, *Logan's Story,* introducing this male associate member of the Baby-sitters club, forthrightly addresses the issue of stereotyping in the first few pages:

> Now, a lot of people think the Baby-sitters club is all girls. I mean, when you think of a baby-sitter, you think of a girl, right? Admit it. But it's sort of like the stereotype of jocks. It just doesn't make sense. Guys can take care of kids, too. They can play games and pick up toys and give baths and make dinner— no big deal.[84]

This positive portrayal of a boy in a principal caregiving role, however, is undercut by the messages sent in other passages of the book. Logan explains that as an associate—not a *real*—member, he "[doesn't] go to regular meetings or pay dues. I just fill in when things get busy." He mentions that he has received some teasing about his association with the Baby-sitters Club, but that "it wasn't so bad at first. Most of the guys didn't even know I had this 'secret life' as a baby-sitter." A few short pages later in the book, Logan refers to his father's lukewarm reaction to his baby-sitting and his father's assumption that he is an associate member only because he is "hot for Mary Anne." To this, Logan says, "(Well, in a way, he's right.) Just in a way, though. I do enjoy kids, and I also like the other club members."

The gender coding replicates on the small screen. Children watch an average of twenty-one hours of television per week. The images they see relentlessly present messages of gender-appropriate behavior. Cartoons, television programs, movies, and advertising all portray girls and boys and women and men in stereotypical occupations and behaviors. While advertising creates an emaciated standard for female beauty, it repeatedly depicts masculinity as rugged individualism, with portrayals of men as military officers and sports figures, tinkering with cars and riding on motorcycles. Males are rarely portrayed in principal caregiving roles. One study of pre- and post-1980 cartoons found that while the picture has changed somewhat for female characters in a less stereotypical direction, in the cartoons evaluated, "male characters were *never* shown as caregivers."[85] A 1996 study showed that boy characters in cartoons are much more likely to use aggression than girls, while girls are twice as likely to demonstrate affection.[86]

One of the most influential children's television forums, *Sesame Street,* has repeatedly tackled the issue of gender stereotypes. In the early 1990s the producers became concerned that all the principal Muppets on the show were male: Bert, Ernie, Big Bird, Oscar the Grouch, the Count, Cookie Monster, Grover, and Elmo. (Miss Piggy, while a Muppet, is not a denizen of Sesame Street.) The writers tried to create strong female characters, but Grundgetta, Prairie Dawn, Rosita, Baby Alice Snuffleupagus, and the Squirrelles (a Motown-sounding trio of squirrels) did not rise to celebrity status. Finally, in 1993, after a quarter of a century of programming, *Sesame Street* acquired a successful girl Muppet with other than a walk-on role. When Zoe, a furry orange monster, joined the cast as a friend of Elmo, a furry red monster, initially she was not a hit with the Happy Meal crowd: too deep a voice, not enough jewels, too androgynous. A marketing survey followed, and children advised the show's research director to dress Zoe in beads, dangly earrings, and hair bows. Once these gender cues were added, Zoe's popularity zoomed.

Zoe's story is a good example of one of the gender feedback loops in operation. Gender differences that are unsupported by real differences in biology, such as clothes and accessories, become so deeply a part of the ways we understand gender that the socially constructed expectations become the reality.

At about the same time that Zoe moved in, the neighborhood was preoccupied with gender issues other than the scarcity of female role models. A fundamentalist minister tried to "out" Bert and Ernie as the first gay couple on children's television: "They live together in a one-bedroom house, never do anything without each other, and exhibit feminine characteristics."[87] *Sesame Street*'s producers issued a press release patiently explaining that Bert and Ernie were puppets and did not have genitalia or a sex life of any kind. That reassurance did not squelch the rumors, although it slowed the flood of mail from concerned parents that their tykes were witnessing a "deviant" lifestyle. As the attempted "outing" of Bert and Ernie shows, media images of gender are continuously shaped by the stereotypic expectations of the prevailing culture.

Domestic Labor

One of the principal influences on gender role identity is observed parental roles. Traditionally in America, mothers have assumed primary responsibility for housework and child care, while fathers have been the material providers. The 1980s and 1990s have witnessed a slight decrease in traditionalism regarding the division of domestic responsibilities, but the basic gendered division of household responsibilities has changed very little. What children witness at home on a daily basis shapes their concepts of gender roles, and what children in America see even today is the gendering of a household.

Even in the late 1990s, a time when more than two-thirds of mothers with young children work outside the home, women shoulder the vast amount of domestic chores in terms of sheer numbers of hours and effort. And the hours spent on domestic labor reflect the gendering of household tasks. Women typically do cooking, cleaning, and laundry and have primary responsibilities for child care and other family demands, while men typically perform major repair projects. The mental picture children will carry with them to adulthood is the vision of mom toting a laundry basket and dad hefting power tools.

Making calculations based on time use studies, and adding the time from paid employment, housework, and child care, sociologist Arlie Hochschild reported that "women worked roughly 15 hours longer each week than men. Over a year, they worked *an extra month of twenty-four-hour days a year*. Over a dozen years, it was an extra year of twenty-four-hour days."[88] In Hochschild's study, only one-fifth of the men shared equally in the housework. The traditional division of labor also affords different dimensions of freedom to the sexes:

> Even when couples share more equitably in the work at home, women do two-thirds of the *daily* jobs at home, like cooking and cleaning up—jobs that fix them into a rigid routine. Most women cook dinner and most men change the oil in the family car. But, as one mother pointed out, dinner needs to be prepared every evening around six o'clock, whereas the car oil needs to be changed every six months, any day around that time, any time that day.[89]

Hochschild's findings are confirmed in a study by two economists, Michael Leeds and Peter von Allmen. In a survey of 4,500 married, dual-career couples between the ages of twenty-five and forty-four, the participants kept track of the hours each week they spent on housework. Fifteen percent of the men responding said they performed less than one hour per week of domestic chores. "[T]he median amount of work for men was about five hours weekly, and the median for women was about 20 hours."[90]

The gendering of housework may run deeper than simply women absorbing a larger share of a finite amount of joint domestic responsibilities. An important additional finding of the Leeds and von Allmen study was that if husbands increased the number of hours they worked around the house, wives did not decrease their work. One possibility is that men and women may be culturally conditioned to believe that certain types of work or a certain amount of work is expected of them.

Men's and women's perceptions about housework diverge markedly. In one survey men's perceptions of who bears primary responsibility for various chores differed substantially from the perceptions of their wives: "Of those men with working spouses or partners, 69 percent said their mates took major responsibility for cooking, whereas 87 percent of the working wives said they did. Similarly, 78 percent of the working women said they were responsible for cleaning, as opposed to 63 percent of men who said their wives did the cleaning."[91]

One reason so many spouses and partners have disagreements over household chores is that men's and women's frames of reference may differ. Men may be comparing the amount of domestic work they perform to the amount their fathers did, which yields a favorable comparison, while women may be comparing the amount of work men are doing to the amount of work the women themselves are doing. The discrepancy in ref-

erence points is part of the cultural transition from traditional to more egalitarian roles.

The conventional division of outside and domestic responsibilities persists in another way: men are expected to be society's breadwinners. Men invest nine more hours per week at the office than women.[92] Men report more
travel in their employment than women, and longer commuting times. The
economic and societal pressures on men to be the principal wage earners
keep them away from home for longer hours, cutting down on the time men
have available for child care. In America fathers spend about forty-five min-
utes per day caring for their children alone, while mothers average more
than ten hours on a daily basis.[93] According to James A. Levine, director of
the Fatherhood Project of the Families and Work Institute, "Women are still
doing twice as much [child care] as men, although 20 years ago they were
doing three times as much."[94]

While popular media depict fathers as significantly involved in their children's lives, the reality has not kept pace with its promotions: "notwith-
standing the discussion of a changing masculinity, few studies have shown
that men are becoming more expressive and intimate."[95] Even when there is
increased paternal involvement with children, "most of these fathers still behave in traditional ways toward their children."[96]

Education

Gender separatism is rampant in schools. Segregation by gender occurs
significantly during middle childhood. First- through fourth-graders possess deeply held beliefs about the opposite sex having cooties or other un-
desirable qualities. But these are not beliefs that spontaneously erupt along
with adult teeth. These beliefs are taught by peers, parents, and teachers. For
instance, the ways teachers or administrators configure the building may
foster the separatism. My son's elementary school has separate coat shelves
for boys and girls, to discourage intermingling of jackets and bookbags, or
perhaps their owners. Gender may also be an easy, efficient way of regulating the use of various school resources: "Girls, you wash your hands at the
sink. When you finish, boys, it will be your turn to wash your hands." And
what second-grade class has not divided into the boys against the girls for
purposes of a game? By middle school or high school, consider the gender
composition of such coeducational public school classes as home economics or shop or such activities as cheerleading, Little League, the chess club,
or synchronized swimming. Add into the equation the millions of girls and

boys each year who join the Girl Scouts, Boy Scouts, YMCA, YWCA, fraternities, and sororities.

Much gender separatism seems to be a matter of individual choice or self-selection. Observational studies of primary school children show that generally boys and girls prefer to play with members of their own sex.[97] Boys move toward games of football or soccer, while girls congregate near the school and participate in hopscotch or foursquare. But what begins as self-segregation can be promoted by a teacher's responsive behavior: "Justin, if you don't lower your voice, you'll have to move over to the girls' table." Teachers, like parents, are a significant source of beliefs and messages about gender-appropriate behavior. Even teachers professing egalitarian gender ideology provide gendered messages. Some teachers will subtly encourage girls toward literary activities by spending more time with girls when they are reading and, similarly, will nudge boys toward math and science. Not only do young children learn what tasks are culturally appropriate for their gender, they are taught to prefer to excel at activities that are considered gender-appropriate. Thus, gender researchers have suggested that since "reading is viewed as feminine, and math as masculine by adults and children alike, . . . this leads children to achieve more in the subject perceived as being more gender-appropriate than in the subject perceived as being less gender-appropriate."[98]

Researchers agree that boys volunteer more frequently and volubly than girls. According to one study, boys are eight times more likely than girls to call out an answer in class.[99] Whether volunteering or not, boys receive more teacher attention. A study by the Gender/Ethnic Expectation and Student Achievement program revealed that "Los Angeles teachers responded four to nine times as often to boys."[100] Teachers generally tolerate interruptions by boys better than those by girls. Education professors Myra Sadker and David Sadker observe, "Whether male comments are insightful or irrelevant, teachers respond to them. However, when girls call out, there is a fascinating occurrence: Suddenly, the teacher remembers the rule about raising your hand before you talk. And then the girl, who is usually not as assertive as the male students, is deftly and swiftly put back in her place."[101]

The attention boys receive is not all positive. The Wellesley College Center for Research on Women notes that "[b]oys, particularly low-achieving boys, receive eight to 10 times as many reprimands as do their female classmates. . . . When both girls and boys are misbehaving equally, boys still receive more frequent discipline."[102] Some teachers seem less concerned about hurting boys' feelings. Boys are expected to be tough and are handled more physically. Other studies show the intersection between boys' academic performance and high-risk behavior. Statistics from the U.S. Department of Justice show that "high school boys are four times more likely than girls to be murdered; they are more prone to abuse alcohol or drugs; boys 12 to 15 run double the risk faced by girls of becoming victims of a violent crime, and 82% of the nation's incarcerated youths 18 and under are male—a percentage that increases to an estimated 95% for adult men."[103]

Boys are more likely than girls to be truant, repeat grades, flunk, and be placed in special education classes. Nationwide, two-thirds of students in special education classes for learning, developmental, and behavioral problems are boys.[104] And boys who are members of racial minorities are much more likely than whites to be placed in special education classes and to be classified as educably mentally retarded. Boys, particularly minority boys, have "a disproportionately large percentage of behavioral problems."[105]

Boys also run a much greater risk of expulsion than girls. One study conducted in the Florida school system by the Department of Education found that while males were 51 percent of the student body, male students accounted for 78 percent of the expulsions.[106] The study also showed strong links between poor school performance and greater discipline, and between race and economic position and discipline: "poor, black male students were overrepresented among students who were disciplined." Nationally, 7.2 percent of boys, compared to 6.5 percent of girls, will drop out of school prior to the tenth grade.[107]

The evidence that boys are more likely to suffer emotional disturbance and educational disabilities or engage in delinquent behaviors raises grave questions about biology, acculturation, and masculinity. The problems may be traceable to a confluence of factors, such as neurological differences between boys and girls, the lack of male role models, and cultural expectations of masculine behavior. Many of those social and even biological forces are changeable, but changes will require sorting out the ways and degrees to which behaviors are biologically influenced and socially created.

At this juncture, we have to ask whether our culture has pathologized behavior that is simply a manifestation of the prevailing construct of masculinity. Characterize a child as "rowdy," "noisy," "obnoxious," "competitive," "belligerent," or "aggressive," and more likely than not you are describing a boy. If a teen is labeled a "juvenile delinquent," chances are most people would mentally picture a male. Our thoughts of what it means to be a boy or a girl are embedded in nursery rhymes (boys are made of "snips and snails and puppy dogs' tails" while girls are made of "sugar and spice and everything nice"), aphorisms ("boys will be boys" is a popular homily that not only excuses a variety of misbehaviors, but carries forward and reinforces the social creation of gendered roles), and truths about appropriate behaviors ("big boys don't cry"). "[T]o some degree, society believes that boys are, by definition, bad."[108]

Society expects boys to develop the traits of dominance: independence, self-reliance, competitiveness, and leadership. Yet if boys learn the lessons too well and are too exuberant in their assertiveness, too extreme in their risk taking, or too defiant in their independence, we diagnose the biological disease of "testosterone poisoning." At times the line between acceptable and unacceptable behavior is dangerously thin. When the news reports first began to roll out about the six-year-old from Lexington, North Carolina, who was disciplined for sexual harassment, I wondered if the case was a good example of the point. According to initial reports, a teacher observed Johnathan Prevette kissing a classmate on the cheek, and he was suspended for "sexual harassment." He became a cause célèbre; America was up in arms that a first-grader was labeled a sex offender. The law of sexual harassment had gone too far, responding to such trivial situations.

Later reports disclosed that it was not the case that a teacher witnessing the behavior had turned Johnathan in as a sex offender, but that the girl had complained about the kiss to a teacher, and that the principal had determined that his behavior was "unwelcome touching"—not sexual harassment—under the school's general conduct code. Johnathan was not suspended, but he was removed from the classroom for a day, missing the group's ice cream party.[109] Then Prevette's parents encouraged him to do the talk show circuit—CNN, the *Today Show,* and *NBC News.* This seems to be where the sexual harassment label was applied. Yet conservative civil rights groups since have touted this case as an example of the misguided nature of sexual harassment laws. Johnathan's parents have threatened litigation unless the school issues a written apology. At a press conference on the courthouse steps, Jackie Prevette, wearing a "Kiss Me Johnathan" button, demanded an apology from the school. And the girl who complained about Johnathan's behavior? She feels guilty for stirring up trouble.

A number of things are wrong with this picture: Johnathan's parents' reaction, the media's reaction, and perhaps even the school's reaction. What seems most tragic about this incident is how quickly the entire country leaped on one side of a gender bandwagon, holding Johnathan up as an example of how sexual correctness has gone too far. This episode may cause a ready dismissal of actual cases of sexual harassment in elementary and secondary schools, a phenomenon that is the norm, while the case of Johnathan Prevette is the exception.

An American Association of University Women survey of 1,600 eighth-through eleventh-grade students found that four out of five students had experienced sexual harassment at school.[110] Sixty-five percent of the girls had been physically touched, grabbed, or pinched in a sexual manner. This peer harassment may consist of bra snapping, breast grabbing, obscene graffiti, sexual comments, catcalls, sexist remarks, unwelcome advances, or solicitation of sexual activity. At an elementary school in Montana, Friday was "Flip-Up Day," during which boys would chase girls to try to flip up their skirts.[111]

Legally, there has been some headway into the problem of peer sexual harassment. Since 1992, educational institutions may be held liable under Title IX for failing to take appropriate steps to eliminate peer harassment.[112] And many school officials are developing programs to educate students about unwelcome sexual conduct. However, parents and peers may model inappropriate behavior. An extreme example of the point was the case of the Spur Posse, a group of popular, athletic high school boys in a Los Angeles suburb who gained national attention by engaging in a sex-for-points competition to see who could sleep with the greatest number of girls. The girls were as young as ten years old. After the incidents came to light, some classmates and family members applauded the boys as studs, and labeled the girls "sluts." The mother of one of the Spur Posse members blamed the girls, saying to a news reporter, "Those girls were trash," while the father defended his son proudly: "Nothing my boy did was anything that any red-blooded American boy wouldn't do at his age."[113]

Even if parents are not condoning statutory rape and schools are condemning sexual harassment, in subtle ways they may be reinforcing gender stereotypes or the process of demarcation that leads to stereotyping. As the case of little Johnathan Prevette indicates, parents, teachers, and the media may be creating the idea that gender disputes have only two sides. Which side do you choose: the side that defends child-victims of oppressive sexual harassment laws or the side that supports child-victims of sexual harassment? Is the unwelcome kiss of a first-grader sexual harassment or was a little boy wrongfully punished for affectionate behavior? Whose side are you on: Johnathan's or the girl's?

People may be quick to seize on exceptional cases and readily categorize them, creating sharply dichotomous choices. One aspect of gender separatism is the construction of these warring dualisms. Perhaps a third side exists, one that recognizes the enormity of the harassment problem, the possibility of victims on both sides, and the delicacy and yet utmost importance of teaching young girls and boys the differences between good and bad touching, without labels, rancor, or blame.

Gendering in Adolescence

By adolescence, boys and girls have been bombarded with messages about what constitutes gender-appropriate behavior. Those messages have come from parents, teachers, peers, literature, television, radio, and movies. They have come also from institutions that establish sports programs, school activities, and employment opportunities. Even those parents who believe strongly in gender equity may feel compelled to socialize their children toward traditional gender norms to avoid seeing their children branded as social misfits.[114]

Parents may subtly perpetuate gender norms in ways they do not consciously recognize. Adolescent and family research demonstrates that fathers and mothers treat teenage boys differently than they do teenage girls. They encourage adolescent boys to work outside the home at an earlier age than adolescent girls. Parents assign household chores so that boys are not encouraged to do domestic chores, while girls are assigned housekeeping duties: "Girls do the dishes, boys do the lawn."[115] Later in life, girls act out the domestic chores they have been taught, while boys make little effort to overcome their learned helplessness in the domestic arena.[116]

Family behaviors regarding chores, benefits, and rules relating to independence (such as curfews and car usage) reflect significant gender biases. Parents transmit the idea that boys need cars more than girls and more supplemental income because they should take girls on dates or provide for their own economic well-being by working independently outside the home. Adolescent males are governed by more permissive rules regarding curfews and use of the family car.[117] Parental responses inculcate and reinforce gender-specific sex role behavior.

A study of gender norms among high school students covering the late 1970s to the late 1980s indicated that boys acquired prestige principally through sports, grades, intelligence, and access to cars, while girls did so through their physical appearance, sociability, grades, and intelligence.[118] One interesting finding of the study was that in the latter part of the 1980s, girls attained more prestige, in the perceptions of *boys*, through participation in sports.

Whether teenagers adhere to traditional models of behavior may depend on race, class, and economic differences. In the fall of 1996, the University of Missouri at Kansas City's Women's Council sponsored a symposium focusing on gendering in teens and young adults. One presentation consisted of panels of students discussing dating behavior. Students from Shawnee Mission North, a relatively affluent, predominantly white high school from a suburb in Kansas, described group dates, coffeehouse meetings, boys asking girls out, and girls asking boys out. A panel of girls from Paseo Academy, a predominantly black high school in the Kansas City, Missouri, metropolitan area, spoke uniformly of more rigid gender roles. They said that at their school, girls would never ask boys for a date, and if a boy were asked out by a girl, he would not agree, "out of respect for her." Some of the panel members from Paseo, almost dispassionately, reported the terms guys would use to describe their girlfriends: "bitch," "slut," and "ho."

Peer behavior and language, commercial products for teens, and music all craft the separation of the sexes during the teen years. The misogynistic lyrics in some gangsta rap music are well documented, such as 2 Live Crew's "Put Her in the Buck": "There's only one way to have a good time—fuck that pussy and make it mine. . . . I'll break you down and dick you long, bust your pussy and break your backbone." Even when women rappers entered the fray to combat the male-dominated, antifemale vocals, some of it was simply parallel trash-talk about the opposite sex. Salt-n-Pepa's hit "Tramp" offers the following advice: "Now what would you do if a stranger said 'hi'? / Would you dis him or would you reply? / If you'd answer, there is a chance / That you'd become a victim of circumstance / Am I right fellas? Tell the truth / Or else I'll have to show and prove / You are what you are I am what I am / It just so happens that most men are TRAMPS."

Other female rockers send messages that define masculinity through women's eyes as deception in relationships or connections made only through sexual encounters. Consider Sheryl Crow's lyrics from "Strong Enough"—"Will you be strong enough to be my man? / Lie to me / I promise I'll believe / Lie to me / But please don't leave"—or Juliana Hatfield's "Lost and Saved": "I can't help myself, I need a hand / Just when I think I'm dead, he turns up again in time for bed / I thank my lucky stars again. . . . I found a way to use my head / I go over and over every word he said." These visions of gender, which bombard teenagers daily over the airwaves, denigrate females and prescribe specific roles and behaviors for males.

The gender divide among teens is apparent in the labels they give their peers. During a date rape prevention program at a Phoenix, Arizona, high school, students described "ideal" men as "macho," "strong," and "domineering." The same students described ideal women as "submissive" and "obedient."[119] Mixed-gender friendships are viewed with suspicion. The divide is visible in teen treatment of sexuality. Guys who have sex with numerous partners are admiringly called "players," while girls who engage in the same behavior are called "whores." The Spur Posse competition, the national attention it drew, and the parental reaction may be exceptional, but the vilification of girls for their sexuality and the condonation of boys who have sex is shockingly commonplace. A national survey of over 200,000 teenagers demonstrated the double standard: "Only 22 percent of boys and 15 percent of girls say it hurts a boy's reputation, while 70 percent of boys and 87 percent of girls say a girl's reputation is damaged."[120] In these inconspicuous but persistent ways sexism becomes normalized among adolescents.

The gender divide is kept firmly in place by the exclusion of alternate sexualities. Gay and lesbian teens have traditionally received the most negative treatment by their peers and parents. Faced with feelings of unworthiness and low self-esteem, "[g]ay and lesbian youths account for as many as 30 percent of teenage suicides, up to 40 percent of teenage runaways, and a disproportionately high percentage of high school dropouts."[121] Although these teens are often the ones most in need of counseling, it is often hard for them to receive guidance because of opposition to gay and lesbian counseling. Parents in Palm Beach County, Florida, objected to a pamphlet that referred teens to a lesbian and bisexual counseling center for fear that youths with other problems would only receive guidance on sexual orientation issues.[122] Even Congress got into the act when members of the House and Senate proposed amendments to the Elementary and Secondary Education Act that would cut federal funding to any school "that has the purpose or effect of encouraging or supporting homosexuality as a positive lifestyle alternative."[123] The state legislature of Utah went one step further and actually passed a bill that allows school boards in Utah to prohibit school clubs that "encourage criminal or delinquent conduct; promote bigotry; or involve human sexuality."[124] The legislation was passed after the Salt Lake City School Board voted to ban all extracurricular clubs, rather than allow a "gay-straight" alliance club to form.

Homophobia and heterosexism are powerful social forces that silence those whose sexual orientation is nonheterosexual. Teenagers are met with traditional institutional expectations about gender roles: since heterosexuality is the norm, homosexuality is abnormal and thus it must be discouraged; gay and lesbian teenagers' experiences will be marginalized, their problems disregarded. These messages about homosexuality reinforce the strict separation of the sexes. The underlying theme is that discrimination based on gender roles is perfectly acceptable, and that crossing the gender divide is disallowed.

Sports

The largest feminist furor over sports has centered on inequality in the distribution of resources. For years, resources were allocated disproportionately to boys' high school and college sports programs. The congressional enactment of Title IX in 1972 was an attempt to level the playing field. Title IX prohibits sex discrimination in the classroom and in athletic programs in schools receiving federal funds.[125] The Department of Education's Office of Civil Rights developed guidelines for Title IX compliance, which require schools to (1) provide athletic participation opportunities roughly in proportion to the enrollment by gender; (2) demonstrate a persistent commitment to expanding program opportunities for the underrepresented sex; or (3) accommodate the athletic interests of the underrepresented gender.[126]

With the passage of Title IX, the government has taken a position as a promoter of women's rights. But the reach of Title IX was sharply limited by judicial interpretation of the legislation. In 1984 the Supreme Court held that no violation could be found by an institution that received federal funds unless the specific program that committed the discrimination directly received the federal money.[127] Three years later Congress passed corrective legislation, the Civil Rights Restoration Act, which reversed the Supreme Court's holding by giving institution-wide Title IX protection to any public program of higher education receiving any federal financial assistance.[128] Title IX is enforced in two ways: through complaints from athletes and compliance reviews. The compliance reviews, though, are periodic and include only a few federally funded institutions at a time. To date, no institution has ever had its funding pulled by the Office of Civil Rights.[129]

Legal action, media interest, and parental encouragement are dismantling some of the formal barriers to girls' and women's participation in high school and college sports. Since 1970 the number of high school girls playing varsity sports has increased ninefold; now, one in three high school girls plays a varsity sport, compared to one out of every two high school boys.[130]

More oblique forms of preferential treatment remain. Boys' teams still receive better media coverage, locker rooms, coaching, playing facilities, groomed athletic fields, equipment, and game times. Girls' teams may have to use tape or chalk to affix numbers to the backs of their jerseys; they have fewer female coaches as role models, and no cheerleaders at their sporting events; they will probably carry their own water jugs. In collegiate athletics, the NCAA Gender Equity Task Force determined that "few, if any, athletic departments complied with Title IX's requirements ... men's programs received approximately seventy percent of the athletic scholarship funds, seventy-seven percent of the operating budgets, and eighty-three percent of the recruiting money."[131]

Male domination in sports has its darker side for the construction of masculinity. The longtime exclusion of girls from sports is mirrored by relentless pressure on boys to engage in and excel at sports. We live in a culture that prizes sports and sees masculinity defined in part by athletic ability. Boys have to be good at sports or they are failures. The repeated childhood experience of choosing teams leads to shame and ridicule for those who are picked last. If boys are athletic, they have friends; if not, they are humiliated in gym class. Sports create hierarchies based on toughness and physical prowess. The sports themselves even have a hierarchy: the culturally more masculine sports, such as basketball and football, are prized over the less masculine sports, such as golf (a noncontact sport) and fencing (which looks a lot like dancing). Through sports, males undergo a socialization process that reconstitutes and transmits masculine hegemony.[132]

Often boys are urged toward sports that celebrate certain qualities traditionally associated with masculinity: physicality, power, strength, risk taking, and competition. Coaches, parents, and peers pressure boys not only to excel at sports but to win. When boys are pushed to be heroes and take risks, the toll is both psychological and physical. According to a report by the Adolescent Health Initiative for the West Virginia Bureau of Public Health, "[b]oys were twice as likely as girls to die in auto accidents, three and a half times more likely to commit suicide, four times more likely to be killed by a firearm and five times more likely to drown."[133]

One subtle effect of sex-segregated sporting teams is the model of team building that is the implicit lesson. Many colleges, graduate schools, and employers look to see if individuals participated in team sports, on the theory that teamwork training builds behaviors of leadership and cooperation. What this means in segregated sports is that boys learn to help other boys.

Certainly, boys learn how to deal with other players who have greater or fewer athletic skills than they do, players who possess more or less confidence, or players with particular abilities; one sort of person they don't learn to work with is someone of the opposite sex.

Sex segregation, coaching tactics that foster discrimination against women and homosexuals, and certain kinds of athletic discipline (such as coaches warning players against having sexual relations before important games) all make sports a training ground for sexism. Numerous studies have linked violence in particular sports with players' acceptance of beliefs about appropriate masculine behavior.[134] Boys are pressured to demonstrate toughness in sports. It is in this arena in particular that boys learn not to cry. Coaching strategies may involve ridiculing players for behavior that is unmasculine with taunts of "wimp," "pussy," and "faggot." I attended a third-grade football practice and overheard a coach yell degradingly at the group of boys: "Come on *girls*, when I tell you to tackle, that means putting your weight behind it. You don't resist linemen like this." The coach made the gesture of a limp-wristed push. Being good at sports is connected with not being a girl. The explicit message is that a boy who does not demonstrate appropriately tough behavior is female or homosexual; the implicit message is that women and gay men are without worth.

Many major universities have had high-profile instances of sexual assaults by athletes. One study, covering thirty Division I colleges, found that "male college student-athletes, compared to the rest of the male student population, are responsible for a significantly higher percentage" of reported sexual abuse cases.[135] In another three-year survey, the National Institute of Mental Health reported that athletes were involved in one out of every three sexual assaults at colleges.[136] Male sexual identity is constructed in part by locker room myths and metaphors. Sociologist Don Sabo describes the link between sports and male sexuality: "Dating becomes a sport in itself, and 'scoring,' or having sex with little or no emotional involvement, is a mark of masculine achievement. Sexual relationships are games in which women are seen as opponents, and his scoring means her defeat."[137] The degradation of women is accompanied by a loss of male insights into sexuality, and, says Sabo, the absence of a "vocabulary of intimacy."

Language

Since language permeates everything, it is unsurprising that the gender separatism reflected in various social spheres is embedded in language.

Conversation defines what humans are. Language is not simply a means for communicating ideas, it is social behavior that creates, conveys, and mediates relationships. A significant body of research explores the communication patterns of men and women.

In the 1980s and 1990s sociolinguists began to explore differences between men's and women's styles of communication. Professor of sociolinguistics Deborah Tannen says that boys and girls grow up in different cultures of communication: "Even if they grow up in the same neighborhood, on the same block, or in the same house, girls and boys grow up in different worlds of words. Others talk to them differently and expect and accept different ways of talking from them."[138] Girls often use language to emphasize rapport in relationships—telling secrets, exchanging compliments, displaying modesty about knowledge, and encouraging group participation. Boys tend to use language to seek status—giving orders as a leader or parading knowledge. These patterns transform into adult behavior. Women characteristically use language to create intimacy, foster consensus, and preserve a sense of community, while men use conversations to attain positions in the hierarchy of social organizations. Tannen says men view life as a contest, in which the objectives are to retain independence and avoid failure. Thus, during everyday conversations, men seek respect and give advice and solutions, while women seek affection and offer understanding.

The works of Tannen and others show how patterns of discourse may result in subordination and domination. Conversation for both sexes is a means of negotiating status, but women and men use conversation in different ways. Men tend to apologize infrequently, while women apologize as a conversation ritual; women are more likely to be indirect in making a point and to minimize the certainty of their statements; men generally dominate in formal conversations through interruptions, topic control, and length of talking time.

In an oddly ironic move, popular authors and readers are using the work of gender sociolinguists as evidence that women and men will naturally and universally misunderstand each other. A friend of mine who is a professor at an East Coast law school tells a story illustrating this phenomenon. He assigned his Gender and the Law class some works by Carol Gilligan and Deborah Tannen. A student in the class read the material and said during the seminar, "Now I know why my marriage didn't work, and why I should never get married again. No way I can ever really talk to a woman." Several other members of the class voiced their agreement. Others in the class, along with my professor friend, tried to convince these students that Tannen and other sociolinguists are attempting to open up possibilities for cross-gender conversations. Their point in doing this exploratory research is that only by recognizing the gap in communication can we ever hope to close it.

The law students are not the only ones drawing the conclusion that differences between the genders are ineluctable. In the last half decade, publishers have released an extraordinary spate of self-help books for gender problems. For instance, there is John Gray's best-selling *Men Are from Mars, Women Are from Venus: A Practical Guide for Improving Communication and Getting What You Want in Your Relationship* and its sequel, *Mars and Venus in the Bedroom: A Guide to Lasting Romance and Passion,* and *its* follow-up, *Mars and Venus Together Forever: Relationship Skills for Lasting Love,* and the *latest* installment, *Mars and Venus in Love.* These training manuals also include Lillian Glass's *He Says, She Says: Closing the Communication Gap between the Sexes,* Justin Sterling's *What Really Works with Men: Solve 95% of Your Relationship Problems (and Cope with the Rest), Men: A Translation for Women* by Joan Shapiro, and Cris Evatt's *He and She: Fascinating Facts about the Differences between Men and Women.*

Some of these workshop leaders, motivational speakers, and relationship gurus magnify the differences between the sexes—whether for purposes of illustration or profit is not entirely clear. The implication, though, is all too clear: the sexes are inevitably separated, members of different species or inhabitants of different planets. John Gray writes, "When you remember that your partner is as different from you as someone from another planet, you can relax and cooperate with the differences instead of resisting or trying to change them."[139] Justin Sterling prefers the species metaphor: "Men communicate through actions, as a German shepherd does. . . . Because dogs can't speak with words, nonverbal communication is all you can rely on to understand your dog. It is all you should rely on to understand a man."[140]

The underlying assumption of many popular cross-gender conversation books is that gender differences are fixed: men and women do not communicate because they are such radically different beings; these differences can be understood and adapted to, but not changed. The inherent financial interest in the existence of differences cannot be overlooked; the industry's continued existence depends on the persistence of differences. A mini industry is being built on making cross-gender conversations possible. On the one hand, these books may be making valuable contributions toward promoting cross-gender dialogue by encouraging recognition of typically gendered behavioral patterns. This comports with the academic message of many sociolinguists. On the other hand, the implicit and at times explicit message is that differences between the sexes are necessary and inevitable. The books written for the popular media tend to promote the *acceptance* of basic differences and devise strategies to cope with the differences, rather than trying to effect any changes in the behaviors that manifest the differences. This is part of a much larger cultural habit to take the given, the norm, as the natural. Until the norms are challenged, the gender line will remain firmly in place, recommunicated every day in ordinary dialogue, and appearing fixed and natural.

Occupational Segregation by Sex

Occupational segregation clusters women in low-wage jobs. Historically, and still persistently, women are often excluded from professional occupations, particularly from the upper echelons of the professions. While nearly half of all paid workers in America are women, women rarely attain senior management positions. "[T]he CEOs for all but five of the Fortune 500 industrial and service companies are men."[141] Although U.S. Bureau of Labor Statistics show that 41 percent of all managers are women,[142] "[w]omen in the executive ranks are over-represented in staff support functions such as communications, human resources, and legal affairs. Few female executives head core business areas such as sales and marketing functions, manufacturing plants, and major operating divisions."[143] These features are significant aspects of the economic subordination of women. They are tied to lesser job training opportunities for women, women's responsibilities as primary caregivers and household workers, and the sociocultural role of women as secondary wage earners, which constrains their occupational choices.[144]

The mirror image of the exclusion of women from professional tracks is the nonacceptance of men in traditionally female occupations. According to the Bureau of Labor Statistics, males accounted for only 2 percent of kindergarten teachers nationwide and 2.7 percent of child care workers, almost precisely the same percentage as two decades ago.[145] This pattern persists in other jobs traditionally associated with women. Men made up only 3.6 percent of receptionists and 6.2 percent of registered nurses. The preclusion of men from certain occupations is a largely invisible form of sex discrimination. Three dissenting Supreme Court justices maintained in 1982 that exclusion of male students from Mississippi University's nursing school did not "present . . . a serious equal protection claim of sex discrimination."[146]

Researchers have demonstrated that if a certain category of people is believed to be less competent in general, then a specific individual's performance is viewed more negatively and that individual's success is more likely to be explained by factors other than ability. The same sorts of gender stereotypes that have hampered women's promotion in various professional arenas apply to men who assume primary responsibilities in the domestic realm. A United States census survey showed that approximately one million fathers stay at home as the primary caregivers of their children, compared to sixteen million mothers. In one survey more than half the full-time dads reported that they were "extremely satisfied" with their career choice. While full-time fathers may have a greater degree of social acceptance in the 1990s than in the past, many describe the stigmas they face, and the ways their self-esteem suffers from societal reactions to their occupying the role of primary parent.

Almost every stay-at-home father has a story about being treated like an anomaly. They report being greeted with suspicion by mothers at playgrounds and playgroups. Peter Baylies, a full-time father and the editor of the newsletter *At Home Dad*, says, "I went to a mothers' playgroup and I sat down and . . . they were pretty surprised to see me. It was almost like being interviewed. Yet, what I do is no different from what they do."[147] The atypicality of the arrangement is reinforced by questions ("Are you laid off for a while?" "Are you babysitting today?" "Giving your wife a break?") and by unsolicited advice from strangers on the clothing and feeding of children. One full-time father described himself as "a freak." Social institutions reinforce the women-only preserve. While some preschools and churches have Parents' Day Out programs, many are still called Mothers' Day Out programs; images of incompetence are depicted in movies such as *Mr. Mom*; elementary classrooms typically still have "room mothers."

For men, staying home with children usually is not an option that is on their plate of choices because of economic necessity and social constraint. Ask a group of men whether they could, if they wanted, stay at home to raise children. It is a question I have asked my law school classes and various social and civil groups. The answer is unwavering: the vast majority of men would feel guilty about not providing for their families. As one man in an audience of lawyers said, "I couldn't do that. It was never a possibility that was in my consciousness; that wasn't the way I was raised."

Indeed, external economic circumstances—rather than initial decisions about preferred social arrangements—are often the driving force behind fathers taking a principal role in child care. Peter Baylies has found from anecdotal evidence that the main reason full-time fathers stay home with their children is that they were laid off from their jobs. Statistical evidence confirms this conclusion. Between 1977 and 1988 approximately 15 percent of children were cared for by their fathers. In 1991 fathers were the principal caregivers for 20 percent of children, but the figure dropped to 16 percent three years later. According to the Census Bureau, this correlates with an economic downturn in 1990 and 1991 and greater employment prospects after 1993.[148]

At the end of the second millennium, men have greater social permission, and concomitantly greater obligations, to engage in child rearing, yet men do not have the freedom not to work outside the home. Although men say they want to take a more active role in their families' lives, corporate America has not caught up with this new reality. Jackie Church, a consultant at Work/Family Directions, says that "the senior men and women at policy and decision-making levels in these companies don't understand. . . . After all, they got to where they are by devoting themselves entirely to their career at the expense of family." [149] The pressures felt by women to balance work and family demands are matched by the tension felt by men to be both a major breadwinner and an involved father. A *New York Times*-CBS poll found that "83 percent of women and 72 percent of men expressed feeling torn between work and family responsibilities."

In 1993 Congress passed the Family and Medical Leave Act (FMLA), which requires private sector employers of fifty or more employees to allow workers up to twelve weeks per year of unpaid leave for the birth or adoption of a child or a serious medical condition of the employee or a family member. Men do not take advantage of parenting leave nearly as much as women: "only 2 percent of men eligible for paternity leave ask for it."[150] While leave is legally available to both women and men, there are enormous social and financial pressures on men not to take time off. Coworkers may demonstrate resentment; supervisors may question the employee's "commitment." It is not surprising that studies show "many men still disguise the true nature of those days off. They either call in sick themselves, take a vacation day or say they are working from home."[151] Finally, most people simply cannot afford the time off. A Gallup poll taken in the year Congress was contemplating the FMLA revealed that seven out of ten workers would be financially unable to take unpaid time off for births or family emergencies.[152] The division of labor that relegates men to the employment arena is a structural barrier to men's participation in child rearing. The gendering of labor is not fixed, but is dictated largely by social and economic conditions.

In addition to facing societal expectations that they must be the primary breadwinners, men confront sharp economic and social consequences for selecting nontraditional career paths. While men may not be attracted to caregiving jobs because of low pay and minimal prestige, they are also culturally shunted away from nurturing and some types of service occupations. Men gravitating toward caregiving occupations may be viewed not just as anomalies but as potential child molesters. Despite beliefs that conceptions of masculinity are changing, recent studies show that men who engaged in nurturant touching of young children were rated as less masculine than men who did not participate in those behaviors.[153] Men in traditionally female occupations take social flack and may be treated as oddities by customers.

Since only 3 to 6 percent of child care workers are male, "they represent the deviant case"[154] and are treated accordingly. When men enter child caregiving occupations, their motives are viewed with suspicion. Are they potential child molesters, or maybe just gay? A field study of male child care workers illustrates the on-the-job difficulties faced by men doing "women's work." The study involved interviews of male and female child caregivers at various child care centers. Some thematic patterns and unwritten rules emerged in the treatment of male workers: "in many centers, men are more restricted in their freedom to touch, cuddle, nap, and change diapers for children."[155] Consider the story of Michael, a male caregiver in a Head Start program. The napping routine at the Head Start center might involve rocking or holding children or rubbing their backs. Every time researcher Susan Murray observed at the center, Michael never participated in napping the children. When she asked the head teacher why Michael was always relegated to lunch cleanup during the napping routine, the head teacher replied, "It's safer this way. You just never know what the parents might think, what kids might say. We really like Michael, and we've always just done it this way."[156]

Michael's story is not isolated. At another center, one male caregiver recognized a father's discomfort in handing his son over to a man and asked that someone else greet that child. Elsewhere, a parent specifically asked that a male child care worker not be allowed to "rub her daughter's back at naptime."[157] Amid fears of potential child abuse accusations and voiced parental suspicions, concerns that children (and male workers) might be suffering real deprivations of intimacy fade into obscurity. Even when they are accepted, men may be treated as tokens and thrust into "manly" roles as substitute daddies in charge of large motor activity. At a child care center that had just hired a male caregiver, a coworker said, "Oh good, now we'll have someone to do truck play with the boys." This pattern of treating male child care workers according to conventional expectations of masculinity, Murray says, "reifies the perception that there is very little that men have to offer children."

For years, feminists have attacked occupational sex segregation by urging women to break down the barriers into jobs traditionally filled by men. The percentages of women entering and rising in male-dominated professions, social associations, higher educational institutions, and legislatures has slowly but steadily increased. No one has devoted much effort toward encouraging men to cross the gender divide into women's occupations. The suggestion seems preposterous: why would men want to crash the pink ghetto when they could obtain higher salaries in other lines of work?

Given the current moral and market undervaluation of "women's work," perhaps the suggestion does border on the absurd. It is not just about power and money; the pervasive gendering of work goes much deeper than that. Influences from home, school, religion, the economy, prestige, and tradition all shape boys for certain occupations and girls for distinctly other jobs. Only in recent years has it been suggested that men might have an interest in entering nurturing or helping occupations. The idea that men might like or excel at these sorts of jobs is of equally recent vintage.

Of course some males in traditionally female jobs are paid higher salaries than females in comparable positions. For instance, female nurses earn only 95 percent of the amount earned by male nurses with equivalent education and training. This fact might be viewed as undercutting the disadvantage argument, since males can still dominate by entering a traditionally female occupation and taking over. Viewing the evidence this way falls back into the zero-sum game mode of analysis. Many different facets of sex discrimination can coexist. Males as a group can be discriminatorily excluded from certain occupational choices while individual males who do enter traditionally female fields can be discriminatorily overpaid. These threads of sex discrimination intertwine.

Apart from a work culture that nudges men toward traditional occupational choices, men also face gender discrimination for making nontraditional career choices and taking time off from work. Management professors Joy Schneer and Frieda Reitman conducted a study of 713 male and female M.B.A.s, of whom 119 had career interruptions. They found that the employment gaps for women were more likely to be voluntary, most frequently for child rearing, while the gaps for men were more likely to be involuntary, such as company restructuring. Controlling for other income determinants, they found that men who experienced a career gap for whatever reason had incomes that were 21 percent lower than the incomes of men without gaps, while the women's incomes were only 9 percent lower than the incomes of women without gaps. These results indicate that men may be punished economically for discontinuous employment histories based on gender-specific stereotypes: "Traditionally, women are expected to leave the work force to have and raise families. Women thus possess a socially acceptable reason for being out of the work force that does not relate to competence, but men do not."[158]

It is almost axiomatic that men dominate the market, while women are relegated to the domestic sphere. What is little acknowledged, though, is the occupational segregation of men. Because of the many economic and social advantages men have accrued, the preclusion of choices for men is a much less visible form of discrimination.

Gender differentiation begins in infancy. In our culture it has led to girls learning nurturing behavior and also passivity, submissiveness, and dependence. Boys are socialized to act aggressively and autonomously, and to achieve. Specific tasks are assigned to members of each sex, and various social activities—from housework to sports to occupations—are considered principally the domain of one sex but not the other. Crossing traditional gender lines is viewed as a violation of cultural norms.

Some sex researchers have demonstrated statistically significant sex-related differences in attitudes, behavioral tendencies, and social actions. While there is considerable confirmation that the sexes *exhibit* differences in behaviors, attitudes, and actions, the evidence is overwhelming that these social behaviors are not solely, and not even primarily, the product of biological sex differences. On the contrary, the most powerful evidence is that gendering is largely a social construct. Much of the biosocial research points toward the conclusion that on the whole, similarities between the sexes are more pronounced than differences, there is greater variability between individuals of the same sex than between the sexes, and socially created gender differences abound.

Even to the extent that some facets of sex differences have biological roots, we build on these differences socially. Individuals are sculpted by their environments, and traditional stereotypes play a large role in constructing gender. The emphasis on differences between girls and boys and women and men can reinforce gender stereotypes. Boys and girls are expected to act in prescribed ways in accordance with their genders. At least in part to receive approval, children will conform to gender role expectations; they will behave in ways that are expected of them. And the match between beliefs about the propriety of gender roles, behavioral expectations of others, and the development of gender role–congruent social skills creates a cycle of gender role reinforcement. Gender differences between females and males will repeatedly manifest because they are expected, taught, adopted, and then displayed in social behaviors. Gender thus becomes a self-fulfilling prophecy.

We live in a culture that celebrates differences—and looks for them. Society continually trains its members in the recognition of differences. Our culture holds deep beliefs in the existence of a natural order. Biology easily becomes the uncritical justification for discrimination.

For those areas at the margins where some sex-based differences exist, the social question remains: do those modest statistical differences justify presumptive differences in treatment of women and men? The nature-nurture debate will not be resolved scientifically during our lifetimes, if ever. Thus, what we face is really a different set of questions. Of what significance are the social differences between the sexes, and, in the face of uncertainty about whether sex differences are biological or social in origin—whether they are hardwired—how should we behave toward gender differences? The idea of difference itself is a social construct. Whether gender differences are innate or cultural or, most probably, some combination of the two, we still must make distinctly social choices about the labels we attach to those differences and the significance we give them. The labeling process—the part that occurs through the passage of laws and the crafting of legal decisions— is the subject of the next chapter.

3

How Courts Enforce
Gender Separatism

> Where the law serves to constrain the range of permissible, or even coherent, sexual meanings, it becomes an instrument of discrimination itself. —Katherine M. Franke, "The Central Mistake of Sex Discrimination Law"

Increasingly, courts are being called on to determine what physical and social differences between the sexes matter legally. Laws and legal decisions send symbolic messages about what it means to be male and female, and those messages play a central part in shaping gender. In many individual cases, judicial constructions of sex facilitate gender separation. Courts consistently employ a naturalistic conception of gender, deeming physical differences between the sexes important when their relevance to issues in the case is questionable; courts hold fast to conventional gender stereotypes in areas ranging from dress and grooming codes to appropriate occupational channels for men and women to hazards affecting men in the workplace; and courts are often blind to the subtle stereotypes that construct masculinity. In short, the courts patrol the borders of gender.

This chapter begins with the Supreme Court's interpretation of differences between men and women in constitutional cases. Embedded in the Court's early decisions are the notions that biological differences between the sexes exist and that they matter. In cases from the mid-nineteenth to the mid-twentieth centuries, the Court repeatedly found that women's innate fragility made them unfit for certain occupations. Even after the constitutional gender revolution in the 1970s—when the Court began applying an elevated level of scrutiny to classifications based on sex—the Court found physical differences between men and women determinative in cases involving civic service responsibilities, the reach of a criminal statute, and the extension of disability benefits. In each of these cases the Supreme Court made a social choice about the importance of male and female physiology. It did not, however, rely on physiology in a consistent way: biological differences were not important to the Court in a case involving pregnancy disability benefits, but they were vital to the Court in determining that statutory rape laws should apply only to males.

Two recent Supreme Court cases—one regarding the admission of women to the all-male Virginia Military Institute (VMI) and the other involving a manufacturer's fetal protection policy—suggest the modern Court's perceptions of gender. In some ways, those perceptions have not changed much in the past century. While the Court rightly refuses to allow schools and employers to exclude women from occupational channels, lurking beneath the surface of the opinions are two forms of gender stereotyping that remain subtle but pervasive. First, the Court has made obvious steps toward occupational gender equity for women, but has ignored men's pleas for equality in the realms of parenthood and reproduction. Second, the Court has tacitly accepted the very idea of gender separatism. To the Court, the existence of some separate educational facilities for men and women seems natural, perhaps inevitable. In the area of gender relations, vestiges of the separate but equal doctrine remain good law.

Moving from the level of Supreme Court decisions to that of lower courts across the nation, we will see what happens when petitioners test everyday practices of gender separatism. In areas as seemingly disparate as the law of voluntary associations, gender-based pricing, and hair and dress regulations, court decisions repeatedly reinforce the gender divide. Numerous decisions of federal and state courts keep the structures of gender separation firmly in place.

The Constitution and the Natural Order: Immutable Differences

The assumption of equal protection doctrine is that similarly situated people and situations must be treated similarly. If they are not, the state must come forward with some justification for the difference in treatment, the requisite strength of that justification depending on the nature of the classification. Equal protection analysis asks first whether there is discrimination or a difference in treatment. If so, the next question becomes whether it can be justified. Governmental reasons for classifications based on race require "the strictest judicial scrutiny," while classifications based on gender require the government to demonstrate an "exceedingly persuasive justification." Equal protection doctrine does not say that differences in treatment cannot exist; it merely says that those differences must be justified by real differences in the situations of the groups subject to disparate treatment. If groups are not similarly situated, dissimilar treatment is not discrimination at all.

The constitutional analysis of gender has focused on a biological model for centuries. Embedded in constitutional decisions about gender is the idea of a natural order. The Supreme Court reads the Constitution in ways that protect this order. Heightened scrutiny is applied to gender classifications based, in large part, on the idea that sex is an immutable physical characteristic. This method of analysis reinforces the impression that the biological differences between men and women matter socially.

The early constitutional cases regarding gender assumed it was a biological category. In 1869 Myra Bradwell passed the Illinois bar exam with high honors and applied for admission to the bar. An Illinois statute prohibited married women from obtaining licenses to practice law. In 1873 the U.S. Supreme Court affirmed the Illinois Supreme Court's decision denying Myra Bradwell admission to the bar, holding that the privileges and immunities of national citizenship under the Fourteenth Amendment did not extend to the right to practice law. In a concurring opinion, Justice Bradley developed the notion of separate "spheres" for men and women. He explained that the legal rights of women were minimal because of prevailing beliefs about women's physical capacities:

> The civil law, as well as nature herself, has always recognized a wide difference in the respective spheres and destinies of man and woman. Man is, or should be, woman's protector and defender. The natural and proper timidity and delicacy which belongs to the female sex evidently unfits it for many of the occupations of civil life. The constitution of the family organization, which is founded in the divine ordinance, as well as in the nature of things, indicates the domestic sphere as that which properly belongs to the domain and functions of womanhood. The harmony, not to say identity, of interest and views which belong, or should belong, to the family institution is repugnant to the idea of a woman adopting a distinct and independent career from that of her husband.[1]

In a companion case, the *Slaughterhouse Cases*, in which butchers argued that the privileges and immunities clause prevented the state from creating a monopoly on slaughterhouses that would put them out of work,

Bradley had insisted in dissent that "citizens of the United States, lay claim to every one of the privileges and immunities which have been enumerated; and among these none is more essential and fundamental than the right to follow such profession or employment as each one may choose, subject only to uniform regulations equally applicable to all."[2] Thus he accepted the argument for the butchers that he rejected in Myra Bradwell's case.

But women were different. According to Bradley, women had a natural "destiny" based on "the law of the Creator," and that mission was "to fulfil [*sic*] the noble and benign offices of wife and mother." Women apparently lacked those qualities of "decision and firmness which are presumed to predominate in the sterner sex." The laws of the country were required to reflect this natural order. That is, "the rules of civil society must be adapted to the general constitution of things, and cannot be based upon exceptional cases."

In 1908 the Supreme Court repeated the idea that women's biological capacities should determine their legal rights. In *Muller v. Oregon*, the Court held that differences between the sexes justified laws restricting working hours for women based on concerns for their reproductive health:

> That woman's physical structure and the performance of maternal functions place her at a disadvantage in the struggle for subsistence is obvious. This is especially true when the burdens of motherhood are upon her. Even when they are not, by abundant testimony of the medical fraternity continuance for a long time on her feet at work, repeating this from day to day, tends to injurious effects upon the body, and, as healthy mothers are essential to vigorous offspring, the physical well-being of woman becomes an object of public interest and care in order to preserve the strength and vigor of the race.[3]

It is no coincidence that the revolutionary litigation technique of the Brandeis brief was first employed in *Muller* to show empirically the need for protective labor legislation for women. To defend the Oregon statute that limited women working in certain occupations to no more than ten hours per day, Louis D. Brandeis, who ascended to the High Court eight years after the famous briefing, and his coauthor and sister-in-law, Josephine Goldmark, collected data from more than a hundred authorities in factory work, hygiene, psychology, sociology, and medicine to show the vulnerability of women from long hours of work.[4] Their 113-page brief contained fewer than three pages of legal arguments. The brief attempted to demonstrate empirically that women, unlike men, were inherently ill suited for manual labor:

> Woman is badly constructed for the purposes of standing eight or ten hours upon her feet. I do not intend to bring into evidence the peculiar position and nature of the organs contained in the pelvis, but to call attention to the peculiar construction of the knee and the shallowness of the pelvis, and the delicate nature of the foot as part of a sustaining column.[5]

When the *Muller* Court upheld the statute's restrictive working hours, thus limiting women's economic opportunities, it did so with an explicit reliance on the Brandeis brief (of course the brief took its father's name). The Court noted that "history discloses the fact that woman has always been dependent upon man," that males possessed "superior physical strength," and that "in the struggle for subsistence she is not an equal competitor with her brother." It concluded that "woman's physical structure, and the functions she performs in consequence thereof, justify special legislation restricting or qualifying the conditions under which she should be permitted to toil."[6] While the meaning of gender was attached to social roles, those roles were thought to be dictated by biology.

Even in midcentury the ideology of *Bradwell* and *Muller* still retained its hold on the Court. In *Goesaert v. Cleary*, decided in 1948, the Supreme Court upheld Michigan's right to draw "a sharp line between the sexes" and to forbid women, except wives and daughters of male bar owners, to work as bartenders.[7] The Court observed that "bartending by women may . . . give rise to moral and social problems" and reasoned that the "oversight assured through ownership of a bar by a barmaid's husband or father minimizes hazards that may confront a barmaid without such protecting oversight." This notion of inherent role differences persisted in 1961, when the High Court found constitutional a Florida statute that required men to serve as jurors, but said that only women who registered would be called for jury duty. The Court found that "a woman should be relieved from . . . jury service unless she herself determines that such service is consistent with her own special responsibilities," reasoning that women are "still regarded as the center of home and family life."[8]

Finally, in 1971, the Supreme Court issued its first decision striking a state law as unconstitutional gender discrimination under the equal protection clause. *Reed v. Reed* concerned an Idaho probate statute that preferred men over women as administrators of decedents' estates.[9] The Court unanimously struck the statute, finding no rational basis to "give a mandatory preference to members of either sex over members of the other." Two years later, in *Frontiero v. Richardson*, a plurality of the Court was willing to use strict scrutiny to invalidate a federal statute that assumed spouses of male service members would be dependents but required female service members to prove the dependency of their spouses to receive benefits.[10] The Court recognized the stereotypic generalizations contained in the assumption that men would be breadwinners and women would be dependents.

These decisions began to acknowledge the ways social institutions create gender differences and make them into advantages and disadvantages. Gender was both a biological and social category. A classification based on gender triggered heightened scrutiny, said Justice Brennan in *Frontiero*, in part because of the immutable characteristic of sex, and in part because the "[n]ation has had a long and unfortunate history of sex discrimination."

The Supreme Court ultimately settled on intermediate scrutiny for gender cases, and of course real biological differences could justify differences in treatment of men and women. The idea of biological differences has, for example, been used to justify separation of the sexes for purposes of athletic activities, since physical differences are thought to be related to performance differences in athletics.

In the 1970s and 1980s the Court was willing to debunk more obvious gender stereotypes and remedy blatant gender imbalances. It appropriately recognized when purported physiological differences were being used by the government as a smokescreen for cultural difference. For example, in *Craig v. Boren*, the Court struck an Oklahoma statute that created disparate drinking ages for males and females.[11] The statute had prohibited the sale of 3.2 percent beer to females under the age of eighteen and males under the age of twenty-one, on the theory that eighteen- to twenty-year-old males were more likely to drink and drive than females at that age. Although there may have been some physical differences, some social differences, and some small empirical differences in arrest rates between young adult males and females, the Court condemned "the stereotype that women mature earlier than men and are more responsible at an earlier age."

Reproduction and Potential Pregnancy: Women

But the underlying theme that men and women are biologically different in ways not manifested in gross anatomy persisted. In several cases the Supreme Court capitalized on the intuitive appeal of the "physiological differences" argument in contexts in which it was less than clear that such differences were at issue.

In 1981, in *Rostker v. Goldberg*, the Court upheld the male-only draft registration, finding that men and women were not similarly situated with respect to the Selective Service Registration Act because only men could fight in combat positions.[12] The Court accepted, without probing, Congress's determination that women were biologically unsuitable for combat positions. Thus women were excluded from the draft because they were excluded from combat. End of inquiry.

In the same year, in *Michael M. v. Superior Court of Sonoma County,* the Court upheld a statutory rape law that imposed criminal liability on males but not females for engaging in sexual intercourse when the female was under eighteen.[13] California attempted to justify its law by arguing that since the burden of pregnancy falls exclusively on women, no additional criminal punishment was necessary for them. The Court was willing to view the possibility of young women becoming pregnant as a real physical difference between the sexes, justifying differences in treatment with respect to the criminal laws. The gender-specific statutory rape law did not violate the equal protection clause because "young men and young women are not similarly situated with respect to the problems and risks of sexual intercourse. Only women may become pregnant, and they suffer disproportionately the profound physical, emotional and psychological consequences of sexual activity."

The Court's location of responsibility in biological differences reveals its unwillingness to probe the cultural and historical creation of statutory rape law and gender. Dissenting in *Michael M.*, Brennan carefully traced the development of the California statutory rape law:

> the law was initially enacted on the premise that young women, in contrast to young men, were to be deemed legally incapable of consenting to an act of sexual intercourse. Because their chastity was considered particularly precious, those young women were felt to be uniquely in need of the State's protection. In contrast, young men were assumed to be capable of making such decisions for themselves; the law therefore did not offer them any special protection.

The gender classification of the law "was initially designed to further those outmoded sexual stereotypes," not to address the problem of teen pregnancies.[14] Pregnancy prevention was never among the law's objectives, but was instead a post facto justification the state created for purposes of the lawsuit. Thus, sex stereotypes—placing punitive social responsibility on males as sexual aggressors—rather than real physical differences lay at the heart of the Court's willingness to punish males but not females for statutory rape. Indeed, as Justice Stevens suggested in a separate dissent, if the state really wanted to eradicate teenage pregnancy, it should punish both males and females for twice the deterrent effect.[15] (Justice Blackmun's concurrence inadvertently reveals the danger behind the stereotypes of male aggression and female passivity: the victim in the case "consented" to intercourse only after she was "hit . . . back down.")

The idea of pregnancy potential was a "real" difference that justified imposing criminal liability only on males. Yet in other contexts the Court has refused to recognize that discrimination based on pregnancy is gender discrimination. In *Geduldig v. Aiello,* a public employer excluded coverage of pregnancy-related disabilities from its comprehensive health insurance plan.[16] In 1974 the Supreme Court upheld this pregnancy exclusion, reasoning that "[t]he California insurance program does not exclude anyone from benefit eligibility because of gender but merely removed one physical condition—pregnancy—from the list of compensable disabilities." In an infamous footnote to the opinion, the Court explained why the pregnancy exclusion was not gender discrimination: "While it is true that only women can become pregnant, it does not follow that every legislative classification concerning pregnancy is a sex-based classification. . . . The program divides potential recipients into two groups—pregnant women and nonpregnant persons. While the first group is exclusively female, the second includes members of both sexes."

Two years later, in *General Electric Co. v. Gilbert,* the Court applied its *Geduldig* equal protection analysis to the similar situation of a private employer sued under Title VII, holding that "it is impossible to find any gender-based discriminatory effect . . . simply because women disabled as a result of pregnancy do not receive benefits."[17] Congress disagreed with the conclusion in *Geduldig* and *Gilbert* that discrimination based on pregnancy is not gender-based discrimination. It passed the Pregnancy Discrimination Act, amending Title VII to include discrimination on the basis of pregnancy as a prohibited act.[18] The *Geduldig* theme that "it does not follow that every legislative classification concerning pregnancy is a sex-based classification" is one that lives on in constitutional jurisprudence. In a 1993 case dealing with the blocking of access to an abortion clinic, the Court refused to find the antifemale animus to establish a violation of a federal civil rights statute because "the disfavoring of abortion . . . is not ipso facto sex discrimination."[19]

A comparison of the holding in *Michael M.* with those in *Geduldig* and *Gilbert* indicates how the Court treats biology and gender. The fact of potential pregnancy is biological, but the Court makes distinctly social choices about when and whether to give that fact social importance. To vest pregnancy with significance for purposes of a criminal responsibility statute (when that was never the statute's intended purpose) and yet not consider pregnancy significant when it affects the work life and health of the mother seems wrongheaded in the extreme.

One danger of giving biological categories great weight is that it diverts the Court from considering the social explanations for the construction of the categories and excuses the Court from taking into account the cultural ramifications of its decisions. Consider what remains unexplored when the Court focuses on biological facts. In *Michael M.*, the Court's ready acceptance of potential pregnancy as a justification for the classifications in the statutory rape law masked the legislature's true intent in constructing those classifications. Left unexamined was the cultural construction of what it means to be male and female. And embedded in that social construct were ideas about male sexual aggression, female vulnerability, and the assumption on the state's part of a need, as Brennan expressed, "to protect the State's young females from their own uninformed decisionmaking."[20]

The same mistake occurred in *Geduldig* and *Gilbert*, with the Court's construction of what are essentially biological—albeit manufactured—categories to resolve the case. The artifice of the distinction between pregnant and nonpregnant persons is transparent. Although the "nonpregnant persons" category includes men and women, the "pregnant persons" category is composed exclusively of women. Once again for the Court, biology dictated the outcome. It was not the physical and social consequences of pregnancy that the Court considered important, but the fact that women (as a biological class) appear in both the "pregnant persons" and "nonpregnant persons" categories. Given the Court's resolution of the case with the biological syllogism, what lay unexplored? The Court's refusal to recognize that pregnancy is a disability deserving accommodation "reinforces cultural stereotypes that pregnancy is a 'natural' status for women, unlike injuries or diseases designated as disabling, and presumes that women will have no need of financial support should pregnancy render them incapable of working."[21]

The biological category is also lacking in integrity and stability. Biology is not the reliable empirical hallmark of gender differences that the Court seems to seek. While "potentially pregnant persons" and women constituted the same class for the Court in *Michael M.*, in *Geduldig* the Supreme Court clearly demarcated between pregnancy and gender.[22] While not all legislative classifications based on pregnancy are equal, what is revealing are the circumstances under which the Court chose to vest pregnancy with significance. The biological reasoning was useful to the Court when it served to confirm social stereotypes about aggressive males and vulnerable females, but was jettisoned when it threatened to impose an obligation on the state to provide insurance benefits for pregnancy. This inconstancy of premises should generate some suspicion of claimed "givens" or "necessities."

The tendency of the Court to look for real (defined as biological) differences comes and goes. In the 1989 case of *Price Waterhouse v. Hopkins*,[23] the Supreme Court found a cause of action under Title VII for employment decisions that are based on sexual stereotypes. "[W]e are beyond the day," Brennan wrote,

> when an employer could evaluate employees by assuming or insisting that they matched the stereotype associated with their group. . . . An employer who objects to aggressiveness in women but whose positions require this trait places women in an intolerable and impermissible catch-22: out of a job if they behave aggressively and out of a job if they do not. Title VII lifts women out of this bind.

But the Court's record on recognizing and exploding cultural stereotypes is less than perfect. For example, the Court recognized a cause of action for hostile environment sexual harassment in *Meritor Savings Bank FSB v. Vinson,* but left the burden on the sexual harassment plaintiff to demonstrate that the sexual conduct was unwelcome—essentially that she did not "ask for it."[24]

In *Mississippi University for Women v. Hogan* the Court again bucked a cultural stereotype.[25] In a five-to-four vote, the Court struck a state-supported university's policy of admitting only women to its nursing school. In her first term on the Court, Justice Sandra Day O'Connor wrote the opinion in *Hogan*, which contains one of the most insightful explications of the construction of gender ever to appear in a Supreme Court opinion.

O'Connor stated that MUW's policy of excluding male students was unconstitutional because it "tends to perpetuate the stereotyped view of nursing as an exclusively woman's job . . . and makes the assumption that nursing is a field for women a self-fulfilling prophecy." In *Hogan* three of the dissenting justices thought the separatism of sexual segregation was not only acceptable but desirable.

In various other cases, the dissenters' refrain has kept alive the idea of biologically based differences. For instance, in *Caban v. Mohammed* the Supreme Court heard a case in which an unwed mother left the biological father of her children to marry another man.[26] When the stepfather wanted to adopt the children, the biological father filed a cross-petition for adoption. The Court invalidated a New York statute that permitted unwed mothers but not unwed fathers to withhold consent to the adoption of their children. While the *Caban* majority condemned "the stereotype that a biological mother always bears a more intimate relationship with a child than does a father," the four dissenters held fast to it. The dissents by Justices Stewart and Stevens (the latter joined by then Chief Justice Burger and Justice Rehnquist) emphasized the unique physical bond between mother and child— "[o]nly the mother carries the child"—which, they thought, should confer exclusive rights on the mother to determine who could engage in the social relationship of fathering the child for the remainder of the child's life. For the dissenters, parenting abilities and possibilities were matters of biology. Thus, even when a majority of the Court condemns stereotypes resulting from outdated notions of social relations, a strong refrain often emanates from dissenters holding fast to the anachronism.

Reproduction and Potential Parenthood: Men

International Union, UAW v. Johnson Controls concerned a Title VII challenge to a battery manufacturer's fetal protection policy that excluded fertile women, but not fertile men, from jobs working with lead. Men were permitted to work at jobs requiring lead exposure exceeding OSHA standards, but women were required to demonstrate their infertility. One of the named plaintiffs, Mary Craig, chose to be sterilized in order to keep her higher-paying job; another, Elsie Nason, a divorced fifty-year-old, was involuntarily transferred to a lower-paying job in another division of the company when she could not prove she was sterile. The company defended its policy on the ground that occupational lead exposure might risk the health of fetuses.

In 1989 the Seventh Circuit Court of Appeals upheld the company's fetal protection policy, accepting the argument that the lead exposure might endanger fetuses and thus determining that female sterility in this workplace was a bona fide occupational qualification. The court based its decision on a finding of "real physical differences" between men and women that justified the difference in treatment. Women, whom the Seventh Circuit described as potential "mothers," might risk the health of their "unborn children."

The Supreme Court reversed, holding that sterility was not a bona fide occupational qualification.[27] The justices unanimously agreed that the fetal protection policy was discriminatory under Title VII because "[w]omen who are pregnant or potentially pregnant must be treated like others." In *Johnson Controls*, the Supreme Court observed the pattern of its decisions since *Muller*, noting, "Concern for a woman's existing or potential offspring historically has been the excuse for denying women equal employment opportunities."

Johnson Controls was widely heralded as a feminist triumph. The decision recognized that women may face sex discrimination because of their reproductive capacity, irrespective of the absence of pregnancy and the lack of any future intent to become pregnant. The victory is far from hollow: women cannot be denied employment based on their reproductive status. But one aspect of this case lurks in the shadows. *Johnson Controls* is a metaphor for the unspoken bias against males in constitutional cases—and in life—and the ways that bias is difficult to detect.

The exclusive focus of the *Johnson Controls* opinion was the discriminatory treatment of women. The Court's initial framing of the case viewed the matter solely as a woman's issue: "May an employer exclude a fertile female employee from certain jobs because of its concern for the health of the fetus the woman might conceive?" Since the Court saw the problem as one of "fertile women in the workplace," the harms to male workers receded from view. One of the named plaintiffs in the case, Donald Penney, was male. A married man who wanted to have children, Penney had requested a voluntary leave of absence to reduce his blood lead levels so that he and his wife could safely conceive a child. This leave of absence was denied.

In finding that the fetal protection policy constituted impermissible sex discrimination in violation of Title VII, Blackmun's opinion for the Court stated, "Fertile men, but not fertile women, are given a choice as to whether they wish to risk their reproductive health for a particular job." That was factually incorrect. The fetal protection policy was sex-specific in not one but two directions, and men were *not* given the option to *avoid* confronting workplace lead exposure that might risk their fertility. Donald Penney was not afforded any such choice.

Masculinist bias—assuming the norm of male workers and thus barring females from workplace hazards—has its dark side for men. The company had not banned fertile men from jobs that exposed them to lead, despite evidence that sperm exposed to lead may cause birth defects. In fact, the health risks to potential future offspring may be as or more serious through paternal exposure to toxins:

> Few studies have been done on the reproductive risks associated with male exposure because of cultural assumptions that mothers are more closely linked to children and are more responsible for children's problems and disabilities than are fathers. The studies that have been done on paternal exposure indicate it is likely that agents posing reproductive risks through maternal exposure are also dangerous through paternal exposure. . . . Often, a fertile male will pose a greater risk to fetal safety than a fertile non-pregnant female. Spermatogenesis, the rapid division of sperm cells in the testes, is an ongoing process, whereas the female's ova all are produced by early infancy, and rapidly dividing cells are more susceptible to a number of injuries. Also, some substances such as lead and cadmium "concentrate in the male reproductive tract [and] are quite toxic to sperm."[28]

The Court did note that the record contained evidence "about the debilitating effect of lead exposure on the male reproductive system." But this evidence was used only to show that women were being treated differently, and thus discriminated against, in a situation in which men and women were relevantly similar. The Court failed to reach the other logical conclusion. Nowhere does the opinion recognize that denying men the ability to avoid exposure to workplace hazards, while requiring it of women, is gender discrimination against men. The Court never addressed Donald Penney's concerns.

Indeed, the Court attempted to distinguish an earlier case, *Dothard v. Rawlinson*, which had held that sex was a bona fide occupational qualification for guards in a maximum-security prison for males.[29] In 1977 the Court in *Dothard* found no equal protection violation in excluding women from contact areas in the prison because some male inmates who were sex offenders might rape female prison guards due to their "very womanhood." On one level, *Dothard* and *Johnson Controls* are easy to reconcile. Implicit in both cases is the assumption that if it is a tough, dirty job, somebody male has to do it.

Donald Penney represents male workers whose harms are not vocalized. The assumed norm of the male employee has excluded women from the workplace for centuries, but it is a norm that has been little explored relative to its effects on men. In *Johnson Controls*, the Court not only assumed that men belonged in the workplace, but virtually ignored their reproductive risks.[30] What assumptions about masculinity are implicit in this vision of the norm of the male worker? Men are risk defying, in need of no protection; and men have no reproductive concerns worthy of mention.

Commentators uniformly read *Johnson Controls* as a great victory for women's rights. But that understanding invites deeper exploration. In one sense *Johnson Controls* typifies the Supreme Court's gender cases, many of which involve outcomes in which women have fought hard for the same opportunities as those available to men, and, as part of the package, the rights to be subjected to the same hazards and punishments that men experience. The female workers in *Johnson Controls* sued to have the same right as men to be exposed to hazardous conditions in the workplace. In *Michael M.*, if women had won, they would have won the opportunity to be prosecuted for statutory rape. In *Rostker,* women wanted to be in combat-ready positions in the military. As we will see in the next section, in *United States v. Virginia* women won the right to the same military education, but also the right to endure the same mental stress, privacy invasions, humiliation, and abuse as male cadets. Of course, the price of fighting for equal treatment is swallowing its disadvantages as well as accepting its benefits. This offers women a Hobson's choice in some gender cases: they could lose by ending up treated as naturally inferior—or they could win and become subjected to the same harms that men experience daily. They win the right to be treated badly too.

In a Constitutional Law class taught by a friend of mine a few years ago, the group was discussing *Rostker v. Goldberg*. One of the men in the class had been in the military for several years and had fought in Vietnam. He was simply perplexed at why women had ever sued for the right to fight in combat in the first place. As the discussion continued he became visibly upset; he told the class, "You just don't know the horror of it. You just don't know how terrible it is. Whoever convinced you that you want the right to fight is full of shit." When my friend recounted the story of the student's plea, I wondered if this failure to comprehend the burdens of masculinity accounts for some male resistance to feminism. Perhaps women do not understand how difficult masculinity can be, just as men do not understand how privileged and advantaged they are.

The Virginia Military Institute and Gender Separatism

In 1996 the Supreme Court decided a case with overtones of the stereotypes of the previous century about the "natural and proper timidity and delicacy" of women. The case concerned the opportunities for women to attend a state-funded all-male military college.

Since its founding in 1839, the publicly supported Virginia Military Institute (VMI) had followed an all-male admissions policy. In 1990, after VMI refused a female high school applicant's admission, the Justice Department sued the school. Virginia defended its decision to maintain a male-only institution based on its provision of "rigorous military training" that was inappropriate for females and effective for males only in a single-sex environment. This "adversative" training includes spartan barracks living, a class system, mental stress, shaved heads, a stringently enforced honor code, a complete absence of privacy, upperclass hazing, and harsh physical training. The trial court's factual findings describe the conditions:

> Entering students at VMI are called "rats" because the rat is "probably the lowest animal on earth." In general, the rats are treated miserably for the first seven months of college. . . . Features of the rat line include indoctrination, egalitarian treatment, rituals (such as walking the rat line), minute regulation of individual behavior, frequent punishments, and use of privileges to support desired behaviors. . . . The rat line is more dramatic and more stressful than Army boot camp or Army basic training. . . . After the rat line strips away cadets' old values and behaviors, the class system teaches and reinforces through peer pressure the values and behaviors that VMI exists to promote. . . . The dyke system is closely linked to the class system, and is the arrangement by which each rat is assigned a first classman as a mentor, called a "dyke." The dyke system provides some relief from the extreme stress of the rat line. . . . The barracks are designed to reduce all cadets to the lowest common denominator. . . . there is literally no place in the barracks that physically affords privacy. . . . The average occupancy rate of cadet rooms at VMI . . . was 3.7 cadets per room. The barracks are stark and unattractive. The windows and the doors ensure that cadets are never free from scrutiny. There is constant intermingling of cadets as a result of the close and intimate quarters and the number of cadets assigned to a room. Ventilation is poor. Furniture is unappealing. A principal object of these conditions is to induce stress. . . . There are no locks on the doors of cadet rooms in barracks, no windows in the barracks doors, no window shades or curtains. . . . On the fourth floor a cadet cannot go to the bathroom or go to take a shower without being observed by everyone in that quadrangle on all levels.[31]

The federal district court denied the government's equal protection complaint, finding that by providing unique "adversative" training, Virginia actually was adding a "measure of diversity" to its educational system. The district court also found that "substantial educational benefits flow from a single-gender environment, be it male or female, that cannot be replicated in a coeducational setting."

The appellate court reversed, holding that while VMI's program of single-sex training was "justified by its institutional mission," Virginia failed to explain "why it offers the unique benefit of VMI's type of education and training to men and not to women."[32] It remanded the case to the district court for construction of a plan to remedy the equal protection violation, suggesting that Virginia might consider admitting women, eliminating state support, or developing an alternative program for women. Virginia responded to the appellate court's decision by creating a separate, parallel program for women, the Virginia Women's Institute for Leadership (VWIL), on the campus of nearby Mary Baldwin College.

A task force headed by the dean of Mary Baldwin College determined that "a military model and, especially VMI's adversative method, would be wholly inappropriate for educating and training most women for leadership roles."[33] So the VWIL program had nothing like the rigors of VMI—no rat line, no dyke system, no barracks life, no uniforms, no hazing—but instead was based on a "cooperative method which reinforces self-esteem." Compared to the approximately 1,300 students at VMI, VWIL was funded based on an expected student enrollment of 25 to 30 students. Mary Baldwin students would be permitted to live off campus or in student dorms, which were described as "plush and comfortable" with plenty of privacy. In lieu of military training, VWIL students would take part in ROTC programs and the "largely ceremonial" Virginia Corps of Cadets, and "would take courses in leadership, complete an off-campus leadership externship, participate in community service projects, and assist in arranging a speaker series."

The VMI Foundation agreed to provide an endowment for VWIL of $5.5 million, while VMI's endowment level was $131 million. The entry requirements for VWIL involved SAT scores averaging a hundred points lower than those at VMI. "VMI awards baccalaureate degrees in liberal arts, biology, chemistry, civil engineering, electrical and computer engineering, and mechanical engineering."[34] Students could be graduated from VWIL only with a bachelor of arts degree. Only 68 percent of the faculty at Mary Baldwin had Ph.D.'s, compared to 86 percent of the faculty at VMI. The Mary Baldwin campus housing the VWIL program offered "[o]ne gymnasium" and "two multi-purpose fields." The physical facilities of VMI included "an NCAA competition level indoor track and field facility; a number of multi-purpose fields; baseball, soccer and lacrosse fields; an obstacle course; large boxing, wrestling and martial arts facilities; an 11-laps-to-the-mile indoor running course; an indoor pool; indoor and outdoor rifle ranges; and a football stadium that also contains a practice field and outdoor track."[35]

The district court upheld this plan, declaring that Virginia was not required "to provide a mirror image VMI for women."[36] A divided court of appeals approved the VWIL program—which was designed to address "the different educational needs of most women"—as "substantively comparable" to VMI.[37] The government petitioned the Supreme Court for certiorari.

Justice Ruth Bader Ginsburg, who, as a lawyer, argued the earliest winning gender cases before the Supreme Court, delivered the opinion of the Court. The Supreme Court found the male-only admissions policy unconstitutional and held that the parallel program at VWIL was inadequate to remedy the constitutional violation: "However 'liberally' this plan serves the state's sons, it makes no provision whatever for her daughters. That is not equal protection."[38] Rejecting Virginia's argument that the single-sex program at VMI promoted systemic educational diversity, the Court found the argument a post hoc rationalization for separatism, since the record revealed no evidence that the male-only admissions policy was prompted by diversity concerns. When VMI was established in 1839 it was not built for the purpose of educational diversity, and its founders assumed that only men could enter military service.

The Court acknowledged that the introduction of women would alter the educational experience at VMI, but noted that predictions that the admission of women would destroy the adversative method or the school were reminiscent of similar dire predictions about the admission of women to the bar, medical faculties, and federal military schools. In making judgments about whether single-sex educational programs were justified by "gender based developmental differences," the state could not rely on generalizations about "typically male or typically female 'tendencies.'" "[G]eneralizations about 'the way women are,' estimates of what is appropriate for most women, no longer justify denying opportunity to women whose talent and capacity place them outside the average description."[39]

Regarding the second question—whether the creation of VWIL as a parallel program for women remedied the constitutional defect—the Court unsurprisingly found the VWIL program at Mary Baldwin College a "pale shadow" of the educational experience at VMI. The Supreme Court noted that "VWIL affords women no opportunity to experience the rigorous military training for which VMI is famed."[40] By all tangible measures—funding, resources, facilities, qualifications of faculty and students, curriculum and degree offerings, educational philosophy—VWIL differed markedly from VMI. The intangible differences of history, pedigree, alumni support, prestige, reputation, and future job opportunities were perhaps even greater. In short, Virginia failed to demonstrate an "exceedingly persuasive justification" for the exclusion of qualified women from the "premier training of the kind VMI affords."

Images of Gender in the VMI Litigation

The outcome of *United States v. Virginia* represents some progress, since the Supreme Court expressed appropriate skepticism of gender separatism. Yet woven throughout the lower court opinions in the case, and even in the Supreme Court's opinion, are conventional assumptions about gender and traditional ways of thinking about gender questions that are representative of why gender separatism persists.

Images of Women

The decisional record of the lower courts in the VMI litigation is rife with gender stereotypes. In the initial district court decision, Judge Jackson Kiser rushed to embrace some of the starkest stereotypes about the biological basis for gender differences. In his findings of fact, Kiser created a heading entitled "Gender-Based Physiological Differences," under which he first remarked that "West Point['s Office of Institutional Research] has identified more than 120 physiological differences between men and women" that are "very real differences, not stereotypes."[41] He specified some of these physiological differences: most women are generally slower, fatter (which "imposes a burden on some kinds of physical performance"), and weaker ("only 80% as strong as males") than most men. He accepted as evidence and reported as fact that female athletes were injured more frequently than male athletes, could perform fewer sit-ups and push-ups, and were generally outperformed by men "on all of the common physical aptitude tests." Paramilitary training obviously would be dangerous for women's delicate constitutions, and they couldn't handle it.

In the next section of factual findings, "Gender-Based Developmental Differences," the district court accepted the testimony of educators and academics that "females and males characteristically learn differently": "Males tend to need an atmosphere of adversativeness or ritual combat in which the teacher is a disciplinarian and a worthy competitor. Females tend to thrive in a cooperative atmosphere in which the teacher is emotionally connected with the students." The court found that women have "distinctive psychological and sociological needs" and that those needs represented "real differences, not stereotypes."[42]

These factual findings related directly to the court's holding that because most women could not measure up to men's standards of performance, VMI was justified in excluding all women from its school. "Even if the female could physically and psychologically undergo the rigors of the life of a male cadet," Kiser wrote, "her introduction to the process would change it. Thus, the very experience she sought would no longer be available."[43] Women, in his view, were fundamentally different from men in ways that would inevitably infect the educational program. The institution should not be required to admit women because it would have to bend to their differences: "the distinctive ends of the system would be thwarted, if VMI were forced to admit females and to make changes necessary to accommodate their needs and interests." In initially upholding Kiser's findings, the court of appeals flatly stated, "Men and women are different, and our knowledge about the differences, physiological and psychological, is becoming increasingly more sophisticated."

Three years later, in upholding the proposed VWIL plan as "comparable" to VMI, Kiser ruled that the physical and pedagogical differences between VMI and VWIL were justified by "real differences between the sexes." Approving the VWIL plan, a divided Fourth Circuit exhibited concerns about the feasibility of "adapting the adversative methodology to women, setting woman against woman with the intended purpose of breaking individual spirit and instilling values."[44]

Images of Men

Less obvious in the court opinions were the stereotypes about men. One stereotype implicit in the trial court opinion upholding the exclusion of women from VMI, the appellate court opinion approving the trial court's "homogeneity of gender" rationale, and the later appellate opinion approving the VWIL remedial plan was the assumption that the all-male composition of VMI was essential not only to the character of the institution but also to the character development of the male students. The federal district court found that one of the benefits of single-sex education for men was that they would be "able to focus exclusively on the work at hand, without the introduction of any sexual tension."[45] This represents a particular construct of masculinity. It first assumes an all-heterosexual student body. Beyond that, an essential ingredient of a good "citizen-solider" was the boys' club mentality indoctrinated into all the cadets. Men were being shaped and defined in large part by the exclusion of women.

In 1839, when VMI opened its doors, women could not enter the military—"men alone were fit for military and leadership roles."[46] It was a model of masculinity that has not changed much in over a century and a half. In the 1990s this microcosm of the country was still raising its boys to be soldiers. Even though only 15 percent of VMI's graduates enter military life, the harsh boot-camp conditions were considered an elemental part of the education. When the federal district court heard the testimony of experts that men benefited from adversative training while women needed a more supportive, nurturing education, it accepted these truisms with little reflection.

VMI's unique "adversative" approach was considered character-building for men.

> He is told where to stack his underwear and where to put his razor. He must submit to an array of theatrical abuses from upperclassmen; he can, for example, be stopped at any time and made to recite a passage from the "Rat Bible" (a compendium of sundry statistics having to do with things like . . . athletic teams); he might be asked what's for dinner (rats must memorize the day's menu); he might be ordered to drop and do 20 push-ups.[47]

Carefully selected professional educators were willing to testify—and the district court was more than willing to accept—that comradeship and virility could be created through brutal and punitive physical conditions. One of those experts testified that "the VMI model is based on the premise that young men come with [an] inflated sense of self-efficacy that must [be] knocked down and rebuilt."[48] It was a system that few female but most male applicants could be expected to tolerate. Just as "shy, self-distrustful young women" could not withstand the "rigors" of adversative training, it was inconceivable that a man might be tender and loving, one who would blossom in a nurturing environment; that would be abnormal.

According to the value system inculcated at VMI, caring and nurturant behavior from men was a necessary evil—part of the system, but a baneful part nonetheless. The "dyke" system, whereby first-year "rats" were mentored by seniors, was an attempt to reintroduce some human concern into a system intentionally stripped of warmth, compassion, and nurturance.

But consider the etymology: when upperclassmen performed this function, they were called by a pejorative name typically used to refer to masculine lesbian women.[49] The clear message is the devaluation of men who do women's work.

As this condensed litany of gender demonstrates, a number of federal judges, at varying levels, were quick to move from obvious biological differences to accepted socio-moral stereotypes. Decisions at different junctures—initial approval of the male-only admissions policy; later approval of the "substantively comparable" VWIL plan—equated sociological stereotypes with biological differences. The lower federal courts expressly relied on gross sexual stereotypes, based on some modest evidence of physiological differences. Even the psychological and sociological differences between men and women were seen through a lens of biology. The trial and appellate courts were ready to accept that unchangeable biological and sociological sex differences exist and to allow those differences to have profound political consequences.

The various judges who ruled on the VMI litigation were not unanimous in committing the biological fallacy. Judge J. Dickson Phillips, Jr., dissenting from the Fourth Circuit's approval of the VWIL remedial plan, was willing to acknowledge the error of consistently equating previous elections of a sexist society with biological necessity: "No conscious governmental choice between alternatives . . . dictated the original men-only policy; it simply reflected the unquestioned general understanding of the time about the distinctively different roles in society of men and women."[50] But the theme of equating gender roles and biology is a persistent one. It resonates in Justice Antonin Scalia's dissent from the Supreme Court's majority opinion. Although only a single voice, Scalia wrote an opinion almost as lengthy as the majority's, in which he waxes nostalgic over "manly" virtues and regrets their disappearance. He quotes at length from *The Code of a Gentleman,* a booklet that the VMI "rats" are expected to keep with them at all times:

> Without a strict observance of the fundamental Code of Honor, no man, no matter how "polished," can be considered a gentleman. The honor of a gentleman demands the inviolability of his word, and the incorruptibility of his principles. He is the descendant of the knight, the crusader; he is the defender of the defenseless and the champion of justice . . . or he is not a Gentleman. A Gentleman . . . does not discuss his family affairs in public or with acquaintances. Does not speak more than casually about his girl friend. Does not go to a lady's house if he is affected by alcohol. He is temperate in the use

of alcohol. Does not lose his temper; nor exhibit anger, fear, hate, embarrassment, ardor or hilarity in public. Does not hail a lady from a club window. A gentleman never discusses the merits or demerits of a lady. Does not mention names exactly as he avoids the mention of what things cost. Does not borrow money from a friend, except in dire need. Money borrowed is a debt of honor, and must be repaid as promptly as possible. Debts incurred by a deceased parent, brother, sister or grown child are assumed by honorable men as a debt of honor. Does not display his wealth, money or possessions. Does not put his manners on and off, whether in the club or in a ballroom. He treats people with courtesy, no matter what their social position may be. Does not slap strangers on the back nor so much as lay a finger on a lady. Does not "lick the boots of those above" nor "kick the face of those below him on the social ladder." Does not take advantage of another's helplessness or ignorance and assumes that no gentleman will take advantage of him. A Gentleman respects the reserves of others, but demands that others respect those which are his. A Gentleman can become what he wills to be.[51]

Scalia's analysis did not go further than simply quoting the military scripture. The premise of the good old days is entirely unquestioned, as is the seeming inconsistency between the qualities of "gentlemen" and the adversative training methods used to construct them.

Separate but Equal

The Supreme Court in *United States v. Virginia* did not state that single-sex programs were categorically unconstitutional. For the Court, it was not a question of "separate but equal" because VMI and VWIL were so patently unequal. Yet even in a majority opinion architected by Ruth Bader Ginsburg, formerly the director of the ACLU Women's Rights Project, there lingers a soft theme of gender separatism.

While attempting to eradicate stereotyping, the majority was willing to accept the idea of important natural differences between the sexes, observing that "'[i]nherent differences' between men and women, we have come to appreciate, remain cause for celebration, but not for denigration of the members of either sex or for artificial constraints on an individual's opportunity." While the Court explicitly addressed overgeneralizations about females in one portion of the opinion ("estimates of what is appropriate for most women, no longer justify denying opportunity to women whose talent and capacity place them outside the average description"), in another portion it indulged in stereotypic presuppositions: "It may be assumed, for purposes of this decision, that most women would not choose VMI's adversative method."[52]

Second, the Supreme Court's VMI opinion was guilty of a serious omission. Conspicuously absent was any reference to *Brown v. Board of Education*. Petitioner's brief to the Supreme Court raised the *Brown* issue, not as one of the specific issues preserved for review, but as representative of the law in the area of segregated education: "Although single-sex education may not necessarily send a stigmatizing message that renders it 'inherently unequal,' cf. *Brown v. Board of Education*, . . . the exclusion of women from VMI does send a powerful, harmful message."[53] Nowhere in the twenty-three-page VMI opinion is *Brown* even mentioned as relevant precedent. The Court never contemplates the possibility that, in the area of gender relations, separate, by its very nature, might never be equal.

In *Brown*, in the context of race, the Court flatly stated that "[s]eparate educational facilities are inherently unequal."[54] The *Brown* Court recognized that the equal protection inquiry regarding racial separatism should not turn on comparisons of the "tangible factors" of educational "buildings, curricula, qualifications and salaries of teachers," but on the symbolic message sent by the "segregation itself": "To separate [grade school and high school children] from others of similar age and qualifications solely because of their race generates a feeling of inferiority as to their status in the community that may affect their hearts and minds in a way unlikely ever to be undone."[55] In *United States v. Virginia* the Court was unwilling even to mention the possibility that gender separatism might send similar messages of inferiority. In *Brown* the Court assumed equality of facilities and tested whether separation of the races was just; in *United States v. Virginia* the Court ignored the issue of separation of the sexes and tested whether inequality in the provision of resources was just.

We can surmise the reasons for *Brown*'s omission from the VMI opinion. The modern Court does not rely on *Brown* even in the racial desegregation cases; its real vitality is almost purely symbolic. To transfer it to another context would have required a certain revitalizing, and there were certainly not five votes for that project. Perhaps the Court also wanted to preserve the possibility of publicly funded all-female math or science classes or inner-city male academies. In a footnote, the VMI Court explicitly left open this possibility that gender-exclusivity might provide a unique educational opportunity, and hence educational diversity: "Several amici have urged that diversity in educational opportunities is an altogether appropriate governmental pursuit and that single-sex schools can contribute importantly to such diversity. Indeed, it is the mission of some single-sex schools 'to dissipate, rather than perpetuate, traditional gender classifications.' . . . We do not question the State's prerogative evenhandedly to support diverse educational opportunities."[56] Certainly the Fourteenth Amendment does not apply to private single-gender high schools and colleges. And an "exceedingly pervasive justification" may well exist to support public single-sex education or classes in a localized way, with a highly contextualized inquiry, showing an empirically demonstrable need and specific benefits flowing from the program.[57] But the Court's reluctance even to mention *Brown* is troubling.

In not explicitly recognizing the stigma associated with the very fact of sex segregation, the Court tacitly condones gender separatism. VMI's practices were not unacceptable because sex-segregated institutions send the wrong message; VMI was in error because it blatantly underfunded the women's program. This raises the question to what extent recognition of a gender dichotomy necessarily means a hierarchy: can there be a separation of the sexes without hierarchy? Given the history of gender relations—since exclusivity in both the public and private spheres for so many years implied a hierarchy of who was worthy to participate publicly—the presumption should probably be that the dichotomy implies a hierarchy. But the Court seems willing to indulge in the opposite assumption: separation of the sexes is fine, as long as the facilities provided are substantially equal.

Perhaps the Court's neglect of *Brown* has something to do with the constitutional framework for equal protection analysis: the different levels of scrutiny applied to race and gender cases. Race cases are deserving of strict scrutiny because the history of racism has been one of invidious or malevolent treatment, while gender cases receive intermediate scrutiny because the history of sexism has been one of "benevolently" paternalistic decisions. The Fourth Circuit had expressly disavowed that this was a case to which the "separate but equal" principle would even apply, since males and females were relevantly different, rather than similarly situated: "When there is a difference between two classes of persons, then separate and different facilities for each class may satisfy equal protection if the difference in facilities is sufficiently related to the nature of the difference between the classes. In this case, we do not espouse a 'separate-but-equal' test and never discuss 'separate-but-equal facilities.'"[58] Instead, the Fourth Circuit, and ultimately the Supreme Court, tested whether VMI and VWIL were "substantively comparable facilities." The truth is, there probably is not a majority of the Court that believes that sex-segregated schools are inherently unequal. They apparently do not contemplate that the rationale in *Brown* extends to gender much at all, let alone with the same force.

Or perhaps the explanation lies in the opposite direction. Maybe gender differences are so sacred and pervasive, so structural to the family, to economics and politics—even more so than racial differences—that it is more threatening to the Court even to consider pronouncements about separation of the sexes. This may parallel the reasoning why certain basic necessities of life, such as food, shelter, and peace, are not guaranteed by or even mentioned in the Constitution—and not because we think they are unimportant. On the contrary, perhaps they are too important. In both instances—the Supreme Court leaving untouched the issue of gender separatism and the Constitution not providing for basic needs—there are unexpressed assumptions about what is appropriate for a government to do. Lucinda Finley explains that the conventional assumptions about gender differences set the standard for constitutional models of equality:

> The idea of separating men and women in certain realms, and of some things being more appropriate for one sex than for the other, just does not strike most people as odd, or repugnant to ideals of equality, as does the notion of forced racial separation. When it comes to sex, the notion often seems appropriate, resonating with deeply entrenched cultural notions about the biologically based dissimilarity of men and women, and the inevitable alterity of masculinity and femininity.[59]

At this juncture, the Court is not going to enter the business of dismantling the walls separating the sexes. Maybe we simply aren't ready for the gender equivalent of *Brown*.

What does it mean to say that the Court was unwilling to touch the gender separatism lurking just beneath the surface of the issues in VMI? In the context of the VMI litigation, it could mean something as innocuous as the absence of a fully briefed issue or as admirable as constitutional restraint in avoiding decisions on unnecessary issues. The plaintiff's litigation strategy was, after all, to prove convincingly that VMI and VWIL were unequal. But Scalia's dissent, deploring the majority's abandonment of *The Code of a Gentleman*, spoke volumes about what was really at issue. The separation of the sexes is at the heart of masculinity. It was an issue that was too deep and too important for the VMI majority even to mention.

In a case that ran parallel to the VMI litigation—Shannon Faulkner's attempt to gain entry to South Carolina's all-male Citadel—the theme of lost masculinity is mentioned explicitly, again in a dissent. Judge Clyde Hamilton, dissenting from the Fourth Circuit's approval of a preliminary injunction ordering Faulkner's admission, lamented that "the majority emasculates a venerable institution by jettisoning 150 years of impeccable tradition and distinguished service."[60] The preservation of traditional forms of masculinity is one of the last bastions of sexism. But it is a huge reservoir, and one that is largely untouched by judicial decisions.

The Defense Litigation Strategy of VMI

Virginia and VMI's defense of one of the only two publicly supported all-male schools in the country consisted of, on the surface, the simple strategy of resisting change and preserving tradition. The roots of that tradition date back to an epic confrontation. Valorie Vojdik, lead counsel for Shannon Faulkner and Nancy Mellette in their lawsuit to gain admission to the Citadel, explains that

> Because the VMI litigation was marked by the absence of any woman who sought admission, the courts were able to frame the constitutional conflict as a battle between Virginia and VMI, on the one hand, and the United States, on the other. Recalling that the parties "first confronted each other" on "the battlefield at New Market, Virginia," the district court envisioned the lawsuit as a continuation of the Civil War involving another "life-and-death" battle over the existence of VMI.[61]

On a deeper level VMI was, quite simply, all about gender separatism: preserving VMI's exclusive all-male admissions policy. VMI professed, though, that its purpose was not to exclude women, but to provide "single-sex" education, which, VMI implied, would ultimately benefit all Virginia's sons and daughters with "system-wide diversity."[62] VMI stressed the pedagogical value of sex-separatism, citing expert testimony regarding the benefits of single-sex education at the college level. "Single-sex education," VMI argued solemnly, "in fact helps to combat gender stereotypes by encouraging students to pursue careers once associated primarily with the opposite sex."[63] The federal district court accepted VMI's expert testimony on the benefits of single-sex education, and found as a matter of fact that "[o]ne empirical study in evidence, not questioned by any expert, demonstrates that single-sex colleges provide better educational experiences than coeducational institutions."[64] The Fourth Circuit was willing to extrapolate from this finding that "single-gender education at the college level is beneficial to both sexes is a fact established in this case."[65]

But the research on which VMI's experts relied, and that the federal trial and appellate courts cited approvingly, was not, as the courts supposed, applicable to the experiences of both males and females. Almost all the studies were conducted at women's colleges and secondary schools, since few all-male schools exist. Many of these studies are of questionable extensibility: the evidence of beneficial effects from single-sex educational experiences are principally studies of "women who graduated from the Seven Sister colleges. They are studies that date back from the 1940's through the 1960's. . . . The fact of the matter is that most of these women came from privileged backgrounds, had tremendous resources, and they were going to succeed no matter where they went. Yet, these studies did not control for socio-economic status."[66] The lower courts' acceptance of the antiquated studies from a limited and unrepresentative sample of schools illustrates the very human tendency to confuse correlation with causation.

The Fourth Circuit did rely on research conducted by Dr. Alexander Astin in a 1977 book, *Four Critical Years: Effects of College on Beliefs, Attitudes and Knowledge,* showing benefits to both sexes from single-sex schooling. Astin, however, testified on behalf of the United States in the VMI litigation and for Shannon Faulkner in the Citadel case, based on his updated 1993 research, *What Matters in College? Four Critical Years Revisited,* that it was "not single sex status per se that yielded the positive effects observed for single sex colleges for men,"[67] since the advantages remained after the all-male schools he studied admitted women.

One well-respected study of sixty nonparochial private high schools (divided equally among boys', girls', and coeducational schools) showed that teachers in all the settings initiated most of the sexist incidents: teaching students to sexually stereotype, actively devaluing females, and promoting male gender domination. According to the researchers, the number of sexist incidents in the different types of schools were "roughly equal," but took different forms. In coeducational schools, sexism appeared more as gender domination and active discrimination against females. More common in the single-sex schools than the coeducational schools were two different forms of sexism: "gender reinforcement—the perpetuation of gender-differentiated 'social definitions' (conventional behaviors or styles typically associated with being male or female)"—and "embedded discrimination—the residual sexism of a gender-stratified society."[68]

Single-sex environments might offer some educational advantages, but "[t]he current research demonstrates that the efficacy of single-sex education may be sex-specific—limited to young women—because it offers an environment free from female-specific forms of educational discrimination, such as silencing, discouragement, and male-peer harassment. The reasons single-sex education can benefit young women obviously do not apply to men."[69] Indeed, "studies of male secondary schools fail to demonstrate any positive effects for male high school students, and some demonstrate a negative effect."[70] The consensus is that in "male single-sex settings there is increased incidence of violence and sexism" and, in the words of one expert in the Citadel case, a "hypermasculine ethos."[71] This could be an enormous problem for the "sons of Virginia" and South Carolina, not to mention their daughters, but the trial court in the VMI litigation discounted any evidence that did not comport with its theories.

It is truly curious that the district court, in one portion of the opinion, was adamant about the existence and pervasiveness of physical differences, psychological differences, and differences in learning styles between males and females, but in another portion of the opinion, was willing to assume blithely that the pedagogical research on the benefits to women from single-sex education applied equally to men.[72] This is evidence of a relentless insistence on upholding traditional images of masculinity, despite realities to the contrary.

The dubious empirical basis of VMI's arguments went well beyond its claims of purported benefits for single-sex schooling. VMI seized on the classic work of educational psychologist Carol Gilligan as justification for its all-male admissions policy. Gilligan, the author of *In a Different Voice: Psychological Theory and Women's Development,* conducted research that showed that traditional psychological theories of human development, based on all-male study populations, gave undue positive weight to typically masculine ways of evaluating ethical issues, such as abstract thinking, rights, formal rationality, autonomy, separation, and detachment, while undervaluing typically feminine ways of thinking about moral problems, such as focusing on care, attachment, interdependence of relationships, and communication.

Relying on Gilligan's work, VMI maintained that men and women develop and learn differently and have different psychological needs. The separate spheres were necessary, VMI contended, because men need adversarial training. Not only would women's presence destroy the all-male atmosphere, but the type of education VMI offered would be all wrong for women: women need supportive education. Integration would be bad for both sexes, VMI said in its briefs to the Supreme Court, because "VMI would be forced to adopt different physical fitness standards and grading criteria for men and women, just as West Point has done,"[73] "the VMI method would be counterproductive for, and have a 'discriminatory impact on,' many women students," and, as the district court found, "the presence of women would add 'a new set of stresses on the cadets.'"[74]

Gilligan and others took the unusual step of filing a "friend of the court" or amicus brief in the litigation to argue that her research was being misconstrued. In the brief, amici first explained that the purpose of Gilligan's research was to point out omissions of classical psychological theory. Her research noted the sampling problem of classical theorists: their work was conducted with all male subjects.

> In a Different Voice . . . addresse[s] a problem [Gilligan] observed in her research on psychological development: that women's descriptions of their experiences and responses to experiences did not conform to descriptions of normal "human" emotional and cognitive development reflected in classical psychological theory articulated by Freud, Erikson, Piaget, and Kohlberg. While these classical theorists concluded there was something wrong with women, Gilligan concluded that there was something wrong with psychological theory.[75]

The amici next told the Supreme Court that VMI's reliance on Gilligan's work was misplaced. She was not describing innate traits of men and women, nor should her conclusions be used to justify sex-segregated education. In fact, amici suggested that "[t]he observations about psychological development patterns that are generally associated with gender in *In a Different Voice* are not based on any premise of inherent differences between the sexes, but on the basis of their different opportunities and experiences." Single-sex schooling, said the amici, would simply instantiate generalizations about men's and women's typical behavior. The point is not the wisdom of single-sex education, but the mistaking of observed differences for inherent differences.

Why did VMI pursue this litigation strategy? Why did VMI argue that men and women are inherently different? It almost seems that the empirically more supportable strategy would have been to argue that men and women are different, and that those differences are culturally constructed, but real nonetheless: that men and women have been made different.

The answer may be that VMI chose the natural differences strategy because that is a theme that resonates with the Court: that is the way the Court understands gender equality. The Supreme Court and lower federal courts still believe in biological constructions of race and gender. If the decisions in *Rostker, Dothard,* and *Michael M.* were any indication, the Court might be most receptive to arguments about the gender-appropriateness for certain jobs based on biological differences. Certainly it is difficult to make a sharp distinction between different treatment based on supposed physical differences and different treatment based on supposed cultural differences. The laws in *Craig, Dothard,* and even *Johnson Controls* and the VMI litigation probably were based on both. But various members of the judiciary seem willing to put their thumbs on the biological side of the scale.

Second, if VMI had conceded the argument that gender is culturally constructed, then it would have implicitly acknowledged the role of the institution in reconstructing differences. Reconstruction is a process that needs to start somewhere. The argument almost had to be one of innate differences. Otherwise, VMI was potentially complicit in the construction of gender differences.

Postscript

The sequel to the VMI and Citadel litigation was like the aftermath of any battle: contentious, contemptuous, and creating its own casualties. Many alumni encouraged VMI to retain its all-male tradition by going private. The Board of Visitors debated for three months after the Supreme Court's decision whether to privatize. The seventeen-member board voted by the narrowest possible margin—nine to eight—to admit women. One of the board members resigned in protest against the vote.

The other all-male, state-supported school, the Citadel, decided two days after the Supreme Court's ruling in *United States v. Virginia* to "voluntarily" admit women. It admitted four women to the 1996 entering class. Of about six hundred cadets, the women cadets constituted *two-thirds of 1 percent* of the class. Unlike other institutions that have gone coed, the Citadel lacked a critical mass of women entrants. The first coeducational class at the Naval Academy had 81 women; there were 119 at West Point, and 157 at the Air Force Academy;[76] they accounted for approximately 10 percent of each of the entering classes. The minority status of the women cadets at the Citadel was painfully visible. And the welcome they received was reminiscent of the welcome given to the Citadel's first woman entrant, Shannon Faulkner.

Shannon Faulkner attended day classes at the Citadel beginning in January 1994, and formally entered the Citadel in August 1995, after a court order requiring her admission unless South Carolina developed a parallel program for women. By the time Faulkner entered the Citadel, she had received numerous death threats, and graffiti had been spray painted on the side of her home. A special room, with a video camera and a panic button, was created to protect her; she entered the gates of the Citadel accompanied by federal marshals. The local citizenry was angry at Shannon—for being overweight, for not having her head shaved, and, worst of all, for being female. They staged demonstrations and picketed at the gates of the college carrying signs and wearing T-shirts that screamed, "Save the Males, Shave the Whale" and "1,952 Bulldogs and one Bitch." They affixed bumper stickers to their cars: "It's a Girl: 186 pounds, 6 ounces." They showed up on campus to tell her she was not welcome.

This scene was reminiscent of a 1994 demonstration at Texas Women's University (TWU) at which female students demonstrated in protest at the Regents' decision to admit males, with signs reading "Better Dead than Coed" and "Raped by the Regents." In a phrase hauntingly similar to those used several years later by students and officials at the Citadel and VMI, a TWU student said at the time, "We're not anti-man. We're for preserving this university's 91 years of tradition."[77] In 1990 a similar student insurrection at Oakland, California's private Mills College caused its trustees to reverse their decision to admit male students as undergraduates.

Faulkner became ill during Hell Week from doing drills in the 102-degree heat and then withdrew from the school after less than a week, citing illness, stress, and isolation. Some of the two thousand male cadets joyously celebrated her departure. They danced victory dances and ran in formation around the quadrangle, gleefully high-fiving, whooping, and chanting "Na-na na-na na-na na-na, hey, hey, goodbye." Twenty-nine male cadets also dropped out that semester, amid much less fanfare.

One year later, in August 1996, four women entered the Citadel. By January 1997, only two remained. Jeanie Mentavlos and Kim Messer resigned from the Citadel because of physical abuse and sexual harassment. Mentavlos and Messer alleged that in addition to general isolation, animosity, and hazing, they were kicked and pushed, subjected to degrading language, rubbed, kissed, shown pornography, and forced to listen to sexually explicit songs. Messer was shoved against the wall with her rifle, and ordered to drink tea until she became ill. A junior cadet ordered Mentavlos to drink alcoholic beverages in the barracks. Messer received a death threat. Upperclassmen put kitchen cleanser in their mouths and poured nail polish remover on their shirts and set their clothes on fire. Three male cadets resigned over the incident, a fourth was dismissed, and ten others were punished with demerits, marching tours, and restrictions to campus.

Maybe the hazing was gender-neutral. Less than a month after reports of the sexual harassment incidents at the Citadel, *Dateline NBC* broadcast a video of the Marine Corps "blood pinning" ceremony. This initiation ritual consists of superior officers pounding newly earned paratrooper wings into the chests of young Marines. Decorated veteran and journalist David Hackworth defended the institutionalized hazing:

> Until war disappears, warriors such as our extraordinary Marine Recon men of the bloodied chests are needed. They're special men. Not stockbrokers, accountants and lawyers. They jump out of perfectly good airplanes, mainly at night, dropping behind enemy lines to slit throats and create instant carnage. They do brutal stuff in training because war is brutal, and they must be macho to survive.[78]

Perhaps listening to Hackworth's cautions, or perhaps attending to alumni concerns that the end result of VMI litigation would be a dilution of military training to a program of "VMI Lite," VMI officials have decided that female cadets will have their heads shaved and—unlike the guidelines at the Army, Navy, and Air Force academies—be subject to the same physical training requirements as male cadets. As VMI Superintendent Josiah Bunting III put it, "It would be demeaning to women to cut them slack."[79] The post-litigation strategy of VMI has been a posture of in-your-face equality: let's see how many women can survive.

Spectators are appalled that adolescent girls will be shaved, stripped of privacy, and subjected to harsh discipline and humiliating hazing. Military sociologist Charles Moskos says, "Unisex physical standards are just a covert way to get women out."[80] VMI's strict equality position has provoked outcries that VMI is just trying to circumvent court order, and is still resistant to change. After losing legally, VMI is still fighting socially to retain its traditional bastion of masculinity by trying to dissuade women from coming. It does seem at the very least disingenuous that an educational institution that convinced itself, and tried to convince the U.S. Supreme Court during the VMI litigation, that there are profound physical and psychological differences between males and females now insists on ignoring all those differences.

These reactions, however, miss an essential point: we should have been protesting the barbarism of this educational approach all along. And yet we have tacitly accepted this treatment of our adolescent boys. The paramilitary educational methods for males were not as unseemly as they now appear to be for females. We had accepted the assumptions of identifying

courage with a shaved head and correlating national independence with absolute individual conformity. We were willing to assume that the virtues we
wanted—democracy, comradeship, and professionalism—could be created
through terror-bonding. We were willing to defer to the institution, rather
than asking of what relevance these behaviors are to the training of soldiers
in a highly technological era in which war has become immensely less physical. We were, at bottom, quite complacent about the separation and differential treatment of the sexes.

If the sad history of *Brown v. Board of Education* is a guide, there will be
flagrant resistance to the requirement of integration. The tragedy is that *the
resistance* will probably be condoned. Certainly these things take time. But
if we not only expect the resistance, but accept it, we risk losing the fight for
gender equality. And that tacit acceptance of token compliance can take
many forms: media stories talked about the Citadel's admitting women.
Four women is barely plural, not even enough to form a rat line. It is an occasion for celebration, but not complacency. Resistance can also involve ignoring the issues. The Citadel's interim president, Brigadier General R.
Clifton Poole, commented on the hazing incidents involving the female
cadets: "But this whole thing, the issue wasn't gender. The issue was maintaining traditions that are important to the school."[81]

Looked at differently, though, it is not VMI's or the Citadel's fault that
there were so few applicants. We don't raise our girls to be soldiers. The
issue VMI brought to the forefront is one that is deeply rooted in American culture: the differing treatment of men and women. We are beginning to explode the myths concerning the limitations on women's inherent capabilities. But what about *men*? Think about what VMI's training
program represents, with its spartan barracks living, hazing, and "rat line."
Adversative training is what we as a culture think it takes to turn boys
into men.

Boy Scouts and Girl Scouts

Society's increasing urban complexity, changing demographic patterns, and
greater female participation in the labor force has broken down some gender barriers, so that larger societal institutions are less segregated by sex. Hit
with aging and declining memberships, faced with demographic facts that
baby-boomer men are reluctant to join all-male groups,[82] and threatened
with lawsuits, sex-segregated voluntary associations have also begun to

open their doors to women. The Jaycees, the Lions, and the Rotary, which formerly had diminutively titled women's auxiliaries like the "Jaycettes, the Lionesses, and the Rotary-Annes,"[83] began to admit women in the mid-1980s, on the heels of lawsuits finding that the exclusion of women was discriminatory.

In 1984 the Supreme Court used a state antidiscrimination statute, the Minnesota Human Rights Act, to hold that the Jaycees were essentially a place of public accommodation and could not exclude women from full membership.[84] Three years later the Court held that the state had a "compelling interest in eliminating discrimination against women" that outweighed the infringement on Rotary members' expressive associational rights.[85]

But the endangered species groups have not rushed to embrace the opposite sex. Some members' reactions to the decision of Lions Clubs International to admit women were less than welcoming. "We don't want them, and 98 percent of Lions feel just like I do. . . . We might close down first," said Clarence Shastal, president of a local Lions Club chapter in Illinois.[86] Not until 1995 did the national organization of the Benevolent and Protective Order of Elks vote to allow women to join. As one member of the Memphis Elks, Loyal Knight Wes Wheelock, said before the Elks vote, "Personally, I'm against it. . . . I don't see why we can't stay a brotherhood."[87] But in 1997, despite the grand exalted ruler of the national organization's urging local Elks chapters to admit women, most have remained all-male.[88] For example, in Hartford, Vermont, seven women were sponsored for membership by the husband of one of the women, but the members of Hartford Lodge 1541, in a secret vote, rejected them. The women are still free to come, as they have for years, to the Lodge's dinners, picnics, and bingo games, and to volunteer their services of cooking, serving drinks, and cleaning up after the events.[89] In a telephone call to the Kansas City Elks chapter, the receptionist (a woman) seemed very proud of their chapter's women's groups, the "Elkettes" and the "Lady Does." The Loyal Order of Moose, with close to two million members, and the Shriners, with over half a million members, have resisted the admission of women.

Self-segregation is part of our daily patterns of social intercourse. People feel more comfortable around others who are like them in various ways: sex, race, religion, and culture. In private groupings, of course, we still divide into traditional, Flintstones-like patterns: while Fred and Barney head off to the Water Buffalos Lodge, Betty and Wilma chat across the fence about domestic chores and put Bronto burgers on the table.

The last decade has been a time of transition for associational law, with legal challenges to exclusionary practices at social organizations ranging from the Boy Scouts to eating clubs to fraternities. While legal decisions in the late 1980s and early 1990s moved somewhat toward encouraging mixed-sex groups, the law generally approves exclusive associations based on sex, as long as those groupings either have a particular expressive purpose or can be characterized as private.

The Supreme Court has recognized a right to freedom of association for intimate or expressive purposes. The family, for example, is protected as an intimate associational group. Organizations that have as their express political purpose the advancement of some gender-based goals, such as a men's rights group or a women's consciousness-raising group, could presumably exclude the opposite sex, because admitting outsiders would impair the political purposes of those particular groups.[90] Clubs like the Jaycees or the Rotary, which are large civic and service organizations that encourage nonmember participation in activities and take no political positions, cannot discriminate on the basis of race or sex.

As long as the organization is not one created principally for expressive purposes, the Supreme Court has left it to the states to regulate. But state public accommodations laws may be interpreted not to reach the provision of services or groups meeting in different members' homes, which is why the Boy Scouts of America—with over 5.3 million youth and adult members nationwide—have successfully excluded girls (and atheists) from membership and prevented women from becoming scout-masters.[91]

The gender divide is deep and firmly entrenched in our cultural heritage. In addition to the 5 million Boy Scouts, there are presently 3.4 million Girl Scouts. The nation's seven thousand fraternities and sororities boast nine million active members. These numbers do not begin to include the tens of millions of alumni of single-sex clubs. The cultural heritage becomes part of the legal landscape. As just one example, when Congress was crafting Title IX of the Education Amendments of 1972, which prohibits gender discrimination in educational institutions that receive federal funds, it specifically exempted fraternities, sororities, and youth service groups out of respect for tradition. Senator Birch Bayh, sponsor of the amendment, argued in favor of the exception: "Fraternities and sororities have been a tradition in the country for over 200 years. Greek organizations, much like the single-sex college, must not be destroyed in a misdirected effort to apply Title IX."[92]

In defense of sex segregation in voluntary associations, First Amendment afficionados would point out that the right to associate must mean the right to congregate in ways that do not meet with government approval: it must include the right to exclude. Legally, the Ku Klux Klan can meet without the presence of blacks or Jews, and a women's encounter group can meet without the presence of men. The law allows racial, sexual, and cultural separatism in the choice of people with whom we affiliate privately. Of course, if the group takes on public characteristics or uses public facilities, it may be legally required to integrate. Only when that public layer is added does the law recognize that associational interests run into equality interests.

Perhaps those equality concerns are something we should think more about in our "private" choice of associations, whether those groupings are a lunch bunch, a book club, or a professional association. They are voluntary associations for people who are in them; they are involuntary associations for people who are excluded from them.

The symbolic message sent by the sex separation promotes an orthodoxy of beliefs. Sex-segregated organizations seduce people into thinking that separation of the sexes is appropriate, even good, and perhaps necessary. But that separatism does not end with childhood. The parents of today's Girl Scout will be the parents of tomorrow's plaintiff in a sex discrimination suit alleging exclusionary employment practices.

Controlling Cross-Dressing

Legal precedents regarding dress codes that regulate identity and gender formation concretize the separation of the sexes. Employers and schools maintain different standards of appearance for men and women, boys and girls, and legal protests against these gendering practices are often futile. Courts generally allow employers and educational institutions to enforce dress and grooming codes that require employees and schools to sacrifice their personal preferences and conform to conventional norms of male and female appearance.

Courts support employers' decisions to maintain rigid separation between skirts and pants. Employers may fire women who wear pantsuits, and they can require men to wear ties while exempting women from the regulation.[93] Women have been discharged from employment for not wearing makeup and for wearing too much of it.[94] Men have not been hired or have been terminated for having long hair and donning facial jewelry.[95] Courts even have local rules about appropriate courtroom attire. A 1994 survey of the rules in federal district courts in Oklahoma revealed dress regulations that explicitly prohibit women from wearing pantsuits and expressly require male lawyers and court personnel to wear coats and ties. In the words of the survey's author, the court's own dress code "purposefully requir[es] women personnel to feminize their professional appearance."[96]

The Equal Employment Opportunity Commission originally weighed in on the side of male employees who challenged hair length regulations for men. The federal appellate courts, however, unanimously supported employers' rights to require male employees to have short hair while permitting female employees to have long hair. The courts held that different standards of dress and different hair length regulations for males and females was not discrimination on the basis of sex, because it was simply requiring employees "to conform to community standards in their dress and appearance."[97] While courts invalidate hiring policies that respond explicitly to customer preferences for one sex over the other (such as passengers' preferences for female flight attendants), they generally uphold employers' grooming and attire requirements that keep employees within the confines of their assigned gender roles, based on "commonly accepted social norms."[98]

The generally accepted justification for allowing sex-differentiated grooming standards is that employers have legitimate image concerns—which may be couched as professionalism, competence, appropriateness, or good taste—all of which are shorthand for preserving the gendered status quo. Not surprisingly, then, employers impose and courts support stronger prohibitions against men's wearing earrings, long hair, and skirts than against women's wearing pants.[99] One commentator summarized her survey of dress cases by saying, "Female employees have been more successful in their challenges of employer dress codes and other appearance standards than their male counterparts."[100] Again, it seems easier to cross the gender divide in one direction than the other.

Parents usually dress children in clothes that convey the child's gender. Of course, these clothing and dressing practices persist into adulthood, sometimes amplified by school dress codes that require girls to wear dresses and boys to wear pants. Many school districts across the country enforce both dress codes and hair length regulations, and these grooming restrictions are routinely upheld by courts. At the elementary and secondary levels, schools can ban clothing that is indecent (although ideas of decency have changed markedly in twenty or thirty years) or that displays gang affiliation, but schools often reach beyond danger and decency to ban clothes that are distracting or inappropriate. For instance, in 1996 middle schools in both Seattle and Salt Lake City adopted "no dress" codes for boys, sending boys who wore skirts to school home to change their clothes. One boy chose to wear a skirt as part of his "gothic" dress style, which included wearing all black clothing; the other two boys wore skirts "because they liked them," not with a purpose to violate school rules.[101] When supporters of the boy in Salt Lake City gathered to protest rules that gave females, but not males, the choice of wearing skirts or pants, the junior high school principal said, "I just told them it wasn't acceptable in society for men to wear skirts."[102]

These school clothing regulations, which impose conventional standards of gender decorum, usually withstand legal challenges. As just one example, the Texas Supreme Court in 1995 rejected an equal protection challenge to the school district's policy that boys could not wear hair past their collars or dangling earrings.[103] The majority accepted the authority, discipline, and hygiene rationales offered by the school district. The dissenting justice recognized the implicit gender messages, noting that girls with long hair also attended gym and biology classes and yet, according to the district, did not present the same health and safety hazards as boys with long hair.

In 1991, when Jimmy Hines was a fourth-grader in Fulton County, Indiana, he began to wear a single gold stud earring to school. Although the elementary school had no written dress code, the junior and senior high schools located in the same building had a rule prohibiting males from wearing earrings. The school superintendent sent Jimmy's parents a letter, stating that their son's earring was in violation of school policy. When Jimmy persisted in wearing the earring, the school's board of trustees then passed a dress code for the elementary school that prohibited jewelry and clothes "not consistent with community standards." Following his suspension for continuing to wear the earring, Jimmy's parents sued the school district, arguing that the earring ban for males only had no rational relationship to the educational mission of the school. The Indiana Court of Appeals ruled that the earring ban was not gender discrimination, and accepted the Caston School Corporation's argument that "the policy creates discipline, a sense of pride, and positive attitudes among students because it discourages rebellion against local community standards of dress, under which earrings are considered female attire."[104]

In *Harper v. Edgewood Board of Education*, a brother and sister were prohibited from attending their high school prom because they came dressed in the clothing of the opposite sex: Florence wore a tuxedo and Warren wore a dress, stockings, heels, and earrings.[105] The federal district court rejected the plaintiffs' First Amendment and equal protection challenges to the school's policy, holding that "the school dress code does not differentiate based on sex. The dress code requires all students to dress in conformity with the accepted standards of the community." Of course the extreme fear is that schools will defer to community standards that say girls don't need to know math or dissect frogs. The more modest and realistic outcome of the deference to community norms demonstrated in these cases is that gender changes in egalitarian directions will be slow, dragged by the inertia of the communities with the greatest resistance to social change.

Attire is a strong form of personal expression, and clothing regulates behaviors as well as appearances. What is lost with gender-coded dress and appearance regulations is more than expressive potential. Dress codes may have some very practical effects: girls and female teachers have less mobility on playgrounds if they are forced to wear dresses; when males are forced to wear jackets and ties, the formality of the dress may create some distance in interpersonal relations. Patriarchy has its couturiers: the rules of dress reinscribe the cultural norms of gender. Women's appearance can be feminized and men's appearance masculinized to comport with prevailing social norms that reflect stereotypes of gender, and may be accompanied by gender-specific behavior. The laws relating to gendered dressing do not just squelch expression, but may also inhibit activities. We lose the ability to cross the gender line in terms of attire, presentation, comfort, behavior, and relations. We carefully dress the gender line.

Even when the rules are not formalized, the social constraints on gender-appropriate dress are huge. In 1997 a student of mine at the law school was clerking for a midsize law firm in the Kansas City area. She wore a tailored suit with pants to work one day. A mildly surprised male partner at the firm said, "You're wearing pants!" With her usual presence of mind, the student replied, "So are you!" Without dress codes or regulations, societal expectations certainly would promote gendered dressing, but judicial decisions give legal imprimatur to the correctness of one of society's most visible means of sex separation.

Ladies' Night

Your neighborhood dry cleaner probably charges more to launder women's shirts than men's. Your neighborhood bar may offer half-price or two-for-one drinks for women, while charging men full price. Your local gas station may offer full-service gas pumping, tire and fluid checks, and window washing for women only at self-service prices. A study of hair salons in five major California cities, conducted by the California Assembly Office of Research, found that 40 percent of the salons surveyed "charged between $2.50 and $25 more for women's services than for similar men's services."[106] A study by Florida legislative staff determined that two out of three department stores charged women for alterations on suits, while offering the same service to men free.[107]

Retail establishments across the country charge men and women different prices for essentially, and often precisely, the same services. John Banzhaf, a professor at George Washington University, encouraged students in his public interest law class to test dry cleaning practices: "A man would bring in [an extra large women's] shirt, pick it up three days later and pay $1.50. He'd walk around the corner, take the shirt out of the wrapper, crumple it up and hand it to a female student to take in to the same cleaners. When she picked up the shirt three days later, the charge was $4.50."[108]

Men waged some of the first attacks on gender-based pricing, claiming that ladies' nights at bars, restaurants, car washes, racquet clubs, and sporting events discriminated against them. A number of the earlier decisions, in the late 1970s and early 1980s, were less than sympathetic, and courts in Illinois, Michigan, and Washington accepted the retailers' rationale for price differentials of wanting to encourage membership and patronage by women—pointing out that men were not refused or denied public accommodations, just charged the "regular" price.[109] Some courts had trouble seeing how men were injured. Reviewing the policy of a dance club to offer discounted drink prices to women, one circuit court commented mildly that the club simply wanted "to increase the enjoyment of the males by enticing the attendance of more females for the males to socialize with."[110]

More recent decisions hold that stocking the bar with babes is not an adequate justification for price discrimination against men. Yet most of these courts base their decisions on the price discrimination rationale, rather than recognizing the harmful effects that giving women preferential pricing may have on gender stereotypes (that women need economic or ability patronization or that women are appropriately sexual bait).[111] Only in the mid- to late 1990s have legislatures begun to enact statutes making illegal the practice of charging a consumer more based solely on gender. California, for example, passed the Gender Tax Repeal Act, which makes it illegal for businesses to discriminate by charging one sex more for similar services.[112] While the act is a step in the right direction, businesses may be able to perpetuate the current discrimination by claiming that delivery of services for one sex is inherently more costly than for the other.[113] Under the act, businesses are allowed to charge higher prices for services that involve more time, difficulty, or cost. This means that a dry cleaner will be allowed to charge more for a plain woman's shirt because it is too small to fit on the regular cleaning press, or a hair stylist will be able to charge more to cut a woman's hair because of the extra time it takes to use a round brush when blow-drying the client's hair.

In response to the legal assault on gender-based pricing, some retailers are discontinuing their promotions; others are blatantly trying to circumvent prohibitions against gender-based promotions. One restaurant, for example, in response to a human relations commissions complaint, replaced its "Ladies' Night" with "Skirt and Gown Night," offering a half-price discount for all patrons wearing a skirt or gown.[114] Since society prescribes different attire for men and women and has many long-standing traditions of single-sex organizations, it should come as no surprise that some retail establishments will continue to engage in gender-based pricing, and that the public often will tolerate or encourage these promotions. They are still part of the social fabric in which subtle forms of discrimination based on gender are dismissed as inconsequential or trivial.

Given the lag time for legal institutions to respond to social changes, it may be unrealistic to expect proactivity on the part of courts in breaking down gender barriers. But courts, at times unwittingly, promulgate separation of the sexes.

The gender line is etched firmly into our social consciousness. It is reinscribed legally with decisions relating to occupations, crimes, dress, voluntary associations, and schooling. Legal analysis in cases ranging from evaluation of statutory rape laws to combat restrictions validates sexual stereotypes—stereotypes that are not based on biological differences, but on the traditional ways of doing things.

4

Making Men
The Socio-Legal Construct of Masculinity

Sometimes—rarely—discrimination results from a malicious prejudice buried deep in our soul. Sometimes—much more often—it results from unconscious biases, the assumptions of competence or incompetence, aptitude or ineptitude, a "fit" that is good or not. But
sometimes—perhaps most often—discrimination is not rooted in the
biases of any individual at all. Discrimination results simply from bu-
reaucratic practices, from the unthinking repetition of the ordinary
ways of operating in the world.
                                       —Robert L. Hayman, Jr., *The Smart Culture*

The purpose of examining the various ways legal doctrines and
the legal system disadvantage men is not to thrust men into victimhood.
Victimhood presents a dilemma. On the one hand, failure to acknowledge
victimization can allow forms of oppression to go unchecked. On the other
hand, speaking in terms of victimization may promote passivity, helplessness, and blaming behavior on the part of victims.[1] If we learn to examine
gender role stereotypes as evidential facts, rather than mere opportunities
for blame, we may be able to sidestep parts of the dilemma.

This chapter explores the ways legal doctrines disadvantage men through
gender role stereotypes. It considers the ways these stereotypes construct
masculinity, particularly how legal decisions require men to suffer certain
types of harms without legal redress and exclude men from caring and nurturing roles.

The Legal Architecture of Male Aggression

It is empirically clear that male aggression is neither mythical nor insignificant. Women in America suffer approximately "two million rapes and four

million beatings" every year; they are more likely to be injured by men they know than by car accidents, rapes by strangers, and muggings combined.[2] It is equally clear that until institutional structures and cultural norms that perpetuate male aggression are exposed, there is little hope of eradicating it. Tracing the origins of male aggression entails exploration of a complex web of social beliefs, behavior patterns, learned interactions, and psychosocial theories.[3] However, even this approach is a relatively modern departure from the traditional view that male aggression is an inescapable part of male physiology.[4]

Only recently have scholars begun to direct attention toward the ways law may reinscribe stereotypes of male aggression. For example, social acceptance of male aggression may be reinforced by rape laws that presume a woman's consent to intercourse in the absence of her resistance.[5] Dorothy Roberts notes the effect of legal decisions on assumptions about male aggression: "The stereotype of the aggressive, 'macho' Black male legitimates the massive incarceration of young Black men."[6] Similarly, labor arbitrators and judges create standards to distinguish acceptable from impermissible levels of picket line violence based on traditional assumptions about male aggression: "assumptions about the 'animal exuberance' of male workers are used to defend and rationalize a tolerance for a minimal level of violent behavior in the 'rough and tumble' of labor activity."[7]

The U.S. Supreme Court has given official imprimatur to the stereotype that males are aggressive. In *Michael M. v. Superior Court*,[8] the Court held that criminalizing consensual sexual conduct for underage males but not underage females does not violate the equal protection clause because only women become pregnant, and, therefore, the genders are not similarly situated with respect to sexual intercourse. Expanding on its justification for upholding the males-only statutory rape law, the *Michael M.* Court depicts females as victims and males as aggressive sexual offenders. In fact, chastity protection was the state legislature's asserted purpose, a fact the *Michael M.* majority ignored in its analysis.[9] Instead, the Court viewed the matter as one of biology, noting that "males alone can 'physiologically cause the result which the law properly seeks to avoid,'" and holding that the "gender classification was readily justified as a means of identifying offender and victim."[10] This assumption of male sexual aggression, and its twin assumption of female passivity, not only offers a legal basis for criminalizing the conduct of only one gender, it also "construct[s] sexuality in limiting and dangerous ways."[11] The Court's ruling in *Michael M.* perpetuates commonly held perceptions about male sexual aggression, while its analysis fosters the belief that this aggression is biologically based.

Just as society has historically tolerated aggression *by* men, it has also tolerated aggression *against* men. The majority of male violence is directed against other men.[12] Men are almost twice as likely to be the victims of violent crime[13] and are treated more harshly in the criminal justice system. Men receive more severe criminal sentences, even when men and women commit precisely the same substantive offense.[14] The percentage of men on death row exceeds the percentage of death-eligible offenses committed by men. In California, of 1,164 defendants convicted of first- or second-degree murder between 1978 and 1980, 5.5 percent were female; but of the 98 defendants sentenced to death, all were male.[15] Of the "16,000 lawful executions in the United States, . . . only 398 (2.5%) [of those executed] have been females."[16] Some of this violence may be turned inward: men commit suicide in much more significant numbers than women.[17]

Consider also the exclusion of women from military combat. Banning women from military combat positions sent distinct messages about the capabilities and appropriate social roles of women. The combat exclusion for women also sent explicit messages about social expectations of and appropriate roles for men. War is a gendered construct: just as women could not be combatants, men were not afforded the option to be noncombatants.[18] Legally, only men could fight in combat. Men were exposed to the physical harms of war. Even more significantly, this rule legally shaped an exclusively male image of combatants.

For example, in *United States v. St. Clair*, a man argued that voluntary military service for women and involuntary registration for men constituted a denial of equal protection.[19] But the federal district court rejected this claim, remarking that "the teachings of history [establish] that if a nation is to survive, men must provide the first line of defense while women keep the home fires burning." For many courts, the constitutional inquiry was determined by inescapable features of male physiology and social psychology: men possessed the strength to throw the grenades, the psychological wherewithal to suffer the indignities of war, and the social authorization to be killed first.[20]

The Supreme Court gave its approval to this construct in *Rostker v. Goldberg*.[21] The High Court has never considered whether the draft exclusion of women is valid, but held in *Rostker* that selective service registration for men, but not women, did not violate equal protection. The *Rostker* reasoning was an exercise in diversion because the Court simply deferred to legislative and executive decisions regarding military affairs. It determined that since women were statutorily ineligible for combat, men and women were not similarly situated with respect to combat duty. Therefore, the combat exclusion for women was valid.

Rostker was not about legitimate physical or social differences between the sexes, but about stereotypic distinctions between warriors and homemakers.[22] Omitted from the Court's evaluation was any social contextualization of the combat exclusion. The Court did not consider that this exclusion might promote other forms of discrimination, such as the barring of women from political office for lack of military credentials, or that the exclusion itself might foster negative attitudes about women.[23]

These are not simply the antiquated decisions of a bygone era; they are the archaic decisions of modern society, as the lower court holdings in the Citadel and VMI litigation attest.[24] Sex-segregated institutions help construct the ideology of masculinity. They are, says Katherine Franke, "much more than all-male educational institutions; they are dedicated to the parodic celebration of, and ritual indoctrination in, the ways of masculinity for men."[25] The social and political ramifications of separating the sexes may be enormous.

Links between gender and aggression are institutionalized and "locked in" legally. Courts seem to accept the notion that men are militaristic; they are the warriors. Men possess the psychological capacity for aggression as well as the physical abilities for combat, while women lack both. The civic obligation of men is clear: the concept of citizenship for men is intricately tied to fighting.[26] The casualties of this legal expression of personhood are not only the subordination of women, but also the construction of a rigid social order in which men have the exclusive sociopolitical obligation to engage in violence, to be the killers.

Male Toughness, Resilience, and Diminished Expectations of Privacy

One other area of legal decisions suggests the stoicism society has come to expect of men, while protecting the "vulnerability" of comparably situated women. In the past two decades, male and female inmates have filed suits complaining about cross-sex monitoring by prison guards. These are not cases of deliberate humiliation. Female inmates simply do not want to be observed by male guards and male inmates simply do not want to be observed by female guards while dressing and undressing, showering, and using toilet facilities. Granted, this is the prison setting, in which inmates have diminished privacy expectations generally. However, as one court observed, it could not "conceive of a more basic subject of privacy than the naked body. The desire to shield one's unclothed figure from [the] view of strangers, and particularly strangers of the opposite sex, is impelled by elementary self-respect and personal dignity."[27] Perhaps central to the problem is this construction of *opposite* sexes,[28] but even leaving that issue aside for the moment, consider how courts have treated parallel claims of privacy infringement by male and female inmates.

Courts have consistently held that if male guards routinely watch female inmates engage in personal activities, this violates their constitutional privacy rights.[29] In *Jordan v. Gardner* the Ninth Circuit Court of Appeals, sitting en banc, issued a thoughtful opinion discussing a prison policy that required male guards to conduct random, clothed body, pat down searches of female inmates.[30] The court determined that the policy violated the Eighth Amendment's prohibition against cruel and unusual punishment, and thus constituted the unnecessary and wanton infliction of pain. Because of the high incidence of prior sexual abuse among the inmates, the court found that women prisoners might be particularly vulnerable to the emotional impact of cross-sex body searches. In a parallel case, *Grummet v. Rushen*, involving female guards conducting pat down searches of male inmates, including the groin area, the court decided that "[t]hese searches do not involve intimate contact with an inmate's body."[31] Other courts have held that out of deference to the privacy interests of female prisoners, male guards can be excluded from the women inmates' living areas.[32]

On the other hand, most courts have been much more reluctant to recognize that male inmates might suffer dignitary invasions if female guards frisk, strip search, or observe them while they are bathing, dressing, or defecating.[33] In *Johnson v. Phelan* a pretrial detainee made the equal protection claim that female guards monitoring male prisoners could observe them naked in their cells and while they showered and used the toilet.[34] This embarrassed him and offended his sense of "Christian modesty." The Seventh Circuit Court of Appeals came close to sneering as it rejected Johnson's claims:

> Johnson's complaint (and the brief filed on his behalf in this court by a top-notch law firm) [does] not allege either particular susceptibility or any design to inflict psychological injury. A prisoner could say that he is especially shy—perhaps required by his religion to remain dressed in the presence of the op-

posite sex—and that the guards, knowing this, tormented him by assigning women to watch the toilets and showers. So, too, a prisoner has a remedy for deliberate harassment, on account of sex, by guards of either sex. Johnson does not allege this or anything like it.

Far more important to the *Johnson* court was the prison's interests in efficiency: "It is more expensive for a prison to have a group of guards dedicated to shower and toilet monitoring . . . than to have guards all of whom can serve each role in the prison." And the court counterpoised the male inmate's privacy interests with job opportunities for women as guards, which the court characterized as a "clash between modesty and equal employment opportunities." "A prison," said the court, "could comply with the rule Johnson proposes, and still maintain surveillance, only by relegating women to the administrative wing, limiting their duties (thereby raising the cost of the guard complement), or eliminating them from the staff." Other courts have not seen the choices as so stark, and some of them have, quite sensibly, adjusted the physical structure of the facilities, job duties of the guards, or surveillance possibilities to accommodate the privacy interests of the inmates, the employment interests of the guards, and the security interests of the prisons.[35]

Reading between the lines, the majority opinion not only failed, as Judge Richard Posner noted in dissent, to recognize the essential humanity of prisoners (and Albert Johnson was a detainee who had only been charged with, not convicted of, a crime), but also diminished male interests in privacy. Cross-sex surveillance was not an unreasonable intrusion into male detainees' privacy.

Other courts, similarly, have diminished the harms suffered by incarcerated males. In *Somers v. Thurman*, Somers alleged that female prison guards "subjected [him] to visual body cavity searches on a regular basis," monitored his showers, and "made 'jokes among themselves.'"[36] These searches "violated prison regulations prohibiting unclothed body inspections by correctional employees of the opposite sex." Despite these contentions of intrusive, demeaning, and unprofessional behavior violating institutional rules, the court held that the guards were entitled to immunity. Discounting some of the female inmate–male guard precedents, the court emphasized the psychological "differences between men and women," and concluded that "[t]o hold that gawking, pointing, and joking violates the prohibition against cruel and unusual punishment would trivialize the objective component of the Eighth Amendment test and render it absurd."

If the same allegations had been made by a female inmate, the decision likely would have looked much different.

Other courts have placed the onus on male prisoners to shield themselves from view: "there are alternative means available for inmates to retain their privacy. The use of a covering towel while using the toilet or while dressing and body positioning while showering or using a urinal allow the more modest inmates to minimize invasions of their privacy."[37] None of the female prisoner–male guard cases obligated the women inmates to cover themselves to protect their privacy. Only one court even attempted to explain the difference between the privacy protection afforded to men and that given to women. The differences in privacy protection were explained by the conclusion-begging statement that "male inmates and female inmates 'are not similarly situated'" and the confusing bit of non sequitur reasoning that different security risks (which might or might not relate to gender) justified the differences in treatment.[38]

In short, female guards can view male prisoners in various stages of undress but male guards cannot view female prisoners similarly disrobed. Women in custody are afforded more privacy than men. Simmering under the surface are assumptions about the motivations of the viewer: women guards would not view men as sex objects, but male guards might be inclined to leer. The tacit assumption is that male guards would perform their jobs with malevolent motives, while women guards are more likely to gaze benignly. Male prisoners have diminished expectations of privacy relative to similarly situated women prisoners. Again, the cultural assumptions about characteristic features of males—men are invulnerable and autonomous, and they can build their own walls—are reflected in legal doctrines determining their rights.

Suffering in Silence

From infancy, men learn to endure suffering silently and in private. Stoicism is ingrained in many and varied ways. Author William Styron says, "Women are far more able and willing to spill out their woes to each other. Men, on the other hand, don't have that. Men are fatally reticent."[39] In describing the "rules of manhood," sociologist Michael Kimmel explains that "[r]eal men show no emotions, and are thus emotionally reliable by being emotionally inexpressive."[40] Various legal constructs reinforce this silent stoicism. Consider the law regarding sexual harassment of men. This is not the only area in which courts accept pervasive social stereotypes, either explicitly or implicitly, in ways that diminish the harms suffered by males,[41] but it provides an important lens through which one can view the legal construction of gender.

Sexual harassment suits by men (which constitute approximately 10 percent of all such suits)[42] often face ridicule. A Minnesota attorney who successfully represented a male city council aide in a sexual harassment suit against a female city council member reported that radio talk show hosts were mocking his client "to the hilt."[43] When eight men sued Jenny Craig International, they complained of both sex discrimination and sexual harassment: that female coworkers had taunted them with demeaning remarks and anatomical comments about their "tight buns," and that because of their sex they were assigned unfavorable tasks and denied promotions in the predominantly female corporate structure. Columnists derided the suit, sarcastically referring to the workplace isolation suffered by "the Boston eight" as "harrowing," suggesting that a number of recent sexual harassment claims by men are "guffaw-engendering," and concluding that while "[i]t is far too late for judges to laugh this stuff out of court . . . that shouldn't stop the rest of us."[44] Even courts have difficulty seeing female-perpetrator/male-victim sexual harassment as equivalent to the prototypic gender model. In *Carter v. Caring for the Homeless of Peekskill, Inc.*[45] a federal district court in New York held that a male employee had no claim for sexual harassment by the female "chairman" [sic] of the board of directors of his corporate employer, with whom he had a prior sexual relationship, since his "former paramour" had no supervisory power over him, even though she suggested he resign from his position "'as a personal consideration' to her."

If men are sexually harassed by other men, they have no legally cognizable injury; if men are sexually harassed by women, they are not believed. The assumptions that the typical perpetrator of sexual harassment is male and the typical victim female are not unwarranted. The vast majority of workplace sexual harassment consists of men harassing women: approximately 90 percent of victims are female.[46] Yet this prototype of male perpetrator and female victim may be transformed into a stereotype about sexual harassment that admits no other victim. The incidence of sexual harassment of men may be greater than people believe: of the total number of sexual harassment cases, between 9 and 15 percent are male victims.[47]

The underreporting of sexual harassment by either gender is not surprising. "Sexual subjects are generally sensitive and considered private; women feel embarrassed, demeaned, and intimidated by these incidents."[48]

Importantly, just as women vastly underreport sexual harassment, so may men. A British Institute of Personnel and Development Survey "found that men were less likely than women to take legal action if harassed."[49] And just as women feel ashamed and humiliated by this harassment, men may feel absolutely silenced. Women fear that people will not believe their sexual harassment claims.[50] In addition to the fear that people will not believe their claims, men may fear that people *will* believe their claims, but will regard them as effeminate.[51] Because society equates being the target of sexual harassment with being something less than male, men may not want to admit that sexual harassment happened to them.[52] This sentiment among individual men is not unrelated to society's denial that males may be victims of sexual harassment. Treating a problem as nonexistent helps keep it that way.

Most significantly, some recent court interpretations hold that the federal employment statutes do not provide a cause of action for same-sex sexual harassment, or for harassment based on sexual orientation, the vast majority of which appears to be men brutalizing other men in a sexual manner.[53] Courts are virtually uniform in rejecting claims of sexual harassment on the basis of sexual orientation. If an employer sexually harasses gay or lesbian employees because of their sexual orientation, the employee has no cause of action under Title VII.[54] A number of these cases include extraordinarily vulgar and abusive comments as well as highly offensive touchings. For instance, in *Carreno v. Local No. 226 International Brotherhood of Electrical Workers*, coworkers performed "simulated sexual intercourse or sodomy" on Carreno.[55] Yet the court reasoned that the coworkers treated Carreno abusively not because of his gender, but "because of his sexual preference."

If, however, an employer sexually harasses an employee not on the basis of the employee's sexual orientation, but on the basis of the employer's sexual orientation, courts are willing to view the predatory activity as sexual harassment.[56] Thus, as claimants, gays and lesbians do not have a cause of action for sexual harassment, yet, as alleged perpetrators, gays and lesbians must defend themselves against such causes of action.[57]

Some courts addressing the issue have held that the right to sue under Title VII for sexual harassment does not apply to same-sex harassment of a sexual nature. Perhaps a majority of courts now allow same-sex sexual harassment cases, although this shift was a phenomenon of the mid-1990s, and some courts still view same-sex sexual harassment as outside the purview of Title VII.[58] As this book was going to press, the Supreme Court granted certiorari on the issue of whether same-sex sexual harassment presents a cognizable claim under Title VII.[59]

Several recent cases illustrate the reasoning that prevailed in same-sex cases until the mid 1990s. In *Polly v. Houston Lighting and Power Co.*, the male plaintiff was subjected to both verbal and physical abuse. Several of the defendants repeatedly called him "a 'faggot,' a 'queer' and a 'fat bucket of . . . sh-t.'" The defendants kissed Polly; they grabbed and pinched his genitals, buttocks, and chest; and "on one occasion, Defendant Ubernosky forced a broom handle against Polly's rectum." Despite this conduct of a distinctly sexual nature, the federal district court held that Polly could not sue under Title VII for sexual harassment since the harassment was not "based upon his sex."[60]

The plaintiff in *Goluszek v. H. P. Smith* suffered similar abuse: "[T]he operators periodically asked Goluszek if he had gotten any 'pussy' or had oral sex, showed him pictures of nude women, told him they would get him 'fucked,' accused him of being gay or bisexual, and made other sex-related comments. The operators also poked him in the buttocks with a stick."[61] Goluszek was a single male who lived with his mother. The court found that Goluszek "comes from an 'unsophisticated background' and has led an 'isolated existence' with 'little or no sexual experience.' Goluszek 'blushes easily' and is abnormally sensitive to comments pertaining to sex." When he complained about the harassment by the other employees, the general manager found the allegations without substance. During his several years of complaints and grievances, which were not pursued or were dismissed for other reasons, Goluszek was reprimanded a number of times for tardiness and waste of time. At one point the general manager informed Goluszek by letter that if he continued to disrupt the workplace and waste company time by complaining about these incidents, it would constitute adequate cause for his termination. The employer ultimately discharged Goluszek for tardiness, an instance of absenteeism, and wasting company time.

The *Goluszek* court found that the plaintiff "was a male in a male-dominated environment," and that "if Goluszek were a woman H. P. Smith would have taken action to stop the harassment." The court concluded that while "Goluszek may have been harassed 'because' he is a male . . . that harassment was not of a kind which created an anti-male environment in the workplace."[62] Thus, although Goluszek's sexuality was attacked, the court relied on the idea that Title VII just does not preclude same-sex sexual harassment. Several subsequent cases have followed the *Polly* and *Goluszek* holdings without additional analysis in order to dismiss claims by males of same-sex sexual harassment.[63]

While courts are taking the statutory dodge by simply holding that Title VII does not prohibit same-sex harassment, it is clear that employers and coworkers are treating some males differently *because of* their gender. Men who do not conform to conventional notions of maleness are punished. Goluszek, for example, was a single, sexually unsophisticated male who lived with his mother and who was offended by sexual conversation. It is precisely this departure from male norms that subjected him to sexual harassment as a male. The notion in *Goluszek* that the company did not foster an "anti-male environment" assumes that only a single type of male exists: one who can ignore an environment constantly charged with sexual innuendos, one who enjoys sexual repartee, and one who can withstand physical abuse. Kathryn Abrams observes that these plaintiffs "challenge accepted notions of what it means to be a man. . . . Their combination of male characteristics—XY chromosomes, male genitalia—and what are usually thought to be female characteristics—sexual naivete or aversion to sexualized talk— seems to make the courts as uncomfortable as it makes their co-workers."[64]

An important additional feature of many same-sex sexual harassment cases brought by male plaintiffs is the courts' approach to the factual allegations of the complaints. Almost uniformly, courts minimize the facts and diminish any possible negative effects when men complain of sexual harassment. For instance, in *Garcia v. Elf Atochem North America* the male plaintiff complained to his union steward that the plant foreman had sexually harassed him on several occasions.[65] The conduct involved the foreman grabbing Garcia's crotch and "ma[king] sexual motions from behind [Garcia]." Before holding that sexual harassment of a male by a male supervisor was not actionable under Title VII, the court noted that the company had received prior similar complaints about the foreman, but determined that "[t]he conduct complained of was viewed as 'horseplay' and was not alleged to be sexually motivated." In contrast, if these same sorts of obscene physical touchings had occurred between a man and a woman, the woman would have a valid cause of action.[66]

In *Hopkins v. Baltimore Gas and Electric Co.*, the male plaintiff related over a dozen incidents of sexual harassment by his male supervisor, including inappropriate gestures, comments, and jokes, as well as direct questions about the plaintiff's sex life.[67] Hopkins alleged that his male supervisor, Ira Swadow, had sent him internal company correspondence with the words "S.W.A.K., kiss kiss" written on it; had kissed Hopkins at his wedding reception; attempted to squeeze into a revolving door compartment with Hopkins; and had asked Hopkins "whether he had gone on any dates over the weekend and, if so, whether any of those dates had culminated in sexual intercourse." Hopkins also testified about the following incidents:

> Swadow entered the men's room at work while plaintiff was using the facilities, pretended to lock the door, and said, "Ah, alone at last." . . .
>
> . . . On one occasion, Swadow approached plaintiff while he was leaning against a table at work, pivoted an illuminated magnifying lens so that it was positioned above plaintiff's crotch, and said, "Where is it?" . . . On another occasion, Swadow and plaintiff bumped into one another, and Swadow said to plaintiff, "You only do that so you can touch me." . . .
>
> . . . On another occasion, in the course of a discussion which Swadow was having with plaintiff and a male vendor concerning the difficulties of surviving an airline crash in water, Swadow said that if he were in such a situation he would "find a dead man, cut off his penis and breathe through that." In his deposition, plaintiff testified that he told Swadow that he was "sick" and that his remark was "inappropriate," particularly in the presence of some one [sic] not employed by the Company.

The court determined that Title VII did not prohibit same-sex sexual harassment, but hedged its bet by also holding that the incidents the plaintiff complained of did not amount to sexual harassment, since "[n]one of the alleged incidents of sexual harassment by Swadow involved implicit or explicit requests or demands for sexual favors." The court observed that "many of the incidents relied upon do not appear at all to have even been 'sexual' in nature, and several others involved essentially trivial conduct which would not in any event be actionable under Title VII." Curiously, the court added that "Swadow never asked that plaintiff go out with him on a 'date,' and Swadow never touched plaintiff in a sexual manner."[68]

Rather than looking at the cumulative pattern of conduct, which courts consistently do in cross-gender sexual harassment cases,[69] the *Hopkins* court viewed the incidents separately, as isolated and trivial events. If this approach to the evidence is adopted in same-sex sexual harassment cases, it will be virtually impossible for a plaintiff to meet the *Meritor Savings Bank v. Vinson* test that the sexual harassment must be "sufficiently severe or pervasive."[70] Moreover, instead of viewing what conduct was present, the *Hopkins* court concentrated on what forms of abuse were not present. Completely absent from the court's interpretation was any evidence of how these incidents made the plaintiff feel.[71]

The same pattern of analysis was replayed in *Vandeventer v. Wabash National Corp.*[72] In deciding that the male plaintiff did not suffer a hostile work environment, the court observed,

> Mr. Feltner alleges *only* that he was harassed by another man. . . . In particular, Mr. Feltner complained to Wabash National *only* that he was harassed by a coordinator (a crew or team leader) named Tremain Gall, who aimed the comments "drop down," "dick sucker," and "crawl under the table" at Mr. Feltner. Mr. Gall made a comment wondering whether Mr. Feltner could perform fellatio without his false teeth. Mr. Gall also asked Mr. Feltner if he would go with him to a gay bar. Those were the *only* comments Mr. Feltner ever complained about.

In rejecting Feltner's quid pro quo sexual harassment complaint, the court noted, "[t]he *only* detriment allegedly suffered by Mr. Feltner was termination and possibly (although unsupported by the record) decreased productivity due to the hostile environment." The language used by the *Vandeventer* court is language of diminishment. The text and subtext read perfectly clearly: Feltner was *only* harassed by one other man (it was a fair fight); he was *only* subjected to comments (and should have taken them like a man); and he *only* lost his job (buck up, pal).

A number of courts take a monolithic view of what constitutes sexual harassment, conceiving it only as the oppression of a female by "a male in a male-dominated environment."[73] In rejecting same-sex claims and sexual harassment claims based on the sexual orientation of the victim, courts draw and reinforce strict gender and sexual orientation lines.[74] If a male had aimed the same sorts of verbal and physical intimidation present in *Polly*, *Goluszek*, or *Vandeventer* toward a female, the female would have a valid sexual harassment claim.[75] In fact, in *Vandeventer*, while the court dismissed Douglas Feltner's claims of a hostile environment, it allowed Lisa Vandeventer's claims of a hostile environment based on derogatory sexual remarks to survive a motion for summary judgment.[76]

Indeed, the anomaly of rejecting same-sex sexual harassment becomes clearer if we add one hypothetical fact to either *Polly* or *Goluszek*. Assume that a female employee had witnessed the events that occurred and filed a claim of sexual harassment based on the hostile work environment. If the same events had occurred and were simply *witnessed* by a woman, the woman probably would have a cognizable claim for a sexually hostile work environment.[77] Thus, while the female bystander could recover for sexual harassment, the direct male victim would not have a remedy.

In holding that same-sex sexual harassment is not an appropriate basis for a Title VII claim, courts send a powerful message about gender roles: when men sexually harass other men, the victims do not suffer legally cognizable injuries. More simply, perhaps the message is that men do not suffer, or that "real men" do not suffer. Courts reveal a general unwillingness to believe that men could be offended by instances of sexual harassment. They trivialize men's complaints about vulgar and insulting comments, and endorse employers' messages that men who complain about these workplace incidents are providing appropriate grounds for their own termination. This approach reinforces social stereotypes of men as tough, sexually aggressive, and impervious to pain. Furthermore, it contributes to a cultural climate in which men cannot express their humiliation, their sense of invasion, or their emotional suffering.

The Exclusion of Men from Caring, Nurturing Roles

The feminist movement has brought us images of competent women at work, but not of caring, nurturing men at home. (Perhaps the critique is not appropriately just of feminism. This is a particular example of the larger question: Who is responsible for constructing the ideology of feminist men? Some feminists might say that it is men's responsibility. My suggestion is that the responsibility is universal.) The images of competent women at work have been presented because feminism enabled women to enter the workplace, and because economic realities forced women into the workplace. True-life images of men at home are scarce, at least in part since those same economic circumstances (with the attendant forms of market discrimination), rather than any failures of feminism, keep women out of and men in the workplace, even if men might prefer a role as the primary child rearer.[78]

To the extent that the legal world reflects social conceptions of gender, men are excluded from family roles. For example, women are able to take parental leave more easily than men. "Men and women are not offered the same leave under present practices. Employers frequently give women more parental leave than men. The many employers who offer pregnancy leave but not child care leave are giving women some parental leave and men none."[79] Even when paternity leave is formally available, subtle or direct employer actions may discourage men from taking advantage of the leave:

Corporations take a far more negative view of unpaid leaves for men than they do unpaid leaves for women. Almost two-thirds of total respondents did not consider it reasonable for men to take any parental leave whatsoever. . . .

Even among companies that currently offer unpaid leaves to men, many thought it unreasonable for men to take them. Fully 41% of companies with unpaid leave policies for men did not sanction their using the policy.[80]

These social and institutional barriers to parental leave for men are a significant impediment to the equal division of child care responsibilities.[81] The approach harms both men and women. If employers give women more generous parenting leave than men, men are excluded from and women are locked into parenting roles. Both genders are damaged because the underlying stereotypes limit their choices.

The legal precedents on this issue are more promising than the social practices of employers. Even several early cases allowed child-rearing leave to men if such leave was available for women.[82] At least one recent decision implies that employers should not draw a stark distinction between maternal and paternal roles regarding child rearing. In *Schafer v. Board of Public Education*, Gerald Schafer applied for a one-year child-rearing leave to raise his infant son.[83] The board routinely granted parenting leave to women. The leave was denied, and therefore Schafer had no choice but to resign from his teaching position. The Third Circuit Court of Appeals held that a collective bargaining agreement that permitted female teachers one year of unpaid leave for child rearing but denied this leave to male teachers violated Title VII. The court distinguished between disability leave for the period of actual physical disability relating to pregnancy or childbirth and child-rearing leave, which could be taken at any time by either sex.

In contrast to parental leave cases, courts have been less adept at perceiving the gender issues in cases that more indirectly present the question of what role a father should play in parenting. Significant evidence shows that courts discount men as potential custodial parents. Courts also subject women to a variety of gender biases in custody cases: mothers, for example, may sacrifice financial security for custody.[84] However, for present purposes, the discussion will focus on the biases against men. While the empirical evidence is decidedly mixed, the cumulative evidence seems to indicate that gender biases run in both directions under different circumstances.

Reversing centuries of fathers' proprietary rights to custody of their children, doctrinal law in the early 1900s began to encompass a preference for maternal custody of children of tender years.[85] In the past two decades, most states have abandoned the formal presumption in favor of mothers being awarded custody,[86] and a number of states use language encouraging shared parenting in their custody statutes.[87] However, gender is still a statutory consideration in several jurisdictions.[88]

The child's best interests standard ostensibly considers more direct criteria of parenting capacity and patterns. Nevertheless, decisions favor mothers in a number of ways. Joint custody law still prefers mothers as physical custodians.[89] The primary caretaker standard, adopted explicitly in West Virginia and Minnesota, and implicitly in a number of other jurisdictions, may be a thinly veiled return to the maternal preference standard, since "[i]t has been assumed that mothers are the primary caretakers of children and therefore the primary or psychological parents."[90] Even in states in which the formal maternal presumption is absent, judges may make decisions as though such a presumption still exists, or may exhibit strong biases against awarding custody to fathers. In one study of judges, approximately half agreed that custody awards may be "based on the assumption that children belong with their mothers." Another survey of attorneys showed that "all but one attorney interviewed believed that some Vermont judges are biased against fathers in custody."[91] Moreover, as an empirical matter, mothers obtain sole custody in an overwhelming proportion of cases. A study conducted in California demonstrated that mothers obtained custody in two-thirds of all cases, while fathers received sole physical custody in 9 percent of all cases.[92]

Fathers normally obtain custody in contested custody cases.[93] A recent study of Utah cases, however, suggests that while the proportion of fathers who obtain custody in the event of a formal dispute is still relatively high when compared to negotiated custody settlements, "sole custody was awarded to the father in 21 percent of the cases and to the mother in 50 percent of the cases."[94] Contested custody cases, though, account for only a small fraction of all custody cases. Less than 2 percent of divorces involving children necessitate a judicial determination of custody.[95] Self-selection may also be a significant factor in determining who contests a custody decision.[96]

Even before the custody hearing, fathers may be discouraged from seeking custody. A survey of fathers reported that 35 percent of physical custody fathers and 10 percent of legal custody fathers wanted more custody than they requested, while only 12 percent of physical custody mothers and 7 percent of legal custody mothers felt this way.[97] Some research suggests that attorneys may advise fathers not to request or fight for custody.[98]

Custody decisions obviously entail consideration of gender, but how gender frames the terms of the debate is not as clear. All too often, analyses of whether fathers or mothers are discriminated against in custody litigation revolve around which parent "gets" the children. It is as if the custody award is a proprietary entitlement, which gives one parent the physical custody of the children and the other parent the right to complain about a gendered decision. Courts and commentators increasingly recognize that the decisional focus must be on the circumstances that are best for the individual child. While some observers acknowledge that custody decisions send messages about the kinds of families a society wants to construct, courts often ignore the larger question of the reconstructive effects of particular tests.

Feminist Legal Theory and Maternal Preferences

Some feminist legal theorists are appropriating the domestic sphere as principally the province of women.[99] Mary Becker, for example, argues that "a conspiracy of silence forbids discussion of what is common knowledge: Mothers are usually emotionally closer to their children than fathers."[100] The article is replete with mothers' stories about their relationships with their children. She includes a couple of fathers' stories, but only for the purpose of attesting to the mothers' close relationships with their children. Thus, in Becker's work, the different voice silences the male voice. Moreover, the article seems to disparage the emotional bonds between fathers and children by asserting, "Most mothers describe father's love as: '[L]ess intense, less caring, or less understanding than mother love.'" Becker relies on one mother's comments to argue that fathers do not have the same empathetic abilities as mothers: "A father just doesn't seem to feel a child's hurts and disappointments as his own the way a mother does."

Becker advocates a maternal deference standard in custody cases. She claims that "judges should defer to the fit mother's judgment of the custodial arrangement that would be best." If this proposal is adopted (which is unlikely for constitutional reasons) or allowed to undergird custody arrangements, it will often prevent men from parenting. Yet Becker is not alone in urging that custody determinations should reflect the special emotional bonds between mother and child.[101]

Of more general concern than the specific standard in custody cases is the approach in the theoretical literature to men as parents. Judgments about males have come in the form of universals, rather than in the form of particulars of individual parents' experiences. Theoretical literature depicts "mothering" as an activity exclusive to women. Fathers will continue to not be custodial parents as long as societal divisions of child care responsibility persist. Feminist theory could do much toward exploding the myth that parenting is a sex-linked trait, and toward fostering an understanding of how men can nurture and take on child care responsibilities.

5

The "F" Word

Feminism and Its Detractors

> Feminism is a dirty word. . . . Misconceptions abound. Feminists are portrayed as bra-burners, man-haters, sexists, and castrators. Our sexual preferences are presumed. We are characterized as bitchy, demanding, aggressive, confrontational, and uncooperative, as well as overly demanding and humorless.
>
> —Leslie Bender, "A Lawyer's Primer on Feminist Theory and Tort"

Why are people, women and men, so scared of the label "feminism"? Why is feminism so aggressively and gleefully demonized? A strong majority of people in this country embrace fundamental concepts of women's rights. Yet a roughly equal percentage of people decline to describe themselves as feminists. Why is this? As we shall see, a principal reason for the denigration of feminism is the extent to which the term has been defined by its opponents. Traditional opponents of feminism have been hugely successful in promoting the negative images associated with it. This is tied to the persistence of patriarchy and a backlash from those unsettled by the successes of feminism. The media are also quite complicit in the discrediting of feminism. Many print and broadcast features depict only the extremes of the feminist movement, rather than its reasoned core.

But the feminist movement itself must also share responsibility for some of its bad press. Historically, and even today, some feminists have engaged in exclusionary practices. In its formation, the women's movement alienated some potential supporters along lines of race, gender, and social class. Many of those deep divisions persist today. Certain feminists, perhaps in attempts to garner publicity or attention to causes, have indulged in a politics of anger. Various individuals and groups within the movement have expended an inordinate amount of time and an extravagant level of vitriolic energy battling with each other. Aside from the internal wars, the feminist movement also has been hampered by a lack of cohesion and, in part due to its political philosophy, an absence of hierarchical organizational structure. This chapter traces the splintering of the movement across dimensions of age, approaches, and political projects.

My purpose here is not to lay blame, but to explore root causes. Honest, self-critical analysis does reveal that some of the disreputability originated from actions taken by feminists within the movement. Feminists must be willing to accept responsibility for, and analytically evaluate the effects of, these actions—the infighting, the publicity grabs, and the alienating consequences of their more extreme theories. Of course, critics selectively cull the most extreme rhetoric and political statements and misuse them to discredit feminism. Let us see how this happens.

Public Opinion: "I Love It!" "I Hate It!"

Many if not most people refuse to label themselves feminists. In a Peter Harris poll conducted at the request of the Feminist Majority Foundation in April 1995, a nationwide sample of 1,364 women and men were asked if they considered themselves a "strong feminist," a "feminist," "not a feminist," or "anti-feminist." The results of the poll showed that "[b]y a close 43% to 41%, a plurality say they are not feminists. However, by 51% to 35% a majority of women say they are a feminist, while by 50% to 30% a majority of men do not."[1] Those polled were then given a dictionary definition of feminism—as "someone who supports political, economic, and social equality for women"—and were then asked if they would identify themselves as feminists according to that definition. Two-thirds of those responding (71 percent of women and 61 percent of men) said they would call themselves "feminists" according to that definition.

Other polls yield less positive statistics. According to a 1996 Wirthlin Worldwide poll of 1,015 adult men and women in America, 60 percent said they were not feminists, while one in four consider and call themselves feminists; the remainder of those polled were undecided.[2] While entire generations of women have shared in the gains won by early feminists, they are reluctant to align themselves with the movement. In a 1993 article, Wendy Kaminer noted that although most women are supportive of efforts to promote equal rights for women, only one-third identify themselves as feminists.[3]

While women and men do not call themselves feminists, they do embrace the ideals of women's rights and equality between the sexes: they share feminist concerns while rejecting the label. An overwhelming majority of women will acknowledge that the women's movement has had a positive effect on their lives.[4] According to a Louis Harris poll, 71 percent of the 3,100 people surveyed support the movement to strengthen women's rights.[5]

Perhaps one of the difficulties with ascertaining popular allegiances lies in the nature of labeling. The unwillingness to identify oneself as a feminist may be a part of the perverse individualism of Americans, who hate to be labeled. Or it may have to do with the nature of fads and trends—the popular conception attached to the label: whether it is presently "cool" or "not cool" to be a feminist. As soon as Phil Donahue became a feminist, many of his detractors must have immediately decided they did not want to be one.

The "trending" of feminism also has some roots in popular press depictions. But even acceptance of the poll results at face value points to the need for clarification about terminology and education about basic definitions. When the subjects of surveys are educated about the meaning of terms, such as basic definitions of feminism, they respond more positively to associations with those terms. Eleanor Smeal, president of the Feminist Majority Foundation, observes, "One fact stands out: The more the public knows about women's rights ranging from affirmative action to abortion, the more favorable they are."[6]

The problem is thus not with the objectives that feminists aim to achieve. Mainstream and radical feminists, probably along with many moderates and conservatives, are concerned about equal employment and educational opportunities, equal pay for equivalent work, abuses of power on both the institutional and personal levels, such as government decisions made without adequate consideration of minority interests, domestic violence, adequate child care, and the lack of economic choices for people at many different stations in life. The problem seems centered on the reluctance of people to identify themselves as feminists.

The reasons offered for this dissociation with feminism are many, but a few themes resonate persistently. Some women perceive that feminists must adopt an orthodoxy of beliefs, such as favoring censorship of pornography or being pro-choice. They may disagree with a specific political position that they perceive as essential to feminism or more generally are reluctant to embrace "a way of life that does not allow for individuality and complexity. [They] fear that the identity will dictate and regulate [their] lives."[7] Others are concerned about the male-bashing they associate with the term. Some of these women feel that calling themselves "feminist" will make them unattractive to men or brand them as strident and humorless.[8] Still others may be wary of the modern divisions of feminism into camps of "equity" feminists or "gender" feminists, or the labeling of the latter group as "victim feminists."

In short, many people avoid identification with feminism to avoid possible negative associations that others might attach to the label, especially ideological ones that they do not share. And people do not want to align themselves with a term that has such an unpopular image.

Images and Ideology: Read the Label Carefully before Opening

The images conjured up by the word "feminist" are often particularly unflattering. Feminists may be stereotyped as militant, unattractive, man-hating, and anti-family, or perhaps as rape-crisis whiners. What has caused such a stigma to become associated with the term "feminism"? Of course there is more to it than just an image problem, more than just a media problem. It is important to recognize that the construction of the image *itself* serves political functions. The identity and purposes of the image makers are vital areas for inquiry, but media images generally do not survive in infertile ground.

The Defense of Patriarchy

Feminism has become defined in great part by its opponents. In politically loaded strategic moves, commentators, politicians, and traditionalists characterize the more radical elements of the feminist movement as representative of the mainstream. And whatever negativism is necessarily a part of the feminist critique is not only highlighted but distorted. For instance, factual statements made by feminists that throughout history men have systematically disempowered women are transformed into accusations of present-day man-hating. Metaphors are intentionally misinterpreted. Radical feminist Andrea Dworkin, for example, has often been cited for the proposition that all heterosexual intercourse is rape;[9] thus, any time June and Ward Cleaver had sex (undoubtedly on Sunday only and in the missionary position), it was rape because of the structure of patriarchy and the socially and politically subordinate positions of women. Dworkin never said that all heterosexual sex is rape, although she did contrast men's experience of sex as subjects with women's experience of sex as objects.[10] The very fact of social critique is treated as a lapse in etiquette. When feminists talk about sex in public, they are excoriated for breaching a sense of decorum that has reigned for centuries.

It is a rhetorical move much like that exemplified in the debate over political correctness. In the past decade, academics' attempts to include different race and gender perspectives and to discuss the virtues of humanism in their courses have been derided by critics as a movement of "political correctness." Media articles on incidents involving protests at photographic exhibits, sexual harassment policies, university speech codes, and professors teaching multicultural curricula raise the specter of tenured radicals on a totalitarian rampage bent on value, language, and thought control.

In *The Myth of Political Correctness,* John Wilson argues that no such movement exists. He exposes the "PC movement" as the fabricated creation of the conservative right, who are posing as the victims of an oppressive— but nonexistent—liberal political order. Wilson carefully details the incidents and evaluates the facts behind the distorted anecdotes giving rise to the charge.

Feminism suffers from much the same exaggeration and definition-by-caricature. Opponents have been extraordinarily successful in constructing the feminist straw woman and then burning her in effigy. In the past two decades, the word has often been used in popular conversation to connote behaviors with which some people disagree: women opening doors for themselves, having a job, living with another woman, or using birth control. In a 1992 fund-raising letter, Christian Coalition founder Pat Robertson derided feminism as a "socialist, anti-family political movement that encourages women to leave their husbands, kill their children, practice witchcraft, destroy capitalism and become lesbians."[11] Patrick Buchanan repeated this description in a speech at the 1992 Republican National Convention.

Conservative radio talk show host Rush Limbaugh coined the slur "feminazi." While Limbaugh originally applied the term to pro-choice advocates and First Lady Hillary Rodham Clinton, it has become a household term, used interchangeably with the word "feminist." What has been almost smoothed over in the popular translation of the derisive label is the unthinking comparison to Nazism. What remains is simply a stark adversarial image of what it means to be a feminist, with a hostile undertone that implies violent extremism.

While Buchanan's and Limbaugh's comments are vivid examples of the twisting of "feminism," we see the same forces at work in the more muted but powerful depictions of feminism in the popular media. Consider, for example, the portrayal of Hillary Rodham Clinton, one of the nation's most visible symbols of feminist ideals: a successful, pro-choice professional who kept her maiden name, a political activist who champions women's rights, named by the *National Law Journal* as one of the nation's hundred most powerful lawyers, and an author whose book *It Takes a Village* demands that the nation shoulder collective responsibility for the welfare of children. Yet she is subjected to relentless caricatures by cartoonists, pundits, and political columnists. Greeting cards spoof her as First Dominatrix; cartoons feature policy advisors taping her mouth shut because she is engaged in the gender-inappropriate behavior of speaking her mind; bumper stickers ask, "Who Elected Her?" or exhort, "Impeach Clinton: Get Rid of Bill, Too." An article in *Life* magazine about "The 50 Most Influential Boomers" dubbed Hillary Rodham Clinton "First Feminist." But Clinton herself avoids identification with the term, which in itself speaks volumes about perceptions of public acceptance of feminism.

A strong woman with political power and savvy, Hillary Rodham Clinton is castigated for traits that in men would bring praise and rewards. While some legitimate questions may be raised regarding her knowledge of events in the Whitewater transactions, think about the negative press she has garnered for other initiatives. She was culpable of having the hubris to expect Congress to approve a national health care reform proposal. When she drew on the African proverb "It takes a village to raise a child" for her book urging communities to nurture children, Hillary Rodham Clinton was castigated for advocating government intrusions into family life.[12] If Barbara Bush or Rosalyn Carter had issued such a message, would not the reception of it have been vastly different? According to his mother, Newt Gingrich, then Speaker of the House, called her a "bitch." If it is nationally acceptable to vilify—with some of the worst gender stereotypes imaginable—the First Lady (a designation that we won't get into at this point), why would any citizen sign up to be a feminist?

A significant amount of the negative imagery associated with feminism may be due to resistance to its ideas borne out of self-interest. As with many insurgent concepts, feminism does threaten the privileged class. For centuries, that has been men. Much of the resistance to feminism was, and still is, simply a defense of patriarchy. It is an understandable defense of a concept of self, appropriate roles, and relations, and a worldview that is pervasively developed in the minds and hearts of many in our society.

But not only men join the crusade against feminism. The idea that feminism might require discarding traditional roles terrifies both men and women. Some women are happy with traditional roles. Many know no other way of life.

Other women may worry about the responsibility that comes with equality. Large numbers of women repeatedly opposed the proposed Equal Rights Amendment out of fears that it would entail compulsory military service for women, institute unisex bathrooms, and rupture their existence. Some opposition to the ERA crystallized among "'family-oriented women' who felt that the ERA endangered and devalued the gendered norms upon which they had built their identities and their lives."[13] Feminism jolted both men and women. It provoked many different kinds of reactions, reactions that varied among women and men and even within individuals, creating sympathizers, unsettling many more, and sending some into a resistant stance.

Some women simply are not feminists, not from concerns about the burdens of equality, but from adherence to the roles traditionally prescribed by patriarchy. Conservatives like Phyllis Schlafly have railed against feminism for decades. A current incarnation, the Independent Women's Forum, which grew out of a group of women who supported Clarence Thomas during his confirmation hearings, sides with more traditional conservative women's groups, such as Schlafly's Eagle Forum and Concerned Women of America, in opposing abortion rights, affirmative action, and legislation like the Violence Against Women Act. These are women who join Schlafly in rabidly antifeminist jibes, such as Schlafly's polemic against "'shrill radioactive feminists' who are taking over Congress" and disrupting family values.[14]

A wide range of politicians and commentators, then, portray feminists as dangerous and dogmatic. Feminism is placed in opposition to "family values." Mere mention of the term sounds internal alarm bells. People pause and take a breath when the word comes up in conversation. Women fear repercussions from being associated with feminism. "A lot of young women don't want to be called feminists because, hey, listen to Rush Limbaugh, and you've heard it all. It's equated with being lesbian, fat, ugly."[15] And the reluctance to use the term probably goes beyond fear of name calling. In 1989 at the University of Montreal, a man who had been denied admission to the engineering school entered a classroom armed with a semiautomatic. He methodically separated the men from the women, and then, yelling, "You are all a bunch of feminists!" opened fire on the women, killing fourteen and wounding many others. Is it any wonder that so many people, principally women, preface their remarks endorsing women's rights with the disclaimer "I'm not a feminist, but . . . . "?

The Media Spin: Pop Culture Feminism

Media images strongly shape popular perceptions. They are what people know, often all that they know, about current events. This shaping influence exists in part because reporting does take from, respond to, and accentuate the threads of popular feelings. In her 1991 book *Backlash: The Undeclared War against American Women,* Susan Faludi graphically depicted the various ways media—film, television, and advertisements—create images of women geared toward keeping women in their traditional places: as vulnerable creatures or victims, passive housewives, sexually available nymphs, traditionally feminine ladies, or pitiable, overworked careerists. Witness the attention-grabbing headlines of newspaper articles that feed popular perceptions of a movement that is dogmatic, dangerous, and possibly delusional: "Power Feminists Can't Afford to Brush Off the Family," "Draft Looks Like Gender Feminist Manifesto," "Fostering Feminist Follies; Women's Studies: Little Thought, Lots of Dogma," "Feminist Group Does Not Live in Real World," "Feminists' Definition of Sexual Harassment Is Exercise in Brainwashing."

Some writers and reporters excel at finding the outré examples, magnifying the provocative labels, and putting a semi-educated gloss on the issues. Other commentators are perceptive in ascertaining what appeals are being made by various modern feminists—appeals to power, to identity, or to the rhetoric of emancipation—but instead of exploring these structures and taking them seriously, they exploit and ridicule them. In so doing, they transform the caricatures of feminism offered by its opponents into descriptions of feminist gospel.

In February 1994 *Esquire* ran a cover story, featuring a topless Drew Barrymore, entitled "Feminist Women Who Like Sex." The title and the text implied, of course, that most feminists do not like sex. Consider the following passage from the article:

> These "sexual agency" or "sexual empowerment" agitators have no collective platform, they often strongly disagree, and they hate being indiscriminately lumped together. But from lesbian eroticist Pat Califia to Clark University

professor Christina Hoff Sommers there's a commonality of interest strong
enough for us to do some discriminate lumpings and declare it a movement,
a movement proclaiming sexual liberation, sexual equality, and the reclama-
tion of men from the scrap heap of theory. Call it "do me" feminism. . . .

  They're going to talk about it—about cocks, about pussies, about fisting
and sucking—ways designed to make the average male blush. . . . The do-me
feminists are choosing locker room talk to shift discussion from the failures
of men to the failures of feminism, from the paradigm of sexual abuse to the
paradigm of sexual pleasure. They want to return sex from the political realm
to the personal. In short, they want to have fun.[16]

In topic, tone, and translation, the article typifies the ways modern feminism is oversimplified and exploited. Sex sells. The article portrays a large
camp of contemporary feminists as predatory, "selfish bitches" whose sexual politics are geared (although not exclusively) toward obtaining sexual
gratification. Naturally, they now bear the media-conferred label "do-me
feminists."

A 1995 issue of *Sassy*, a magazine for teenage girls, contains an article entitled "Is Feminism the New 'F' Word?" The opening paragraph implies that
feminism may be dogmatic, dispensable, and obsolete: "We couldn't care
less what the 'experts' have to say—what the media feminists have been
stuffing down our throats. We wanted to know how *you* feel about the
movement that defined your mother's generation, and how—if at all—you
incorporate feminism into your daily lives."[17] The article invites women to
view feminism not only as unfashionable and passé, but as little more than
a fashion statement, and a dubious one at that.

Modern feminism is portrayed as a matter of individual choice and, thus,
individual responsibility. And for some, individualism is one of the highest
goods, in splendid isolation from cultural beliefs, socialization patterns, and
the influence of structural relations on "choices." The cultural construction
of feminism as individualism has another important consequence: it misdi-
rects attention away from collective responsibility or action. Some commentators have performed a monumental disservice in reshaping issues of
collective importance as problems solvable by individual acts of self-im-
provement:

  Celebrated best-sellers offer cautionary tales of both success and failure, but
  their underlying message is much the same. Whether the topic is super-
  moms and how they manage, or Women Who Can't Say No and the Men
  Who Control Them, the moral is that solutions for women's problems lie
  with individual women. It is just a matter of choosing the right man, the

right wardrobe, the right career sequence, or the right time-management techniques.[18]

The negative imagery attached to feminism is fed by the publicity given to extreme views. Consider the extraordinary media coverage given to Katie Roiphe's first book, *The Morning After: Sex, Fear, and Feminism on Campus*, and the unquestioning acceptance of its premises that incidents of rape on college campuses ("date rape") are wildly exaggerated by "rape crisis feminists." When Katha Pollitt, finalist for the National Book Critics Circle award for her book *Reasonable Creatures: Essays on Women and Feminism*, championed reason in the service of feminism, she received a sprinkling of laudatory reviews. When Camille Paglia slams "yuppie feminists," journalists are entertained by the outrageous things she says, and write literally thousands of columns about her.

And the media articles are about "her"—Paglia herself, or Betty Friedan, or Gloria Steinem. They are articles about the players, but not the ideas. We can read about Camille Paglia's attire of big, black boots and a knife on a belt around her hips, the graying of Betty Friedan, or the sexy but intellectual looks of Gloria Steinem. Newspapers give airplay to personal details of the lifestyles of feminists, such as National Organization for Women president Patricia Ireland, who has both a husband and a longtime female companion. Catharine MacKinnon's relationship with Jeffrey Masson or whether she wears her hair in a bun receives a significant amount of media coverage by reporters who seem less interested in her theories about how legal doctrines and institutions promote patriarchy. Perhaps the critique is not unique to reporting on feminism. The press may glom onto the people in a movement because characters are more interesting to readers than ideas. But besides the striking absence of reflective pieces on subtle differences between the theorists' theories, something else seems to be at work.

This focus on personalities smacks of the irrelevancy of ad hominem reasoning. Illogic of many kinds is there: emotive-persuasive appeals to popular prejudices, vast overgeneralizations, and nonrepresentative sampling. Worse, centering attention on the personalities of feminists leaves intact the worldwide degradation of men and women in all its economic, psychological, religious, political and familial forms. It deflects attention away from the systemic critiques offered by feminist theories. The concentration on feminist figureheads is reminiscent of the now largely discredited "great man" theory of history—the idea that great individuals shape the direction of history. One difference, though, is that in this "great woman" theory of feminist history, the women are depicted as not so great.

In *Who Stole Feminism? How Women Have Betrayed Women,* Christina Hoff Sommers describes a feminist movement populated by "gender" feminists and "equity" feminists. According to Sommers, gender feminists have dominated the women's movement with an ideology of women as victims and men as abusers, while equity feminists, like Sommers, simply want women to have equal rights. Sommers also accuses gender feminists of "falsehoods and exaggerations" regarding evidence of gender bias, anorexia, and battering of women.[19] Sommers's scathing indictment of "the feminist establishment" was extraordinarily well received in the popular media, drawing praise from reviewers in the *Chicago Tribune, Wall Street Journal, Denver Post, Washington Times,* and *Boston Globe.*

What is remarkably curious is the vast amount of spotlight attention the popular media have given to Paglia and Sommers, given that their ideas about women's agency are a repackaging of concepts discussed by academics for years. American studies professor Patrice McDermott makes clear that ideas such as those in the works of Paglia, Roiphe, and Sommers, ideas of feminist victimology and constructions of female sexuality, have been the subject of feminist academic debate for more than a decade. McDermott points out that the media championing of these selective critiques of feminism "promotes a version of women's studies that trivializes feminist analyses of power, undermines attempts to effect social change, and casts feminism as a hegemonic bully on American campuses."[20]

By and large the media are owned by rather conservative capitalist interests; they operate with the necessity of selling, and this often pushes toward sensationalism. And reporters are journalists, most of them proponents of informational rights or at least significantly influenced by individualistic conceptions of freedom. McDermott suggests that this latter feature—the shared ideology of liberal individualism—offers at least a partial explanation of why academics like Paglia and Sommers prefer to publish in the popular press.

Feminist academics have generally accepted a vision of feminist theory that connects individual injustices and larger institutional structures: families, schools, corporations, and other social organizations. Critical academic feminism focuses on the power relations among various classes of people along many dimensions of identity, such as sex, race, and economic conditions. Most feminist academic scholarship acknowledges a variety of epistemological issues in the analysis of women's history and experiences. It develops the idea of multiple perspectives—that an individual black woman, for example, sees the world as a black, as a woman, as a black woman, and as a black woman from a particular set of economic and social circumstances. Academic feminism points to the delicate interplay between subjectivism and objectivism in interpretation—as just one example, the mechanisms by which personal experiences are translated into empirical statements about the condition of women. And academic feminism discusses the constraints of existing power and social relations on the very ways people are able to think about gender.

Pop culture feminism, on the other hand, offers a single view of women, one ringing with the hallmarks of traditional essentialist individualism: women are free agents, strongly sexual beings, and not passive victims. In the works of Paglia and Roiphe are numerous comments about women's responsibility for engaging in risky behavior that solicits male aggression. Katie Roiphe argues that sexual harassment should be handled by individuals rather than through collective action or etiquette codes.[21] In *Sex, Art and American Culture,* Paglia writes that if a woman is raped, she "must accept the consequences and, through self-criticism, resolve never to make that mistake again."[22] And Paglia believes women are willfully stupid for remaining in abusive relationships. Diminished or ignored are the subtle and complex ways women have been conditioned by oppression and their efforts politically suppressed. The epistemological constraints on understanding about women's behavior are nonexistent.

Such depictions of women as either free agents or the products of coercion involve fruitless dichotomizing. Elizabeth Schneider explains what she calls "the false dichotomy of victimization and agency" in the context of battered women:

> [A]lthough an appreciation of women's experiences as victims [is] necessary and important, an exclusive focus on women's victimization [is] incomplete and limiting because it ignore[s] women's active efforts to protect themselves and their children, and to mobilize their resources to survive. At the same time, . . . an exclusive focus on women's agency, reflected in the emphasis on why the woman ha[s] not left the battering relationship, [is] shaped by liberal visions of autonomy, individual action, and individual control and mobility, which [are] equally unsatisfactory without the larger social context of victimization.[23]

Kathryn Abrams suggests that a more realistic vision encompasses both poles of these antinomic choices. Feminist theorizing, social programs, and laws should "reflect the partial agency of women . . . while addressing the underlying conditions of women's oppression."[24]

In many ways, popular writers perform such a disservice to feminism. Emphasizing the focus on themselves as personalities, rather than on issues, is one example. Creating simple demarcations between strands of feminism is another. Some popular culture writers promote a belief that there is a coercive and univocal orthodoxy to feminism. We see it in Katie Roiphe's description of "rape crisis feminists" or Christina Hoff Sommers's simplistic division of feminism into camps of "gender feminists" and "equity feminists." Even historian Elizabeth Fox-Genovese, writing for a mass audience, embodies the idea of insularity in the title of her most recent book, *Feminism Is Not the Story of My Life: How Today's Feminist Elite Has Lost Touch with the Real Concerns of Women*. Fox-Genovese also promotes the idea of feminist orthodoxy, referring in the text to advocation of the pro-choice position as "the litmus test" of feminism. Very generally, this dissociation between academic feminism and the feminism of popular culture disregards the shadings on so many issues, and ignores the complexity of individuals and situations.

An odd disjunction exists in media reporting between the particular and the general. At the one extreme, press coverage centers on individuals, but only high-profile individuals. At the other extreme, little attention is given to the everyday experiences of men and women making choices about issues of reproduction or child care, or having those choices limited, but much is made of the general issue of abortion or parenting or birth control. Deborah Rhode points out, "Articles on Medicaid funding are typically cast in terms of political skirmishes among elected officials or contests between prolife and prochoice advocates. Seldom do we hear anything from or about the women, particularly low-income women of color, whose lives are permanently marred by the absence of birth control or prenatal services."[25] In the process of sensationalizing the political battles, the abstraction comes to the forefront, and people's experiences are lost.

The media give inordinate attention to extreme views because they are simply more interesting. Those in the sensible middle never get the same forum. Coverage of particular issues is provided in sound bites, in which "reporters commonly offer a sampling of the most radical comments and then make special efforts to interview hostile onlookers or 'regular' women on the street who are alienated from such rhetoric. . . . [One] result is that debates among women are cast as catfights."[26] The focus on extreme positions misses many of the simple, mainstream messages of feminism, such as equal rights for women or the need for men and women to be free of gender stereotypes. It also presents a picture of a movement populated by extremists and polarized on most issues of significance. Omitted is any extensive coverage of the issues themselves. Perhaps this is one of the reasons so many people, female and male, are willing to champion women's rights but disavow any connection to feminism.

Misperceptions of Radicalism

One of the most pervasive perceptions of feminism is the equation of feminism and radicalism. This may have to do with the circumstances surrounding the birth of modern feminism, its embrace of sexual liberation, and its battles—viewed as revolutionary—to change the social and political terrain of gender.

From Civil Rights to Feminism

Feminism became part of the popular consciousness after the grassroots civil rights movement. The timing may have been unfortunate in several ways. First, people were "burned out," to borrow a phrase from the era, by the fights for equality. Feminism surfaced in the decade immediately after massive resistance to racial integration. By the late 1960s and early 1970s, the nation had just finished experiencing extensive litigation, race riots, domestic military intervention, and the virulent rhetoric of racism. In the inaugural words of Governor George Wallace, "Segregation now! Segregation tomorrow! Segregation forever!" President Eisenhower had ordered federal troops to Central High School in Little Rock, Arkansas, after Governor Orval Faubus called out the National Guard to prevent nine black children from attending it.

Far more terrifying events rocked the country: church bombings and desecrations, the assassinations of black leaders Dr. Martin Luther King, Malcom X, and Medgar Evers, Ku Klux Klan lynchings of activists, and the brutal murders of civil rights volunteers, black and white, who worked to register black voters. In one of the church bombings, at the Sixteenth Street Baptist Church in Birmingham, four black girls were killed; they had just finished their Sunday school lesson. There were "sit-ins" at lunch counters in Greensboro, North Carolina, "swim-ins," "read-ins," and "pray-ins" to desegregate pools, libraries, and churches, political battles culminating in the passage of the Civil Rights Acts of 1957, 1960, and 1964 (which made it a crime to obstruct persons trying to comply with civil rights orders) and the Voting Rights Act, marches, protests, boycotts, prosecutions, court injunctions, arrests, police dogs, mob violence, jeering, spitting, and a climate of fear and hate.

On the heels of these decades of social unrest, hostility, and violence, women were suddenly demanding rights too. And the problems raised by the women's movement ran deeper than simply a national unwillingness to reenact the tumultuous 1960s. The social upheaval threatened by the uprising of women was in some ways far more pervasive than the demands of racial minorities for social and political rights. The women's movement potentially included not a mere 10 percent of the population, but literally half of the population, of all races. And it involved people one lived with: wives, partners, mothers, sisters, daughters. The radicalism of feminism was exaggerated in the minds of the defenders of traditionalism not only because of the dangers of widespread social and lifestyle changes, but also because this insurrection was emotionally charged with betrayal. It was as though women, who were expected to be docile, supportive, and nurturing, were being unfaithful.

The feminist movement promised a revolution that could not be confined to certain areas of the country or neighborhoods or to certain kinds of relief. The problems of the racial civil rights movement were more easily defined. The problems of the women's civil rights movement were more complex and slippery. There was a vague sense of inequality, but women were not being told they could not sit at certain lunch counters. And feminism shook deep, pervasive, widely and subjectively accepted beliefs, habits, behaviors, and roles. Women wanted an equality that went beyond removing barriers. They wanted what was viewed (oxymoronically) as extreme equality; they wanted equality of results. Americans, when they think about equality, think about equality of opportunity: an absence of formal barriers, no prohibitions in admissions criteria, job training programs, and scholarships, to name but a few examples. The American public's notion of equality has never extended to equality of results. These may be some of the historical reasons that in popular consciousness, feminism as a political movement is associated automatically with radicalism.

The Sexual Revolution: Offending Sensibilities

Another aspect of feminism that promoted its connection in the popular mind with radical behavior was the high-profile intertwining of feminism with the politics of sexual liberation. The sexual revolution's redefinition of sexuality provoked attention to patterns of sexual interaction and provided enlightenment and information about a wide variety of sexuality issues. Information about anatomy and sexually transmitted diseases was no longer hidden. Women received cultural permission to enjoy sex. Contraception became a joint responsibility between sexual partners. Questions were raised about traditional assumptions about women and sexuality: that women were expected to be sexually inexperienced at the time of marriage and always sexually available to men. As the U.S. Supreme Court recognized in 1973 in *Miller v. California,* the sexual revolution of the previous few years removed "layers of prudery from a subject long irrationally kept from needed ventilation."[27]

During the sexual revolution discussions about repressions and inhibitions were not simply, and probably not even primarily, about sexual practices and appetites. These discussions instead signaled deeper concerns about sexual power and autonomy, about who should be in control of women's sexuality. The debate, for example, regarding the "myth of the vaginal orgasm"—a question of whether women's erotic pleasure was necessarily tied to procreative acts—was a dialogue about the acceptance of popular assumptions that contributed to sexual oppression. For feminists, sexual politics were tied to a broader discourse of liberation. The sexual revolution changed popular thinking about sexual expression, gender roles, relationships, and responsibilities. Yet in a country still heavily influenced by the mores of the Victorian age, some perceived this sexual openness as purely licentious behavior. Pope John Paul II and numerous other leading religious figures of various denominations have linked feminism with the excesses of the sexual revolution.[28]

And, as always, there were the media accounts of burned bras and man-hating. The issues in the spotlight of feminist concerns, then and now—such as the connections between sexual freedom and economic independence—were not those that drew media attention. Susan Faludi depicts how the media foster—and even create—myths about feminism. She tells the story of how feminists became one with bra-burners. At a protest outside the Miss America pageant in 1968, "a few women tossed some padded brassieres in a trash can. No one actually burned a bra that day—as a journalist erroneously reported. In fact, there's no evidence that any undergarment was ever so much as singed at any women's rights demonstration in the decade."[29] Faludi continues by noting that "[t]he only two such displays that came close were both organized by men, a disc jockey and an architect, who tried to get women to fling their bras into a barrel and the Chicago River as 'media events.' Only three women cooperated in the river stunt—all models hired by the architect."[30]

Bra-burning is just one example of an isolated, media-sponsored event, but the politics of sexual excess became viewed as representative of the movement. The images persist, despite the facts. In some ways, the media reduced the sexual revolution to fads of women going braless, tales of communes, and experimental interpersonal relations such as "open" marriages and free love. Commentators were much more voyeuristically attracted to reporting on the varieties of sexual behavior rather than the politics of sexual relations.

Some viewed the sexual revolution as being merely about sexual permissiveness. To them, the challenge to traditional assumptions about chastity and gender roles was inextricably linked with perversion and moral decay. And at the time, some of the participants were willing to capitalize on one interpretation of the movement's message of free love, while eliding its more complex political messages: "orgasms, now that anatomy had been clarified, were easier to achieve than equality."[31]

The women's movement's connection with sexual liberation offended along another dimension as well. Leaders in the movement sought abortion and contraceptive rights for women, which they viewed as essential to women's rights of self-determination. This aspect of the sexual revolution was intended to liberate women from oppressions associated with their reproductive functions and to make nonmotherhood a socially acceptable state. The religious right condemned both abortion and contraception and blamed feminism for their availability. Of course, the reproductive choice controversy is a double-edged sword—garnering both adherents and opponents for the feminist movement. In the early months of 1989, after the Supreme Court accepted certiorari in *Webster v. Reproductive Health Services*, a case that threatened a reconsideration of *Roe v. Wade*, the National Abortion Rights Action League and the National Organization for Women each gained fifty thousand new members.[32]

Even today, some conservatives see discussions of sexuality not as key to women's emergence from repression and oppression, but as triggers in the breakdown of "family values." As Irving Kristol would have it, women's sexual liberation means "liberation from husbands, liberation from children, liberation from family. Indeed, the real object of these various sexual heterodoxies is to disestablish the family as the central institution of human society, the citadel of orthodoxy."[33] Extreme conservatives are not the only ones to hold feminism responsible for the excesses of the sexual revolution. In *Feminism Is Not the Story of My Life,* Elizabeth Fox-Genovese notes the dark side of feminism's successes in separating sex and morality. She maintains that one of the consequences of sexual liberation is the rise of single motherhood, which has translated into abandonment, particularly for poor women.

Advocating Change or Fomenting Insurrection: What Is Radicalism Anyway?

Almost all significant social movements have had a contingent of participants who recognize that their job is to push the envelope. In the feminist movement, those originally considered radical had to upset settled constitutional doctrine, employment and property laws, and historically embedded traditional roles and social definitions of gender in order to change the political, social, and domestic landscape for women. For centuries women could not earn wages, sue, possess property, or make contracts in their own name, let alone hold political office. In the early nineteenth century, only Quakers permitted women to speak in public at religious gatherings. Not until 1920, and then only grudgingly, were women given the right to vote. Issues we now consider matters of basic human rights—women's voting, keeping their own wages, and making political speeches—were, in the not-distant past, shockingly radical concepts.

It was radical feminists in the 1960s, whom Betty Friedan accused of waging "a bedroom war," who located marriage and family relations as a source of women's oppression. These discussions were precursors of the modern debates about the politics of housework. Radical feminists mobilized women to recognize and fight rape and other violence against women. But angry rhetoric by some early radical feminists about men as the agents of oppression made it easy to dismiss the entire movement as hopelessly flawed.

In the modern era, radical feminist Catharine MacKinnon stretched the boundaries of the possible by creating the concept of a cause of action for sexual harassment. Instead of viewing the systematic mistreatment of women with sexual innuendos and improper touchings as a matter of tort law or employment law, MacKinnon recognized that no legal constructs existed that comprehended and remedied women's experiences as recipients of unwanted sexual attention in the workplace. In 1979 she wrote *Sexual*

Harassment of Working Women, defining "quid pro quo" and "hostile work environment" harassment. She described sexual harassment as a group-based wrong to women inadequately recompensed under prevailing tort theories. Her theoretical work prompted the EEOC to acknowledge sexual harassment as sex discrimination in violation of Title VII. A decade and a half later, the law of sexual harassment is entrenched and evolving.

Part of the persistent linkage of radicalism and feminism has to do with the nature of social change. Any sort of political resistance to an entrenched social order is viewed as tantamount to radicalism. Particularly with feminism, the mechanisms of change necessitated fundamental restructuring of laws, relationships, social institutions, and concepts of appropriate cultural roles. The movement was a threat to traditional understandings of identity. It demanded reallocation of power and decisional responsibility. It would change social, political, and economic roles for all time. In short, the sweeping transformations envisioned by feminism are the very sorts of fundamental changes that define political radicalism.

But it is essential to distinguish means and ends. Feminism was radical in its transformative expectations. Its objectives, however, of equal political, social, and domestic rights for women were modest. The feminist movement wanted to obtain for women the rights men had enjoyed for centuries. Sure, feminism is radical, if you think of equal rights as radical.

When the term "radical" is used to describe some innovative or outlandish strategy of modern feminism, it is all too easy to forget that women's rights were forged in the crucible of revolution. Now we take for granted the once radical ideas that women should be able to vote, hold political office, use birth control, and work in environments free from sexual harassment. As the Reconstruction amendments, the Nineteenth Amendment, and the Constitution itself all attest, the radicalism of this moment in history may be the well-entrenched rights of the future.

But the equation of modern feminism with radicalism relates to the political tactics discussed at the beginning of this chapter. Painting feminism as an insurrectionist movement or focusing on some of its smaller excesses may be part of a systematic strategy to discredit it. It is unfortunate that the radical leaders of the movement are remembered for a publicity-seeking tactic or an intemperate statement, rather than for the fundamental reforms they inspired. The perception of the entire feminist movement as radicalism reverses the core and the extremes. This misguided view of feminism as a radical fringe movement may be one of the most significant impediments to its advancement.

Feminism and the Vestiges of Exclusionary Thinking

The stereotype of feminists as opposed to family values is insultingly erroneous. The stereotype of most feminists as man-hating is a distortion. But the question must be asked whether some feminists have promoted those negative associations, or whether the intemperate versions of *some* thinkers on *some* issues are spun out as feminist extremism and repackaged as central to feminism. We also need to tease out the ways early incarnations of feminism or some arguments of a few feminists may have alienated potential supporters.

The Early Women's Movement and Racial Alienation

By the time "feminism" emerged as a popular term in the 1970s, the women's movement had a long history. In this country that history began with the late eighteenth-century fight for political rights. One unfortunate facet of that history was the early alienation of a core of supporters.

Some of the earliest supporters of suffrage saw the parallels between the enslavement of blacks and the cabining, silencing, and possessing of women. Abolitionists like Angelina and Sarah Grimké made an early attempt to connect women's suffrage and voting rights for blacks. The very reluctance of some reformers to allow the inclusion of women in the fight for abolition prompted women to recognize the need for their own emancipation. While the two causes were linked in the minds of some early suffragists, those in power failed to see the connections. The Fourteenth Amendment seemed to specify its applicability only to males.[34] When the Fifteenth Amendment was proposed, and it conferred voting rights only on black men, several leaders of the suffrage movement, including Susan B. Anthony and Elizabeth Cady Stanton, lobbied against it. Anthony and Stanton even sparked a petition drive against black "male suffrage."[35] Others, such as Myra Bradwell and Lucy Stone, viewed the granting of voting rights to black men as a matter of a broader history of incremental successes that would inure to the benefit of women.

But it was at this point in history that some white women began to fear the conflation of suffrage for women (read: white women) and suffrage for blacks (read: black men). Some suffragists thought that only one group—white women or black men—would gain voting privileges. In the mid-nineteenth century Susan B. Anthony refused to assist black women in organizing a chapter of the National Women's Suffrage Association.[36] In 1851, at the Akron Convention on Women's Suffrage, white suffragist Frances Gage was urged to not allow Sojourner Truth on the platform: "Don't let her speak, Mrs. Gage, it will ruin us. Every newspaper in the land will have our cause mixed up with abolition and niggers, and we shall be utterly denounced."[37]

Former slave and early black feminist Sojourner Truth spoke eloquently about the exclusion of black women from both suffrage movements: "There is a great stir about colored men getting their rights, but not a word about the colored woman; and if colored men get their right and not colored women theirs you see the colored men will be masters over the women and it will be just as bad as it was before."[38] Truth's emphasis on the cause of feminism as opposed to abolition is a matter of some historical dispute,[39] but feminism's exclusion of black women is well supported in the historical record.

Over the next few decades, some movement leaders adopted the distinctly racist political strategy of appealing to white men to safeguard continued white domination by arguing that white women would better protect their interests than would black men. The National Suffrage Association proclaimed that "granting suffrage to women who can read and write and pay taxes would insure white supremacy without resorting to any methods of doubtful constitutionality."[40] Omitted from the white women's suffrage movement, black women created suffrage organizations of their own, but were forced to choose whether to align their interests with those of white women or black men.[41]

This early schism—white women selling blacks out to advance their own interests—laid the groundwork for the alienation of black women from the feminist movement. Unsurprisingly, minority women have some mistrust of the feminist movement. Lucretia Murphy observes that "[m]any black women associate 'feminist' with racism because of the history of racist platforms used by the feminist movement."[42] The distinct competition between the interests of women of color and those of white women has replayed itself in modern history. Women of color maintain that they have been excluded from feminist theory and organizing, their experiences essentialized, and their special needs ignored.

Black feminists like Angela Harris argue that the predominantly white feminist movement's focus on gender as the pivotal issue makes women of color invisible.[43] bell hooks has pointed out that Betty Friedan's book *The Feminine Mystique* described the lives of white middle-class women.[44] Women of color's voices have been silenced by the essentialism of writing about categorical "women's issues." Audre Lorde has explained that white women and women of color do not suffer the same oppression simply because they are women.[45] Others, like author Alice Walker, write that the struggles of racism and sexism are intertwined, demanding attention to discrimination at the intersection of oppressions and inviting the development of integrating theories, such as "womanism," as a means of eradicating the intertwined oppressions.

In the legal literature of today, feminists of color are writing about concerns specific to the intersection of race and gender. Authorities punish poor pregnant black women for drug addiction as a means of controlling their reproductive choices. The child welfare system is more likely to remove black children from their homes due to misunderstanding of and "fail[ure] to respect the longstanding cultural tradition in the Black community of shared parenting responsibility among blood-related and non-blood kin."[46] The images of black womanhood include the sexually promiscuous breeder, the lazy, irresponsible worker, and the factually erroneous stereotype of the welfare "queen."

Only recently has the jurisprudential literature recognized the plight of minorities of other racial and ethnic hues, who face individual hardships unseen by those outside the culture. Asian Americans, women and men, face the difficulty of being a "model minority" whose economic and academic successes render discrimination against them invisible.[47] Latina victims of domestic violence may lack access to resources because of language barriers or because they are not citizens or legal permanent residents. Native American women endure sterilizations at a rate far greater than other ethnic groups.[48] Jewish women face the problem of spousal battery in a particular religious environment that denies the existence of the problem, amid a larger culture teeming with anti-Semitism and popular stereotypes that Jewish women are spoiled and domineering.[49] Focusing on the different interests of various types of feminists presents the concern of isolating individual groups. A warning against the insular attention given to the injuries of particular groups is offered by law professor Charles Lawrence. He argues that a focus on the individual harms of various ethnic groups risks jeopardizing collective action against cultural domination by a white majority.[50]

In exploring those facets of feminism that may have disenfranchised or overlooked the inclusion of possible categories of supporters, we must recognize that the original goal of feminism may not have been the empowerment of people on every axis of identity. But in its central focus on women's issues, feminism never meant to exclude the development of other political liberation movements. And it may be a distortion of the feminist mission to suggest that in the modern era the intent was exclusionary.

Lesbian Feminism

In the popular mind and press, feminism was and still is associated with lesbianism. There are perceptions that "feminist orthodoxy . . . holds that heterosexuality is the basis of men's exploitation of women."[51] This simplistic assumption bears little relation to historical fact. The lesbian movement and the feminist movement grew up differently, but with some overlap, and the misunderstanding of feminism *as* lesbianism is drawn from a misinformed reading of the intersection of the movements.

Lesbian feminism threatened the social order on several levels. It was a defiance of sexual conformity, "a form of insubordination: it denies that female sexuality exists, or should exist, only for the sake of male gratification."[52] The sexual preferences of lesbians made some men fear their obsolescence. Statements of independence from mainstream feminists like Gloria Steinem, who made popular the one-liner that "a woman needs a man like a fish needs a bicycle," became associated with lesbianism. Lesbianism was pathologized by such respectable emissaries as Freud and demonized by several major religions.

Commentators also saw any questioning of the reign of heterosexuality as a form of lesbian chauvinism. For instance, Adrienne Rich made the point in her well-reasoned and referenced article "Compulsory Heterosexuality and Lesbian Existence" that "[h]eterosexuality has been both forcibly and subliminally imposed on women."[53] Her purposes were to show the branding of homosexuality as deviance, to make visible how the coercive social constraints of heterosexuality complicated women's choices of sexual preference, and to demonstrate the marginalization of lesbians from mainstream feminism. Even today Rich is misread by journalists writing about the state of feminist theory: "To top it all there is Adrienne Rich, who believes that heterosexuality is the root of all oppression."[54]

Lesbian feminism opened a broader critique of the sex/gender system. Lesbian feminist writings not only challenged the idea of heterosexual norms, they opened a wide range of inquiry into sexual practices and identities. Once sex and gender were separated, all social roles were up for grabs; the sexual boundaries between men and women were obliterated and gender was no longer visible. In some ways lesbianism presented one of the ultimate challenges to the vestiges of biological roles: it raised the specter of an all-out assault on the binary construction of gender—the possibilities of bisexuals and transsexuals and a continuum of gender. Lesbianism highlighted the extraordinary cultural anxiety about the classification of gender.

Some lesbian feminists did link the causes of lesbianism and feminism, but their comments were both blown out of proportion and seized upon as representative of feminism. A handful of lesbian feminists did declare that "feminism is the theory, lesbianism the practice."[55] Radicalesbians, a group launched by novelist Rita Mae Brown, issued a now classic position paper denouncing phallocentricity and male domination, and proposing "woman-identification" as essential to the political struggle of feminism. It made the link between lesbianism, feminism, and anger in its opening salvo: "A lesbian is the rage of all women condensed to the point of explosion."[56] Some writers, such as Charlotte Bunch in "Lesbians in Revolt," did advocate lesbian separatism: "Being a lesbian means ending identification with, allegiance to, dependence on, and support of heterosexuality. It means ending your personal stake in the male world so that you join women individually and collectively in the struggle to end oppression."[57]

Some high-visibility lesbian theorists and demonstrators did claim the mantle of mainstream feminism; this claim was misleading, however. In many ways lesbian feminists were omitted from the mainstream of the feminist movement. While the relations between lesbianism and feminism were and are complex, like any other reform movement, feminism faced the critical questions of what issues and groups would be embraced by the movement. Lesbianism crystallized the tension between the need for a movement to be popularly accepted and its need to be true to some of its adherents.

Despite popular perceptions that feminists were "all a bunch of lesbians," in actuality, explorations of lesbian identity were omitted in significant part from mainstream feminist theory and from feminist legal theory.[58] Straight feminists wondered how to get their husbands and partners to assume greater child care responsibilities, while lesbian feminists worried about losing custody of their children. Lesbians experienced compound discrimination, treatment as deviants, and legal detriments (no marriage, health insurance, or custody rights), concerns unshared by many other feminists and unaddressed in their literature. In the feminist movement of the 1970s and 1980s, lesbians' experiences, stories, and issues were omitted and their concerns viewed as a diversionary threat to central women's issues. The early history of the second wave of feminism saw active exclusion of lesbians from the movement as mainstream spokespeople hushed discussion of the need for a distinct lesbian theory to rebel against phallocentricity. One high-profile example was Betty Friedan's denunciation of gay and lesbian rights activists as "the lavender menace."

These divisions and even basic differences between feminism and lesbianism gained little recognition in popular consciousness. Isolated examples of lesbian exclusivity combined with stigmatization to create the popular image of feminism as little more than the sexual politics of lesbianism. In some ways, the existence of lesbians in the feminist movement simply offered another way for feminism to be dismissed as an unorthodox "attack on the American (heterosexual) way of life."[59] Thus, the feminist movement suffered the sting of homophobia through associational guilt.

The intimation that a feminist was a lesbian had tremendous political force: "'Lesbian' is the word, the label, the condition that holds women in line. When a woman hears this word tossed her way, she knows. . . . she has crossed the terrible boundary of her sex role. She recoils, she protests, she reshapes her actions to gain approval."[60] To avoid the stigma of the label, some feminists distanced themselves from lesbian theory, creating further divisions within the feminist movement.

The Alienation of Men

Feminism is at its core a critique of women's oppression, which necessitated identification of patterns of oppression. There was no other way to describe the experiences of oppression: the indictment of patriarchy required pointing out the domination of men. For some feminists, though, this involved not just a structural analysis of the institutions of patriarchy, but a personification of men as the oppressors. The "Redstockings Manifesto" identified men as the enemy: "We identify the agents of our oppression as men. . . . All other forms of exploitation and oppression (racism, capitalism, imperialism, etc.) are extensions of male supremacy. *All* men receive economic, sexual and psychological benefits from male supremacy. *All* men have oppressed women."[61]

In the early years of the second wave of feminism, a few radical feminists took an oppositional stance toward men: patriarchy was the abstraction of the evil, but individual men were the perpetrators. In 1968 Valerie Solanas, author of the *SCUM (Society for Cutting Up Men) Manifesto*, shot Andy Warhol for allegedly stealing some material from a play she had written. Although Solanas was the founder of SCUM and the only member of the organization, her virulent tract, which described maleness as a disease and called for the selective killing of men, magnified men's fears of feminism. The single-member SCUM "group" conjured up visions of a society filled with feminists so revolutionary and twisted they had become homicidal. SCUM was implicated in a hypothetical conspiracy that allegedly had dumped estrogen in the water supply of several major western cities, resulting in a decline in sperm count.[62]

In her 1977 novel *The Women's Room*, one of Marilyn French's characters says, "All men are rapists and that's all they are. They rape us with their eyes, their laws and their codes." Even on into the 1980s, the titles of some of feminists' writings, such as Andrea Dworkin's 1988 *Letters from a War Zone: Writings, 1976–1987*, emphasized the antagonistic nature of what has come to be popularly known as the "gender wars." Other radical feminists of the era disavowed connections to the antimale rhetoric of their compatriots. While the New York radical feminist group Cell 16 emphasized celibacy, separatism, and karate,[63] a spokesperson for Cell 16, Dana Densmore, wrote an article in 1970 entitled "Who Is Saying Men Are the Enemy?"[64] And some of the statements, such as Gloria Steinem's "We women have become the men we once wanted to marry" were not antimale; rather, they were proclamations of independence.

Viewed more charitably, many of the radical feminists who were describing male chauvinism were intent on identifying patterns of behavior rather than perpetrators. It is also difficult to talk about the history of patriarchy without discussing some of its agents, who principally were males. The rhetoric may have been a necessary catalyst to action, stemming from justified anger at male violence against women, lack of reproductive freedom, economic suppression, and lack of political and social power. And oppression may appear different to those who are experiencing it firsthand than to those looking at it from a more secure position through the filter of history.

But even apart from the extreme of separatist rhetoric, hate-filled or not, on the part of a few radicals in the feminist movement, some of the methods of the early women's movement were isolationist in purpose and effect. At its grassroots center were consciousness-raising (CR) groups. In the late 1960s and early 1970s tens of thousands of women came together in smaller and larger groups to exchange experiences and discuss the political meaning of their personal experiences. Journalist Anita Shreve writes, "In the year 1973 alone, some 100,000 women belonged to CR groups nationwide—

making it one of the largest ever educational and support movements of its kind for women in the history of this country."[65]

An essential feature of the vast majority of these groups was that they were for women only. Women needed an atmosphere of nonjudgmental nurturance and respect for their fears, insecurities, and complaints of daily life. The idea of consciousness-raising was that the sharing and validation of experiences in this for-women-only space would promote self-esteem and foster awareness of various personal forms of oppression. Its ultimate political objective was to move beyond the personal therapy it afforded toward collective action to combat shared oppressions. But inherent in this creation of community was a dimension of exclusion: women built solidarity between and among themselves and omitted men. Thus, the unity of sisterhood meant in some respects both militancy and separatism.

This need for separatism from men may have been a transitional one, but its legacy continues. The gender separatism of men and women is inscribed in even some of the most genial contemporary discussions of feminism. Paula Kamen discusses women who describe themselves as people who "prefer the female way of life, not the male one."[66] Many more incendiary statements exist, such as those in the 1991 collection of essays *Angry Women*: "I think it's man's basic nature to exploit power, position, authority, money, and it stems basically from greed. . . . I still see chronic domination by white middle-aged men in positions of power who will remain there forever, because *they decide who gets to decide.* Nothing short of *total war between the sexes* is going to eliminate that!"[67]

Some of this oppositional behavior persists. As just one anecdotal example, a feminist jurisprudence Internet discussion group recently engaged in a conversation about whether feminism is a set of principles and beliefs or a state of consciousness. At the conclusion of one message the writer, speaking to an audience of feminist women and self-proclaimed profeminist men, included this astonishingly vitriolic denunciation: "If you want to be regarded as a profeminist man, you live it, you earn it. And from what I have seen, most of you guys have a long way to go before you've evolved past being some sub-species of misogynist." One reading of this message is the unobjectionable demand that profeminists live their professed ideals. The alternative message, colored certainly by the seething tone, is that cybersisterhood is a quasi-exclusive group: no guys (without proven credentials) allowed. The personalization of theoretical views, particularly when coupled with combativeness, can undermine moves toward reasoned dialogue.

The Politics of Anger

Some of the most revolutionary moments of the feminist movement were born of anger. The NOW demonstration at the 1968 Miss America pageant attacked the exploitation inherent in commodifying a sexual image of women. The 1969 Stonewall riots in New York City were a symbolic streetfight for sexual liberation. The draw of early consciousness-raising groups was the comfort of an environment in which to vent anger about personal problems. From this resistance came the realization that shared private experiences were representative of collective oppression, a recognition capsulized in the slogan "the personal is political." Radical feminist groups such as New York Radical Women, Cell 16, Redstockings, the Feminists, New York Radical Feminists, and the Furies engaged in various guerrilla theater demonstrations to protest various types of exploitation of women. Feminist anger can be extremely varied in its own dimensions, in its shapes and intensity, and with respect to the objects to which it attaches (all males, a given situation, various manifestations of a system of patriarchy).

Part of empowerment is the ability to express negative emotions without fear of censure. As one of Toni Morrison's characters says in *The Bluest Eye*: "Anger is *better*—there is a *presence* in anger." Anger had its purposes in the history of the women's movement: to mobilize and to convey the oppression to which women had been subjected for centuries. The early politicization involved denunciation of a system that denied women education, jobs, and control of their own bodies. Mary Joe Frug made the argument that "the anger and pessimism connected with negative feminism produces a more positive political residue than the form of sentimental boosterism that often accompanies cultural feminism."[68] In terms of immediate, pragmatic results, she had a point. In a number of instances feminist anger was the catalyst that inspired political action. For example, the Anita Hill–Clarence Thomas sexual harassment "trial" fueled the rage of tens of thousands of American feminists. In the months after the Thomas confirmation hearings, contributions to feminist groups increased by 30 to 50 percent.[69]

The anger has provided the movement with some of its most attention-grabbing rhetoric. But it has also fueled a profound sense of alienation for its targets. It is the anger or the slogan, and not the metaphor or central message, that is remembered. "Never trust a man with testicles"; "If they can get one man on the moon, why not the rest of them?"; "When God created man, She was only joking." The media weigh in with helpful reports about "feminists" and "anger"; from the headlines one gets the sense that many feminists exist in a perennial state of rage. The male-bashing horrors of television talk shows and stand-up comedians are legendary. Cartoons make jokes about "male patterned stupidity." Even popular television programs like *The Simpsons* and *Home Improvement* portray inept and more or less boorish (yet somehow endearing) men. The central premise of the situation comedy *Men Behaving Badly* is the capacity of men for idiotic behavior, such as using dirty underwear in lieu of coffee filters.

Beginning in the late 1980s, an industrious marketing of novelties played on this antimale theme. The coffee mugs, T-shirts, desk calendars, stationery, and books (*The Dumb Men Joke Book, 101 Reasons Why a Cat Is Better Than a Man, Men and Other Reptiles*) share the assumption that "all men are bastards." On the serious side, men have been banned from anti-rape rallies and women-only conferences.[70] Academics engage in pensive discussions about whether men can even be feminists.

The symbolism of the John and Lorena Bobbitt episode was compelling. Lorena Bobbitt cut off her husband's penis with a kitchen knife while he slept, later claiming he had raped her earlier that evening. The incident polarized men and women by sex. Some feminists quite appropriately took the opportunity to point out that women in countries all over the world have been subjected to genital mutilation for centuries. Others very inappropriately cheered the act as justified retaliation. In a *Vanity Fair* article, Kim Masters writes of "the Lorena supporters who have transformed the V-for-Victory sign into a symbol of solidarity by making scissorlike motions with their fingers." Even Barbara Ehrenreich, usually a voice of reason, remarked on the Bobbitt incident with tacit approval of violence—not just as a defensive measure but almost as an offensive strategy in case the feminist movement stalls: "Personally, I'm for both feminism and nonviolence. . . . But I'm not willing to wait another decade or two for gender peace to prevail. And if a fellow insists on using his penis as a weapon, I say that, one way or another, he ought to be swiftly disarmed."[71]

The argument that feminists should control their anger runs the danger of playing into the hands of a stereotype: that expressions of anger by women are unfeminine, and therefore inappropriate and jarring. To argue that feminists should control their anger may be seen as yet another form of silencing. I hope to sidestep the stereotype. Anger exhibited by anyone—male or female—does not, as a continual conversational strategy, foster reasoned discourse.

In defense of the angry rhetoric, one might question whether it was ever intended to be a conversational strategy. The expressions of moral outrage, frustration, and defiance were not about promoting dialogue. Their constructive side instead was concerned with internal liberation and unity of purpose, and much less with communication to a neutral or unsympathetic audience. This raises the broader question of revolutionary strategies. What is an appropriate strategy at one point in time may lose its force or even become counterproductive. It is more than a matter of impolitic style. Even if the emotions behind the rhetoric are justified as retribution for years of oppression or dumb blond jokes or whatever, antimale comments are extremely offensive. And the anger can be self-defeating in a number of respects.

Anger can empower and motivate, but its destructive potential is enormous. Not only does anger alienate the people against whom it is directed, it also risks antagonizing people who might otherwise be supportive. bell hooks explains that "[a]nti-male sentiments alienated many poor and working class women, particularly non-white women, from the feminist movement. Their life experiences had shown them that they have more in common with men of their race and/or class group than bourgeois white women."[72]

Several distinct phenomena are at work here. First is the anger, which is real, which is probably often justified, and which may need to find expression, although most likely at a price. Second are the ideas that need communicating, some of which are too difficult to convey without anger because they hardly exist without anger. Third is communication, which is sometimes hampered by anger, but at times is facilitated by anger. Finally, there is rhetoric; hyperbole sometimes helps communication and sometimes hinders it.

Modern feminists need to rethink the strategy of anger. A significant part of this contemplation involves investing thoughts in the objectives and methods of feminism. Recent feminism has been significantly reactive—eliciting counterposed reactions to the horrors of a rape trial or instances of domestic violence or Supreme Court confirmation hearings. As I elaborate in chapter 8, the conscious strategy of the next generation of feminism must involve reaching out not to converts, but to nonsupporters, nonfeminist men and women, with reasoned dialogue. The principal and consciously analyzed approach must be one of reason.

Fragmentation of the Movement

Infighting: The Factionalism of Feminism

Many women are alienated from the feminist movement. Some of the alienation may result from a misperception that there is a feminist orthodoxy—that feminists must be career women or pro-choice or antipornography. Another thread of alienation may include the factionalism implied by some pop culture figures, which may surface simply as feminist-bashing, or as a tendency on the part of some feminist writers to reduce honest intellectual disagreements to the personal level.

Some of the early theorists, such as Shulamith Firestone, who described motherhood and procreation as sources of oppression, offended many traditional homemakers by speaking of the roles in which some women had invested themselves as forms of enslavement. In her 1970 classic, *The Dialectic of Sex: The Case for Feminist Revolution*, Firestone wrote that "[t]he first demand for any alternative system must be. . . . The freeing of women from the tyranny of their reproductive biology by every means available." She proposed the technological neutralization of the social impact of sex differences through test-tube reproduction and communal child rearing. While Firestone and others were making critical theoretical points about institutions, the high theory was lost or perhaps mistranslated, and the idea devolved in the popular mind into an attack on motherhood.[73] Some traditional homemakers perceived that the feminist movement, in championing abortion rights, was indifferent to their concerns about quality child care. In the "dismissive shorthand" of the 1980s, "feminism came to mean denigrating motherhood, pursuing selfish goals and wearing a suit."[74]

While critics have counterposed feminism and motherhood, many prominent feminist theorists have long argued that feminism must address concerns of mothers and children. In 1981 Betty Friedan, in *The Second Stage*, strenuously advocated the inclusion of men's and children's concerns in the feminist agenda. The "second stage" that Friedan envisioned was an integration of work and home, feminism and family.

Particular issues have disunited feminists, few as seriously as abortion. One feminist commentator has asserted an inherent antipathy between the pro-life position and feminism, stating, "pro-life feminism, as currently formulated, is a contradiction in terms."[75] Others, such as Kathleen McDonnell in *Not an Easy Choice: A Feminist Re-examines Abortion*, find more room in the feminist movement for a difference of opinion. Pro-life feminists have argued that in several very significant senses reproductive choice does not liberate women, but instead relieves men of parental responsibilities, makes women sexually available, and values individualism over a communal ethic of care. In *Abortion and the Politics of Motherhood,* sociologist Kristin Luker describes the ways women divide along ideological lines in the abortion debate in terms of their perceptions of motherhood. Luker concludes that pro-choice supporters are generally better-educated and economically better off than pro-life activists. Interestingly, several students in a Women and Law class taught by a colleague of mine were resentful of Luker's conclusions, arguing that her underlying message and tone prompted divisions along class lines, by implying that the appropriate side of the issue was populated by those with superior educations and wealth.

This same sort of inquiry repeats in debates concerning other areas. Must one oppose pornography to be a feminist? Can one be a feminist and not believe in the propriety of affirmative action? In short, must a person subscribe to a particular set of normative conclusions to be a feminist? In response to questions such as these, law professor Lea Brilmayer observes,

> What the core [of feminism] consists of is certainly contentious, and disagreement over its content is an important debate.... We have tendencies to each choose the issue that matters most to us, and then insist that it's not possible to disagree with our position on that issue and still be a feminist. But even the most one-dimensional of feminists must realize, on some level, that theirs is not the only issue feminism must deal with.[76]

Many of the philosophical schisms of feminism were healthy and intellectually invigorating. Feminist legal theorists split over whether the accommodation of pregnancy in state and federal pregnancy discrimination acts would institutionalize the view of women as workers with essential differences in need of protective legislation (a view that has been used against women harmfully in the past) or remove a source of workplace disability for women. In the recent feminist debate over pornography, antipornography feminists made powerful arguments that the graphic sexual depiction of women in positions of subordination was part of a collective social construction of women.[77] Anticensorship feminists responded with compelling arguments about sexual repressiveness, the dangers of censorship in society generally and specifically to women (protecting women from sex might limit women's sexual choices or lead to further protectionist legislation), and the misdirection of attention away from individual perpetrators of violence against women.[78]

Some of the political polarization, however, has been taken to a level of personal vitriol. Leanne Katz, executive director of the National Coalition against Censorship, describes "the extraordinary name-calling tactics of anti-'pornography' feminists against feminists who oppose them.... We are charged with being manipulated by 'pimps,' with being the mouthpieces of 'pornographers.' We are accused of being indifferent to violence against women, and with being the Uncle Toms of the patriarchy."[79] Katz tells the story of a conference at the University of Chicago Law School in 1993 on "Speech, Equality and Harm: Feminist Legal Perspectives on Pornography and Hate Speech" at which a singular perspective was imposed: "to be a feminist, one must support measures for censorship. Feminists who disagreed were brushed aside and insulted away."

Wendy Kaminer and Naomi Wolf maintain that one reason many women avoid identification with feminism is that recent editions of feminism involve copious whining. Women are tired of being told they are victims and hearing about other women who are victims. Of course, one of the reasons feminism was invented was that many women, for many years, in many different ways, were victimized by the constructs of patriarchy.

Among people who self-describe as feminists, a recent battle has arisen over ownership of the term. Various camps accuse other individuals and groups of not being "real" feminists and of distorting feminism's central purposes. In *Who Stole Feminism?* Christina Hoff Sommers asserts that "gender feminists" have pirated the feminist movement. "Their primary concern," Sommers says, "is to persuade the public that the so-called normal man is a morally defective human being who gets off on hurting women."[80] Sommers stoops to personal jibes and mixes them with hyperbole. She calls Catharine MacKinnon "a chronically offended fanatic who has convinced first-year female law students that American society is a Bosnian rape camp."[81] Gloria Steinem, according to Sommers, is "head of the Ministry of (Ms) Information. A gender warrior who cannot help fighting battles long since won." In response, Susan Faludi calls Sommers and a handful of other writers "anti-feminists."[82] Camille Paglia joins the fray by launching salvos at mainstream feminists' "third-rate minds" and "women's studies ghettos."[83]

There have been intensely personal skirmishes. Award-winning *Guardian* columnist Suzanne Moore was quoted (now allegedly misquoted) as saying that if Cambridge academic Germaine Greer had a voluntary hysterectomy, it would be a "major statement." In response, Greer, a longtime opponent of hysterectomies as unnecessary "surgical castration," ridiculed

Moore by saying she must be "a feminist of the younger school . . . with hair bird's-nested all over the place, fuck-me shoes, and three fat inches of cleavage. . . . So much lipstick must rot the brain."[84]

The concerns seem centered on slogans and adjectives. Or perhaps some people interested in their own celebrity are using feminism as a marketing strategy to promote "books, images, and careers, instead of promoting equality and social justice."[85] Forgotten are commonalities and history and the fact that terms may have complex meanings. Ignored is the possibility that the most visible differences may be on ancillary matters. Abandoned is the search for shared beliefs. Concessions are rare. Might not Camille Paglia have a point that men are omitted from feminism? Does Rene Denfeld make a valuable comment that intolerance of some feminists could repel potential supporters? Could Naomi Wolf be right that victimhood has its dark side? Martha Minow observes the disempowering effects of the rhetoric of victimization: it shifts attention from the realm of collective political action to a focus on therapeutic individualism, creates feelings of powerlessness in those evaluating their identity in terms of victimhood, and "blurs evaluations of degrees of harm and degrees of responsibility in both the lives of individuals and the larger structures of society."[86]

Some of the divisions are inevitable, and, as I argue later, point to the increasing internal strength of the movement. But an enormous distinction exists between divisions and divisiveness. A political mistake is committed when the divisions become the central focus, when the points of departure incite and inspire more than the commonalities. The factionalism is undoubtedly related to some people's reluctance to identify with feminism; they feel they must carefully sign up for an appropriate feminist camp. Perhaps some of this is inevitable with the popularization of an idea, that it comes with a great deal of glitz. But we should be more careful with things that matter so much.

Must the popular culture icons of feminism spend their time railing at each other rather than rallying around issues? Did we not learn anything from the various strands of theoretical feminism—the gender or difference theorists' emphasis on the virtues of cooperation and collaboration or the liberal or equity feminists' focus on the principles of humanistic treatment? It is a crisis of spirit reminiscent of Yeats's "Second Coming": "Things fall apart; the center cannot hold. . . . The best lack all conviction, while the worst are full of passionate intensity."

Not all, and perhaps not even most, feminists spend time feminist-bashing. Even some of those who critique feminism in ways with which others do not agree may be trying to gather supporters around unifying concepts, as does Elizabeth Fox-Genovese with her emphasis on "family feminism." And there are voices of tremendous reason, such as Katha Pollitt, whose essays in *Reasonable Creatures* and the *Nation* combine sophisticated theory with pragmatic advice for middle America. But a little damage can go a long way, particularly when it plays out in splashy headlines.

Some of the tactics in this feminist infighting display the fairly typical tendencies of reductionism and oversimplification that many commentators (including this one) tend to lapse into in the description of social movements. But many of the manufactured and emotive language displays could easily be eliminated—terms such as "gender warriors" or "faux feminists"—and movement made toward reasoned dialogue. Highly charged rhetoric substitutes for rational discourse. This sort of emotivism is logically fallacious in its attempts to discredit a whole position rather than a concrete set of arguments, and it is counterproductive on a much larger political level, playing into some of the worst stereotypes about women.

The attacks against people are not only impolitic and impolite; ultimately they are logically impotent. They are a form of hypostatization, a specific instance of reductionism, in which the characterizing essence of anything is simply located in some entity or person. Personal slurs against individual feminists reduce a complex set of social relations and problems—the theoretical divisions of feminism—into a very weak argument that this other lousy person is wrong. It moves feminism from the level of collective theoretical discussions to the level of the personal or individual, allowing the meaning of the movement to be defined by its most visible personalities.

Splintering of the Movement

Even more generally than infighting and factionalism, the feminist movement suffers from splintering along age and issue lines, and limited networking and coalition building. As with any social movement that has a history and a future, feminism has fragmented generationally and philosophically. As the second wave of feminists, the feminists of the 1960s and 1970s who effected so many fundamental legal reforms, passes the torch to a younger generation, people and groups nationwide are gravitating toward sometimes narrow concerns.

Feminism in the 1990s has many faces. There are liberal feminists, cultural feminists, radical feminists, neoradical feminists, socialist feminists,

Marxist feminists, postmodern feminists, and post-structuralist feminists. Feminism can be linked with particular political or social action positions, as with ecofeminism, lesbian feminism, and antipornography feminism. Within given academic disciplines, there can be many incarnations. In legal theory, for example, liberal or "sameness" feminists battle with relational, cultural, or "difference" theorists over the origins and appropriate consequences of gender differences. Radical feminists offer a structural or institutional analysis, while pragmatic feminists emphasize attention to situations, context, and dialogue. The anti-essentialist critique in jurisprudence questions the existence of a unitary woman's experience, and points to a diversity of experiences at the intersection of race, gender, ethnicity, class, and religion, among other characteristics of identity. Of course these divisions are not discrete groups; numerous categories of feminists exist, and still others defy categorization.

Regarding organizational structure, there are the more traditional feminist organizations, such as NOW and the Feminist Majority. NOW has more than 600 chapters in all states and approximately 280,000 members nationwide. Special-interest coalitions lobby for reforms in specific issue areas such as child care, political rights, pay equity, welfare reform, pension rights, abortion rights, birth control, and lesbian rights. The National Abortion Rights Action League (NARAL) and Planned Parenthood are two of the most prominent national organizations campaigning for reproductive rights, but there are also other national groups, such as the National Abortion Federation and the Religious Coalition for Reproductive Choice.

A multiplicity of women's organizations focus on specific topical areas. Organizations such as 9 to 5, the National Association of Working Women, the Coalition for Labor Union Women, Southerners for Economic Justice, Federally Employed Women, La Mujer Obrera, Sweatshop Watch, the Coalition of Labor Union Women, and the National Committee on Pay Equity lobby for equal pay and employment. Ecofeminists, who link the oppression of women and the domination of nature, focus on issues of animal rights, vegetarianism, and organic farming. Antipornography feminists have a cadre of organizations, such as Women against Pornography and Feminists Fighting Pornography, while the anticensorship forces have their own groups, Feminist Anti-Censorship Taskforce and Feminists for Free Expression. Groups fighting domestic violence include the National Coalition against Domestic Violence, Human Options, the National Domestic Violence Project, the National Network to End Domestic Violence, the Family Violence Prevention Fund, Hispanic Women in Action, and the Coalition to

End Domestic and Sexual Violence. The national groups in particular interest areas have their regional counterparts, such as the Bay Area Coalition for Our Reproductive Rights, as well as local chapters.

Other feminist groups, such as the Asian Pacific Women's Network and the National Black Women's Health Project, work at the intersection of race and gender politics and employment or health issues. Political action committees, such as Emily's List, a fund-raising group for pro-choice Democratic political candidates, and the Joint Action Committee for Political Affairs, a pro-Israel, pro-choice group, support individual candidates. Nationally, regionally, and locally, women are spread across various political and social action causes, committees, and coalitions: the Intelligent Black Women's Coalition, the National Women's Political Caucus, the American Association of University Women, Radical Women, the American Business Women's Association, Feminist Alliance Against Rape, the National Women's Health Network, the Older Women's League, the Women Against Military Madness, Women's Action for Nuclear Disarmament, National Council of Catholic Women, National Council of Career Women, National Council of Jewish Women, National Council of Negro Women, the Young Women's Christian Association of the U.S.A., the Woman/Earth Institute, Women in Film, Feminists for Animal Rights, and literally thousands of others. There are other groups nationwide, such as the ACLU, the NAACP Legal Defense and Education Fund, whose principal missions are targeted toward other causes, but are generally sympathetic to feminist issues. Puerto Rico has a Coordinating Body of Feminist Organizations; in contrast, in the States, heavy reliance is placed on the largest existing feminist groups, such as NOW and the Feminist Majority Foundation, for coordination.

Some networking efforts cross national boundaries, but still seem topically defined, such as the International Network for Feminists Interested in Reproductive Health and the International Women's Rights Action Watch. There have been some recent networking efforts of note. In February 1996 the Feminist Majority Foundation organized "Feminist Expo 96," a gathering of approximately three thousand women from three hundred feminist organizations, who discussed affirmative action, federal economic priorities, and political action. But as several commentators observed, "despite the energy and enthusiasm it generated, the Expo stopped short of envisioning or planning for the future of the women's movement."[87] Virtual Sisterhood (http://www.igc.apc.org/vsister) is an Internet group trying to assist women's organizations worldwide network in cyberspace. Nominally, however, Virtual Sisterhood seems exclusive to women, and in its priority statement, it defines feminist organizing in terms of women's issues. There seem to be almost too many women's organizations, divided into sometimes broad and at other times somewhat narrow issue or interest areas.

Part of the fragmentation of feminism is undoubtedly tied to its philosophical underpinnings. From its beginnings, the structural model of the women's movement involved an absence of administrative hierarchy. The movement was instead a decentralized set of many different branches, loosely connected through networking, friendships, and overlapping memberships. This was connected to the ideological premises of the movement, which involved mobilizing at the grassroots level and avoiding rigid hierarchical structures.[88]

The modern attention to local concerns rather than national participation may be connected to broader currents, such as decentralization and shrinkage in larger civic group participation, if Robert Putnam's "Bowling Alone" thesis is to be believed.[89] Perhaps given the number of women and men working at full-time jobs, people prefer to commit only to projects with shorter time frames, or perhaps they like local projects—adopting a one-mile stretch of highway, volunteering at a local battered women's shelter, or refurbishing a Habitat for Humanity home—where they can see concrete results.[90]

A significant problem, though, is that the concerns of the individual organizations are looked at in isolation from the larger, more complex and interwoven patterns of society. While the small battles must be fought—seeking better treatment for female sports teams and complaining about demeaning language—the focus on the particular seems to have elided the general. An inordinate amount of energy and resources are devoted to minor causes—skirmishes, for example, about the spelling of "woman" or "womon" and "women" or "womyn." In addition, fragmentation is evident in some of the episodic events staged by social groups and by the rise and fall of the groups themselves.

More youthful radical groups have staged a number of attention-grabbing protests. The Third Wave, with five hundred members in thirty-three states, composed principally of younger feminists in their twenties, conducted a bus tour and voter registration drive in the summer of 1992 that registered twenty-five thousand people, many of whom were low-income women and women of color. The Women's Action Coalition, with chapters in Europe and more than twenty cities in the United States, picketed outside the Supreme Court after the confirmation of Clarence Thomas, and demonstrate against rape and domestic violence outside courthouses during celebrated trials. Pissed Off Women has staged protests blocking access to urinals to demand reforms in health care. At the high school level, groups like FURY (Feminists United to Represent Youth) and YELL (Youth Education Life Line) mobilized in support of sex education.

These feminist groups diverge not only along lines of interest, but also in tone, manner, and methods. There is the in-your-face style and aggressive, punk rock lyrics of power and liberation of Riot Grrrls. Guerrilla Girls is a New York–based underground network of activist female artists who protest discrimination against minorities in the arts by plastering posters on walls of public buildings and making public appearances (incognito in gorilla masks). Women's Health Action and Mobilization protested against regulations banning abortion counseling by draping a gag over the Statue of Liberty. Lesbian Avengers, whose logo is a smoking bomb, is a group dedicated to increasing the visibility of lesbians and fighting for their civil rights. Their attention-grabbing protests and activities have included fire-swallowing demonstrations, Dyke Marches during San Francisco's gay pride week, kiss-ins at airports to demand partnership rights for gays and lesbians, Christmas caroling at malls with nontraditional holiday songs such as "Ronda the Lesbo Reindeer," and more incendiary actions. For example, a handful of Lesbian Avengers showed up at a Massachusetts elementary school on Valentine's Day, wearing T-shirts emblazoned "We Recruit" and passing out homemade candy, leaflets explaining that "girls who love girls and women who love women are OK!" with phone numbers of two homosexual youth groups, and an 800-number phone-sex hot line. Many of these protest activities achieved the desired result of drawing attention, though much of the attention was highly critical. In addition, the event-based focus of these groups necessarily means that attention to feminist concerns will be both episodic and issue-specific.

The fact of splintering, in one sense, speaks to the strength of feminism. One testament to the strength of any social movement is its ability to conduct self-critique. The movement is strong enough now to withstand internal dissension and tolerate dialogue and diversity. Feminists need not band tightly together to withstand opposition from without. And feminism has endured so long that we are seeing a generational baton being passed to the third wave of feminists. Many of the core activists in NOW and the Feminist Majority are in their forties and fifties, although women in their twenties are beginning to occupy leadership positions in some chapters across the nation. NOW even has high school chapters in a dozen states. At recent colloquia, these groups have made a conscious effort to highlight the participation of younger feminists.

Yet there is evidence of estrangement between older and younger generations of feminists. Joannie Schrof reports, "[M]any members of the third wave say the older generation isn't interested in making room for young women or their concerns. Young women tell story after story of seeking the guidance of older feminists only to be told, 'I'm not dead yet' or 'That's my issue, I've been working on it for 20 years.'"[91] For their part, some elder stateswomen of the feminist movement, such as Bella Abzug, Betty Friedan, and Gloria Steinem, formed the Veteran Feminists of America (VFA), an organization that is open only to activists from the early years of the feminist movement. According to Jacqui Ceballos, former NOW president, VFA members are drawn together by their alienation from younger feminists: "Some of the women's groups we were working with years ago are so tremendous in size now that they don't even remember us. And we were the ones who started everything. But now if we try to help some of the younger women work on an issue, they don't want our help. They turn us down like we were their mothers."[92]

Apart from territorial battles, some dissociation between older and younger feminists may be based simply on interests. Some of the core activists of the second wave of feminism are focusing their attention on issues of aging women. Betty Friedan began the embrace of aging with her 1993 book *The Fountain of Age*. In her new book, *Getting Over Getting Older: An Intimate Journey*, Letty Cottin Pogrebin writes about issues of women as they age: physical changes, depression, mortality.

Younger feminists seem to be turning inward as well, but in a different direction. Many seem less centered on issues of collective rights and more concerned with those of individual expression or self-actualization. Eighteen-year-old Kate Bedford, head of California NOW's Young Feminist Issues Committee, lists among her topics of greatest concern "self-defense . . . [b]ody image, bulimia, anorexia, body hatred . . . self-esteem . . . smoking . . . [v]egetarianism."[93] Barbara Findlens assembled an anthology entitled *Listen Up: Voices from the Next Feminist Generation*, which offers insights into the new wave of feminists. The stories in *Listen Up* are predominantly voyages of self-discovery: stories about family relationships, tales of personal struggles in the face of disadvantages and disempowerment, sexual coming of age stories. Most are thoughtfully crafted, and some are beautifully written. Sadly, though, very few of the writers have connected their personal experiences with larger social issues.

In *Listen Up,* one reads about anorexia and fat oppression, playing ball, hair-dyeing, poor parenting, wearing jeans, self-defense, incest, teenage mothering, aerobics, dating, personal mentors, and body hatred and acceptance. The pages are laden with "me" and "I" and subjective examination of the writer's own ego. Yet the self-exploration is rarely linked to any intricate analysis of government policies, broader cultural tides, or social activism. Most of the authors seem uninterested in experiences outside their own.

For many of the writers, feminism is about *them.* As one of the essayists proclaims, "I consider it [shaving my head] one of the most profound, daily statements of my feminist struggle."[94] Instead of moving from their individual experiences outward to larger social issues, they absorb the larger issues into self: "I'm learning to connect the dots. One dot for woman-hate, one for racism, one for classism, one for telling me who I can fuck. When I connect all the dots, it's a picture of me."[95]

Rebecca Walker's *To Be Real: Telling the Truth and Changing the Face of Feminism* is another collection of young feminist voices. The essayists here have somewhat more success in outer-directedness and in connecting the personal with larger social issues. Indeed, one of the writers, Gina Dent, issues a reminder about the need for linking personal revelations and feminist theorizing: "By declaring that 'the personal is political,' feminist theorists held that to start from your own point of view was to help explain something larger than yourself; to legitimate that which was not yet part of the public dialogue; to make the language of politics less remote; to widen the sphere of viable life choices."[96]

Others of the essayists, unfortunately, lapse into the same self-focus that captivates those in *Listen Up.* Many of the topics circle around glorification of the self: deep concerns about appropriately expressive attire, confessions of sexual excitement at violent images, developing an affinity for hip hop music, and protracted discussions about what surname marital partners should adopt. Again, the message seems to be that feminism's most important purpose is to pave the way for supreme individualism.

Each feminist generation unquestionably needs to raise its consciousness anew, but some of the members of Generation X seem to have plateaued at the level of self-actualization. Lost is the connection of self to other people, others' issues, and broader currents. If the importance of feminism in the nineties is only how it makes an individual feel, the seventies' notion of consciousness-raising—"the personal is political"—becomes a tautology. Wendy Kaminer is sharper in her criticism of the introverted fascination:

[S]ocial and political commentary requires detachment from the self as well as engagement in its dramas. . . . Almost all the young contributors to *Listen Up* focus on themselves with the unchecked passion of amateur memoirists who believe that their lives are intrinsically interesting to strangers . . . most seem to equate political commentary with the telling of a personal story. They write about feminism by writing about growing up.[97]

For some, the feminist liberation movement of the 1990s has moved not toward communalism but toward individualism. The preoccupation is with individual well-being, with self. Sociologist Susan Alexander observes, "Today's twentysomethings believe they can achieve equality as individuals. Identifying oneself as feminist or seeking membership in a women's organization are seen as unnecessary steps for maintaining equality."[98] Other younger feminists are working toward more global integration of feminist issues with environmental issues, political participation, and work against violence and racism. Observers of third-wave feminism must not overlook the voter participation drives, development of environmental consciousness, and efforts to integrate men.

One point to consider is that the feminist movement of the 1990s is unlikely to have the revolutionary fervor of the 1970s, and not only because the initial rebellion has occurred. In part because of the successes of early feminism, there are fewer people with time available for organizing. Anita Shreve observes that "One of the ironies of the Women's Movement is that in preparing the ground for greater career opportunities for women, it sowed the seeds of its own demise. It's a matter of simple physics. Women who combine career and family life simply don't have any time left to devote to feminism or CR or activist issues."[99]

Part of the absence of coalition building has to do with limitations not unique to feminism. Some tension exists between tax-exempt organizations and those that can engage in political activity. And, according to Carla Mahaney, cochair of the Kansas Choice Alliance, which networks with NOW, the ACLU, the Women's Political Caucus, the League of Women Voters, and other organizations regarding issues of reproductive rights, coalitions work best relative to short-term, specific-purpose matters, after which the coalition activity dissipates.

There is no central organizing issue, no present, single crisis of modern times—as there was with suffrage or with *Roe v. Wade*. Political organizing is difficult in the face of so many issues and the divergence of interests and positions. Apart from event-specific unity, only modest coalition building occurs between feminist organizations and groups representing other oppressed peoples. The coalition-building efforts appear episodic, but effective when they occur, such as the 1996 "March to Fight the Right" in San Francisco, which brought together 650 advocacy groups from Catholics for Free Choice to NOW to the AFL-CIO.

Is Feminism Passé?

Many women and men coming of age during the 1990s may take for granted rights feminists in the 1970s fought hard to garner. Rights to equal pay and access to employment and graduate educational opportunities, reproductive rights and rights of sexual autonomy, and the right to a working environment free from sexual intimidation are all inventions of the mid-' 1970s to late 1980s. The courts dismantled many of the formal barriers to women's participation in economic, educational, and political life during those years; at least nominally, the legal playing field was leveled. Many men and women who will reach voting age in the next millennium will have grown up with mothers who worked outside the home and an abundance of other professional female role models. The National Organization for Women, founded in 1966, will have been in existence for their entire lifetimes.

Younger feminists have inherited a world several decades removed from women's struggles for basic human rights. The gains in reproductive rights, the dismantling of obvious employment barriers, the construction of sexual harassment laws, and other interpretations of Title VII all may lead people to assume that many of the most important problems feminists rallied around in the 1970s have been solved. After interviewing a number of women in their twenties, journalist Claudia Wallis concludes, "The long, ill-fated battle for the Equal Rights Amendment means nothing to young women who already assume they will be treated as equals."[100] In one sense, the lack of direct experience with discrimination may be an enormous benefit: those who have grown up with foundational equality, who have not experienced discrimination, may be unwilling to tolerate it if it occurs.

It is difficult to generalize whether young people appreciate the history of the feminist struggle. It is also difficult to test the negative proposition "don't know much about history." Some evidence does suggest an ahistorical approach to feminism. A 1995 National Assessment of Educational Progress study measuring the historical knowledge of U.S. high school seniors in public and private schools showed that 57 percent of the students failed to demonstrate knowledge of basic aspects of American history; only one out of every hundred students reached the advanced level of proficiency.[101] And many history courses may include only a modest amount of recent history. As just one anecdotal bit of evidence, a colleague of mine, Rob Verchick, says that each year in his Gender and Justice and Property courses, he senses surprise when he talks about how recently women acquired voting and property ownership rights: "I think for some students, their perception of the timeline is that this absence of women's rights was a medieval phenomenon." Although at first blush this might seem like progress, it is an attitude that may give institutions more credit for rights protection than they are due. Students may be much too trusting of institutional decisions, if they perceive those decisions emanating from decision makers who, they think, have not discriminated in the recent past. The constant need for lessons of the past is in some ways reminiscent of the "Never forget" teachings of the Shoah: the reminder of the need for eternal vigilance against brutal forms of group hatred.

Part of the lack of esteem for feminism may have to do with a lack of recognition of even its popular culture icons, let alone its theoreticians. A 1994 survey by *Esquire* magazine of one thousand women aged eighteen to twenty-five asked the participants who had the most to say about their lives: Camille Paglia, Phyllis Schlafly, Susan Powter, Susan Faludi, or Clarissa Pinkola Estes. While each of those women received between 2 and 6 percent of the votes, 74 percent of those surveyed said they were not familiar with any of the above.[102]

A poll conducted by R. H. Bruskin for Whittle Communications "found that only 16% of college women 'definitely' considered themselves feminists."[103] The 1994 *Esquire* survey was only mildly more optimistic, showing that 34 percent of the eighteen- to twenty-five-year-old respondents were willing to be called feminists. Perhaps in not self-describing as feminists, the next generation achieves some form of integration, but it risks invisibility for the movement. And the mainstream women's movement may be having trouble attracting younger women as activists.[104]

The core issues of feminism have not changed. Sexism, gender stereotyping, and the persistence of traditional gender roles are still epidemic, although in the late 1990s they may come in more subtle incarnations: occupations that are still predominantly male or female preserves, lower wages for women, rampant domestic violence, regulation of various aspects of reproduction (waiting periods, parental consent, reporting requirements), sexual harassment in elementary schools with "skirt-flipping days," the assault of rap lyrics, gender bias in pricing at hair salons and dry cleaners, ladies' nights at bars, and the indistinct ways language leaves the imprint of gender. The list—I will avoid the term "laundry list"—is virtually endless.

It may be argued that identification with the feminist battles of the second wave is not vital, if there is a present willingness to fight against gender disparities whatever their manifestation. But one danger of an ahistorical perspective is that of complacency. To view the horrors of the past *as* past discounts the residual effects of prior centuries of discrimination: the job opportunities realistically available to women and men in all walks of life; the economic worth given to those occupations; and the continued, conditioned social roles into which males and females are shaped. Without an understanding of history, it is difficult to move forward with wisdom. What is lost is not only context, and the richness of the feminist theoretical project, but also its momentum: the collective sense of struggle.

The villainization of feminism is only partially self-inflicted, and it is largely undeserved. Some feminist excesses from the early history of feminism are relentlessly replayed by opponents of feminism and by the media as representative of modern feminism. Some pop culture feminists have helped discredit feminism with media-seeking divisiveness and personal attacks on other feminists themselves: not the theories, the people. In the midst of the historical blunders, the bad press, and the infighting, modern feminism is splintering along dimensions of age, issues, and methods. While the diversity of feminists itself is a strength, the differences have led to fragmentation of the movement.

There is a need for unification among feminists. There is a need for intergenerational collaboration. That collaboration must include comprehensive reflection on commonalities rather than differences, core assumptions, discussion of appropriate methods of argumentation, inquiries conducted with reason rather than rhetoric. There is a need to recognize the connectedness of different kinds of oppression and to build broader coalitions between feminists and workers in other liberation movements. And there is a need for a recommitment to feminist first principles. In chapter 8 I make the case for the rehabilitation of feminism.

6

Feminist Legal Theory and the Treatment of Men

And they thought men were ridiculous and delicious and terrible, taking every opportunity to let them know that they were.
—Toni Morrison, *Jazz*

Feminist legal theory has not concerned itself much with the sympathetic construction of white maleness. Jurisprudential scholars have focused on the masculinity of nonmajority males. In the past decade, critical race scholars have centered attention on the differential treatment of black, Asian, and Latino males, principally as a matter of racial subordination. During roughly the same time frame, sexual orientation theorists have demonstrated the deep connections between heterosexuality and patriarchy, pointing out the ways military, employment, housing, custody, adoption, and sodomy laws discriminate against gay males.

The interest of feminist legal theorists in masculinity has concentrated on the ways institutional male power structures and interests reproduce themselves and exclude or disserve women: the explicit and more subtle forms of male domination in the workplace, male violence against women, and masculinity in various substantive areas of law as exercises of dominance, privilege, and power. These theorists touch kindly on the construction of masculinity only incidentally. The men who populate feminist legal theory, for the most part, are either perpetrators or the unwitting dupes of patriarchy.

Over the past two decades a dialogue about men and masculinity has occurred in disciplines other than law. The explorations of masculinity by various men's movements have developed on a path apart from and rarely intersecting with feminist legal theory. Largely missing from feminist legal theory is a sympathetic critique of the ways the ideology of majority group masculinity is constructed by law.

This chapter has two parts, and the bifurcation is almost a metaphor for the argument. The first part evaluates men's movements in popular culture and some of the theoretical work in the social sciences regarding masculinity. The second part looks at the ways feminist legal theory has constructed maleness. In some ways, the situation of men in feminist theory parallels the treatment of women in traditional theory: initially excluded, then admitted at the margins, and—this reaches into the future—perhaps moving more toward the center of inquiry.

Men's Movements

The 1990s have seen diverse attempts to redefine masculinity in the social sciences and popular culture, in reaction to male frustrations and feelings of disempowerment. A multilayered, amorphous collection of men's organizations has burgeoned nationwide: a mythopoetic men's movement, spiritual and semipolitical revival programs, the formation of men's rights groups, study groups, and coalitions, and some profeminist men's organizations. In *Wildmen, Warriors, and Kings: Masculine Spirituality and the Bible,* Patrick M. Arnold predicted that the developing men's movement would become among "the strongest forces in American culture during the 1990s."

Men's Rights Groups

Reactionary men's rights groups constitute one of the largest branches of the men's movement. Based largely, and very explicitly, on a defensive reaction to feminism, organizations espousing men's rights developed early in the second wave of feminism. The focus of almost all these organizations is the rights of men. The paramount concerns are that ex-wives drain men financially while denying them access to their children, although recently some groups have expanded to consider the correlative responsibilities of their participants.

The Men's Defense Association (MDA), one of the oldest groups, was created in 1972. A letter from Richard Doyle, founder of the organization, explains the purpose of the MDA: "The male of the species is under increasing attack legally, politically, economically, and culturally. It is our mission to defend the interests of men, in opposition to the enormity of anti-male forces and opinion." The MDA originally kept a file of "sad stories" of men losing custody and visitation rights, until the accumulation of stories presented a filing problem.

The National Coalition of Free Men includes among its objectives the laudatory goal of "promot[ing] awareness of how gender based expectations limit men legally, socially and psychologically." Its literature explains how men are culturally conditioned to be competitive, feel inadequate in the child care arena, and think that "violent action confirms and enhances their manliness." So far, so good. But Free Men then suggests that men are disempowered by having no reproductive rights and are "disadvantage[d] in the work place because of female hiring quotas." The group is quick to blame feminism, a "shrill political movement" with "hostility for the nuclear family," and the women's movement, which "has gone unchallenged and this has contributed greatly to the breakup of American families and the social ills which follow: high rates of teen pregnancy, high rates of juvenile crime, high rates of teen suicide, depression, and poor school performance."[1]

The American Fathers Coalition (AFC) is a 100,000 member lobbying organization representing approximately 250 separate men's rights groups. It recently created an umbrella organization, the American Coalition for Fathers and Children, to promote shared parenting. AFC activities include lobbying for reduced child support payments if children spend more time with their fathers, urging courts to enforce visitation orders, and organizing picket lines to protest sexist stereotypes in movies like *The First Wives Club*. Stuart Miller, a single father and lobbyist for AFC, maintains that men are excluded from families: "The majority of men really do want to support their kids," he says; but he complains, "If someone takes your car, how much longer are you going to keep making payments on that car?"[2]

The National Organization for Men (NOM), with twenty-five thousand supporters, lists as its purposes the protection of men's rights and the prevention of "the further erosion of men's status." Laced throughout NOM's literature are denunciations of the feminist movement (for perpetrating myths that men are responsible for a large portion of domestic violence) and "lesbian propaganda" (allegedly contained in the Ms. Foundation's Take Our Daughters to Work Day information kit). The Men's Rights Association produces a monthly newsletter, the *Liberator*, whose purpose is "to marshal manpower in defense of men, masculinity and the family. Our definition of men's liberation is freedom to be (not from being) men." One of the issues of the *Liberator* included in its humor section the following joke: "Q: What is the difference between a terrorist and woman's libber? A: You can negotiate with a terrorist."[3]

A handful of men's rights groups proclaim an interest in egalitarian approaches, and a few are sympathetic to equal treatment views of feminism, but oppose anything smacking of special treatment or cultural feminism. Some men's groups skip over the egalitarian rhetoric and extend the battleground of gender to wage war against affirmative action, pay equity (pejoratively dubbed "sex pay"), and abortion rights—anything that is perceived as promoting special treatment of women. One example of the new struggles looming on the men's rights horizon is the issue of male reproductive choice. The National Center for Men is constructing a lawsuit that it believes will be the male counterpart to *Roe v. Wade*. The organization argues that men should be allowed to terminate their parental rights and responsibilities postconception during a limited time period.

Some organizations are specifically interested in fathers' rights. Groups like the Men's Defense Association, the American Fathers Coalition, Fathers' Rights and Equality Exchange (FREE), and Dads against Divorce Discrimination (DADD) focus most of their energy on issues affecting single and divorced fathers, such as custody, visitation, child support, and divorce reform. Some of the fathers' advocacy organizations, while prompted by discrimination against fathers in divorce and custody battles, seem less concerned with apportioning rights between divorced mothers and fathers and most concerned with encouraging shared parenting, to keep fathers actively engaged in the lives of their children. Groups such as Mad Dads, for example, are neither antifeminist nor misogynist in their rhetoric or undertakings, but try to promote the image of men as responsible fathers.

Many men's rights groups blame feminism for a host of ills, chief among them the breakdown of the family. Ken Pangborn of Men International, a national coalition of over 130 men's rights groups, described the group's estimated 25,000 to 50,000 members as "absolutely death grip foes of feminism."[4] Fred Hayward, head of Men's Rights Inc., concurs, but views being "pro-male" as a necessary defense, since, he says, "The logical extension of feminism is to eliminate men."[5]

The Mythopoetics

The mythopoetic men's movement originated in the 1980s with various men's retreats, and skyrocketed in popularity in the early 1990s, after the publication of Robert Bly's *Iron John: A Book about Men* and Sam Keen's *Fire in the Belly*. *Iron John,* one of the most successful nonfiction works in 1991, sold more than a million copies and spent sixty-two weeks on the best-seller list. The mythopoets use myths, poems, and other literary works to examine men's historical roles and seek guidance for modern male socialization and personal growth.

Bly and other mythopoets argue that men lack positive male archetypes, and that they have lost touch with an essential masculine force: the wildman within. Since most fathers are removed from their families by workforce commitments, the raising of sons is left to women, who turn their resentment of their husbands toward shaming their boys. Boys are cut off from their feelings and from each other at deeper emotional levels. With their masculinity chastised, boys are left to grow into men without appropriate initiation rituals. Men need an initiation into manhood that only other men can provide. Men's attainment of masculinity is connected to departing from home and leaving women behind.

The ideas are shared through men's centers, gatherings, books, tapes, conferences, and retreats. Bly himself has led many of these wildman spiritual retreats or initiation rituals, at which men drum and dance around bonfires, hug one another, participate in talking circles during which they share their troubles, strip naked to engage in sweat lodge rituals, chant, recite myths and poetry, tell stories, organize into clans, and provide support for one another. An estimated 100,000 to 200,000 men have attended such events.

Mythopoetic adherents encourage men to acknowledge their vulnerability, focus introspectively, and engage in dialogue about their feelings. Men are prompted to overcome their isolation from one another, and to seek and receive nurturance from other men. Mythopoets view the separate spheres of men and women as vital to formation of male identity. Healing, in the mythopoetic view, can come only through reparation to Jungian archetypes and an emphasis on father-son relationships. "[T]he mythopoetic warrior's quest is to rediscover his masculine core and experience a bond with his psychic ancestors."[6] This necessarily creates distance from women and sets up a blame situation. Most mythopoets see relations between men and women as inevitably adversarial, and criticize mothers for shaming their sons. Bly cautions that the mythopoetic movement "does not seek to turn men against women," yet it links the empowerment of women and the emasculation of men. "Soft males" are often found in the company of "strong women."[7]

In its embrace of the central ideas of the gender identity paradigm—the existence of male and female essences, and the proposition that boys need male guidance to turn into men—the mythopoetic movement is accepting outdated psychoanalytic theory. "The [mythopoetic] men's movement . . . misses one of the central insights of social science—that gender is a product of human action and interaction, that our definitions of masculinity and femininity are the products of social discourse and social struggle."[8]

The promotion of male bonding to the exclusion of women creates little opportunity for dialogue between the sexes. Sociologists Michael Kimmel and Michael Kaufman suggest that the mythopoetic men's movement's flight from femininity is ultimately damaging to gender relations:

> Perhaps more than anything else, it is through the social practices of parenting that men may connect with the emotional qualities that they have rejected in real life—nurturing, compassion, emotional responsiveness, caring. These emotional resources will not be adequately discovered reading a book or stomping through the woods hugging other men who have taken totemic animal names. They are to be found in the simple drudgery of everyday life in the home. Cleaning the toilet, ironing, or washing dishes are not romantic—you don't have to be a "golden eagle" to keep your nest clean. But they are the everyday stuff of nurture and care. They are skills that are learned, not received by divine revelation after howling at the moon in the forest. We need more Ironing Johns, not more Iron Johns.[9]

The Evangelical Men's Movement

In October 1995, Louis Farrakhan and his Nation of Islam organized the Million Man March in Washington, DC. Estimates of attendance ranged from 300,000 to 1.2 million African American men. It was billed as "a holy day of atonement and reconciliation" whose purposes were to exhort black men to "reclaim" their roles as heads of their families and as community leaders, rediscover religion, and take personal responsibility for their mistreatment of each other and of women. Women were excluded from the gathering. Farrakhan asked supportive women to demonstrate solidarity with the march by staying home from work, school, and shopping to instruct children in values of unity and esteem.

Promise Keepers, another men's movement that is sweeping the nation, is a mostly white evangelical Christian group that is planning its own million man march. Since its inception, close to two million men have attended

Promise Keepers meetings in football stadiums across the country. The gatherings are male-only, have a spiritual orientation, and promote fatherhood. Founded in 1990 by former University of Colorado football coach Bill McCartney, the organization uses rhetoric similar to that enunciated in the Million Man March. Promise Keepers pledge to honor Jesus; pursue vital relationships with a few other men; practice spiritual, moral, ethical, and sexual purity; build strong marriages and families through love, protection, and biblical values; support the mission of the church; reach beyond racial and denominational barriers toward biblical unity; and influence their world. Promise Keepers has inspired the formation of dozens of Christian men's groups across the country, such as Christian Men's Network, Career Impact Ministries, Men Reaching Men, and Dad the Family Shepherd.

In the religious men's movement, women are relegated to subordinate positions. In response to men's collectives, supportive Christian women's groups have sprung up across the country, with appropriately subservient names: Promise Reapers, Chosen Women, Heritage Keepers, and Suitable Helpers (not suitable leaders, but "helpers"). These women's auxiliaries believe they can best assist their husbands' missions by returning to traditional gender roles and adopting submissive postures with respect to their husbands' wishes, following biblical teachings. One survey by the Promise Keepers organization showed that at Promise Keepers conferences, where attendees are exclusively male, 48 percent of the volunteers are women. These "unpaid servants" serve meals, assist the handicapped, and attend to the needs of those on the stadium floor. For the wives and girlfriends of evangelical followers, the movement represents a trade-off: the price of men's commitment to their families and religious communities is "gender traditionalism—the idea that men and women generally have different social and familial roles, that these roles tend to reflect inherent psycho-emotional differences, and that men and women generally feel more fulfilled when they perform their respective roles."[10]

The ideal vision is of a return to a stark public-private distinction in which men are the public actors and women are relegated to the domestic realm. Louis Farrakhan has attempted to defend his Million Man March— "We're not saying that a woman's *place* is in the home. We are saying that a woman's *base* is in the home"[11]—but it seems to be a distinction without a substantive difference. Women are segregated and limited to home duty, while men conduct the public meetings. Men are the protectors, and women are in need of their support. Men are encouraged to treat their wives fairly, so that the wives will accept their authority. The message equates responsibility with patriarchal control.

Feminist/Profeminist Men's Groups

Feminist or profeminist men see the ways both women and men have suffered from sexism. They engage in a sympathetic critique of masculinity, and look at the ways social groups and institutions shape gender roles. Most view gender as a social construct and want to dismantle traditional sex roles. They oppose sexist, racist, and homophobic behavior, believe in shared responsibility for nurturing children, and engage in lobbying projects for women's rights and gay rights. Michael Kimmel, sociology professor and spokesperson for the National Organization for Men Against Sexism, says the impetus for profeminist men's organizations is "[m]en recognizing that their lives as men are impoverished because women are not equal—that we will live happier and better lives when women are our equals."[12] As Kimmel and Thomas Mosmiller detail in their book *Against the Tide: Profeminist Men in the United States, 1776-1990,* some men have supported feminist causes, particularly in discrete issue areas, such as voting, education, and reproductive rights, since the founding of the Republic. Beginning with the second wave of feminism in the 1970s, contemporary profeminist men supported women's struggles for economic, social, and political equality, although this backing often consisted of individuals aligning with women's groups, rather than collective efforts by groups of men.

Some feminist men aligned with radical feminism, others with liberal feminism. The former were more willing to assail men as women's oppressors, while the latter emphasized the ways gender roles constrain both sexes. Even with feminist men's groups, a dance of essences occurs: in the later 1970s, when men sympathetic to feminist causes organized collectively to combat sexism, they "took the label *profeminist* rather than feminist because they recognized the personal experience of being a woman as an important component of being a feminist."[13]

Feminist men joined consciousness-raising groups with women and worked with women's organizations such as NOW. They began writing political tracts and more academic pieces, published in journals like *Changing Men: Issues in Gender, Sex and Politics, Signs,* and *Genders.* Each year since 1975, feminist men's groups have held conferences on Men and Masculinity: the Los Angeles conference in 1978 centered on "Men Overcoming Sexism," the 1989 M & M conference in Pittsburgh was titled

"Menergy: Celebrating the Profeminist Men's Movement"; Minnesota hosted the 1997 conference on "Spirituality, Community, and Social Change." The National Organization for Men Against Sexism (NOMAS), the "largest national organization for profeminist men," had its earliest incarnation in 1981.

Paralleling the growth of feminist men's political groups was the development of the academic discipline of men's studies, which grew from fewer than fifty courses nationwide in the early 1980s to more than ten times that number today, with a high concentration of courses in California, the Midwest, and the Northeast.[14]

Some profeminist groups today take an active role in combating sexual harassment and violence against women by encouraging awareness, acceptance of responsibility, and prevention strategies. Many of these activities are simple, grassroots acknowledgments of gender issues through programs, protests, conferences, educational ventures, counseling, and media blasts. For example, NOMAS's task force on Ending Men's Violence conducted a GOTCHA campaign on the Duke University campus. A group of three students approached men walking alone across campus at night and put a sticker on them, to emphasize the vulnerability of women to sexual assault. Another member of the group would then hand the individual a pamphlet that addressed women's risks of violence when they walk alone.

The White Ribbon campaign originated in Canada to commemorate the anniversary of the December 6, 1989, University of Montreal massacre of fourteen women. During the first year over a hundred thousand men wore white ribbons. In Canada the campaign has evolved to a week's worth of events—films, concerts, discussion groups, walks, building lightings, vigils, posters, buttons, bookmarks, and corporate sponsors—to protest male violence against women. It has filtered into the United States, where some men's groups on college campuses wear white ribbons to signify their opposition to sexual harassment and violence against women. Cities like Syracuse, New York, have created parallel White Ribbon events to create awareness and fund raising for anti–domestic violence efforts.

Other groups hand out antisexist leaflets at Andrew Dice Clay concerts, develop student organizations to discuss how gender issues affect men, provide counseling for abusive men, and attempt through public actions and seminars to campaign against sexism and violence.[15] Ken Fisher, spokesperson for Men's Network for Change, which bills itself as "Canada's only coast-to-coast pro-feminist, gay affirmative, anti-racist, male positive network," says he used to "see a woman with a black eye and I'd look away. I wouldn't generalize and I wouldn't get involved. Men have to stop looking away."[16]

Profeminists are the smallest branch of the men's movement, with an estimated two thousand adherents, many of them academics. As with other camps of the men's movement, the number of official members may not tell the whole story. Tens or hundreds of thousands of other men who have not joined an organized men's group may embrace feminist visions and be supportive of feminist ideals through their lived experiences: voting, vocalizing, promoting egalitarian policies in the workplace, and sharing traditionally female responsibilities at home.

Competing Masculinities

At one level, the widely varying groups in the men's movement are engaged in battle over the definition of masculinity. This competition over the meaning of masculinity itself borders on a stereotype, but it stems from shared impulses to assert and define gender and to seek foundational truths.

For example, Robert Bly criticizes the passivity of feminist men, calling them "soft males"—men who reject their natural tendencies toward aggression.[17] Men's rights activists dismiss the weekend warriors as indulging in "New Age nonsense,"[18] and some view profeminist men's groups as traitorous. Profeminist groups try to distinguish and distance themselves from organizations that conduct male-only retreats. Some profeminists have been harshly critical of men's rights groups: "For these men, the question of unfair divorce settlements, child-custody cases, and the like are a ruse used by some men who favor perpetuating their own dominant status in society."[19] Men's rights adherents cling to traditional notions of the family, which is antithetical to the profeminist view. It is no accident that Promise Keepers meetings occur in sports stadiums. This negotiation over the construction of masculinity is an aggressive and intensely politicized discourse.

Competitive infighting even occurs within different camps of the same branch of the men's movement. Doug Haugen, president of the North American Conference of Church Men's staff, a fellowship of ministers from twenty-two denominations, said that he and other workers who have been in Christian men's ministry for years have experienced some resentment at the instant commercial success of Promise Keepers. But, Haugen says, he and the other pastors at the Promise Keepers Atlanta clergy conference "confessed and repented of their jealousies."[20]

These various men's movements cut across axes of identity other than sex. They are about race, power, economics, religion, and psychological identification. Participants in mythopoetic men's weekend retreats are overwhelmingly white, straight, well educated, and middle-class. The evangelical men's movement is not only closely related to religion in general and the Christian right in particular, it is largely a lower-middle-class, working-class, and minority phenomenon. In terms of social class and general social power, the envisioned nationwide collective of men is empowering. But these men are not jockeying for leadership positions in the new corporate-technological society; they feel removed from the traditional power structures. It is a battle for domination of the sub-institutions, families, communities, and churches that support those power groups.

The Less Sympathetic Critique of the Men's Movements

GENDER SEPARATISM

While members of the spiritual men's movement, evangelical groups, and men's rights advocates hold widely disparate views of masculinity, the movements have some strong thematic connections. First, most of the men's movement collectives other than profeminist men's organizations have a notable absence of women participants and an utter lack of interest in the intersections of men's and women's issues.

The various men's movements' insistence on men's separation from women goes to the heart of their constructs of masculinity: maleness means, in part, an affirmative exclusion of women. At one extreme, some men's rights advocates conduct their work in oppositional existence to feminism. Men International's Kenneth Pangborn says one purpose of his organization is to combat the myths and "the constant venom spread by feminists and picked up by the media."[21] The theme of gender separatism is repeated in the religious revivals and the mythopoetic retreats: women are forbidden to attend either event.

For men's rights groups, evangelical groups, and mythopoetic organizations, the primary synergy and support come only from other men; they make no efforts to bridge the gap between the sexes. In short, the most influential men's movements, with, collectively, several million adherents, and influence far beyond that, promote a return to sex segregation.

THE RETURN TO STEREOTYPIC PATTERNS OF MASCULINITY

It is not a historical accident that in the 1990s there has been a resurrection of all-male groupings and calls for a return to the archetypes of traditional masculinity. In times of instability, humans seek out the familiar. There is nostalgia for a simpler era, a time when men were men, and women were less trouble.

Consider the religious men's movement's template for gender relations. The vision of millions of men gathering as a collective to pledge their faith and commit themselves to their families is one that embraces unity, brotherhood, and family values. But the ideal is simply a traditional view of the family, one with subservient women subscribing to autocratic male leadership.

Many of the evangelical methods of reinventing masculinity are retrospective, with archetypes borrowed from Christian theology and *Father Knows Best*. Nowhere in the picture is a partnership between men and women ever contemplated. In fact, some of the Promise Keepers literature says that the breakdown of the family can be attributed to "the feminization of the American male."[22] Reverend Tony Evans elaborates: "I am trying to describe a misunderstanding of manhood that has produced a nation of 'sissified' men who abdicate their role as spiritually pure leaders."[23] The Nation of Islam and the Promise Keepers associate male empowerment with the repression and domination of women. While the origins of the Islamic faith have always embodied separatism between the sexes, and the resurgence of interest in Islam may have to do in large part with racial and economic currents, some of its modern attractiveness is undoubtedly related to the male exclusivity.

Some fathers' rights groups and most evangelical groups overlap in their implicit assumption of male supremacy. Religious groups rely on biblical teachings to construct their views of gender ideology. They explicitly want to return men to their rightful "head of household" position. One favorite Promise Keepers scriptural quotation is Ephesians 5:22–23: "Wives, submit yourselves unto your own husbands, as unto the Lord. For the husband is the head of the wife even as Christ is the head of the church." The implicit messages also reinforce the gender hierarchy. The second of the seven Promise Keepers promises (right on the heels of a commitment to honoring Jesus Christ) is the commitment to "pursuing vital relationships with a few other men, understanding that he needs brothers to help him keep his promises." The idea is that the most worthwhile bonds of connection that men will forge should be to other men.

The visions for male-female relationships reach only to the limits of the traditional family—with men in positions of power. Promise Keepers speaker Tony Evans explains how men should take responsibility as leaders in their families:

> The first thing you do is sit down with your wife and say something like this: "Honey, I've made a terrible mistake. I've given you my role. I gave up leading the family and I forced you to take my place. Now I must reclaim that role." Don't misunderstand what I'm saying here. I'm not suggesting that you ask for your role back, I'm urging you to take it back. If you simply ask for it back, your wife is likely to simply [refuse]. . . . Be sensitive. Listen. Treat the lady gently but lovingly. But lead![24]

With men's rights groups, the male supremacy theme may be more subtle. Dads Against Discrimination, for example, is an organization created by divorced, separated, and unwed fathers who "pledge to PRESERVE, PROTECT, and DEFEND the FATHER headed family, and to pass the history of FATHERHOOD to subsequent generations." According to Richard Doyle, head of the Men's Rights Association (MRA), "Women are the ones who should be the nurturers," but the MRA's newsletter, the *Liberator,* is more explicit, often carrying articles blaming women for "most divorces, for all male misery, and for the breakdown of the American family."[25]

One thematic strand crossing over several men's movement groups is tied to the military posture of masculinity. The network of Promise Keepers is a hierarchical organization, with "key men/ambassadors" serving as "recruits" to introduce Promise Keepers to church officials. This hierarchical approach to male leadership is repeated in the mythopoetic organizations, with surrogate father figures or "teachers" offering men the father-love that has been missing from their lives, and in some men's rights rhetoric suggesting that women have deprived men of their rightful roles as family leaders. Even some of the nonmisogynist groups, with laudable social objectives, such as MAD DADS (Men Against Destruction—Defending Against Drugs and Social Disorder), are out on patrol. MAD DADS, consisting of twenty-five thousand members in forty-five cities, is essentially community policing, with groups patrolling neighborhood streets at night to confront gang members and stop drug use and property crimes.

The ideas of male accountability and responsibility from the evangelical movements are fed by fairly conventional ideas of men as breadwinners and providers. Similarly, the mythopoetic ideal accepts as a given that men need isolated retreats from their work and family responsibilities, rather than investing thought in changing the institutional structure of work. Can the attempt to reshape the image of masculinity through the trope of equating male strength with being "good" husbands and fathers be separated from male autocracy? Not if the rhetoric that accompanies it envisions male leadership, defines wives as "helpmates," and directs men to avoid anything feminine or "sissified." For mythopoetic, men's rights, and religious men's groups, sensitivity to women's issues is often linked to softness and emasculation.

INTERNALISM, ESSENTIALISM, AND THE NATURALISTIC CONCEPTION OF GENDER

Tied to traditional notions of masculinity is the belief in biological essences, promoted by both religious and mythopoetic groups and even some men's rights advocates. According to mythopoets, men have lost touch with their male essences, their inner warriors, the wildman within. Some men's rights groups concur with this belief in "essential maleness."[26] David Blankenhorn, chair of the National Fatherhood Initiative and a supporter of Promise Keepers, says that men "are by their natures inclined to 'promiscuity, abandonment, and violence.'"[27] The purpose of the Million Man March was to call for African American men to take their "rightful place as men." The fact that African American women have traditionally been the leaders was upsetting the "natural order of things," in which a man is "the protector and provider and defender of [the] family."[28] This naturalism is a theme that resonates even among masculinity theorists who are otherwise sensitive to some aspects of the social construction of gender. In *Warriors and Wildmen*, Stephen Wicks suggests that women's and men's places in society are set by natural forces that are largely impervious to human intervention: "So deeply rooted and pervasive is sex, that to attempt to subvert its energy radically and quickly by social arrangement is to tamper with nature itself, a potentially risky and ultimately futile endeavor."[29]

A strand connecting the evangelical and mythopoetic movements is the emphasis on internal feelings (the shaming and wounds in the mythopoetic movement), individual experiences, and proclamations and words (the evangelical groups' proclamations of love for their families and Jesus), as opposed to external behaviors or progressive social and economic reforms. The therapeutic focus of both groups is introspective: dancing, hugging other men, praying, crying, and telling stories of personal growth. The mythopoets and religious men's movements' emphasis on inner, spiritual development relieves the participants of the need to address pressing social, economic, race, and class issues.

The internal and essentialist features of these men's movement themes are limiting in several ways. They turn inward, toward the experiences of single individuals, rather than outward, either for verification or toward social reform. Even among men's rights advocates who want sweeping legal reforms, the reforms themselves look at an isolated slice of the whole social picture: men's rights. The advocates' interest inevitably seems to stem from their own bitter divorce or custody experiences. They don't want anyone else to suffer personally as they have.

Not only are social differences explained by the inherent differences between men and women, but as Ken Clatterbaugh says, "[b]ad things are bound to happen if change is introduced that goes against essential natures. Women are women and men are men and what men and women traditionally have done reflects their real natures—unhappiness, and possible social chaos, is the price of trying to alter gender roles."[30]

The More Sympathetic Feminist Read of the Men's Movements: Seeing the Reconstructive Possibilities

The easy task of critique is to spot the socially conservative values underlying some of the men's movements and to herald the dangers of reincarnating traditional, sexist gender roles. A button circulated among critics of men's retreats capsulizes the dismissive attitude: "Men's Weekends— when 365 days a year aren't enough."[31]

The more difficult task is to find a charitable reading of these men's movements, one that acknowledges their promising inclinations. A supportive feminist reading of the themes in the men's movements would recognize the good impulses while criticizing those aspects that appeal to the traditional ideology of a given order, whether biological, historical, or religious.

What lessons can feminism learn from the various men's movements? Sifting through the complaints of reverse sexism, the blame language that castigates women for the breakdown of the family, and the anti–affirmative action, anti–reproductive rights, antifeminist rhetoric is not simple. But if one can distill legitimate complaints out of the anger, what might they be?

Men are rightfully resentful about being locked into the social roles of breadwinner, protector, and provider. It is no coincidence that men's rights groups seek custody, evangelical groups seek to form closer relations with their family and their faith groups, and profeminist groups actively want to assume more child care responsibilities. The thematic complaint resonates with empirical experience: social forces have excluded men from the arena of nurturing. This is a mirror image of feminist concerns that society has delegated principal child care responsibilities to women.

All the men's movements, from evangelical to profeminist, are struggling to reconstruct masculinity. Some of the groups recognize the emotional impoverishment of traditional models of masculinity, particularly the cultural training in distancing oneself from feelings and emotions. Men are meeting in relatively apolitical therapy and support or discussion groups concerned with issues of stress, grief, self-esteem, health, aging, and impotency. In 1991 over 1,500 such groups met in the United States.[32] This may be the beginning of breaking down the notion that it is unmanly to discuss personal problems. (On the other hand, since these groups seem relegated to the therapy arena, maybe they still perpetuate the myth of manhood: only sick or troubled men are those who need to talk about their problems.)

While some of the methods remain largely internal, self- or group-focused, they signal the development of a new dimension to masculinity: men yearning to express emotions. Whether through dance and drumming rituals or participation in support groups or commitments to rebuild families and religious communities or seeking custody of and involvement with their children, hundreds of thousands of men across the nation are constructing a new masculinity, one with a softer side, one that connects them to other people on an emotional level. Unpacked from its trappings—the ceremonial drumming and chanting rituals, mythical archetypes, and weekend warrior quests—the mythopoetic movement, for example, offers promise in its search for emotional fulfillment, particularly in fatherhood. Consider a poem written by Robert Bly, "For My Son Noah, Ten Years Old":

> and slowly the kind man comes closer, loses his rage,
> sits down at table.
> So I am proud only of those days that pass in undivided
> tenderness,
> when you sit drawing, or making books, stapled, with
> messages to the world,
> of coloring a man with fire coming out of his hair.
> Or we sit at a table, with small tea carefully poured.
> So we pass our time together, calm and delighted.[33]

Certainly, this male integration of traditionally female pursuits occurs within the sexual polarity of the movement's theories, but at least it sees part of men's work as child care. In this respect, the interests of those in the men's movements are, if not one with feminists' concerns, at least closely related.

One of the most hopeful readings of the men's movements and attention to masculinities is that they seem to be following the developmental pattern of the second wave of the women's movement. Just as feminism began in opposition to a masculine stronghold, the more conservative men's movements began in opposition to the dominance of feminism in gender studies. It is vital to distinguish those portions of the men's movements that are just reactionary attempts to cling to privilege. But the very fact of oppositional existence—to the extent that it is thoughtful and reasoned—would at least seem to necessitate an understanding of gender discourse.

The male-bonding, developing male intimacy, self-questioning, and focus on self-awareness of the male-only retreats parallels women's consciousness raising groups. Part of the inquiry into masculinity promotes the idea of introspection. Even though this is subject to the critique that it is simply internal, it does encourage men to think seriously about their commitments, responsibilities, and places in the family and in larger community settings.

The women's movement later branched into social reforms. Even if the social reforms of this generation of men's rights groups are men seeking quid pro quo custody reforms, the recognition exists that the movement must turn outward toward broader social impacts. Whether the mythopoets can move beyond personal growth or self-actualization is an unanswerable question. Some evangelical groups have begun the process of building outward: in their efforts to dismantle denominational and racial barriers and reinvest in social communities, the Promise Keepers seem interested in having a larger cultural impact. Left open is whether the group will try to reach beyond interfaith barriers.

Looking at the ways men are constructed, we cannot help but gain insight into the construction of women. Even if some of those revelations presently take the form of point-counterpoint (such as who is favored in custody determinations, and in what ways), future dialogue does not have to be structured this way. Work in both feminism and men's studies should benefit from engagement and constructive challenge. Consider, for example, the battle about domestic violence statistics. Some men's rights groups have assailed numbers showing that men are typically the perpetrators of domestic violence and women its usual victims with evidence that women are more likely to physically assault their spouses and partners.[34] What may well be happening in some situations is that women in abusive relationships initially do provoke physical violence. This is consonant with contemporary domestic violence theory: perhaps some women have learned that the physical encounters will be less serious if the explosions occur earlier in the cycle of battering.[35] Moving the discussion away from blame—who hits earlier, harder, or more often, men or women?—and analyzing instead the relational cycle of violence may increase understanding of the mechanisms of violence and ways to end its cycles.

Dialogue between feminists and adherents of various men's movements has such possibilities. Are the consciousness-raising themes of men's groups any different from the second wave of the feminist movement? Is the cycle of self-awareness different for men and women? If some men seek greater roles in child care, what institutional and personal changes are necessary to permit this? The tendency of both feminist and men's groups has been to act in terms of opposition to the other sex, instead of toward general, unifying aims. Apart from work by profeminist men, the prospects for men's movement theorists and feminists to join together in challenging traditional sex roles remains largely untapped.

Academic Constructions of Masculinity

Academic work on the ideology of masculinity shows that manliness is not a monolithic ideal, but is contingent on categories of class, race, and sexuality. Crossing these substrata of demographic characteristics, though, is a "constellation of standards and expectations that individually and jointly have various kinds of negative concomitants. . . . including achievement, emotional control, antifemininity, and homophobia."[36] Research suggests that the ideology of masculinity itself influences men's behaviors: in following their social gender "scripts," men engage in unwarranted risk taking, suppress emotions, and distance themselves from family members.[37]

The various meanings of masculinity spread of course beyond the camps of the men's movement, although the movement itself is in large part about defining masculinity. The Christian men's movement, for example, is vocal about its disapproval of homosexuality. Promise Keepers has issued a press release saying that although it believes homosexuality is "a sin which violates God's design," gays are welcome to attend Promise Keepers rallies.[38] More broadly, though, men who do not conform to heterosexual gender expectations suffer exclusion, torment, and physical violence. Our culture censors gay-positive works: Washington, DC's Corcoran Gallery of Art canceled a retrospective of the works of Robert Mapplethorpe, a gay photographer whose pictures graphically depicted gay sex practices; the fact that the National Endowment for the Arts funded some displays of Mapplethorpe's works has threatened public funding for the arts; and school libraries across the country have removed books about being gay, such as *Daddy's Roommate, Daddy's Wedding, His Athletic Shorts,* and *The Drowning of Stefan Jones,* from their shelves.

The hierarchies of masculinity include stereotypic images of men of color: black men "are constructed as criminal, violent, lascivious, irresponsible, and not particularly smart," while Native Americans are lazy, alcoholic, "menacing, hostile, and threatening."[39] The stereotypes translate into treatment. Men of color are the principal targets of police brutality. One of my colleagues, an African American male, pulled into his own driveway in an affluent, predominantly white suburban neighborhood. Two officers patrolling the area forced him to spread-eagle against the side of his car for being "suspicious." Marvin Jones, a black law professor at the University of Miami, says that when he walks down a street he hears "a symphony of car doors locking." Negative stereotyping is not exclusively a matter of demonizing images. Asian American males, for example, may be portrayed as mild-mannered, intelligent, studious, or effeminate. But the social construction of masculinity is a process of creating outsider classes and hierarchies of worthier and less worthy males.

Modern academic thinking about masculinity in psychology and sociology has focused on men in various institutional domains: the gender role conflicts experienced by men juggling differing expectations at home and work, the changing construct and expectations of fatherhood, the prospects of psychotherapy for men, and areas of dysfunction for men as social actors: problems of competition, aggression, violence, and intimacy.

Theorists in psychology have reevaluated traditional theories of masculinity. Post-Freudian theories of gender identity development suggested that psychological health depended on developing a coherent gender role consistent with one's biological sex. Some gender identity theorists thus posited that the development of appropriate masculinity required little boys to reject their strong psychic attachment to their mothers and distance themselves from feminine behaviors. This traditional approach to masculinity was influenced by popular wisdom and, reciprocally, sifted into popular consciousness as stereotypic injunctions about appropriate male behavior. Deborah David and Robert Brannon cataloged these admonitions as "No Sissy Stuff," "Be a Big Wheel," "Be a Sturdy Oak," and "Give 'em Hell."[40]

Contemporary theorists reject the binary and essentialist nature of identity theory, which "pressures an individual to conform to a gender role that is restricted to one of only two possibilities" and point to the lack of empirical basis for it.[41] Most modern psychologists and men's studies scholars accept some variation of the "gender role strain" paradigm, which "sees gender differences as a result of cultural pressures on individuals to conform to gender role norms. Gender roles are seen as operationally defined, internally inconsistent, constantly changing, and inevitably producing a degree of psychological dysfunction in all people."[42]

The movement from gender identity theory to relational theories of psychological development may enhance social acceptance of less restrictive gender roles, and the necessity of more fluid gender roles is being confirmed with empirical research. Clinical studies have evinced an increasing awareness of the importance, for both fathers and children, of fathers' participation in children's lives, as well as the benefits to the entire family of more egalitarian parenting.[43]

But what of the risky, irresponsible, and violent behavior that males demonstrate in abundance compared to females? Men become alcoholics at a rate five times that of women; "over 85% of drug offenders are male"; ultimately, "[m]en die 7 to 10 years sooner than women," due principally to poor health management, higher rates of accidental injury, and much greater tendencies to indulge in risk-taking behaviors.[44] Men commit 94 percent of all violent offenses; they are 50 percent more likely than women to be its victims.[45] The wealth of psychosocial data supports what psychology professor Louise Silverstein and psychiatry professor Gary Brooks theorize about "dark side behavior": these behaviors are not the products of aberrational males; they are instead the expected consequences of typical gender socialization. Culturally, we train males toward violence as a problem-solving strategy.

Cross-cultural studies have demonstrated that the traditional definitions of manhood are neither genetically fixed nor inevitable, and that sex and gender can be separated. The people of Tahiti, the Semai of the Malay peninsula, and the Vanatinai of Papua New Guinea are examples of nonpatriarchal cultures with minimal gender role differences: "In Tahiti, women are permitted to do virtually everything that men do, even holding political office, and men are not afraid of appearing effeminate. . . . within this cultural context, the male role is defined as almost the opposite of macho: Passivity, timidity, and no taste for competitive striving are valued traits."[46] The women of Juchitán, Mexico, descendants of an Amazonian Indian tribe, "dominate both the local economy and the men." Not only are the Juchitán women "physically dominant over men (in terms of size and strength)," they are also the primary economic actors, "while men assume most of the child care responsibilities."[47]

Sexual and social "gender transitivity" is exhibited among English schoolboys, in ancient Greece, and in the Native American berdache. The berdache of Mojave, Navaho, Pima, Sioux, and Zuni cultures were "socially cross-gendered" men and women who assumed the characteristics, dress, and social roles and responsibilities of the opposite sex. Their "socio-sexual identities constituted an independent and unique gender category that transcended 'male' and 'female' genders; on this basis, berdaches generally were highly regarded by their communities, respected and powerful because they personified a unity of dualities that helped to cohere the larger cosmology of Native American society."[48]

These are not shadowy figures of yesteryear. In Lepurosh, Albania, Sema Brahimi was one of four sisters and an infant brother who lost their father when Sema was fourteen. Northern Albania is a culture in which women wear head coverings and must obey their husbands, fathers select wives for their sons, and each family must be represented by a man. When Sema's father died, she cut her hair, became a field worker to earn money for her family, and adopted the masculine version of her name, "Selman, and her mother and sisters began referring to her with the pronouns 'he' and 'him.'"[49] She later selected a wife for her brother and "wore a suit and tie at his wedding, assuming the role of father of the groom." In other words, to be able to play the political part of man, one must also play all the social roles. There is nothing particularly forward or progressive about a culture that requires family representation by a man, except at some level where the community makes no pretense that the biological fact of gender has such significance and that in certain social circumstances a cultural construct can supplant biology. The situation is a curious but explicit recognition that the construct of gender is cultural.

Simply put, it is culturally possible to socialize males and females away from aggression, competition, and even gender role differentiation. Academic inquiries into manhood raise new possibilities for constructions of masculinity that acknowledge power differentials in the present construction of gender relations, yet see the prospects for empathetic understanding of traditional male roles.

Despite this wealth of recent developments in men's studies—regarding the hierarchies, complexities, and malleability of masculinity—many feminist legal theorists have not incorporated the new social science evidence into sympathetic constructions of males or masculinity. The men who populate feminist legal theory remain, for the most part, yesterday's patriarchs.

Feminist Legal Theory and the Construction of Masculinity

The explorations of masculinity in the social sciences have not yet sifted into legal theory. Feminism in law has focused on the unjust subordination of women. Central to feminist legal theory are several premises. First, feminism maintains that culturally, politically, economically, and legally, women have been, and still are, subordinated, oppressed, degraded, and ignored. Second, feminism argues that law is in many ways gendered, it is an exercise of power, and it operates "to the detriment of women."[50] Finally, feminist legal theory contends that this pervasiveness of patriarchy is unjust. "[F]eminism in law means advocacy to end restrictive treatment of all women."[51]

Liberal Feminism or Equal Treatment Theory:
Men as Objects of Analysis

Feminist legal theory has evolved through stages into several different camps. The equal treatment theorists, or liberal feminists, were the first wave of feminist legal theorists.[52] These theorists argued for the abolition of all gender-based classifications.[53] The hallowed building block of liberalism, that all men are created equal, was recast to include women.[54] The goals of liberal feminism were assimilationist in nature: making legal claims that would ensure women received the same rights, opportunities, and treatment as men. Thus, liberal feminists demanded equal pay, employment, education, and political opportunities.

Equal treatment theory viewed men as the benchmark, the norm. Male experiences were an accepted and unquestioned reference point. As theorists emphasized the need for women to achieve equal opportunities, the obvious focus was on the opportunities, rights, and powers men possessed that women did not. Most references to the treatment of men were descriptions of past and present conditions, rather than evaluations of whether those norms were good or bad.

The model of formal equality was reinforced by court decisions. A significant number of the more prominent early cases seeking equal treatment for women were constructed as challenges to gender classifications that burdened men, thereby stigmatizing women as incapable of shouldering those same burdens.[55] Often these cases entailed strategic choices on the part of feminists to attack gender-based classifications using male plaintiffs.[56] As director of the American Civil Liberties Union's Women's Rights Project (WRP), Ruth Bader Ginsburg developed the strategy of proceeding with cases featuring male plaintiffs to press for formal equality for women: "Her briefs consistently characterized sex stereotypes as double-edged. She argued that rigid sex roles limited opportunities for freedom of choice and restricted personal development for members of both sexes."[57] However, it is clear from the cases taken and arguments made that male plaintiffs were being used by women instrumentally, principally to advance women's rights:

> In all of the cases that the WRP has argued before the Court, women's rights were presumably the central concern. In *Kahn v. Shevin,* for example, the WRP undoubtedly had little concern for the extra fifteen dollars added to Mel Kahn's annual tax bill because Florida gave widows, but not widowers, a limited property tax exemption. Similarly, in *Craig v. Boren,* the WRP did not participate simply to protect the right of eighteen to twenty-one year old boys to buy 3.2 beer in Oklahoma. In all of the cases . . . women suffered the critical wrongs, but men were the legal complainants. Use of a male plaintiff was the only way, in many cases, to meet standing requirements. Because the Court did not yet recognize the harm women suffered, a male plaintiff who suffered pecuniary harms was essential.[58]

This litigation strategy did create a standard that was user-friendly to both sexes in the sense that it was gender-blind. Although the initial rubric was gender-neutral, its application in some cases has not yielded gender-neutral results, and instead has served to reinforce traditional role expectations.[59]

Equal treatment theory was necessary to eradicate the worst forms of disparity in treatment of women. Liberal feminism was justly concerned with women's systematic and intentional exclusion from educational and vocational opportunities. These early feminists focused on basic disparities in the treatment of women, and approached the resolution of those disparities from a rhetoric of equality for women. Equal treatment theorists were primarily interested in opposing stereotypes of women as needing special protection. Even though these theorists made arguments about the dual disadvantages of gender stereotypes, they did not spin out the systematic implications of a wide variety of rules and laws that perpetuated gender role stereotypes that harmed men as well.

Cultural Feminism or Difference Theory: Men as Other

The second wave of modern feminists were the difference theorists, also referred to as cultural or relational feminists or special treatment theorists. These scholars would agree with liberal feminism's insistence on gender-neutral laws for most issues. However, they maintain that formal equality, particularly with regard to reproduction and child raising, denies important social and biological differences between women and men.[60] They critique equal treatment theory for providing equality of opportunity only to the extent that women are the same as men, but not for accommodating the ways women are different from men. In their view, equal treatment theory will ultimately fail to arrive at gender equity due to fundamental differences between men and women.

The difference theorists call for acknowledgment of the differences between the sexes, and recognition of the biological or social and cultural construction of gender roles. Some of them advocate the need for preferential treatment in the areas of reproduction and child rearing,[61] while others more moderately support accommodation only for actual childbearing.[62]

A central claim of difference theory is that women have distinctive methods of acquiring knowledge and making moral decisions. Women and men typically display different emotional and cognitive patterns, different social skills or characteristics, possibly stemming from innate physiological traits or from different life experiences. Women operate with an ethic of care and are concerned about relationships and collaborative resolution of issues.[63] Men reason toward an ethic of rights; they prize autonomous individualism and attempt to resolve issues with hierarchical and objective methods.[64] Women speak in a "different voice": whereas men are aggressive and competitive, women are sensitive, empathetic, and nurturing.[65] Men are given identity in difference theory only through their differences from women.

In legal theory, cultural feminists argue that the differences between women and men justify different legal treatment on a range of issues.[66] In the area of maternity leave, for example, difference theory necessitated the recognition that notions of formal equality could operate to the detriment of women.[67] Furthermore, at the institutional level, cultural feminists suggest that when women's experiences and methods of reasoning are brought to bear on legal issues, they shape and alter not only traditional outcomes, but also the processes by which those outcomes are reached, in fundamental ways.[68]

Margaret Jane Radin and Robin West have argued that by demonstrating traits that, through biology or acculturation, are predominantly possessed and employed by women, difference theory was not only important empirical work, but was a necessary form of political legitimation for women.[69] Moreover, difference theory was an important form of compensatory scholarship, since it socially validated women's experiences, which, for many years, simply did not count.

At a minimum, cultural feminism focuses on gender similarities and differences. In emphasizing capacities possessed distinctly or predominantly by women, the theory highlights differences between men and women. At the extreme, this has led some theorists toward a wholesale exclusion of men on a number of levels. First, on the theoretical level, the focus of analysis is women, rather than people. Second, difference theory, with its construction of the dichotomous categories of women and men, excludes those who do not fit neatly into either category. The essentialism of difference theory does not admit that there may be gradations of differences—that gender may be a continuum. Third, in significant respects, a number of cultural feminists may be interpreted as promoting the separatist philosophy that men cannot be reconciled with or included in feminism. Robin West, for example, argues that men are "incapable of empathic knowledge regarding the subjective well-being of others."[70] Christine Littleton concurs, stating that "women's experience [is] a necessary prerequisite for doing feminism" and maintaining that "men who wanted to use the label 'feminist' would have to spend a significant number of years living as women to qualify."[71]

In the social sciences more than in law, these gender differences have been interpreted as an indication of women's moral superiority.[72] A number of theorists writing about the sociology of consciousness have suggested that women are epistemologically privileged.[73] Certain characteristics (female) are celebrated, while others (male) are not. The contention of some standpoint epistemologists is that the underprivileged position of persistent oppression creates an ability in women to discern reality more objectively than men.[74] They also contend that because women's nurturing or caring faculties are better developed, they are able to do different, and perhaps more exploratory, research than men. Some theorists make the stronger argument that feminist ethics should be privileged over masculinist values, and that the application of feminine ideology creates better social outcomes.[75]

Arguments about the superiority of the feminine difference are one response to the marginalization experienced by women for centuries. Some of these arguments may have functioned correctively by adding the omitted accomplishments and contributions of women. Even the stronger argument that women hold a privileged epistemological status may have been a necessary step in claiming legitimacy for gender differences or in reversing an established hierarchy so that it could be examined, but such an argument comes with a price. On the level of discourse, this framework meant that dialogue was a competition. The form of the argument—that women's ethics should prevail over men's—sets up a discourse that is at best competitive, at worst combative. Whose values should prevail?

Dominance Theory or Radical Feminism: Men as Oppressors

A third group of feminist legal theorists analyze the inequality in power relations between women and men.[76] Instead of focusing on gender differences, dominance theorists, or radical feminists, emphasize women's subordination. They describe how men's cultural and sexual domination structures social and legal relations between the sexes. They assert that legal concepts, crafted by men, operate to control patterns of behavior between men and women.[77] Dominance theorists call attention to the fact that the male norm in law and society is universal and unchallenged.

Dominance theory dwells less on the individual experiences of women and is much more concerned with the class-based oppression of women. These theorists call attention to the social institutions and practices that promote gender inequality as well as the oppression of women. They cite pornography, prostitution, sexual harassment, restrictions on abortion, and inadequate responses to violence against women as examples of social phenomena that contribute to the oppression of women: "Pornography, in the feminist view, is a form of forced sex, a practice of sexual politics, an institution of gender inequality."[78] Radical feminism argues for dramatic social transformation and redress of the power imbalance.

Dominance theory may tend to promote a circumscribed view of both men and women by representing men negatively and portraying women as the victims of centuries of male oppression. Under this theory, men subordinate, ignore, invade, harass, vilify, use, and torture women. They are, quite literally, the bad guys. The essential social relations between men and women are those of domination and submission: male domination and fe-male victimization. Gender is constructed as social position and political prowess. Sexuality is the practice of subjugation. As Robin West capsulizes it, radical feminists believe that "the important difference between men and women is that women get fucked and men fuck: 'women,' definitionally, are 'those from whom sex is taken.'"[79]

Importantly, not even the "good guys" are exempt from this description, for all men are potentially bad.[80] Dominance theory opens the door to an essentialist position for the viewing of men as a uniform collective: none are better, some are worse, and all are guilty.[81] Note that radical feminists are not the only ones to blame men: "To be blunt, it is almost impossible *not* to blind oneself to the violence in the world of which you are an indirect if not direct beneficiary, and most men do indeed benefit, at least in the short run, from the sexual violence from which many women fear or suffer."[82]

In addition to viewing men as the perpetrators, dominance theory views gender discourse as a finite-sum game in which there must be winners and losers. For dominance theorists, gender equates with and is defined by power. They argue that gender equality can come only through a shift in power: "Equality means someone loses power. . . . The mathematics are sim-ple: taking power from exploiters extends and multiplies the rights of those they have been exploiting."[83] If women can attain equality only by "taking power from those who have it," that is, men, this sets up a fundamental an-tagonism between the sexes.

Postmodern Feminism: Men Omitted

Much of modern feminist legal scholarship has moved beyond the same-ness-difference-dominance debate, although a number of ideas from cul-tural feminism are being adopted and implemented as mainstream social practice. A principal current focus of feminist exploration in law is post-modern feminism. Feminists influenced by postmodernism emphasize that there is no monolithic female experience, but many experiences that vary according to a woman's race, class, ethnicity, and culture.[84] Femininity is so-cially constructed, and knowledge, rather than consisting of objective, time-less truths, is situational and constructed from a confluence of multiple per-spectives.

Another insight of postmodern feminism is that abstract theorizing should give way to pragmatic, contextual solutions.[85] An important facet of postmodernism generally, and postmodern feminism in particular, is that discourse, perhaps especially legal discourse, constructs social understanding. Some authors suggest that to prevent gender hierarchies from self-reproducing, postmodern feminist theory must focus on the structural conditions perpetuating patriarchy.[86]

Postmodern feminism is concerned with the dilemma of essentialism: how feminists can remain unified on gender issues and yet recognize that feminists are shaped as much, if not more, by characteristics of race, class, and ethnicity.[87] Feminists drawing on postmodernism want to avoid unitary truths and acknowledge multiple identities.

In struggling with the "no woman, many women" concept, much of postmodern feminism simply omits men. Of course, the postmodern perspective that women's identities are shaped by their cultural and social situations necessarily includes their interactions with men. The postmodern exploration of this subject considers the social construction of gender differences and the self.[88] Nevertheless, the idea that many incarnations of women exist is a woman-centered theory—the focus is on women. Even postmodern feminist ideas about the cultural composition of gender concentrate primarily on women. Thus, the reason for the omission of men from postmodern feminism is not that men are irrelevant or that they are evil, but principally that the concentration is on a different subject: woman or women.

Feminist Legal Theory in Perspective

None of this analysis is meant to suggest that the various incarnations of feminist legal theory are wrong or that they have not been helpful. They have been absolutely critical in redressing the institutional blindness to the subordination of women, affirming women's experiences, empowering women, and elevating their social and political status. Although feminists have paid attention to the condition of men, their attention was for a particular purpose. Feminist arguments about how men have been disadvantaged were employed principally to create equal opportunities for women.

Much of feminists' inattention to men is understandable since women lacked the attention for centuries. In its nascency, feminist theory needed to focus on the situations of women. The establishment of women's identity and group consciousness may have required at least the temporary separation of the interests of men and women.

Feminism requires opposition to the unjust subordination of women. Underlying this definition, though, are broader suppositions that gender role stereotyping is unjust, that categorical assumptions about people must be closely examined, and that an awareness of the social, cultural, and political ramifications of any categorization must be considered. Gender disparities exist only as relational differences. We know gender stereotyping only by comparing the treatment of one group of people (women or men) to another group of people (men or women), while bearing in mind both differences and similarities in situations, functions, needs, and rights. The focus of feminist scholarship for the past two decades has been on how women differ from men, how women have been disadvantaged relative to men, and what corrective actions are needed to secure the financial, social, and political status of women.

Gender role stereotypes include both male and female stereotypes. Clearly, any discrimination against men may ultimately result in harm to women. For example, punishing only men for statutory rape reinforces the model of males as aggressors and affords women "protection" while denying them sexual freedom.[89] But it is vital to acknowledge that the indictment of gender role stereotypes reaches further than harms to women. Stereotypes that create constructs of masculinity harm men both directly and indirectly.

While some have recognized that perpetuation of sex role stereotypes harms men as well as women,[90] there has been no systematic application of feminist theory to situations that injure men. Although the equal treatment theorists examined the burdens of stereotypes on men as well as women, they employed this strategy to advance the role of women. Furthermore, feminism in the modern era has done little to examine the more sophisticated and subtle ways stereotypes, particularly those stereotypes that have been internalized, affect men. Feminist legal theory has not comprehensively explored the negative effects that gender role stereotypes have on men, or it has relegated consideration of such effects to footnotes.

In disciplines other than law, feminists have begun to address the various situations of men and concepts of masculinity.[91] Importantly, the topic of masculinity was essentially nonexistent until feminists began to write about the centrality of gender in the construction of work, domestic life, and identity. Michael Kimmel writes,

> So how is it that men have no history? Until the intervention of women's studies, it was women who had no history, who were invisible, the "other." Still today, virtually every history book is a history of men. If a book does not have the word "women" in its title, it is a good bet that the book is about men. . . . These books do not explore how the experience of being a man structured

the men's lives, or the organizations and institutions they created, the events in which they participated. American men have no history as gendered selves; no work describes historical events in terms of what these events meant to the men who participated in them as men.[92]

Masculinity has received little attention in feminist legal theory. Only quite recently, and then only minimally, have legal theorists explored the ways legal theory and doctrines help to shape concepts of maleness. Not until the mid-1990s did a small number of feminist legal scholars, such as Mary Ann Case, Katherine Franke, and Kenneth Karst, writing about divergent topics, even venture into empathetic discussions of majority group masculinity.[93] Katherine Franke, for example, argues that sex discrimination laws, in making a sharp separation between sex and gender—assuming the former is a matter of biology and the latter of culture—ignores the ways discrimination based on sex is actually discrimination based on traditional gender roles. In its focus on biological sex, Franke argues, "antidiscrimination law strives for too little" and can never reach situations of discrimination against transgendered individuals or effeminate men or women with masculine characteristics or interests.[94]

In a discussion of the military's exclusion of homosexuals and women, Kenneth Karst has described the ideology of masculinity, with its tenets of domination and male bonding. "The exclusion policy," he says, "is part of a vigorous effort to keep the gender line clearly marked." Karst carefully traces the ways legal institutions (such as court approval of the combat exclusion for women) shape traditional images of masculinity:

> War is man's work. Biological convergence on the battlefield would not only be dissatisfying in terms of what women could do, but it would be an enormous psychological distraction for the male who wants to think that he's fighting for that woman somewhere behind, not up there in the same foxhole with him. It tramples the male ego. When you get right down to it, you have to protect the manliness of war.[95]

These are promising beginnings, but much greater inquiry needs to aim at discovering the ways legal constructs are interwoven with the social practices that define what it means to be male in this culture.

Many of the insights from the different incarnations of feminist theory can be applied to the treatment of men. To the extent that caring, contextualizing, unmasking, raising awareness, and emphasizing connections between people are important operating principles, they should be applied to men's relations to legal theory and doctrine.

Pragmatic feminism teaches the importance of looking at specific situations and the danger of universals.[96] Feminists have argued for greater contextual analyses of the categories of identity—such as race, gender, class, ethnicity, and sexual orientation—that shape people's decisions and attitudes. These contextual methodologies can be applied to various situations and roles that shape the constructs of masculinity.

An important methodological tool of feminism is unmasking gendered biases or assumptions made by social groups and institutions, laws, and legal doctrines. It is a process that consists of evaluating whether rules operate in a neutral manner and, more generally, of making gender visible. The treatment of men by various legal doctrines reinforces stereotypic notions of maleness. For example, the law defining the kinds of injuries that are compensable under Title VII describes, legally, who can suffer. It speaks volumes about the ways law views men as impervious to emotional pain.

Feminist legal theory is ready to move beyond the singular interests of women. Men have not been invited into the theoretical discourse; they have not been invited to the table (you should excuse the expression). The next two chapters move the discussion from the level of theory to practice. They suggest ways gender role stereotypes are both constructed and perpetuated in social relations and by legal doctrine.

7

Reconstructing Images of Gender in Theory

> Until women committed to the feminist movement fully accept men
> as comrades in struggle who have every right to participate in the
> movement (and no right to dominate) and recognize that they (men)
> would then be called by political accountability to assume a major
> role in feminist struggle to end sexism and sexist oppression, the
> transformative vision of revolutionary feminism will not be con-
> cretely actualized in lives.
> —bell hooks, quoted in *Angry Women,* ed. Andrea Juno and V. Vale

This chapter revisits the reluctance of some feminist scholars to include men as subjects of analysis and political allies. Some of feminism's inattention to men is understandable, some has been retributive, and some has been the result of resource allocation: equality issues for women needed more immediate attention. But feminism has reached a stage where it both can and must turn part of its attention to the sociopolitical and legal analysis of masculinity issues.

Part of the gender work of the future will require restructuring feminist theory to incorporate theories about masculinity into feminism, invite and actively include men in feminist discourse, and direct attention to the gendered situations of men. This chapter proposes ways feminism generally, and feminist legal theory in particular, can become more inclusive.

Overcoming the Resistance of Feminism to Integration

Abandonment of the Retributive Approach

A common response to the recitation of the harms that men suffer is that these are injuries that men sustain—and the double meaning is intentional.

When I was describing to a feminist friend the harms gender role stereotypes inflict on men, such as requiring them to be the only ones to serve in combat, she responded, "Yes, but men are the ones to declare war. They made their bed, let them lie in it." Although the metaphor was oddly mixed, the argument deserves serious attention: the substantive inequities underlying these stereotypic classifications result from a worldview that men have architected and perpetuated. More simply, men have achieved various benefits from patriarchy, thus they must accept the downsides.[1]

This argument is retributive in nature. It claims that men deserve their injuries from the system "they" have constructed, and that their injuries result from a rational distribution of privileges and burdens. The next deductive step in this line of reasoning is that since men created these constructs that are now disadvantaging them, women have no obligation to intercede on men's behalf. The retributive response is actually a package of somewhat interrelated arguments about prestige, comparative advantage, and responsibility to make social changes.

A related claim is that in terms of financial, social, and political status, men have money, clout, and power. The argument is that men are harmed not cumulatively, but only at the margins. And that even though gender stereotyping harms men, it harms women much more. In so many cases, legal rules favor men. Even seemingly neutral rules operate to favor men. Thus, some feminists claim that because patriarchy hurts women much more than men, women's situation deserves to be the focus of attention.

Most people would agree that harms to women simply swamp harms to men. But the issue is not whether the collective harms to women exceed those to men. Historical facts are not deniable. However, viewing this on a collective level at all times risks overgeneralization. The question instead should be whether individual injustices are warranted.

Women, on the whole, are disadvantaged much more seriously and persistently than men. This is not a response to my point; it is my point: feminist theory should not engage in this *sort* of response, otherwise it becomes a bizarre game of one-upmanship or one-downpersonship. In fact, the real disservice may be in the repeated attempts to deemphasize the experiences of men and to diminish the harms of being male. The focus on comparing the disadvantages of men and women reinforces on a theoretical level what society says on a social level: Suck it up. Be tough. Be a man.

It is important to abandon the retributive approach to males—the "that's what you get for constructing patriarchy, sucker" approach. Instead of constructing an argument of blame, we must ask what is a responsible approach for the future in the sense of justice, fairness, and rational ethics. As Professor Angela Harris notes, "The tendency to think about oppression as an all-or-nothing concept—one is either 'an oppressor' or 'a victim'—prevents us from seeing how groups can be oppressed and privileged at the same time."[2] Just as privilege is often invisible, so are the ways stereotypes trap members of dominant groups. The questions that are not being asked are how are men constrained into masculine gender roles that keep them from expression, inhibit certain social contacts, and preclude "crossing over" into traditionally female roles? And how might women and men, gays and straights, children and parents, and society as a whole benefit more from relational, rational, and constructive perspectives than from a combative, win-lose perspective?

The Distributional Argument

Some feminists take the position that feminism is exclusively about women. For them, the concerns are distributional in several ways. First, feminism has limited intellectual resources and must expend them on improving the conditions of women. Second, in a world of scarce material resources, people must make choices. If providing benefits for men who are operating in traditionally female spheres or roles uses up some resources, this leaves fewer available for women.[3]

For instance, Christine Littleton argues that including men necessarily results in the exclusion of women.[4] Her example is the Family and Medical Leave Act (FMLA), which, she argues, would have provided far more extensive coverage for women if it had left men out of the equation. Littleton argues that in its rush to include men as covered family members entitled to medical leaves, the legislation excluded several categories of women: lesbians (whose partners cannot be spouses under present law), women living in nontraditional or extended families, and working women unable to afford the unpaid leave provided by the FMLA. But, as Littleton acknowledges, legislators exhibited no inclination to include the excluded categories of women.[5] No evidence exists that the marginalized subgroups of women *were* sacrificed to make room for men.

The distributional argument may collapse on itself in a far more important way. The assumption in the FMLA example is that the inclusion of men excludes women politically by diminishing their collective political clout. In fact, the FMLA may be a good example of recent legislation that became law due to its policy of including men.[6] At least the vehicles need to be in place to permit men to engage in parenting roles. If legislation providing benefits relating to traditionally female roles applies only to women, it institutionalizes the gender stereotype and makes it impossible for men to participate in these roles.

While Littleton's example is the easy case to challenge, her general proposition—that working on men's issues may siphon credibility or resources away from women's issues—may be accurate in one sense. If women's organizations devote precious resources to educating the public about, say, the sexual harassment of effeminate men, they risk losing both time and credence with conservative or moderate groups that are not ready for these changes. Redirection of feminist attention will exact a price in the short run. But the prospects of far greater long-term gains from the initial investment of resources, once these issues sift into public consciousness, outweigh the short-term losses.

The resource scarcity argument suggests a corollary: if feminists focus their attention on how men are disadvantaged by gender role stereotypes, it may provide fuel for male backlash against feminism under the guise of male suffering. If men have been advantaged in so many ways for so long, why focus on their burdens? Won't this simply perpetuate patriarchy?

Opportunism can always rear its ugly head. But if the disadvantages to men from gender stereotypes prove to be the result of patriarchy, this finding will not provide an intellectually honest venue to complain about women or feminism. The harms of patriarchy are not harms to only one sex. Nor should the description of those harms be a competitive event between the sexes. The very squaring off in competition freezes us in time, habit, structure, and mind-set, preventing a cooperative examination of gender issues.

Addressing the False Consciousness Problem

The argument about men's opportunistic use of the disadvantages of their gender points to a more fundamental problem of acknowledging the negative consequences of gender stereotypes. A third feminist response might question whether these disadvantages of being male are real—real in the sense of being harms acknowledged by men and being something other than an artifice or device of backlash. Some feminists would say that all the disadvantages are true, but that men do not seem to mind that they get the best of it. If the average man was told, "You really are disadvantaged. You poor schmuck. You are more likely to die in a fight. You belong to the only gender that can fight in a war. You are less likely to be given parental leave so that you can stay home with an infant," many men would say, "So, what's the problem?" In fact, some men may enjoy the seeming disadvantages of traditional roles or may be willing to accept them in exchange for greater advantages.

One might decide that some men are so mesmerized by patriarchy that they do not recognize the problem. This conclusion may be the flip side of the feminist false consciousness argument, which is that women internalize the ideology of patriarchy and assume, falsely, that their choices are their own.[7] Many women make "choices" that reinforce their historically assigned roles. If prevailing political and social ideologies are such potent forces, they may operate on members of dominant as well as subordinate groups.[8]

Just as women have internalized stereotypes of inadequacy,[9] men may have internalized the stereotypic images and behaviors of prevailing norms. A significant body of literature demonstrates how subordinate groups adopt the cultural assumptions and negative stereotypes of the groups that dominate them.[10] Similar work applies the internalization thesis to members of dominant groups: "Dominants respond to subordinates' challenges by citing the group differences that supposedly warrant differential treatment. . . . Serious challenges often give rise to attempts to demonstrate biological differences scientifically. The nineteenth-century antislavery and women's rights movements led reputable scientists to try to prove that women's and Blacks' brains were underdeveloped."[11] Many men may be captivated by the psychological construct of masculinity. It is utterly unsurprising that members of a controlling social group would accept, act out, and even exaggerate stereotypes that favor their social interests.

Perhaps our culture has not given men the opportunity to see any alternatives, or has distorted their choices. Habits, attitudes, and positions of authority may be so deeply ingrained that some men are unable to see themselves as agents of domination or as victims. The less charitable reading is that men's acceptance of gender stereotypes is not due to the coercion of a governing ideology, but is a process of making conscious choices shaped by powerful incentives of self-interest.

In any event, whether through choice, controlling ideology, or, more likely, a combination of the two, patriarchy will continue to perpetuate itself unless we examine and dismantle it. Feminist scholarship has focused on the ways men subjugate women, rather than the complex system of structures and beliefs that impel the perpetual superiority of men.[12] To the extent that men unthinkingly accept the dominant ideology, transformation is possible only through an understanding of the methods of cultural transmission and replication.

Changing the Construct of Masculinity

No simple solutions, rules, or guidelines can readily solve the pervasive gender inequities. Such inequities are historical, social, psychological, legal, economic, and linguistic. The sources of patriarchy are many: historical male dominance replicating itself, social constructs that perpetuate traditional roles, and laws that entrench the traditional constructs. Moreover, these forces—history, social roles, legal rules, and individual postures and inclinations—are significantly intertwined. What follows are some suggestions toward unpacking the structural and institutional biases in order to change the prevailing construct of masculinity. The recommendations encourage discussion of men's experiences, recognition of intertwined oppressions and subtle stereotyping, legal emphasis on the social construction of gender, and development of legal doctrines that promote rather than inhibit crossing over traditional gender lines.

Encouraging Recognition of Men's Experiences

As feminist theory teaches, the personal is political. Private lives are inextricably connected to cultural and political contexts. A wealth of research attests to women's gendered existence, explaining that women experience reproduction, sexual violence, employment circumstances, and other events in ways that men do not. These works explore how men and women exhibit different attitudes, behaviors, interests, priorities, modes of reasoning, and styles of speaking and listening.[13] An assumption underlying many of these writings is that men have universal experiences that women do not share.[14] This assumption is probably based not on a belief that all men have identical experiences, but instead on a lack of exploration into the varieties of men's experiences.

The popular media have made some attempts to validate men's personal and social experiences. However, antifeminist rhetoric often accompanies these efforts, and they may be part of a broader social backlash to recoup rights "given" to women. Some jurisprudential writings address the social and legal experiences of men of color.[15] Others focus on the collective treatment of gay men.[16] Yet experiential discussions regarding the various dimensions of maleness and ideological discussions regarding the construction of maleness are largely missing from the jurisprudential universe. Some feminist legal theorists are beginning to give attention to men's experiences, but this does not constitute a large body of literature.[17]

Mari Matsuda has developed a theory of multiple consciousness, which posits that outsiders, such as women and people of color, develop the ability to shift their perspectives between the viewpoint of a marginalized group and the viewpoint of a dominant culture, while belonging to both.[18] The broader point is that no category of identity, whether it is race, gender, class, ethnicity, or some combination of those or other groupings, is coherent or stable. While Matsuda sees the phenomenon of multiple consciousness as relating particularly, if not exclusively, to the experiences of the disempowered, Carol Gilligan suggests that men as well as women possess "double vision."[19]

The phenomenon of multiple consciousness may apply to the ways men are disempowered. Maybe men do fill all the roles they are assigned: the subjects of false consciousness, perpetrators, collaborators, and victims. Perhaps only a moderate-sized group of men become the monolithic male—a white, middle- or upper-middle-class, able-bodied, heterosexual male with traditional values. Stereotypic masculine virtues may not inure to the benefit of that group. Recall which gender mainly constitutes American society's breadwinners, prisoners, warriors, and killers. At least some resentment may stem from the restrictions of these role expectations.

Of course, the reactionary fervor is apparent in some camps,[20] but the disempowerment may not just be a loss of power in the sense that the group has always enjoyed power. At a deeper, less reactionary level, being a stereotypic white male may not be as easy as it seems.

Much greater inquiry needs to be directed toward the cultural, economic, racial, and class circumstances that shape different men's experiences. In what ways are men's experiences not monolithic? How are men who do not identify as typically male treated? How have men been hurt as men? The group-based treatment of men may not be the result of subordination as was the case with women, but may be due to compulsions to engage in dominant behavior, rigidified role expectations, a lack of cultural mobility, and a narrow range of acceptable psychological responses or social behaviors. Even if men's experiences are "the norm," we must explore the norm by asking who is the generic man that typifies the norm, and what are the experiences, characteristics, and social expectations of nongeneric men? If gender and perspectives based on gender are fundamental to knowledge, law, and social relations, attention must be given to the gendered experiences of men.

The methodology of consciousness-raising promoted by a number of feminists could be particularly suited to this task. Katharine Bartlett suggests that consciousness-raising involves "seeking insights and enhanced perspectives through collaborative or interactive engagements with others based upon personal experience and narrative."[21] Some theorists might object that men cannot engage in consciousness-raising because their consciousness *is* the world. "White men don't need a support group because they already have one. . . . It's called the United States of America."[22] Although one specific purpose of the methodology is to create a voice for people who have not been heard, consciousness-raising is not a method reserved exclusively for women.[23] In fact some of the early consciousness-raising groups of the 1960s had both female and male members.[24]

Men, in groups with other men and women, should be encouraged to engage in consciousness-raising to test the ways society has relegated men to stereotypically male roles. One might immediately recoil from a vision of white men engaged in a "testosterone drenched"[25] weekend retreat at which they complain about being victims of the feminist movement. It is vital, therefore, to make a sharp distinction between consciousness-raising as a practice of psychological support and consciousness-raising as an epistemological method.

Some methods of consciousness-raising are indoctrinative in that they are directed principally at cultivating ideological or psychological confederates.[26] More promising for purposes of promoting inquiry and rationality are the support groups that move toward epistemological advances—those that have to do with questioning, testing, and ultimately reaching reasonably justified propositions—as was usually the case in the feminist movement. Consciousness-raising should be used not simply to solidify or strengthen directions already known, but to examine whether beliefs are warranted.[27] Thus, for example, the notion that feminism sanctions discrimination against white men needs empirical testing. To the extent that traditional gender roles hurt men, consciousness-raising may enable men and women to view men's injuries in ways they might not otherwise expose.

Importantly, consciousness-raising and, more generally, communication about gender differences need not be relegated to either gender in an exclusive grouping. If, as sociolinguists are establishing, men and women are acculturated to view the world and the process of discourse differently, it is vital to encourage dialogue across genders.[28] Bridging perceptual and experiential gaps requires conversation, not unidirectional messages.

Recognizing Intertwined Oppressions

The discussion has proceeded as though male and female were sufficiently explanatory categories, and as though identity was dependent solely on gender. It is crucial to recognize that various forms of oppression—types of choicelessness and powerlessness—are intertwined. Oppressions of gender intersect with other oppressions, including those of race, sexuality, class, and ethnicity.[29] Isolating gender for analytic purposes may be a less than fruitful endeavor, because gender has no single meaning. Just as feminist theory runs the risk of essentializing women,[30] so does any analysis of male disempowerment risk essentializing men.

Cultural stereotypes at the intersection of race, gender, and sexuality classify offenders and crimes.[31] Assumptions about race and gender may lead to suppositions about sexuality.[32] Depictions of "typical" welfare recipients reinforce stereotypes at the intersection of class, race, and gender: "The all-too-prevalent public stereotypes of the poor are the black female unmarried welfare recipient with many children and the black male 'hustler' who lives off the welfare checks of the various women whose children he has fathered."[33] Attitudes about gender and sexuality pathologize nonheterosexual lifestyles, and preclude gays and lesbians from parenting roles.[34] Research is only beginning to explore the interplay of multiple structures of oppression and the simultaneous operation of several interlocking stereotypes.

Analytically, it is often extraordinarily difficult to consider at once the disadvantages of race, gender, class, age, nationality, sexual orientation, disability, geography, and even institutional prestige.[35] But it is vitally important not to let facets of oppression become excuses for intransigence or isolationism. Economic necessity, for example, may impose certain constraints since some families cannot afford to have one parent stay at home, and "[t]he father's primary role in providing economic security functions as a barrier to increased parental involvement in the family."[36] But this fact does not mean that men cannot be feminists or cross gender lines in the area of domestic responsibilities, nor does it mean that the economically entrenched social positions are inalterable over time.

Minimizing the Significance of the Biological Construct

In the recent decade, a significant amount of research has explored biological, psychological, and social differences between the sexes. The wealth of this research attests to a strong cultural location for gender, although almost all the works point to a confluence of constitutive biological, social, economic, and institutional forces.[37] Some feminist literature, though, has concentrated on the biological as opposed to cultural determinants of gender.[38] Undeniably, real differences exist between the reproductive physiologies of males and females, and, to a lesser extent, their physical capabilities. Scholars have rightly criticized the Supreme Court for its failure to acknowledge the reality of these differences and accommodate their impacts.[39] Yet some feminist literature and legal doctrine unjustifiably emphasize the biological construction of gender in areas in which differences are products of socialization as well as physiology.

Joan Williams notes the dangers of relational feminism's embrace of the values of domesticity, which thereby highlights the dichotomous structure of the biological differences model. Contemporary research, she points out, disputes the traditional idea that biology compels social behaviors: "More recent studies . . . challenge the notion that patterned differences between men's behavior and women's are attributable to permanent (and perhaps innate) psychological differences. An example is a study of men who 'mother,' which found that men exhibit the 'nurturing' characteristics commonly associated with women when they play the primary parenting role conventionally assigned to females."[40]

Significant evidence is accumulating that attests to the malleability of "biological" roles and their variability over time, space, and cultures.[41] To some extent, perceptions of biological differences may reflect not empirically significant facts but social stereotypes: "a gender classification [may be] so woven into the entire social understanding of women that it reflects what the judiciary itself still perceives as a genuine gender difference."[42]

Other theorists have also acknowledged the cultural construction of gender[43] and have explored specifically how the association of caregiving tasks and responsibility with women is the product of acculturation.[44] One of the lessons of postmodern theory is that a clear division between biological and social experiences is no longer a tenable one. Almost everything is bio-social, for even where biological bases for conduct exist, socialization exacerbates the tendencies.[45]

The mistaken notion that certain biological impulses are imperatives is also embedded in legal doctrine. In fact, the Supreme Court's scrutiny of gender differences is based significantly on the biological differences model. In *California Federal Savings and Loan Ass'n v. Guerra*, the Court upheld a California statute requiring employers to provide leave to women for pregnancy and childbirth, even though the statute had no parallel provisions for men affected by pregnancy, childbirth, or any other disabling conditions.[46] This holding clearly reinforces the idea that only women need parenting leave. Even when the biological differences are not the important ones, a court may place tremendous legal weight on the historical and biological accoutrements of gender. Legalizing combat for men only, as in *Rostker v. Goldberg*,[47] and criminalizing sexual intercourse for men but not women, as in *Michael M. v. Superior Court*,[48] both illustrate this biologism.

Let us revisit, for a moment, the path the Virginia Military Institute (VMI) case took on its way to the Supreme Court. The touted "uniqueness" of the VMI educational experience[49] is directly traceable to the idea that innate biological differences justify separation of the sexes. On appeal to the Fourth Circuit, appellees argued that the VMI educational experience was a "highly specialized program for the distinctive physiological and developmental characteristics of males."[50] In holding that if VMI were forced to admit women, it would "materially alter the very program in which women seek to partake," the Fourth Circuit Court of Appeals' ruling in the case reinforced the idea that these biologically located differences were outcome determinative.[51] The testimony offered regarding the VMI model concerned psychological and sociological differences between the sexes.[52] Yet the court treated the evidence as though it pointed to inalterable aspects of male physiology, rather than reflecting a more malleable process of socialization.[53]

Even though the Fourth Circuit remanded the case to the trial court, requiring Virginia to defend its policy of providing only one single-sex program, the reasoning of the original decision, and of the appellate decision after remand, held intact the concept that single-sex education is constitutional.[54] The U.S. Supreme Court's decision in VMI, although recognizing the dangers of stereotyping about "typically male or typically female 'tendencies,'" did not dispel this conclusion, and, in fact, expressly left open the possibility that single-sex education might be appropriate under some circumstances.[55]

The social message of single-sex educational programs is unmistakable: there is something problematic about the presence of women in all-male bastions, or the presence of men in traditionally female domains. This message is frighteningly reminiscent of the rationales racists advanced in favor of "separate but equal" racially segregated schools. Yet the arguments that were persuasive to the Supreme Court in *Brown v. Board of Education*—that a "badge of inferiority" would inherently attach and stigmatize in a dual system—are notably absent from the recent single-sex education opinions.[56] Rather, underlying many of the decisions is the notion that inherent differences between the genders justify the separatism. Courts thus depict gender differences as fundamental and enduring traits. The social, political, and institutional scaffolding that constructs these differences recedes into the background.

Trying to allocate responsibility between the biological and the cultural in law, particularly at a time when the wealth of empirical evidence points to deep interactions of the two, seems at a minimum unhelpful. At the extreme, allowing evidence of socialized gender differences to masquerade as innate biological differences is dangerously misleading. Associating genders with distinct constellations of physical, emotional, and mental characteristics has important political consequences: overemphasis of the biologic construct can reify gender differences.[57]

At this juncture in history, people should accept instead that gender is biosocially determined, and emphasize that much can be done with the cultural construct. A substantial body of literature asserts that learned behaviors can reinforce or defeat traditional stereotypes.[58] A cumulative lesson of critical legal studies, critical race theory, and feminist theory is that representations of reality often have the extraordinary ideological power to shape reality.

Encouraging the Crossing of Traditional Gender Lines by Creating Awareness of Subtle Stereotypes

Gender stereotyping is pervasive, persistent, subtle, and often unconscious. It is an amorphous subject in part because generalizations about the characteristics of a gender may be made for a wealth of reasons, ranging from heuristic efficiency to prejudice. Moreover, the conceptions of appropriate social roles for men and women are deeply embedded in society. Stereotyping is also a proactive social force that often shapes behavior and constrains choices.[59] Gender role stereotypes create and maintain occupational segregation by sex, inhibit women's upward mobility, limit women's earning power, and shunt men away from domestic roles:

> Almost half of all employed women work in occupations that are at least eighty percent female, and over half of employed men work in occupations that are at least eighty percent male. . . . [S]ex-typed traits commonly associated with a job often have little inherent connection with performance; instead the perception that a job requires masculine traits typically derives from associating the job with its incumbents.[60]

Coupled with the insidious nature of gender stereotypes are the social enforcement mechanisms that rigidify gender roles. Males who act in stereotypically feminine ways are significantly more likely to be teased, ostracized, and perceived negatively than males who display gender-congruent behavior.[61] Many subtle gender stereotypes are socially entrenched and legally enforced. For example, employment requirements about dress and appearance that are acceptable under Title VII may simply reflect community norms based on gender role stereotypes.

Attention must be directed toward the subtle ways legal doctrines perpetuate gender role segregation. In some areas, the easy targets of gender prejudices have already been exploded. Categorical gender exclusions in particular occupations violate Title VII,[62] and employment decisions may not lawfully depend on explicitly gender-linked characteristics.[63] Yet the process of stereotyping makes exposing assumptions, generalizations, and decisions based on gender extremely difficult. "[W]hen a female applicant for a given position (*e.g.*, litigator) does not fit the evaluator's prototype (*e.g.*, aggressive male), her credentials will be judged with greater skepticism."[64] Legally documenting this subjective skepticism is often close to impossible.

On the doctrinal level, cases challenging subtle and pervasive gender role stereotypes have not fared well. Even to the extent that male plaintiffs have been successful in sex discrimination litigation, they have been victorious only when they established direct economic disadvantages.[65] Were a male plaintiff to bring a claim of subtle discrimination based on gender role stereotypes, he might be laughed out of court, just as some women have been.[66]

For instance, what would the Supreme Court have done with *Andy Hopkins v. Price Waterhouse*? In *Price Waterhouse v. Hopkins*, Ann Hopkins was a candidate for partnership in an accounting firm.[67] Initially her employer placed her candidacy on hold and later denied her consideration for partnership. Hopkins's personnel file contained evaluations by various partners of her qualifications for partnership. The partners complained that "she is a lady using foul language," that although she was "at the top of the list or way above average," she was too "macho," "overly aggressive," and that she should be required to take a "course at charm school."[68] One of Hopkins's supporters commented that Hopkins had matured from a "tough-talking, somewhat masculine hard-nosed manager to an authoritative, formidable but much more appealing lady partner candidate." The partner who explained the board's decision to Hopkins advised her to "walk more femininely, talk more femininely, dress more femininely, wear make-up, have her hair styled, and wear jewelry."[69] The *Price Waterhouse* Court ultimately held that "[i]n the specific context of sex stereotyping, an employer who acts on the basis of a belief that a woman cannot be aggressive, or that she must not be, has acted on the basis of gender."[70]

What if the stereotype had not been that Ann Hopkins was "too aggressive" and "should go to charm school," but that *Andy* Hopkins was "too passive" in seeking out clients, "not competitive enough," and too deferential to others in the office?[71] Perhaps the Court would have relied on the rubric about not "second-guessing" an employer's business judgment.[72] The Court might have stated that Price Waterhouse was entitled to require certain attributes in its partners. It is a decent bet that the Court would not have viewed such a case as presenting a gender stereotyping question.[73]

The Supreme Court's latest message about gender stereotyping in *Price Waterhouse* may mislead observers into thinking that stereotypes are readily recognizable. *Price Waterhouse* was the easy case; it presented direct evidence of overtly gendered comments. Yet language in *Price Waterhouse* implies that many cases will contain readily identifiable stereotypes. Indeed, in referring to the role the expert testimony played in *Price Waterhouse*, the Court observed that "it takes no special training to discern sex stereotyping in a description of an aggressive female employee as requiring 'a course in charm school.'"[74]

Moreover, in focusing on the most blatant evidence of stereotyping, the *Price Waterhouse* Court may have overlooked the more subtle evidence in that case. The Court drew a sharp demarcation between language it found to promote gender stereotypes—adjectives like "macho" and "masculine"—and language it determined was an appropriate, albeit unfavorable, evaluation of Hopkins's personality—adjectives like "brusque" and "harsh."[75] Implicit in this separation of gendered comments from purportedly gender-neutral evaluative remarks is the idea that comments that cumulatively indicate that a person acted unconventionally by not conforming with the norms of his or her gender are *not* gendered comments.[76]

In most instances, gender stereotyping will not be the result of explicit references to gender, as in Ann Hopkins's case. Instead, the stereotyping will occur without explicit references to gender, or will consist of a gender stereotype couched in purportedly neutral language. Most gender stereotyping cases probably will entail much more subtlety than *Price Waterhouse*—shrugs, glances, gestures, code words, with nothing written or memorialized in a file. In order to prevent stereotyping, courts must tune into these subtle forms of gender discrimination.

In particular, courts should recognize that adverse employment actions for nonconformity with conventional gender role expectations are employment discrimination on the basis of gender. At present, however, society punishes those employees who cross over into nontraditional roles and occupations, and the legal system leaves them without redress. Deviation from gender norms incurs tremendous social disapproval and even ritualized violence.[77] Disapproval of those who cross the gender divide is one method of permanently entrenching that gap.

Legal sanctions reinforce these social norms and inhibit men from moving into traditionally female occupations. When men adopt traditionally female roles, they are punished for their cross-gender behavior. For example, in *Strailey v. Happy Times Nursery School*, the Ninth Circuit Court of Appeals allowed the firing of an effeminate male preschool teacher who wore a gold earring—someone who explicitly defied conventional gender role expectations in his choice of employment and attire.[78] The court held that Title VII offered no relief for discrimination based on nonconformity to traditional gender roles: "[D]iscrimination because of effeminacy . . . does not fall within the purview of Title VII."[79]

Part of the chastisement process may be for *being* essentially female; thus males who occupy roles associated with females are subordinated in the same ways as females. But some of the punishment may be for adopting characteristics associated with women—the crossing of traditional gender lines may be the sanctionable offense. Society patrols gender lines by penalizing men for crossing into nontraditional occupations. A striking example of this disparate treatment occurred in *Spaulding v. University of Washington*, in which male and female members of the university's school of nursing faculty sued for sex-based wage discrimination.[80]

The suit sought to remedy historically depressed wages in the predominantly female school of nursing compared to wages in other departments composed primarily of male faculty members. While the male faculty member in the nursing school argued that "he received a salary 'infected' by the discrimination the female faculty members suffered," the Ninth Circuit held that he had no standing to sue under Title VII or the Equal Pay Act because he made "no claim that he received a lower wage because of *his* sex."[81] Thus, although the male faculty member suffered an injury identical to that experienced by the female faculty members, and although this injury flowed from the depressed wages of a traditionally female occupation, the court found that the male lacked standing to redress his economic injuries.[82]

The image of working women has changed dramatically over the past quarter century. Some legal constructs, such as Title VII, are now in place to eradicate barriers to female entry into male-dominated occupations. Of course, significant social impediments—such as the glass ceiling phenomenon—largely unreachable with antidiscrimination laws, remain. In contrast, the image of working men has remained remarkably constant, and no legal constructs attempt to promote men into traditionally female roles. Not only are positive social images of men who embrace female qualities limited, but men are legally disadvantaged if they adopt female roles. Indeed, as *Strailey* and *Spaulding* demonstrate, occupational segregation is made determinate through case law. Since role fixity may be deeply unconscious, gendered assumptions will persist unless theorists repeatedly expose them. In addition, direct reversals of established legal doctrines are necessary to make crossing gender lines realistically possible.

Feminism and Reason

The standards for change must draw on principles that come from feminism and the criteria of rationality.[83] The visions for the future must be based on moral, rational principles, and founded on the use of reason—questioning assumptions, evidentially analyzing arguments, and focusing attention on cumulative, comprehensive, and converging evidence. Egalitarianism is one way of saying no prejudice, no prejudgment. Feminist theory should not distance itself from rational cooperative inquiry, particularly at a time when basic conceptions of science and reason are changing rapidly. "Reason" as a formal, mechanical, deductive process is being abandoned. Philosophers are questioning various rigidities and pretensions of science and reason and are focusing instead on probabilistic theories of knowing. Even the concept of objectivity is changing from one based on claims of independent, external reality to one based on transactional, procedural, and methodological criteria.[84] That rational—including scientific—epistemologies require certain kinds of values, attitudes, and emotions, even passionate commitments, is being increasingly recognized.[85] Modern conceptions of rationality demand awareness of inquiry-debilitating blinders, acknowledgment that moral responsibility extends beyond one's own passionate beliefs, and realization of the need for cooperative inquiry on social questions.[86] Some feminist legal theories are moving in this direction of collaborative rational inquiry by, for example, crossing the boundaries of jurisprudential schools,[87] or connecting feminist theory to larger, foundational philosophical questions.[88]

Transformation of social institutions necessitates acceptance of a wide variety of methods of knowing and the use of reason that is informed by, but not confined to, social class, gender, identity politics, or economics.[89] The deconstruction and reconstruction of gender require acknowledging experiential knowing[90]—a recognition that one's own experiences may be contradicted by others' experiences—and yet acknowledging that this epistemological method is necessarily partial.[91] Changing dominant values and creating abilities to self-reflect and to imagine empathetically what it means to be of a different gender will necessitate openness on both an epistemological and a sociopolitical level, concentration of thought and resources, and time on a large scale.

8

Remaking Gender in Practice

Looking Forward

> [I]f the imagination is to transcend and transform experience it has to question, to challenge, to conceive of alternatives, perhaps to the very life you are living at the moment.
>
> —Adrienne Rich, "When We Dead Awaken"

Is feminism worth salvaging? Why try to resurrect a term and a movement that are to some ambiguous, irritating, offensive, and perhaps unnecessary? Feminism possesses a unique heritage: on the theoretical level, it has created increasingly refined methodologies (from consciousness-raising to questioning hierarchies and exclusion); on the political level, it is the history of a social revolution. This past would be devitalized if its theoretical project were solely humanism and its political action arm limited to a women's movement. If the feminist movement is to become an increasingly powerful force, it must concern itself with issues beyond women's rights. To dismantle the gender line, feminist scholars need to engage concepts of masculinity.

Considering the wealth of evidence demonstrating that gender is significantly a social construct, what will happen if we remake gender? Will the projected horrors of gender identity disorder and unisex bathrooms come to pass—and what will we lose in the way of diversity?

Finally, this book recognizes that while what is legal and illegal affects public opinion, much if not most sex discrimination cannot be remedied legally: it is not perpetrated by government actors; it does not rise to the level of actionability; it occurs in private settings outside the purview of Title VII; it happens in everyday life. So the book concludes not with any systematic program of proposed changes in legal doctrines, but with some suggestions of ways to recognize and avoid gender separatism and stereotyping.

Reclaiming "Feminism"

If it is so reviled, how can feminism remain a politically useful label? If feminism, stripped of slants, refers to basic principles of egalitarianism and humanism, why retain the concept and the much maligned label? If a majority of people are willing to recognize and tolerate, if not champion, "women's rights" and "women's issues," why relentlessly adhere to the contaminated and misunderstood term "feminism"? The first question is whether feminism is worth fighting for as a concept, given its image problems and the factionalism within the movement. The second question is whether feminism is too exclusive—semantically, historically, and politically—to include men.

Some may contend that if feminists avoid labels, more people will join the bandwagon. Most people are "for" equality and human rights. Labels are unimportant, the argument goes, if feminist values are widely embraced. So why not move in new directions, assemble around a different flag, "humanism" perhaps or something less exclusionary than "*fem*inism"?

Even if people are willing to adopt many of the values of feminism, the word is still important at this juncture in history. To abandon "feminism" in lieu of "humanism" or "egalitarianism" or some other banner is to disavow centuries of cultural struggle. Implicit in the statement "I'm not a feminist, but . . ." is a rejection of a rich social heritage. "Feminism" stands for a concept that empowered generations of women. It is the theoretical project that, quite literally, changed the world.

Perhaps more important, self-definition holds political power: "The power to name is frequently also the power to define. The power to name a group can be the power to position it socially and politically."[1] One of the achievements of feminism is its questioning of men's historic power to define experiences and roles, set standards, and control knowledge. As Martha Minow observes, "Feminist work has thus named the power of naming and has challenged both the use of male measures and the assumption that women fail by them."[2]

This is one of the lessons feminism can draw from gay and lesbian theory. The description of someone as "queer" used to be a toxic epithet, which translated into immediate social dismissal. Gays and lesbians have neutralized if not reclaimed the term as a preferred form of self-identification with the development of "queer theory." Some of the essays in Michael Warner's *Fear of a Queer Planet: Queer Politics and Social Theory* describe the ways the reclaiming of "queer" confronted homophobia, deconstructed negative cultural definitions of homosexuality, and reconstructed a pejorative label into a positive social identity. While "queer" is a term most prevalent in academic circles, it is no longer a popular term of derision, and its use is slowly spreading outside essays and articles to social groups and the mass media.[3] The proud adoption of the term in political and social theory did more than recapture a once derogatory label. It offered a central rallying point that unified various theories of sexual identity for a host of different opinions with respect to gay, lesbian, bisexual, and transgender issues. In this sense, feminism may benefit from a moniker that is marginalized—it keeps the revolutionary spirit alive. And in fighting against its own negative publicity, feminism conveys the sense of historical struggle.

Perhaps "feminism" is worth fighting for precisely *because* the opposition's caricature has become its overwhelming symbol. Do we tell other groups not to self-name because it might offend? The power of naming is important not only for definitional purposes but also for possession. If we give up the fight on this word, what other words, what other concepts will be taken away? University of Kentucky professor of educational and counseling psychology Judith Worell says she uses the "'F-word' as often as possible" to "tak[e] the sting out of it—like an allergist exposing his patients again and again to whatever makes them sneeze until they no longer react to it."[4]

Feminism offers an umbrella concept for various individual groups in the splintered women's movement. It is important to have ideas about gender equality associated with one concept or construct. The feminist movement has room for various stripes of feminism—difference theorists, equity theorists, and anti-essentialists (an oxymoron of an appellative), among others—and varying political agendas—pro-choice and pro-life, for example. Central to the spokes of the feminist wheel is the hub concept of a focus on gender equality. Although feminism must be linked with other theories, such as theories of rationality and critical race theory, it has an independent core. The word "feminism" serves as a useful reminder that the fight for gender equality is not just a civil rights battle or a struggle of humanism.

An important question is whether feminism, which seems to contain only a single gender—female—is too exclusive. In the perhaps not too distant future, the feminist movement may be reinvigorated by another, more inclusive-sounding term: "relational justice" perhaps, or some other term. But that move should be made consciously, collectively, cooperatively with men, and not reactively: the future of feminism should not turn on the successes of its detractors or the excesses of its advocates.

Inclusive Feminism

Feminisms

Feminism has been both reduced and, in a curious sense, promoted by its factionalism. In the tradition of "any press is good press," at least people are talking about feminism. But a competing aphorism—"this does more harm than good"—comes to mind. The sense is one of spectators at a boxing match watching feminists of various hues accuse each other of being "antifeminist" or "not feminist enough." Some have recognized that feminism could use some updating and promotional advertising—that feminism must find ways to appeal to middle America with mainstream, populist feminism, and to reach younger generations with both the messages of history and the contemporary relevance of feminism. If feminism is to retain stability and coherence, its advertising needs to steer away from labels like "power feminism" or "equity feminism" and toward cooperative, convergent dialogue.

What may be most productive is for those who use the word to reexamine its meanings. Certainly the various camps of feminism share some commonalities. Rather than warring—"who's most feminist of them all"—feminists of different interests and philosophical locations should search for areas of commonality between and among different brands of feminism, and look for central, cohesive principles.

What is at the heart of feminism? At a minimum, the core theory envisions equal rights for women and men and equal social opportunities for both sexes. Gender is paramount, but not exclusive: other features of identity, such as race, sexual orientation, and economic circumstances, also are critical. Feminism is grounded in a commitment to listening to experiences, particularly the experiences of those without power. Beyond that, feminism contemplates an acknowledgment of diverse choices and a commitment to exposing choicelessness. Perhaps, in practice, this means a recognition that all parents—whether they stay at home with children or perform a job outside the home—are working parents. Feminism demands respect for the variety of choices that both women and men make and the removal of barriers that constrain or inhibit the possible choices. Perhaps a commitment to the ideal of feminism will foster discussions, on a less emotive level, about shared principles and about differences in aims, means, and styles.

Much of the work toward convergences in feminist thinking is attitudinal. It requires, as Lea Brilmayer has suggested, a spirit of inclusivity:

Inclusive feminism requires defining the core to include more people rather than fewer. It means taking at face value, and treating in good faith, a person's claim to identify with the feminist movement. It means genuinely preferring to see others as feminist if they wish to be seen that way, and only reluctantly concluding that the definition is not broad enough to encompass their set of views. It means treating differences of opinion as being different, legitimate views about what feminism requires. It means not trying to silence others by ostracizing them or by calling them traitors or "honorary males," and it means keeping the door open to "girls" who play bridge, read *Good House-keeping,* or defend freedom of expression.[5]

A number of feminists already have adopted a methodology of inclusion toward people, groups, and ideas.[6]

It may be that some oppressed groups will have difficulty finding a home under the feminist umbrella, not because they disagree with the substance, but because they do not want to run the risk of co-optation. Richard Delgado warns that "[g]ains are ephemeral if one wins them by forming coalitions with individuals who really do not have your interest at heart. It's not just that the larger, more diverse group will forget you and your special needs. It's worse than that. You'll forget who you are. And if you don't, you may still end up demonized, blamed for sabotaging the revolution when it inevitably and ineluctably fails."[7]

Delgado may be right that smaller interest groups—ecofeminists or African American feminists or lesbian feminists—may have their interests submerged in the larger project. It is essential, though, not only for the larger group but for the smaller groups as well, to be part of a community that does not simply parrot what they think they are about. Smaller partisan groups are uniquely positioned to challenge and change larger interest groups. Feminists of various racial, religious, sexual, and political affiliations will not share a single agenda, and their prioritizations of shared goals may differ dramatically, but this should not undermine the search for the commonalities, the networking and coalition building.

This may be the largest challenge feminism faces in the future—the building of not a monolithic enterprise, but a house with many rooms. The successes of feminism over the generations—suffrage, women entering professions, the national provision of child care and leave policies—have shown the power in numbers. It may be close to a truism that social movements with more adherents generally have boasted more successes. One should of course consider the purposes of the group and the measures of success. Trappist monks may vow silence; an artist colony may wish to exclude all non-cubists. But feminist precepts urge inclusivity and connectedness: one of the purposes of the social side of feminism is communalism.

The challenge is to create commonalities while avoiding universalizing notions of feminism. Linda Lacey says succinctly, "Feminist authors should not let a healthy caution about essentialism keep us from talking about what we have in common, because it is exploration of similar experiences (and differences) that gives us a sense of identity and purpose."[8]

Drawing Men to Feminism

For some, the threat of focusing feminist attention on situations of men is more than a resource issue. The predominant concerns of feminism were to challenge the hegemonic rule of male inquiry, to carve out a space for inquiry into women's issues, problems, and concerns, and to look at the world from a female vantage point. For too long, the world has concerned itself mainly with men's needs and experiences:

> Men's physiology defines most sports, their health needs largely define insurance coverage, their socially designed biographies defined workplace expectations and successful career patterns, their perspectives and concerns define quality in scholarship, their experiences and obsessions define merit, their military service defines citizenship, their presence defines family, their inability to get along with each other—their wars and rulerships—defines history, their image defines god, and their genitals define sex.[9]

Laws were male, history was made by men, and social life constructed to suit them; women were omitted, and it is far too soon, some may argue, for a fledgling social movement to open its doors to the oppressors.

On an academic level, a question often repeated is why feminist theory needs to reach out to men. The thematic refrain across disciplines is "Why do we need to theorize about men? Legal theory, or psychology, or sociology, *is* the theory of men." But a distinction exists between maleness as "a normative referent" and masculinity as an ideological construct.[10] Traditional scholarship in the sciences, social sciences, humanities, and law has committed the androcentric fallacy, treating "generic man as the human norm," which, as Harry Brod has pointed out, "in fact systematically excludes from consideration what is unique to men *qua* men."[11] Missing from all the disciplines until recently has been inquiry into the varieties of masculinity, the concrete experiences and emotional needs of men, and the ideological construction of maleness over time and cultures.

To realize its potential, feminism cannot center on a politics of separation. The feminist movement may have difficulty acquiring converts if a central tenet of the movement includes vilifying some of the people to whom it needs to appeal. Men will never come to believe in the principles of feminism if they are the enemy or the outsider. The dialogues of the future can be carried on with an anger—"You just don't get it"—that ensures there will never be understanding, or they can be carried on with reasoned discourse that holds promise for cooperative resolution. The rhetoric of anger has outlived its usefulness. Hopefully, feminism has reached a stage where its advocates can separate strands of passion directed at ideas from anger targeted toward people.

For feminism to succeed in promoting large-scale societal change, not only must it be nonexclusionary within its ranks, but a critical mass of men must become feminists. Notions of femininity and masculinity must be redefined. One cannot simply change the way women are, one must also change men. By considering feminism as exclusively the province of women, feminism may risk losing the interest of women who intuitively feel that men should take part.

The lessons of the social movements in the past attest to the need for a broad base of support for fundamental reforms. Members of the white majority played significant parts in the successes of the civil rights movement.[12] Evidence exists that some men have played and are currently playing key roles in encouraging the breakdown of traditional gender barriers: "Struggles for women's equality in the United States have included male activists from the very start. About one-third of the signatories at the 1848 Seneca Falls Convention were men."[13] Whether for their own parenting interests or for the interests of their wives and daughters, some men in the 1990s have been instrumental in creating the possibilities for parenting leave policies at their work.[14] Changes in male consciousness have accounted for significant cultural and political shifts on gender issues.[15] History contains numerous instances of male alliances with and support of feminist causes.[16] (Others, of course, have mounted fierce opposition to the women's movement, and many others oppose feminism in their daily behaviors, expectations, and operational values, even without deliberate, expressed, or focused opposition to the movement.)[17] In many ways, society is just beginning to experience the variety of men's responses to the second wave of feminism.

Given the range and variety of men's responses to feminism, can men generally be encouraged to recognize and understand the oppression of women? Further, can large segments of the male population be drawn to the cause of feminism and see the deeper, broader, more inclusive principles it expresses? These questions go to the heart of feminism's sociopolitical struggle, since many men (and women) resist efforts to include them in the feminist enterprise. Part of the answer may lie in feminists extending an open invitation to men to participate in exploratory dialogue. Inclusion of majority group members may diffuse misconceptions and resentment, as well as help avoid political and social backlash.[18] Encouraging recognition of the ways patriarchy harms men may be another part of the answer, so that women do not exclusively appropriate the harms of a gendered universe. This approach requires that both women and men view victimization as less of a political or epistemological stance and more of an evidential one.

The broader project includes inspiring men to become feminists. This possibility is distinctly underexplored, probably because of the historical and oppositional postures of men and feminism, and because variations exist among different racial, social, economic, and political groups, as well as within individual ideological positions. Considerably more research and commentary exists on what draws women to feminism, what gender, race, and class characteristics correlate with existing feminist orientations, and what qualities of feminism repel men.[19]

In her pioneering work, *Gender Politics: From Consciousness to Mass Politics*, Ethel Klein identifies three principal "paths" to feminism: self-interest, group-consciousness, and political or ideological values. Relying on a national voter study conducted in 1972 of 2,705 men and women, Klein determined that "[m]en and women took different paths to feminism. Women developed a group consciousness while men supported feminism because of the ideological concerns and values expressed by the movement."[20]

Many men become feminists because they believe in the goals of feminism, and are persuaded by the anecdotal, narrative, and empirical evidence offered to support its propositions. Men may develop "sympathetic feminist consciousness" because of their perceptions that women do not have sufficient political capital or mobility.[21] Thus, to promote the creation of feminist consciousness or sympathy among men, feminists must be relentless in their critique of gendered situations. They must continue to unmask the gendered nature of teaching, learning, scholarship, and legal doctrine.

More recent research indicates that variables other than moral or religious factors may be more important influences than previously thought in creating support for or opposition to feminist beliefs and values. A random telephone survey of four hundred people in Muncie, Indiana ("Middle-town"), conducted by the Social Science Research Center at Ball State University, confirmed Klein's hypotheses that among women, support for feminist beliefs and values was related to personal experiences and group consciousness.[22] For men, however, stronger correlations existed between social class and ideological variables: "Financial dissatisfaction was negatively related to feminism; unlike women, it is men satisfied with their finances who support feminism."[23] To cultivate support for feminist precepts, feminists must pay greater attention to the class effects of particular policies and laws.

Feminists should also try to foster men's interest in writing about gender issues and interpreting, adopting, expanding on, and reacting to feminist ideals and methodologies.[24] Theorists in disciplines such as English, modern languages, history, and psychology have shown significantly more interest than legal theorists have in men's relations to and alliance with feminism.[25] Historian Natalie Zemon Davis maintains, "We should not be working on the subjected sex any more than a historian of class can focus exclusively on peasants. Our goal is to understand the significance of the sexes, of gender groups in the historical past."[26]

One of the more important misconceptions about feminism is the idea that most women's issues are solely about or for women. For example, viewing child care as a women's issue—while factually appropriate since women typically shoulder the major portion of child care responsibilities—has ideological ramifications. Continually categorizing child care as a women's issue reinforces the idea that society's traditional allocation of child care responsibilities to women is appropriate. This falls into the trap of taking what *is* as what must be. It is a mistake to view issues concerning wages, status positions, or employment opportunities as only issues about women, or even solely as gender issues, without attention to race, social class, and migration patterns.

As long as certain issues are seen only as women's issues, one half of the population is definitionally excluded from interest in them and participation in solving them. I spoke this year on sociolinguistics, gender, and trial tactics at a Kansas Trial Lawyer's Association conference called "Tips for Women Litigators." The audience, unsurprisingly given the exclusive invitation in the conference title, was 99 percent female. The messages of all the speakers contained sensible advice for both sexes: asset protection strategies for the initial stages of divorce cases; what constitutes powerful as opposed to powerless (filled with intensifiers, qualifiers, hesitation, and polite forms) conversational styles; and negotiation approaches that require knowing the opposition's social circumstances, such as children, recreational activities, and social habits (which sounded like a softer, gentler version of Sun Tzu's *Art of War*). The advice, though, was heard only by women and one lone man.

The philosophy and marketing of modern feminism needs to explicitly avoid being antimale, and to consciously strive toward gender inclusivity. Identifying issues as important social issues—without a gender designation—may be a good strategy. For example, calling a feminist jurisprudence course "Gender and the Law" seems more inclusive than a "Women and the Law" course. At the Association of American Law Schools annual convention of law professors in 1996, one of the workshops centered on the teaching of gender and the law. We discussed whether to approach students regarding feminist issues directly or by using more politically neutral terms like "humanism" and "equal rights." Most of the participants favored some combination of the direct and "stealth" approaches: initially discussing ideals for the treatment of people in terms of equality and rights, discussing the history of feminist thought and resistance to the term, and ultimately defining feminism in ways that make clear that it encompasses egalitarian ideals.

One issue in the debate about men as feminists is why many men would voluntarily give up positions of dominance and privilege to endorse rights for women. Implicit in the question is an assumption that patriarchy hinges on the present motivations of men, which are viewed by some, at the extreme, as a conspiratorial intent to stay in power. Neil Thompson emphasizes that sexism is not simply an issue of the "intentionality of social actors," but a much more complex matrix of social conventions, patterns, and rigid expectations of men that perpetuates daily actions that reinforce patriarchy.[27]

We need to explore the ways social and legal constructs define masculinity. Encouraging the recognition that gender role stereotypes harm both genders should not feed backlash. Instead, men may be more likely to become feminists if they identify with an oppressed group. Paul Lichterman describes the results of his research into why men joined one antisexist men's organization, Men Overcoming Violence ("MOVE"): "The men at MOVE want to fight male battery as a concomitant of what they consider a patriarchal society. At the same time, they want MOVE activities to focus on their personal feelings as men."[28] As the struggles of early feminists attest, the development of a political commitment to issues of gender justice is directly tied to the development of personal consciousness.

These explorations will need to move beyond ideas of "victim" and "wrongdoer," while still considering past injustices. In so doing, they must examine the larger ideological issues, such as which social and legal arrangements most fairly and effectively promote child rearing.[29] The concerns of feminism for so many years have centered on promoting women's participation in social and political processes. Now women and men must work together to transform social institutions and encourage men to more fully participate in social spheres reserved exclusively for women.

Media Spin Control

One task of inclusive feminism is to get a moderate message across to the general populace. Many feminist issues that do attract media attention are played out in incendiary, confrontational settings. The battles are seen as simple, binary confrontations, often with men and women positioned as warring opposites: Anita Hill v. Clarence Thomas, Mike Tyson v. Desiree Washington, Patricia Bowman v. William Kennedy Smith, John Bobbitt v. Lorena Bobbitt.

These encounters deal with some of the most volatile issues of our time: rape, sexual harassment, physical assault, social positions, and power. Unfortunately, the questions asked by commentators are often the most simplistic ones—looking for single causes; bemoaning the treatment of a victim (assuming, of course, that there can be only one); and replaying the arguments of the participants, each claiming the moral high ground on the issue of being wronged. When the media have centered attention on these celebrated cases they have spawned a vocabulary that packages complex ideas in reductionistic and inaccurate sound bites, like "date rape."

Perhaps it is unrealistic to expect more of the immediate news vehicles than the McNews format and pink v. blue coverage. Maybe one can hope for more thoughtful commentary from weekly or monthly journalists. Then again, those expectations may be disappointed. In May 1997, cover stories in both *Newsweek* ("The Myth of Quality Time: How We're Cheating Our Kids, What You Can Do") and *U.S. News and World Report* ("The Lies Parents Tell about Work, Kids, Money, Day Care and Ambition") proclaimed that parents (translation: mothers) dump their children in less than adequate day care arrangements so that they can enjoy work.[30]

The *U.S. News* piece begins with a story of a mom dropping her daughter off at day care, and crying "the whole way" as she drove to work. The article then discusses some statistics from sociologist Arlie Hochschild's recent book, *The Time Bind: When Work Becomes Home and Home Becomes Work,* showing that many parents seek refuge from the irrationality and unpredictability of children's demands by going to work—at least in the one Fortune 500 company that Hochschild studied. (Would a waitress or a file clerk in a small office have the same "reward" structure or work environment?) The article declares it a fabrication that both parents must work because the family needs the money for necessities or taxes, a lie that "day care is perfectly good," and an utter falsehood that fathers would stay home with their kids if they could.

The article is part of a larger newsfest tossing shame and guilt at working mothers, and it is a prime example of the reductionistic approach to news: simplistically presenting child care and work dilemmas as matters of individual choice. While the text of the article attempts to use the gender-neutral language of "parents," the structure of the article, information sources (e.g., questions to an Internet bulletin board called "Women's Wire"), quotes, stories from stay-at-home moms, and citation to poll results demonstrating a "widespread belief that the ideal way to raise kids is with a parent, preferably Mom, at home" all indicate the implicit conclusion: the solution is for dual-earner couples to reevaluate their priorities and cut costs so that Mom can stay home with the kids (because, remember lie number 4, Dad will not gladly stay home with the kids).

In the article's defense, it talks about the traditional construct of masculinity according to which most men feel they must be the family's breadwinner, and the subtle ways women can undermine men's assumption of domestic roles. But so many considerations are not in the picture: omitted are single-parent families, the working poor, and the role of institutions. Why not continue to question inflexible institutional structures that contribute to the work-family dilemma? While companies may make parent-friendly programs available in theory, workers who use them are penalized in pay raises and performance reviews. What about questioning basic political assumptions? Unlike in, say, Sweden, where the state often is the provider of child care, we in the United States assume that child care is a matter of individual rather than collective responsibility. Even if one buys the premise that perhaps one of the primary parents should stay at home, why mothers, or why not both parents alternatively or sequentially? If we continually accept the "givens" (most dads don't want to stay home with the kids; most poll respondents think moms should stay home with kids), we will wind up with an unthinking return to traditional roles, with little consideration for all the participants.

Again, perhaps it is unfair to criticize weekly journalism for being weekly journalism. But as the media move toward use of sociological evidence, the interpretation of it needs more analytical depth. Perhaps this journalistic style is representative of a society in fairly rapid transition, becoming conscious of its ambiguous self. The sadness is that it offers very little thinking outside the existing boxes of institutional and domestic roles.

The onus, though, is not just on the media, but also on feminists writing about these issues not to indulge in binary thinking. As people take emotively laden positions on a specific issue, the potential for explorative reflection and dialogue often is ignored. Some of the lessons coming from these cases were overlooked, while other aspects of the cases were overexploited. Making Lorena Bobbitt into a folk heroine is just one example of indulgence in hostilities that sends a misguided message. On the other hand, a good example of the educative use of high-visibility cases comes from the Clarence Thomas confirmation hearings.

Despite the notoriety of the participants, the Thomas hearings represented a fairly typical example of sexual harassment allegations writ large, and the media airplay given to the case was really the first time the American people received an education on sexual harassment law. The backdrop and some of the side dramas of the confirmation hearings, though, were immensely significant for feminists. Viewers saw Senator Arlen Specter browbeat and twist the words of the sexual harassment complainant, law professor Anita Hill. Outside of viewing range, and only later revealed, was the Senate Judiciary Committee's failure to call several witnesses who would have corroborated Hill's testimony about Thomas's sexually inappropriate behavior, a technique of silencing that spoke volumes.[31] When the people of the country watched the all-male Senate Judiciary Committee hearings and saw Nancy Landon Kassebaum, half of the women in the Senate at the time, vote in favor of Thomas (a vote she later regretted), they recognized the political vulnerability of women without adequate representation.

Similar gendered (and classist) patterns occurred in other cases garnering media attention. In the William Kennedy Smith rape trial, the nation watched money buy innocence. Alan Dershowitz's defense of Mike Tyson was, in some respects, high-profile theater. These cases sparked the beginning of a national dialogue about appropriate sexual behavior, and the heavy dose of media attention to the issues surrounding rape, sexual harassment, and domestic violence gave exposure to previously hidden injuries. Their aftermath saw a soaring number of lawsuits charging sexual harassment, the adoption of sexual harassment policies in workplaces across the country, heightened sensitivity on the part of men about how their actions in the workplace were received, and a voter uprising that elected 200 percent more women to the Senate (up to a whopping six).

During the Thomas confirmation hearings, some writers drew attention to these less visible institutional structures: the dearth of women in positions of political power, the absence of company policies to forestall sexual harassment, and the importance of speaking out even if one is not immediately believed. They stepped back to get a broader, more comprehensive view of the situation, rather than lapsing into simple partisanship in a dichotomous confrontation. This sort of rhetoric adjustment and contextual (rather than advocacy) focus is not divorced from combating the immediate harms of a situation, but it brings forward the parts of gendered realities that become lost in the drama of battle.

Remaking Legal Images

In many ways, current legal doctrines foster a separatist ideology. They reflect and reinforce the sharp separation of the genders and promote a construct of masculinity that does not admit of feminine qualities, characteristics, or roles. Laws and legal doctrines contain implicit assumptions about masculinity. To the extent that legal precedents shape gender differences, the message is inescapably clear: real men embody power; they are society's breadwinners, criminals, and warriors; and they feel no pain. The legal system reinforces these social images and their psychological attendants of stoicism and emotional isolation, and these legal messages sift into the public consciousness.

One can tell a great deal about a society by examining who populates that society's criminal and warrior classes. This country protects women from aggression and places men in roles that demand it. Until the 1996 Supreme Court decision in *United States v. Virginia*, educational institutions segregated males and females solely on the basis of sex. Other decisions, such as those concerning criminal sentences, same-sex sexual harassment, and child custody, rigidify gender roles.[32] In these cases courts are making choices, and they are repeatedly choosing to view certain biological differences between men and women as having social significance.

Courts should be taken to task for showing their receptiveness to constructs of biological gender and their cowardice in not taking a stand on the institutional construction of gender. They should be encouraged to look at both the biological and the social evidence constructing gender, rather than the first principle of looking only for real (i.e., biological) differences. These legal doctrines form pieces of the American cultural mosaic, and they must change to allow realistic social transformations. Relegating women to domestic roles, reserving militaristic roles for men, and punishing any attempts to cross traditional gender boundary lines are interrelated phenomena that offer an impoverished view of both women and men.

One way attorneys can prompt courts to consider the social composition of gender and the lived experiences of individuals is through the use of narratives. As just one example of the point, consider the amicus curiae ("friend of the court") briefing technique used by the National Abortion Rights Action League (NARAL) and the NOW Legal Defense and Education Fund. NARAL and NOW developed a litigation strategy of presenting the U.S. Supreme Court with amicus briefs in abortion cases that contain stories of women's experiences with both legal and illegal abortions.[33] Known as "the Voices Briefs," these first-person accounts of reasons for having an abortion are intended to convey to seven older men and two older women—none of whom presumably has ever had an abortion—what the abstract right of reproductive choice means on an experiential level. The strategy was intended to focus the Court's attention not on the theoretical or moral justifications for or against abortion regulations, but on the experiences of those most affected by them: to make law respond to women's interests and reflect their concrete, lived experiences.[34]

The feminist technique of using personal experiences as political tools could open courts to alternate visions of gender roles for both women and men. Where are the stories of men who have fought for child custody (out of a true desire to be the primary parent) and lost, or who were dissuaded from ever fighting that battle? Where are the stories of men who confronted considerable obstacles in becoming flight attendants, primary school teachers, or nurses, or breaking into sporting events like synchronized swimming? As Robin West has noted, "Principles and reason do not make the case . . . moral convictions are changed experientially or empathically, not through argument."[35]

Change will come as women enter previously male-dominated occupations, as women redefine the gender of combatants in the military, as child-rearing practices change, and as women and men create new social relationships. Law can lead or lag behind social transitions: *Brown v. Board of Education* is a good example of the former; many of the gender cases exemplify the latter. The argument that courts should consider the ways law reflects stereotypic views of masculinity does not push law ahead of the curve or even in directions it will not already be going; it just urges speeding up the evolution. With courts articulating the theory of equality in the abstract (but not applying it to the gendering of men), we have enough indicators that law is ready to become more cognizant of various incarnations of gender stereotyping.

Legal Ideology and the Zero-Sum Game

Schools across the country watched the class action lawsuit brought against Brown University by thirteen female student athletes, fearing that providing women's sports opportunities would dismantle their profitable and much-viewed basketball and football programs. The case originated when Brown, faced with financial strains, demoted four varsity sports—women's gymnastics and volleyball and men's water polo and golf—from university-funded to donor-funded status.

The defense of the suit against Brown is full of ironies, adversarialness, and arrogance. A school with a politically liberal climate, an innovative and flexible curriculum, and a student body comprising almost one-third minorities, Brown was the first school to institute a women's hockey program.[36] It also funded sixteen other women's sports (twice the national average), and, relative to other colleges and universities, did not invest enormous resources in men's football or basketball programs—making it one of the most egalitarian university sports programs in the nation. In response to a demand letter, Brown's president, the well-respected, politically liberal Vartan Gregorian, "was furious that anyone would tell him how to run the university."[37]

In 1994 the parties were able to agree to a partial settlement of the issues regarding provision of equipment, facilities, and practice schedules, but remained at loggerheads regarding participation opportunities for female athletes. Fifty-one percent of the student body was female, but only 38 percent of its athletes were female. In a 1995 opinion the federal district judge found that this disparity between females enrolled at Brown and females participating in athletics at Brown violated Title IX.[38] The district court also found that although the school had "an impressive history of program expansion," Brown had not added a women's varsity sport to its roster since 1982, and thus had no continuing practice of program expansion. Finally, the district court rejected Brown's argument that since it was not accommodating the interests of its male athletes, it was not compelled to meet the needs of its female athletes. The court determined that Brown did not effectively accommodate the interests of female athletes in gymnastics, water polo, skiing, and fencing, since its funding level "prevented each of these teams from reaching its athletic potential."

The trial court left it to the university to devise a plan to comply with Title IX; solutions could range from adding positions to women's sports, to cutting positions from men's sports, to eliminating athletics completely. Witnesses for Brown had testified that cutting or capping the size of men's teams was the only way it could comply. On the other hand, one of the plaintiffs' witnesses, Donna Lopiano, executive director of the Women's Sports Foundation, testified to the "false dichotomy posed" by the idea that adding to women's sports necessarily means cutting sports for men: "[I]t's unfortunate that across the country that in the name of maintaining the standard of living of football team[s] or the standard of living of one or two special men's sports, that men's sports are being cut and women's gender equity under Title IX [is] being blamed for that." The appellate court affirmed the district court's findings that Brown University violated Title IX, and allowed Brown to submit a proposed compliance plan; the Supreme Court denied certiorari on the case.[39] This ruling leaves intact the trial court's holding that the athletic participation ratio must be substantially proportional to the percentage of women students enrolled at Brown, and signifies a rejection of Brown's argument that it should fund sports programs in proportion to the numbers of women "interested" in them.

Brown probably needed to be take-no-prisoners litigation. Title IX has been on the books for a quarter of a century, and women's opportunities for participation in collegiate athletics are still woefully inadequate. Many schools have exhibited patterns of foot-dragging and resistance to the mandates of Title IX. Less than one in ten Division I schools (28 out of 303) are even close to compliance with the proportionality guideline.[40] Across the country, women's sports programs receive 23 percent of operating revenues, while men's programs command three times that share. One week after the Supreme Court's denial of certiorari in *Brown*, the National Collegiate Athletic Association released the results of its five-year Gender Equity Survey. The study indicated that women's sports are a decade or more away from equality in operating expenditures, coaches' salaries, recruiting budgets, athletic scholarship money, and participation rates.[41] The athletic universe needed a watershed event.

But we're watching a zero-sum game of the girls against the boys. The same paradigm we saw played out in the employment context is being reenacted in other realms. It took some time to get folks worked up about sports, but once the inequities were noticed, the institutional resistance forced the use of the same 1970s equal treatment game plan and language: how many sports programs are for men and how many are for women? The recognition of gender disparity became the central battle: boys on one side, girls on the other, competing for scarce resources. Some of this was necessary, since a large part of the disparity observed by the NCAA was caused by a huge funneling of money to men's sports: operating expenses for women's sports grew by 89 percent between 1992 and 1996, while operating expenses for men's sports swelled by 139 percent; at the same time, participation in women's sports increased by 6 percent, and fell by 10 percent in men's sports.

Why have we accepted the notion of finite resources? Administrators have chosen to ax men's sports rather than increase overall funding for sports programs. Do we need to tear down men's sports to build up women's? As Donna Lopiano capsulizes, "I think it's unconscionable to cut men's programs. It's just against all principles of correcting discrimination. The last choice should be cutting opportunities for men."[42] And why are the teams sex-segregated for training purposes in the first place? What could Brown have done in terms of sports funding with the more than $1 million it chose to expend on its own attorney and expert witness fees (to say nothing of the estimated $1 million more it will have to pay for the plaintiffs' legal costs)?

Examples of prominent college and university sports programs across the country demonstrate that Title IX compliance specifically—and gender equity negotiation generally—need not be a win-lose game. For instance, when the University of Kansas faced a Title IX complaint in 1992, it reached a settlement with the Office of Civil Rights in which it agreed to provide more sports and scholarships for women student-athletes, without diminishing its football program or its nationally acclaimed men's basketball program.[43] Today, Kansas's ratio of women student-athletes (48 percent) almost mirrors that of its student body (50 percent).

Similarly, the University of Pennsylvania recently negotiated a settlement to a suit filed by women athletes and their coaches, complaining about the allocation of $1.2 million for men's sports and $80,000 for women's sports. Although details are confidential, the school used money that otherwise would have gone to attorneys' fees to enhance its women's athletics program. Under the settlement, the university will upgrade the women's locker room, provide equal resources for training and game trips, purchase more weight-training equipment for both women and men, renovate the boathouse, hire additional coaching staff, and convert some women's part-time coaching positions to full-time. No money will come from men's programs, and the school will conduct an athletics fund-raising drive. The university, which was not required to admit to a Title IX violation, will also construct a gender equity committee that will report to Penn's athletic director. Penn offers an example of a school's decision to negotiate a favorable outcome that invests in both male and female athletes, and one that makes the school look good in the process.

Unless we radically revisit concepts of gendering and abandon strategies that necessarily create winners and losers, we will be left with cases like *United States v. Virginia* and *Brown*. And this will mean intransigence and foot-dragging on the part of sex-segregated institutions, legal action to compel minimal concepts of equal treatment, and ultimately an uneasy truce at the gender line, with some border skirmishes, and the boundary between the sexes firmly ensconced.

Affirmative Action

In a book that takes the strong stance of an egalitarian approach to gender roles, it may seem surprising to find an endorsement of affirmative action in the employment arena. But to the extent that affirmative action is about realizing possibilities and choices, and because under-opportunitied groups may require generations to catch up, we still need to take steps to create those possibilities and choices for adults. That entails context-specific preferences for both women and men in occupations traditionally foreclosed to them. This may necessitate, for example, affirmative hiring preferences for males as nurses, caregivers, or elementary school teachers.

While the continuation of affirmative action for adults is still a necessity, this approach, when used as pedagogy, is generally the wrong one for children's programs. If we adopt the same affirmative action model for the education of children, we may be limiting their choices and options.

To suggest that the distinction is chronological may seem simplistic, but children and adults are not similarly situated with respect to volition or life options. Most adults already have been trained to conceive of differences, gender and otherwise, in hierarchical terms—to perceive male as normal in the workplace, and female as inferior. Most children are still under construction.

My suggestions are more complicated than simply endorsing affirmative action for adults and not for children. Consider the reasons behind affirmative action programs generally. One assumption is that without special efforts, discrimination will occur, so affirmative action is a way of combating hidden, direct discrimination. Another ground for affirmative action is remedial: to compensate for past inequities and provide opportunities for minorities either through role-modeling or teaching. If gender acculturation begins at birth, we still may need affirmative action plans for children in some contexts.

A need may exist to actively encourage children toward nontraditional gender roles to make up for diminished opportunities already affecting them. Many, if not most, second-grade girls, for example, are probably already disadvantaged in their abilities to become engineers because they have been taught to play with dolls instead of blocks. Most boys in the same age group probably have relatively diminished abilities to become good child care givers because they have been subtly channeled away from that role playing. If one aim is to equalize opportunities and possibilities, then perhaps modest "affirmative action" measures will need to occur even in the elementary and secondary grades: consciously hiring boy baby-sitters, urging girls toward blocks and trains and tools, staving off learned helplessness by giving boys more kitchen tasks, and consciously including girls in neighborhood basketball games and boys in dress-up play.

Regarding the education of children, though, the affirmative action model may send some counterproductive messages. As an example, consider this. In 1992 the Ms. Foundation for Women launched Take Our Daughters to Work Day, a campaign encouraging parents to bring their nine- to sixteen-year-old girls to the workplace to develop the girls' self-esteem and promote role modeling. In the days prior to the 1997 day, a battle raged over the symbolic significance of the day: girls needed their own day of introduction to corporate America, claimed the Ms. Foundation. Critics chided that the exclusive emphasis on girls punitively excluded boys.

There were several sources of inspiration for the Daughters' Day. One was a 1977 book by Margaret Henning and Anne Jardim entitled *The Managerial Woman*, which reported that women who became successful corporate executives all recounted the childhood experience of frequently accompanying their fathers to work. Another study by the American Association of University Women showed that young girls lose self-esteem during adolescence and, as a result, their schoolwork suffers. The Ms. Foundation also cites an American Medical Association report stating that adolescent girls are five times more likely than boys to attempt suicide.

In 1995 an estimated twenty-five million adults and girls in eleven countries participated in the day. According to the Ms. Foundation, almost half of the population in the United States has heard about the day, and nine out of ten Americans view it positively.

The critics, though, have come from every corner. In Little Rock, Arkansas, a religious group called FamilyLife sponsored a "Take Your Daughter Home Day" to encourage mothers "to have the courage to bring their girls home and teach them to be a homemaker."[44] On the other end of the political spectrum, self-described "equity feminist" Christina Hoff Sommers has censured Daughters' Day as based on an "anti-male philosophy."[45] She is quick to criticize as punitive the guided imagery exercises that the Ms. Foundation offers for boys who remain in the classroom while girls embark on a "gender-divisive holiday." Boys are urged to imagine living inside a box and are asked questions about the social constraints represented by the box: "What do people say to girls to keep them in a box? What happens to girls who step outside the box? How do some of these assumptions of what it means to be 'manly' box you in and limit your choices?"

Many critics have pointed out that the research cited by the Ms. Foundation as the basis for its Daughters' Day program is incomplete. They note that the American Medical Association report is quoted selectively. It does state that the adolescent girl attempted suicide rate is five times that of adolescent boys, but goes on to state that "adolescent boys are 4 times more likely actually to commit suicide." Other evidence cited to rebut the premise that girls need their own day is the higher school dropout rate among boys and the larger percentage of girls who graduate and attend college.

In response to the suggestion that Daughters' Day be modified to Take a Child to Work Day, the Ms. Foundation and some other commentators strongly oppose the inclusion of boys. The foundation cites some anecdotal evidence that at companies that included boys, the boys dominated the day by grabbing the chairs or monopolizing the conversation.

Some of the participants on both sides in the debate over Daughters' Day are misguided in tone, tenor, and focus. Those who argue for inclusion of boys are relying on a threat of backlash to impel action: won't the boys be resentful if the girls go off to play? Those who argue for the exclusive attendance for girls are thinking of the day as pure affirmative action. We cannot afford to let the value of this day go unnoticed, but we need to go beyond symbols, beyond days, and beyond affirmative action. While affirmative action is vitally necessary when barriers to participation exist, it is a beginning, not an end in itself. The goal is certainly not to see if we can get the suicide statistics of boys and girls to match up. Nor should it be to contest whether boys or girls are hurt worse by social conditioning. The ultimate objective should be to acknowledge and understand culturally constructed patterns of gender differences in order to move beyond them.

Daughters' Day should become Take a Child to Work Day. The day should be viewed as a broader part of a cultural education package, in which both sexes obtain exposure to their possibilities in the working world, and see women in positions of power and responsibility. Approximately one-third of participating companies have opened the day to boys as well as girls.

The sociological data on which both sides rely in their attempts either to preserve the day for girls only or to argue for the inclusion of boys paint a larger, intricately interwoven picture of gendering in childhood: both boys and girls are disenfranchised. Girls learn cultural submission while boys learn cultural domination and emotional stoicism. If we can better educate our children to recognize stereotypic patterns of gendered behavior, there will be less need for programs based on the pure affirmative action model.

Ah, but what should happen if boys dominate the day at the office—take the chairs, ask all the questions, control the conversation? If in some offices boys (or girls) tend to dominate the discussion or edge girls (or boys) out of a hands-on experience, those behaviors should be pointed out, not as opportunities for blame, but as evidential facts about gendering or as matters of courtesy.

Some have suggested a Daughters' Day and a separate Sons' Day for boys. Corporate America seems reluctant to devote its resources to two days of children at work. Moreover, the separatism implies that boys and girls cannot learn together. Boys and girls need to understand that they can engage in the learning experience about employment responsibilities alongside one another. The workforce of the future, presumably, will include roughly equal proportions of women and men, in positions of comparable responsibility and power. Separatism as a teaching tool seems at odds with the premise that sex segregation in the workforce is wrong.

One day at work—one day of anything—will not solve the problem of teen suicide or elevate self-esteem. This day, however it is ultimately constituted (Daughters' Day, Sons' Day, Gender Day, Children's Day, Role Reversal Day), is a symbolic beginning and an opportunity to focus on gender.

Unfortunately, the day is being seen and fought over as if its structure is *the* symbol of gender relations.

The day must be accompanied by 364 others each year in which society pays attention to the silent language of gender and the ways stereotypes affect the behavior of children. The gender messages in our culture are so much a part of everyday life that they become the ever-present, never-challenged backdrop: What second-grade class has not divided into "the boys against the girls" for purposes of a game? What parent or child has not noticed the boys' and girls' toys in McDonald's Happy Meals, the boys' and girls' toy aisles at Toys 'R Us, or the construction of gender-specific clothing, advertisements, room decorations, and teacher expectations?

Daughters' Day was an excellent beginning in a massive and hopeful cultural experiment toward education about gendering and gender equity. It reflects the process of educating a populace about appropriate workplace and home roles for girls and for boys. It requires recognition, on a national scale, of sociological evidence that speaks volumes about gendering. And it demands taking cooperative institutional responsibility—through schools, media, and corporations—for gender. As with any good social experiment, the purposes behind Daughters' Day should come under reexamination and its methods should be open to change and betterment.

Creating a society that teaches its children to recognize gender inequity will require many lessons of varied kinds for both genders. The visualization exercises suggested by the Ms. Foundation are fine. But both boys and girls together should learn to see the boxes and to see outside them.

Reconstructing Gender

The social origins of sex differences may be underattended. The orchestrated and consistent everyday patterns, habits, and social conventions—morning to night, inside the family and out, in sports, books, television, the workplace, and even in language—relentlessly reconstruct traditional gender roles and expectations. Gender roles and the process of gendering are not immutable or unchangeable: gender roles in modern America have changed markedly in the past quarter century alone. It is undisputable that gender is, in large part, taught. To the extent we are intentionally constructing gender, we can change its shape; to the extent that the construction is less than conscious, the challenge is to make the constructive processes visible.

The Process of Differencing

The sameness-difference model is perplexing, for biologists, psychologists, sociologists, and jurisprudential thinkers. Part of the dilemma seems to be rooted in the idea of what difference means. One notion that seems to be fostered by sex differences research is the idea that difference *itself* can be immutable as opposed to culturally constructed. Differences are not qualities that people or groups possess.[46] No ultimate measure exists of similarities or of differences. When we discriminate among similarities and differences, it is always in terms of certain purposes, norms, and background habits of discrimination. We must continually attend to our purposes for discriminating differences. Indeed, the fact of difference is relatively uninteresting and unimportant until people attach some significance to the difference—and that is a cultural move.

Whether gender differences are natural attributes or social constructs, we must still make cultural choices about what labels we attach to what we identify as gender differences. So, in some contexts, gender matters because of the history we have constructed around it. But that is very different from saying that natural abilities or inclinations based on gender exist and matter in all contexts. It is easy to lose sight of the idea that the differences we chose to say are meaningful in some contexts do not have to be meaningful in other contexts. As Justice Thurgood Marshall observed, sex-segregated bathrooms may not be troublesome: "A sign that says 'men only' looks very different on a bathroom door than a courthouse door."[47]

Thus, to the extent that biologically rooted gender differences exist, of what significance are they? Even if the functional organization of male and female brains differs for various tasks, of what social significance are the differences? What matters most significantly is what difference researchers, theoreticians, the media, and parents make of the differences. If people are willing to believe that biology is destiny—or even the more modest version that gender differences are rooted in biological causes—they may feel it is futile to try to upset settled social arrangements. If gender is seen in this light, any social changes that would upset this perceived natural order are wrong.

These questions are not intended to suggest that biological differences should be denied or remain unexplored; instead, they recognize that in some ways, it may be less productive to take a fixed position on the strands of influence between nature and nurture. Much more fruitful is to inquire how to proceed regarding gender in the face of uncertainty about its origins.

How should we act, socially and legally, if we cannot determine at this juncture in history whether sex differences are more influenced by biology or culture? This same focus on genetic determinants is seen in the battles over whether genes may predispose people toward alcoholism or homosexuality. As a practical matter, one still needs to deal every day with taking a drink or living out gender stereotypes.

Hazards of Dismantling the Gender Line

Gender Identity Disorder

If we do away with gender default rules based on sex, and people no longer have the security of sex stereotypes, how will they know what to do? I gave a talk on the topic of feminism for men at the Central States Association of Law Professors annual meeting. A man who has practiced as both a psychiatrist and a lawyer came up to me afterward and said his concerns were about gender identity disorder. "These are the people," he said, "who wind up on my couch."

The traditional model of identity theory in psychology maintained that individuals would not mature with proper gender identity unless they "manifested . . . sex-appropriate traits, attitudes, and interests that psychologically 'validate' or 'affirm' their biological sex."[48] In 1973, when the American Psychiatric Association reclassified homosexuality, no longer describing it as a pathological disease, the association shifted its focus from "curing" adults of homosexuality to "preventing" children from becoming homosexual. Thus, in the 1980 edition of its *Diagnostic and Statistical Manual (DSM-III)*, the APA created the category of "gender identity disorder," characterized by "a strong and persistent cross-gender identification" and "a persistent discomfort about one's assigned sex or a sense of inappropriateness in the gender role of that sex."[49] Numerous commentators have appropriately critiqued this pathologization of gender nonconformity,[50] but the question remains: if the standard trappings of gender roles become less traditionally masculine and feminine or even less defined, will boys and girls become confused about their sex or their sexuality?

Most modern theorists question the conventional paradigm, principally by showing a distinction between gender roles and gender identity. Studies show that once people establish awareness of their gender identity—male or female—"variations in gender role do not cause psychological problems."[51] One key aspect of gender identity is gender constancy, the recognition that one is permanently a boy or a girl. Researchers are consistent in their findings that gender constancy "is remarkably independent of other components of gender-related behaviors.... Gender constancy is unrelated to sex-typed toy choice, to the imitation of same gender models, to the correct attributions of stereotypes to male and female figures, to measures of gender schematic processing, to attitudes toward boys and girls, and to gender discrimination in reward allocation."[52] In short, the consensus is that males and females will not have difficulties identifying their gender, nor will their sexual orientation be affected by changes in the contours of gender roles and ideals.

The Specter of a Unisex Universe

The suggestion that we make it easier to cross gender lines into nontraditional domestic and occupational roles raises fears of an androgynous world: qualms about unisex bathrooms and unidimensional humans. This provokes a couple of questions. Is dismantling of gender lines necessarily a call for an androgynous society? And why do people fear androgyny?

To answer the latter question first, fear of androgyny may be, in large part, an investment in traditional roles. Some qualms about androgyny certainly shade into concerns about sexual preferences. The more benign explanation is that people recognize diversity as a good—even if much of that diversity is culturally, rather than naturally, defined. People like living in a world with feminine and masculine cultures; they distrust melting pot concepts; and they worry about watering down distinctiveness, whether racial, ethnic, or gender.

The plea for "diversity," though, is somewhat curious in this context, since what is usually sought are the traditional gender differences: we want people to be different on the axis of masculinity and femininity. I presented these ideas on a radio call-in show. One of the callers was the father of a six-year-old girl, who liked his daughter's feminine qualities: her sweetness, cuddliness, and nurturing behavior. They sounded like terrific qualities for any six-year-old, male or female.

The alternative is to retain masculine and feminine qualities, but not to attach either to a particular sex. We have tacitly accepted for so many generations that gender differences are the ones that matter. Why not emphasize other forms of diversity between people: on the scales of creativity, endurance, linguistic abilities, recreational interests, or empathetic qualities? Rather than engage in labeling qualities feminine or masculine, what we really must confront is the choice of qualities and skills we as a culture value most. Three-quarters of a century ago, John Dewey urged this move away from a retrospective search for essences, necessaries, and givens, and a move forward toward desirables. We can emphasize the human qualities we want all people to have, such as confidence, independence and interdependence, nurturing behavior, risk taking, competition, cooperation, independence, and caring, without giving them a gender.

Maybe competition can be directed toward feminist ends? One of my colleagues is an ardent feminist and probably also the best cook on the faculty, although he was raised in a very traditional southern home as a minister's son. I asked him how he started cooking. He laughed and said it began as a competition: he and his male college roommate had cook-offs, trying to best each other in the kitchen with more innovative recipes, obscure ingredients, and elaborate sauces. (The 1996 Pillsbury Bake-off winner was, for the first time in the thirty-seven-year history of the competition, a male.)

Some cultural gender associations already are becoming less strong over time. The androgyny chic of popular culture figures in the 1980s and early 1990s (Michael Jackson, Sinead O'Connor, Annie Lennox, David Bowie, Boy George, k. d. lang, Dennis Rodman, and Grace Jones) gave way in the late 1990s to unisex cosmetics, fragrances, clothing, and haircuts. Some of this seems to be more than a transitory fashion stage. It is increasingly more acceptable for men to wear longer hair, ponytails, and body jewelry, for women to wear jeans or pants in the workplace. The 1980s fad of men carrying purses has yielded to both sexes wearing nylon fanny packs to carry their ID, money, and keys. Some college campuses have unisex bathrooms and coed dorm floors. Many of these fashion and lifestyle changes are for utilitarian reasons of comfort, function, or efficiency. Androgyny no longer carries the shock value it once did: we express less horror, and perhaps more amusement (remember Pat, "just Pat," from *Saturday Night Live*?), if we can't figure out if someone is male or female.

Some of the suggestions may not require challenging the differences themselves, but reconstructing the significance we attach to those differences. I do not want to deny the fact or the possibility of differences, providing that everyone can participate in the construction of those differences, and assuming that those differences do not automatically get translated into better and worse in hierarchical terms. But not all people currently participate in the construction of differences or in saying whether they matter.

Of course, we may lose something positive, or at least interesting, as gender redefinition occurs. We may see increasingly fewer generalized sex differences in clothing, hairstyles, language, or tasks. Particularly those who are secure in old traditions may have something to lose—which is true of all transitions. But that looks only at the debit side of the equation. If we move toward egalitarian gender relations, we are going to gain something that is much more valuable than what we lose: we increase the range of choices for both sexes. We might lose frilly pink dresses, the men who open doors for women, the mom who can bake ten kinds of pies from memory. We might replace those losses with expectations that all people, males and females, act protectively of their communities, nurture their families, care for their elderly parents, and participate in the nation's political life.

Making Gender Visible

Gendering persists because it is relentless, pervasively reinforced, and almost invisible. We are bombarded by its images, so much so that the cultural decisions to invest situations with gender become background noise. One of the ways to de-gender is to make gender visible. In my Gender and Justice course, I try to do this through two exercises. The first is to let the students collectively teach one class session on gender and popular culture. The students bring in anything from the popular media that sends a gendered message, a message about the appropriateness or inappropriateness of particular behaviors for women or men, or positive images and icons that suggest a movement away from gender stereotypes.

The students bring in toy catalogs, the Sears wish book, pink computer software. They tape sitcoms, cartoon squibs, and commercials. Barbie, Pocahontas, and Jessica Rabbit (begging people to save Roger and blowing kisses) have all made appearances. Fashion images are popular. Women's magazines. Advertisements depicting the ideal woman: anorexic, coifed, and wearing knock-me-down-and-fuck-me pumps. The absence of men in caretaking roles in advertisements. Together we ponder the Diet Coke break commercial, during which women office workers gather each day to watch a male construction worker strip off his shirt and down a Diet Coke. Is this egalitarian and empowering—equal opportunity ogling—or is the metamessage about how men and women should relate to each other—as sexually charged subjects and objects—damaging? We talk about "chick flicks," Madonna, Mortal Kombat, and the comic strip Cathy.

The second exercise for Gender and Justice is a two-page paper, due anytime during the semester, about any cultural event the students have attended having to do with gender. The purpose is to make visible the gendering in the everyday events of life. The students write about events such as a domestic violence awareness rally, a panel discussion on attitudes about sexuality, the dearth of women candidates at a political fundraiser and the differing uses of male and female campaign workers. One of my students, Ann Tran, described the gendering in the ordinary event of Christmas shopping:

> In a hopeful attempt to beat the mad dash of holiday shoppers in December, I embarked on my toy shopping expedition early Sunday morning. Unconsciously, I headed straight for the "Barbie" aisle to purchase the respective dolls that my 5 and 3 year old cousins had cited on their wish lists. As I [navigated] the aisle marveling at the vast number of permutations Mattel had generated off the blonde anorexic doll, I nearly fell over a young girl crying on the floor in the middle of the aisle. Just as I noticed her, her mother approached from the opposite end holding the hand of a little boy, and with an exasperated sigh took the "Barbie doing laundry" set off the shelf and put it into her cart. Just as she had finished doing so, she turned to find the little boy who, following his sister's footsteps, had grabbed a "Barbie having tea" set and brought it to his mother for her approval. With a horrified glare, his mother quickly snatched the set from him and returned it to the shelf, reprimanding him for requesting a "girl's toy." "We will pick you out a nice Tonka truck right now," she consoled him. . . . Determined not to perpetuate a cyclical problem, and realizing they would have enough sexual influences later in their lives, I opted to get my cousins some Nerf sports equipment in lieu of the stereotypical girls' toys. As I brought them to the register, the cashier smiled and conversationally remarked, "Oh, your little boys will love these; mine do." I only smiled and mused on how many more generations of Barbies would be grocery shopping, cooking, and doing laundry.

The visibility exercise is not just a matter of law school classroom gymnastics. It is a way of critically seeing and continually inquiring about the necessity and wisdom of cultural patterns of gender differentiation that parents and teachers of the young must begin in the earliest years. This requires examining language, domestic tasks, and behavior patterns that promote sex segregation. Consider, on the simplest level, some of the products that construct our lives: other than price and nominal gender, is there a difference between "Lady Speed Stick" and men's "Speed Stick" deodorant? Are the "extra moisturizers" in Barbasol Pure Silk shaving cream for women worth the 342 percent price differential over the men's version?[53] Do personal care items necessarily have a gender?

Beyond clothes, books, and toys, pay attention to the continual bombardment of gender-coded images amid all the paraphernalia of childhood. Susan Hoy Crawford, in *Beyond Dolls and Guns: 101 Ways to Help Children Avoid Gender Bias,* offers suggestions on ways to recognize sexism in children's lives, such as "the racism test" (substituting race for sex in a situation—parents might overlook a little boy's comment "I hate girls," but would respond if a racial term were used) or "the workplace test" (a classroom sheet of telephones and addresses with boys and girls listed in separate columns might not cause a stir at home, but would if it were handed out in an employment setting).

It is normal human behavior to latch onto colloquial expressions. But some expressions carry a huge amount of cultural baggage. Gender stereotypes and role expectations compress into little verbal packages such as "He's all boy!" or "Boys will be boys" or "Isn't she sweet" (or "cute" or "pretty"). They assume that gender is the primary identifier. They also assume that certain characteristics of a gender are a given. The challenge is to replace those naturalistic and gendered linguistic markers with words reflecting more desirable character traits—such as cooperative, critical, and socially contributory—that we want all children to have.

Even those of us who approach gender with the best of egalitarian intentions can unthinkingly reinforce traditional expectations and roles. I offer as just one anecdotal example a conversation I had with my husband when our second child was just under a year old. Seven years before, Tim had taken a year off from practicing law and stayed home as the primary caregiver for the first year with our son, Aaron. Under our familial version of an equal time arrangement, I took primary responsibility for the second child during infancy. Our daughter, Dylan, came to work with me for the first six months of her life. One evening when Dylan was a few months old I was heading to bed early and asked Tim if he would do the final diaper change of the night. "She'll probably need you to put on socks and a sweater; it may get cold tonight," I said. "Will do," Tim said. "Oh, and don't forget to put the crib side up," I said on the way out of the room. (He had, after all, left it down once.) "Shall I also take the scorpions out of her crib?" Tim asked politely.

As I apologized for my rudeness in giving orders to someone who had more primary baby-care experience than I did, I realized I had begun to feel proprietary about our second child. Since I was Dylan's primary caregiver, I thought I knew what was best for her and presumed incompetence in her father. The incident made me wonder whether other mothers might also unwittingly encourage "learned helplessness" on the part of fathers by assuming the existence of a single correct parenting style.

The gender separatism that begins so early in life follows us, and we become reluctant to test it later on. While a group, such as an association of women lawyers, may begin as a single-sex association, the group's experiences could be enriched and the message spread more widely with the inclusion of sympathetic males. Put the group to a mirror: what if male lawyers created a men lawyers' association? Female attorneys would be in an uproar about the old boys network affirmatively excluding women from participation in a professional organization.

The situation is different, some might argue, since men have not suffered the professional exclusion that women have. This is true, but it is a purely retrospective justification for the group's existence. The group needs to think about what it wants for the present, which, as Alfred North Whitehead observed, is the home of both the past and the future. If the reason for the group's existence is solely to combat the history of discrimination against women, and the organization insists on exclusion based on sex, it is a group that will linger in the past and not move toward the future. Since the integration of male and female lawyers, in an ideal world of legal practice without gender bias, should be among the objectives of the group, the women lawyers' association should move in that direction.

So should the law dismantle sororities, fraternities, the Girl Scouts, and the Boy Scouts? First Amendment associational law follows First Amendment expression law: combat bad speech with more speech; contest single-sex private organizations through competing groups. If mixed-sex groupings are successful, they will win in the marketplace of ideas. Yet we can't get there from here if the predominant single-sex groups continue to be allowed legally to exclude members of the opposite sex.

At this point, parents determine the appropriate social arrangements for their children. They should be asking what it is that Boy Scouts and Girl Scouts do. Are their purposes related to gender? Is exclusion of the opposite sex necessary for a Girl Scout's proficiency badge in geology or video production or an Interest Project patch in canoeing or global understanding? Does a child have to be a boy to be "Trustworthy, Loyal, Helpful, Friendly,

Courteous, Kind, Obedient, Cheerful, Thrifty, Brave, Clean, and Reverent"? Don't we want our girls to also "Be Prepared!" and "Do a Good Turn Daily"? Is the "supportive all-girl environment" promised by the thought bubble propaganda on the back of the Girl Scout cookie box (168 million boxes sold nationwide in 1996) worth the trade-off in gender exclusivity?

Must boys and girls be forced together in groups for all purposes to avoid the effects of sex segregation? What about sports—won't this again put girls at a competitive disadvantage when they cannot compete against the boys? Boys and girls do not need to be together at all times for all purposes. Sex segregation may be sensible for some purposes. But we need to carefully reconsider the need for segregation, rather than readily slipping into it.

How many elementary schools have adopted explicit antisexist policies designed to focus attention on gendering in early childhood? Such policies could be crafted to discourage "boys' tables and "girls' tables" or boys against girls in games. They could also commit to exploring the attention-giving behavior of teachers. Are teachers aware of gender research? Are they trying to encourage participation of girls? Are they trying not to respond to boys with extra attention, or with extra negative attention? What happens if teachers do not respond to disruptive elements? To the extent those elements are gendered, will girls be crowded out if attention is not given to disruptive behavior? We need to start asking questions, rather than accepting the way things are as the way they ought to be.

Almost everything has little immediate effect. But the fact that one man makes a decision to cook dinner a couple of nights a week may make a couple of children think differently about the gender of people in the kitchen. Even if a couple generally divides chores along gender lines, if a mother mows a lawn once in a while and a father folds laundry sometimes, these simple acts send the message that the gender line is navigable. If we change some of the realities now, we change thinking over two or three or four generations.

Gender role stereotypes harm both men and women, and stereotyping harms to one gender also rigidify role expectations of the other gender. Feminist theory needs to explore more fully how legal doctrines construct masculinity, and feminists must reach out to men as compatriots.

We may wonder, even if feminist legal theory turns its attention to the situation of men, what good it will do if the fundamental power structures in society—peers, families, churches, the media, and the more or less silent acculturation processes—have such force in shaping gender. Formidable institutions take strong positions that gender equality should not exist.[54] Perhaps the gendered assumptions and practices among well-intentioned, equality-seeking individuals are also intractable: "Daily social practices that reinforce existing arrangements stand in the way of efforts to expose unstated assumptions about the power behind attributions of difference."[55] The power of unconscious racial stereotyping may exceed that of intentional, invidious discrimination.[56] Similarly, deleterious gender stereotypes of both women and men are subtly perpetuated. This gendered content becomes locked into assumptions, and the assumptions transform into rules. Gender equity will necessitate massive changes in social and psychological development, shifts in the division of labor both inside and outside the home, and transformations in parenting roles. One of many places to begin is legal ideology.

Laws and legal doctrines contain ideological messages. What courts say and do matters, since legal language shapes and reinforces social meanings.[57] Courts and commentators must critically examine the social and legal constructs that keep both genders in their prescribed roles. Unless it becomes acceptable for men to feel hurt, for men to leave roles that foster aggression, for men to complain about the effects of gender role stereotypes, and for men to participate more fully in realms traditionally occupied by women, feminism has little chance of moving forward or expanding its audience. Feminist legal theorists need to explore constructs of masculinity toward the end of promoting practices and politics of masculinity that comport with feminist objectives.

We are in a period of large-scale institutional change—nations forming, collapsing, and defining themselves; the end of the Columbian era of expansionism; the rise of postmodernism; the shaking up of societies and of psyches. These currents mean that fissures exist in large power blocs, as well as in individual attitudes, postures, and inclinations, especially among middle class and professional groups. The time is ripe for theory to change and for social practices to alter. The regnant institutions will not impel change. Early childhood shapings, pervasive socialization, and later, more consciously "chosen" legal and political ideologies will inevitably meet. We must work on ourselves to move from absorbed customs, now our own predilections and habits, to more critically selected aims and means. Theory can help reshape deeply embedded social practices, but first theory must evolve. As the history of feminist thought attests, the very asking of different questions often heralds that change.

Notes

1. Kenneth Karst, *The Pursuit of Manhood and the Desegregation of the Armed Forces*, 38 UCLA L. REV. 499, 503 (1991).

2. MARTHA MINOW, MAKING ALL THE DIFFERENCE: INCLUSION, EXCLUSION, AND AMERICAN LAW (1990).

3. While some feminist legal theorists have specifically disavowed the possibility of men embracing feminist objectives, others have been cautiously optimistic and more welcoming. *Compare* Christine A. Littleton, *Reconstructing Sexual Equality*, 75 CAL. L. REV. 1279, 1294 n.91 (1987) (stating that while "[p]ro-feminist men play an important role in disseminating and implementing feminist ideas," they do not share women's experiences and thus cannot claim to be feminists) *and* Suzanna Sherry, *Civic Virtue and the Feminine Voice in Constitutional Adjudication*, 72 VA. L. REV. 543, 584 n.172 (1986) ("[Professor Kenneth] Karst is correct to disclaim the ability of a male to explore a feminine paradigm") *with* Katharine T. Bartlett, *Feminist Legal Methods*, 103 HARV. L. REV. 829, 833 n.7 (1990) (favoring "a definition of 'feminist' that allows men, as well as women, to make this choice"), Patricia A. Cain, *Feminist Legal Scholarship*, 77 IOWA L. REV. 19, 39 (1991) (urging feminist scholars to reach out to those who are not currently feminists, and stating, "I hope my male colleagues will listen and join the conversation"), *and* Ruth Colker, *Feminist Consciousness and the State: A Basis for Cautious Optimism*, 90 COLUM. L. REV. 1146, 1162 (1990) (suggesting that "men are capable of empathizing with women's situation in society if they are informed concretely about the conditions of women's lives").

4. Notable exceptions are Brian Bendig, *Images of Men in Feminist Legal Theory*, 20 PEPP. L. REV. 991 (1993); Mary Anne C. Case, *Disaggregating Gender from Sex and Orientation: The Effeminate Man in the Law and Feminist Jurisprudence*, 105 YALE L.J. 1 (1995); Francisco Valdes, *Queers, Sissies, Dykes, and Tomboys: Deconstructing the Conflation of "Sex," "Gender," and "Sexual Orientation" in Euro-American Law and Society*, 83 CAL. L. REV. 1 (1995); Joan C. Williams, *Deconstructing Gender*, 87 MICH. L. REV. 797 (1989).

A number of articles have discussed how men fare in discrete issue areas. *See, e.g.,* Judith Bond Jennison, *The Search for Equality in a Woman's World: Fathers' Rights to Child Custody*, 43 RUTGERS L. REV. 1141 (1991); Karst, *supra* note 1.

5. *See, e.g.,* EUGENE R. AUGUST, MEN'S STUDIES: A SELECTED AND ANNOTATED INTERDISCIPLINARY BIBLIOGRAPHY (1985); KENNETH CLATTERBAUGH, CONTEMPORARY PERSPECTIVES ON MASCULINITY: MEN, WOMEN, AND POLITICS IN MODERN SOCIETY (1990); WILLIAM G. DOTY, MYTHS OF MASCULINITY (1993); DAVID D. GILMORE, MANHOOD IN THE MAKING: CULTURAL CONCEPTS OF MASCULINITY (1990); THE MAKING OF MASCULINITIES: THE NEW MEN'S STUDIES (Harry Brod ed., 1987); MEN, MASCULINITY, AND THE MEDIA (Steve Craig ed., 1992); VICTOR J. SEIDLER, REDISCOVERING MASCULINITY: REASON, LANGUAGE AND SEXUALITY (1989).

6. R. W. Connell, *Men and the Women's Movement*, SOC. POL'Y, Summer 1993, at 72, 73.

7. Mary Conroy, *Women Still Clogged in Executive Pipeline*, WIS. ST. J., June 26, 1996, at 1C.

8. Neve Gordon, *Clinton Policies No Favor to Poor Women*, NAT'L CATH. REP., Feb. 21, 1997, at 33.

9. FEDERAL GLASS CEILING COMMISSION, GOOD FOR BUSINESS: MAKING FULL USE OF THE NATION'S CAPITAL 12 (1995).

10. Martha Ezzard, *Where Are the Women? Women Can Win—If Only They'll Run*, ATLANTA J. & CONST., Aug. 4, 1996, at Q02.

11. Ronald F. Levant, *The New Psychology of Men,* 27 PROF. PSYCHOL.: RES. & PRAC. 259, 262 (1996).

12. ANTHONY ASTRACHAN, HOW MEN FEEL 28 (1986).

13. Richard Locker, *To Win You Have to Run*, COM. APPEAL, July 31, 1995, at 1A.

14. James L. Tyson, *Mother's Day an Increasingly Longer Day: Work vs. Family*, CHRISTIAN SCI. MONITOR, May 9, 1997, at 1.

15. *Congressional Testimony before the House Committee on Ways and Means Re FY 98 Budget Education Issues*, Mar. 5, 1997, 1997 WL 8220041 (statement of Stanley O. Ikenberry, President, American Council on Education).

16. *See* ROYDA CROSE, WHY WOMEN LIVE LONGER THAN MEN . . . AND WHAT MEN CAN LEARN FROM THEM 81 (1997).

17. Carolyn Poirot, *Why Do Women Live Longer than Men?*, FT. WORTH STAR-TELEGRAM, May 7, 1997, at 1.

18. Betty Friedan, *Beyond Gender*, NEWSEEK, Sept. 4, 1995, at 30.

19. Ellis Cose, *How Real Is Male Privilege*, NEWSDAY, June 21, 1995, at 4.

20. A NEW PSYCHOLOGY OF MEN 2 (Ronald F. Levant & William S. Pollack eds., 1995).

21. Christine Littleton, *Does It Still Make Sense to Talk about "Women"?*, 1 UCLA WOMEN'S L.J. 15, 33 n.84 (1991).

22. NAOMI WOLF, FIRE WITH FIRE 139 (1993).

23. Marc A. Fajer, *Can Two Real Men Eat Quiche Together? Storytelling, Gender Role Stereotypes, and Legal Protection for Lesbians and Gay Men*, 46 U. MIAMI L. REV. 511, 632 (1992).

24. *See* Heather R. Wishik, *To Question Everything: The Inquiries of Feminist Jurisprudence*, 1 BERKELEY WOMEN'S L.J. 64, 77 (1985).

NOTES TO CHAPTER 2

1. *See* Don Colburn, *Physical Activity Lags in U.S. Leisure Time*, WASH. POST, Jan. 9, 1996, at 5.

2. Laura Hilgers, *Sports: No Longer Just a Man's Game; Women Athletes Starting to Catch Male Counterparts*, ARIZ. REPUBLIC, Feb. 15, 1994, at D1.

3. Brian J. Whipp & Susan Ward, *Will Women Soon Outrun Men?*, 355 NATURE 25 (1992).

4. Bert Rosenthal, *Will Women Run Faster? Experts Dispute Claim*, CHI. SUN-TIMES, Feb. 23, 1992, Sports, at 28.

5. Emma Lindsey, *Body Battle of the Sexes: Who Makes the Most of What They're Given?*, DAILY MIRROR (LONDON), Feb. 27, 1995, at 24–25.

6. Bennett A. Shaywitz et al., *Sex Differences in the Functional Organization of the Brain for Language*, 373 NATURE 607 (1995).

7. Ruben C. Gur et al., *Sex Differences in Regional Glucose Metabolism during a Resting State*, 267 SCIENCE 528 (Jan. 27, 1995).

8. *See* Randy J. Buckner et al., *Dissociation of Human Prefrontal Cortex Areas across Different Speech Production Tasks and Gender Groups*, 74 J. NEUROPHYSIOLOGY 2163 (1995).

9. *See* ANNE FAUSTO-STERLING, MYTHS OF GENDER: BIOLOGICAL THEORIES ABOUT WOMEN AND MEN (2d ed. 1992).

10. Roger Highfield, *Brain Scans Show Sexes Are Not on Same Wavelength*, DAILY TELEGRAPH (LONDON), Jan. 27, 1995, at 11.

11. Larry Hedges & Amy Nowell, *Sex Differences in Mental Test Scores, Variability, and Numbers of High-Scoring Individuals*, 269 SCIENCE 41, 44 (July 7, 1995).

12. Janet Shibley Hyde, *How Large Are Cognitive Gender Differences?*, 36 AM. PSYCHOLOGIST 892, 894 (1981).

13. Janet Shibley Hyde & Marcia C. Linn, *Gender Differences in Verbal Ability: A Meta-Analysis*, 104 PSYCHOL. BULL. 53, 60 (1988).

14. Janet Shibley Hyde et al., *Gender Differences in Mathematical Performance: A Meta-Analysis*, 107 PSYCHOL. BULL. 139, 150 (1990) ("[t]he overall gender difference is small at most ($d = 0.15$ for all samples or -0.05 for gender samples)").

15. Bill Hendrix, *Psychological Differences between Sexes Are Linked to Neurons*, HOUS. CHRON., Nov. 27, 1994, at A4.

16. Hedges & Nowell, *supra* note 11, at 41.

17. Howard N. Snyder & Melissa Sickmund, Office of Juvenile Justice and Delinquency Prevention, Juvenile Offenders and Victims: A National Report 100 (1995).

18. Lynn Smith, *'90s Family: They're Made of Snakes and Snails and . . .*, L.A. Times, Sept. 29, 1996, at E3.

19. *See, e.g.,* Andrew Ahlgren & David W. Johnson, *Sex Differences in Cooperative and Competitive Attitudes from the 2nd through the 12th Grades,* 15 Developmental Psychol. 45, 45 (1979).

20. *See, e.g.,* James M. Dabbs et al., *Saliva Testosterone and Criminal Violence in Young Adult Prison Inmates,* 49 Psychosomatic Med. 174 (1987); Leo E. Kruez & Robert M. Rose, *Assessment of Aggressive Behavior and Plasma Testosterone in a Young Criminal Population,* 34 Psychosomatic Med. 321 (1972).

21. *See* Alan Booth & D. Wayne Osgood, *The Influence of Testosterone on Deviance in Adulthood: Assessing and Explaining the Relationship,* 31 Criminology 93, 102 (1993).

22. *See* Benoist Schaal et al., *Male Testosterone Linked to High Social Dominance but Low Physical Aggression in Early Adolescence,* 34 J. Am. Acad. Child Adolescent Psychiatry 1322 (1996).

23. *See* Christina Wang et al., *Testosterone Replacement Therapy Improves Mood in Hypogonadal Men—A Clinical Research Center Study,* 81 J. Clinical Endocrinology & Metabolism 3578 (1996).

24. *See, e.g.,* Robin West, *Jurisprudence and Gender,* 55 U. Chi. L. Rev. 1 (1988); Richard A. Epstein, *Gender Is for Nouns,* 41 DePaul L. Rev. 981 (1992).

25. *See* Beatrice Whiting & Carolyn Edwards, Children of Different Worlds: The Formation of Social Behavior 270–73 (1988).

26. *See* Eleanor E. Maccoby, *Gender and Relationships: A Developmental Account,* 45 Am. Psychologist 513, 513–15 (1990).

27. Madeline E. Heilman, *Sex Stereotypes and Their Effects in the Workplace: What We Know and What We Don't Know,* 3 J. Soc. Behav. & Personality 3, 5 (1995).

28. Alice H. Eagly, *The Science and Politics of Comparing Women and Men,* 50 Am. Psychologist 145, 149–50 (1995).

29. Rachel T. Hare-Mustin & Jeanne Maracek, *The Meaning of Difference: Gender Theory, Postmodernism, and Psychology,* 43 Am. Psychologist 455, 457 (1988).

30. *See* Louise B. Silverstein, *Fathering Is a Feminist Issue,* 20 Psychol. Women Q. 3, 17 (1996).

31. Sara L. Mandelbaum, in Beth Willinger, *Single Gender Education and the Constitution,* 40 Loy. L. Rev. 253, 269 (1994). Marcia Angell of the *New England Journal of Medicine* makes the point regarding epidemiological research: "Authors and investigators are worried that there's a bias against negative studies." *Epidemiology Faces Its Limits,* 269 Science 164, 169 (July 14, 1995).

32. John Archer & Barbara Lloyd, Sex and Gender 7 (1982).

33. Stephen Jay Gould, Dinosaur in a Haystack 125 (1995).

34. *Id.* at 126.

35. Deborah Blum, *Do Gender Differences Reach into Our Brains*, Fresno Bee, Oct. 24, 1995, at A8.

36. Jacquelyn B. James, *His and Hers*, Boston Globe, May 25, 1995, at 19.

37. Mark Bowden, *Men, Women Use Brains Differently*, Portland Oregonian, Jan. 28, 1995, at A15.

38. Gayle Hanson, *At a Price: Exploring the Mystery of Genes*, Insight, Dec. 28, 1992, at 12.

39. Charles C. Mann, *Press Coverage: Leaving Out the Big Picture*, 269 Science 166 (July 14, 1995).

40. Lisa Popyk, *The New American Family: Goodbye Ozzie and Harriet*, Cin. Post, Dec. 21, 1996, at 1A.

41. Silverstein, *supra* note 30, at 17.

42. *Id.* at 18.

43. *Id.* at 11.

44. *Crime Rate for Girls Jumps*, Chi. Sun-Times, Dec. 4, 1996, at 40.

45. Carol Sanger, *Girls and the Getaway: Cars, Culture, and the Predicament of Gendered Space*, 144 U. Pa. L. Rev. 705, 751 (1995).

46. *In Mutual Funds, Women Remain Silent Majority*, Hous. Chron., Nov. 19, 1995, at 5.

47. Carol Lauer, *Variability in the Patterns of Agonistic Behavior of Preschool Children, in* Aggression and Peacefulness in Humans and Other Primates 172 (James Silverberg & J. Patrick Gray eds., 1992). While the contrast between boys and girls within the Israeli kibbutzim groups was greater than in the American groups, "for more than half of these [Israeli] groups, boys are no more frequent participants in agonistic encounters than are girls." *Id.* at 177.

48. *Id.* at 184.

49. *See, e.g.,* Clayton A. Robarchek & Carole J. Robarchek, *Cultures of War and Peace: A Comparative Study of Waorini and Semai, in* Aggression and Peacefulness in Humans and Other Primates, *supra* note 47, at 189; Michael J. Strube, *Meta-Analysis and Cross-Cultural Comparison: Sex Differences in Child Competitiveness*, 12 J. Cross-Cultural Psychol. 3, 15–16 (1981).

50. Dennis Kelly, *SAT Adjustment Worth 100 Points*, USA Today, Aug. 23, 1996, at 1D.

51. Rachel Shteir, *Get Smart: Did the SAT-Makers Wise Up with a New, Unbiased Test?*, Village Voice, Jan. 17, 1995, at 4. Brigham later renounced these views. *See* Nicholas Lemann, *The Structure of Success in America*, Atlantic Monthly, Aug. 1, 1995, at 41.

52. Howard Wainer & Linda S. Steinberg, *Sex Differences in Performance on the Mathematics Section of the Scholastic Aptitude Test: A Bidirectional Validity Study*, 62 Harv. Educ. Rev. 323, 330 (1992).

53. Katherine Connor & Ellen J. Vargyas, *The Legal Implications of Gender Bias in Standardized Testing*, 7 BERKELEY WOMEN's L.J. 13, 25 (1992).

54. *See* Elaine Woo, *Firms Agree to Alter Standardized Test Education: Changes in PSAT to End Alleged Gender Bias Could Shift Millions in Tuition Aid to Girls*, L.A. TIMES, Oct. 2, 1996, at A20.

55. Sharif v. New York State Educ. Dept., 709 F. Supp. 365 (S.D.N.Y. 1989).

56. Fausto-Sterling, *supra* note 9, at 57–58.

57. Lesley Krueger, *Brainstorm: Differences between Men's and Women's Brains*, 68 CHATELAINE 72 (Dec. 1995).

58. STEPHEN JAY GOULD, THE MISMEASURE OF MAN 104 (1981) (quoting Paul Broca, *Sur le volume et la forme du cerveau suivant les individus et suivant les races*, 2 BULLETIN SOCIETE D'ANTHROPOLOGIE PARIS 153 (1861)).

59. *Id.* at 104–05 (quoting Gustave Le Bon, *Recherches anatomiques et mathematiques sur les lois des variations du volume du cerveau et sur leurs relations avec l'intelligence*, 2 REVUE D'ANTHROPOLOGIE, 2d series 60–61 (1879)).

60. R. C. LEWONTIN, BIOLOGY AS IDEOLOGY 33 (1991).

61. Richard A. Epstein, *Two Challenges for Feminist Thought*, 18 HARV. J. L. & PUB. POL'Y 331, 342–43 (1995).

62. Michael Levin, *The Feminist Mystique*, 70 COMMENTARY 25, 28 (Dec. 1980), cited in Fausto-Sterling, *supra* note 9, at 6.

63. Mike Dorning, *Poll Details Global Role of Gender Bias*, CHI. TRIB., Mar. 27, 1996, at 1.

64. Deborah A. Rhode, *The "No Problem" Problem: Feminist Challenges and Cultural Change*, 100 YALE L.J. 1731, 1748–49 (1991).

65. *Id.*

66. *See* Janet K. Swim, *Perceived Versus Meta-Analytic Effect Sizes: An Assessment of the Accuracy of Gender Stereotypes*, 66 J. PERSONALITY & SOC. PSYCHOL. 21 (1994); Alice H. Eagly & Wendy Wood, *Explaining Sex Differences in Social Behavior: A Meta-Analytic Perspective*, 17 PERSONALITY & SOC. PSYCHOL. BULL. 306 (1991).

67. Bem P. Allen, *Gender Stereotypes Are Not Accurate: A Replication of Martin (1987) Using Diagnostic vs. Self-Report and Behavioral Criteria*, 32 SEX ROLES 583, 599 (1995).

68. *See* Carol Lynn Martin, *A Ratio Measure of Gender Stereotyping*, 52 J. PERSONALITY & SOC. PSYCHOL. 489 (1987).

69. Azy Barak et al., *Traditionality of Children's Interests as Related to Their Parents' Gender Stereotypes and Traditionality of Occupations*, 24 SEX ROLES 511 (1991).

70. *Id.* at 3.

71. *See* Amos Tversky & Daniel Kahneman, *Judgment under Uncertainty: Heuristics and Biases*, in JUDGMENT UNDER UNCERTAINTY: HEURISTICS AND BIASES 3 (Daniel Kahneman et al. eds., 1982).

72. Heilman, *supra* note 27, at 6–7.

73. Katherine Hildebrant Karraker et al., *Parents' Gender-Stereotyped Perceptions of Newborns: The Eye of the Beholder Revisited*, 33 SEX ROLES 687, 688 (1995).

74. *See* Jacqueline McGuire, *Gender Stereotypes of Parents with Two-Year-Olds and Beliefs about Gender Differences in Behavior*, 19 SEX ROLES 233 (1988).

75. *Compare* J. Z. Rubin et al., *The Eye of the Beholder: Parents' Views on Sex of Newborns*, 44 AM. J. ORTHOPSYCHIATRY 512 (1974) (finding that parents described their newborns in gendered terms) *with* Karraker et al., *supra* note 73 (finding that parents', particularly fathers', gender-stereotyped ratings and interactive behaviors with their infants have diminished).

76. Clyde C. Robinson & James T. Morris, *The Gender-Stereotyped Nature of Christmas Toys Received by 36-, 48-, and 60-Month-Old Children: A Comparison between Nonrequested vs. Requested Toys*, 15 SEX ROLES 21, 30 (1986).

77. *See* Claire Etaugh & Marsha B. Liss, *Home, School and Play—Training Grounds for Adult Gender Roles*, 26 SEX ROLES 129, 136–37 (1992).

78. *See* Beverly I. Fagot, *The Influence of Sex of Child on Parental Reactions to Toddler Children*, 49 CHILD DEV. 459 (1978).

79. SANDRA LIPSITZ BEM, THE LENSES OF GENDER: TRANSFORMING THE DEBATE ON SEXUAL INEQUALITY 150 (1993).

80. Marc A. Fajer, *Can Two Real Men Eat Quiche Together? Storytelling, Gender Role Stereotypes, and Legal Protection for Lesbians and Gay Men*, 46 U. MIAMI L. REV. 511, 617 (1992).

81. Roger Clark et al., *Of Caldecotts and Kings: Gendered Images in Recent American Children's Books by Black and Non-Black Illustrators*, 7 GENDER & SOC'Y 227 (1993).

82. Carole M. Kortenhaus & Jack Demarest, *Gender Role Stereotyping in Children's Literature: An Update*, 28 SEX ROLES 219, 226–30 (1993).

83. Ellen Handler Spitz, *Good and Naughty/Boys and Girls: Reflections on the Impact of Culture on Young Minds*, 51 AM. IMAGO 307 (Sept. 22, 1994).

84. ANN M. MARTIN, LOGAN'S STORY 4 (1992).

85. Teresa L. Thompson & Eugenia Zerbinos, *Gender Roles in Animated Cartoons: Has the Picture Changed in 20 Years?*, 32 SEX ROLES 651, 669 (1995).

86. Jennifer Mangan, *Fine Tuning Diversity and Realistic Roles Sought for Girls on Television*, CHI. TRIB., May 26, 1996, at 1.

87. Stephen Rae, *The Fierce, Furious March of the Fundamentalists*, COSMOPOLITAN, Jan. 1, 1995, at 158.

88. ARLIE HOCHSCHILD, THE SECOND SHIFT: WORKING PARENTS AND THE REVOLUTION AT HOME 3–4, 8 (1989).

89. *Id.*

90. *See* Marilyn K. Melia, *Housework: Is the Division of Labor Unfair? There Are Other Explanations than the "Men Are Scum" Theory*, CHI. TRIB., May 7, 1995, § 6, at 1.

91. Ellis Cose, *The Daddy Trap: After All the Talk about Equality of the Sexes, a Man Is Still Expected to Be the Breadwinner*, CHI. TRIB., June 18, 1995, Sunday Magazine, at 12.

92. Carol Kleiman, *Men Clean Up on Wages as Women Keep House*, CHI. TRIB., Sept. 18, 1989, at 5.

93. Jerry Adler, *Building a Better Dad*, NEWSWEEK, June 17, 1996, at 61.

94. *Id.* Polls reveal discrepancies in assessments of parenting responsibilities. In a 1996 poll of over eight hundred parents with children under age eighteen, 54 percent of the fathers surveyed said they shared parenting responsibilities equally with their spouses, while only one-third of mothers said that they and their spouses did the same amount of parenting. *Freeze Frames*, WASH. TIMES, June 16, 1996, at A2.

95. Thomas R. Rane & Thomas W. Draper, *Negative Evaluations of Men's Nurturant Touching of Young Children*, 76 PSYCHOL. REP. 811, 811 (1995).

96. *Id.*

97. BARRIE THORNE, GENDER PLAY: GIRLS AND BOYS IN SCHOOL (1993).

98. Sarah B. Hechtman & Robert Rosenthal, *Teacher Gender and Nonverbal Behavior in the Teaching of Gender-Stereotyped Materials*, 21 J. APPLIED SOC. PSYCHOL. 446, 447 (1991).

99. MYRA SADKER & DAVID SADKER, FAILING AT FAIRNESS: HOW AMERICA'S SCHOOLS CHEAT GIRLS 48 (1994).

100. Lynn Smith, *Teacher Attitudes; Sexism in Classroom—A Purge*, L.A. TIMES, Sept. 10, 1987, at 1.

101. SADKER & SADKER, *supra* note 99, at 43.

102. Jeff Jacoby, *"Alarming Facts" about Boys, Girls*, BOSTON GLOBE, Feb. 6, 1996, Op-ed, at 15.

103. Kristina Sauerwein, *90s Family Boy Trouble*, L.A. TIMES, Nov. 23, 1994, at E3.

104. *Id.* (citing the U.S. Department of Education's National Longitudinal Study of Special Education).

105. Russell Bradshaw, *All-Black Schools Provide Role Models: Is This the Solution?*, 68 CLEARINGHOUSE REV. 146, 146 (Jan. 1995).

106. Diane Rado, *Race, Gender Tied to School Discipline*, ST. PETERSBURG TIMES, Jan. 20, 1995, at 1B.

107. Jacoby, *supra* note 102, at 15.

108. Michael D'Antonio, *The Fragile Sex: By All Accounts Boys Are in Trouble*, L.A. TIMES, Dec. 4, 1994, at 16.

109. *See* Ellen Goodman, *The Truth behind "The Kiss,"* BOSTON GLOBE, Oct. 13, 1996, at D7.

110. HOSTILE HALLWAYS: THE AAUW SURVEY ON SEXUAL HARASSMENT IN AMERICA'S SCHOOLS (1993).

111. *See* Jerry Adler & Debra Rosenberg, *Must Boys Always Be Boys?*, Newsweek, Oct. 19, 1992, at 77.

112. Franklin v. Gwinnett County Pub. Sch., 503 U.S. 60 (1992).

113. Jill Smolowe, *Sex with a Scoreboard*, Time, Apr. 5, 1993, at 41.

114. John F. Peters, *Gender Socialization of Adolescents in the Home: Research and Discussion*, 29 Adolescence 913, 915 (1994).

115. Gina Pera, *The Difference between Girls and Boys*, USA Weekend, Sept. 8, 1996, at 4.

116. Peters, *supra* note 114, at 917.

117. *Id.* at 916–32.

118. J. Jill Suitor & Rebel Reavis, *Football, Fast Cars, and Cheerleading: Adolescent Gender Norms, 1978–1989*, 30 Adolescence 265, 271 (1995).

119. Karina Bland, *Illustrating Crime: Comic Book Teaches Teens about Date Rape*, Phoenix Gazette, Sept. 14, 1993, at B1.

120. Pera, *supra* note 115, at 4.

121. John Nichols, *A Counselor's Guide for Gay, Lesbian Teens*, Wis. St. J. June 14, 1996, at 13A.

122. Larry Barszewski, *School Panel: Pamphlet OK to Hand Out to Teens*, Ft. Lauderdale (Fla.) Sun-Sentinel, Apr. 18, 1996, at 1B.

123. *Outing on the Floor: Gunderson's Secret Revealed*, Wis. St. J., Aug. 4, 1996, at 1A.

124. Utah Code Ann. § 53A-3-419 (1996).

125. *See* 20 U.S.C. § 1681 (1994).

126. 45 C.F.R. § 86 (1996).

127. Grove City College v. Bell, 465 U.S. 555 (1984).

128. Civil Rights Restoration Act of 1987, Pub. L. No. 100-259, 3(a), 20 U.S.C. § 1687 (1990).

129. Susan M. Shook, Note, *The Title IX Tug-of-War and Intercollegiate Athletics in the 1990's: Nonrevenue Men's Teams Join Women Athletes in the Scramble for Survival*, 71 Ind. L.J. 773, 782 (1996).

130. Herb Gould, *Women Say Issue Is More than Sports*, Chi. Sun-Times, May 7, 1995, at 25.

131. Diedre G. Duncan, Comment, *Gender Equity in Women's Athletics*, 64 U. Cin. L. Rev. 1027, 1042 (1996) (citing NCAA Gender Equity Task Force, Final Report (July 26, 1993)).

132. Michael Messner, *Boyhood, Organized Sports, and the Construction of Masculinities*, 18 J. Contemp. Ethnography 416, 417 (1990).

133. Jennifer Bundy, *Boys' Risk-Taking Often Turns Fatal, State Researcher Reports*, Charleston Gazette, Apr. 1, 1996, at 2B.

134. *See, e.g.,* Marc D. Weinstein et al., *Masculinity and Hockey Violence*, 33 Sex Roles 831 (1995).

135. Clarence Page, *The Truth about Domestic Abuse*, Chi. Trib., June 2, 1996, at C17.

136. Paul Levy, *Studies Find More Violence by Athletes*, Star Trib. (Minneapolis-St. Paul), Jan. 9, 1996, at 1A.

137. Don Sabo, *The Myth of the Sexual Athlete*, in Sex, Violence & Power in Sports: Rethinking Masculinity 36, 38 (Michael A. Messner & Donald F. Sabo eds., 1994).

138. Deborah Tannen, You Just Don't Understand: Women and Men in Conversation 43 (1990).

139. John Gray, Men Are from Mars, Women Are from Venus: A Practical Guide for Improving Communication and Getting What You Want in Your Relationships 5 (1992).

140. Justin Sterling, What Really Works with Men: Solve 95% of Your Relationship Problems (and Cope with the Rest) 65–66 (1992).

141. Heilman, *supra* note 27, at 3.

142. Jeanne M. Norris & Anne M. Wylie, *Gender Stereotyping of the Managerial Role among Students in Canada and the United States*, 20 Group & Org. Mgmt. 167 (June 1995).

143. Bickley Townsend, *Room at the Top for Women*, Am. Demographics, July 1, 1996, at 28.

144. *See* Marion Crain, *Between Feminism and Unionism: Working Class Women, Sex Equality, and Labor Speech*, 82 Geo. L.J. 1903, 1909 (1994).

145. Cathleen Ferraro, *Few Men Jumping into Traditional Women's Jobs*, Sacramento Bee, Oct. 22, 1995, at A1.

146. Mississippi Univ. for Women v. Hogan, 458 U.S. 718, 742 (1982) (Powell, J., dissenting).

147. Diane E. Lewis, *Stay-at-Home Dads Gain Support, Acceptance*, Boston Globe, Dec. 26, 1995, Economy, at 68.

148. Barbara Vobejda, *As Jobs Return, Dad Care Reverts to Day Care; Surge in Fathers Minding Youngsters Has Come to an End, Study Says*, Wash. Post, Apr. 24, 1996, at A1.

149. Allison Bass, *Amid Changes, Grindstone Still Wears on Fathers*, Boston Globe, June 16, 1996, Metro, at 1.

150. Adler, *supra* note 93, at 64.

151. *Id.*

152. Vivian Pospisil, *They Can't Afford Unpaid Leave*, Industry Week, July 19, 1993, at 8.

153. Rane & Draper, *supra* note 95.

154. Susan B. Murray, *"We All Love Charles": Men in Child Care and the Social Construction of Gender*, 10 Gender & Soc'y. 368, 372 (1996).

155. *Id.* at 378.

156. *Id.*

157. *Id.*

158. Joy A. Schneer & Frieda Reitman, *Effects of Employment Gaps on the Careers of M.B.A.'s: More Damaging for Men than for Women?*, 33 ACAD. MGMT. J. 391, 394 (1990).

NOTES TO CHAPTER 3

1. Bradwell v. Illinois, 83 U.S. 130, 141 (1873) (Bradley, J., concurring).

2. 83 U.S. 36, 119 (1873) (Bradley, J., dissenting).

3. Muller v. Oregon, 208 U.S. 412, 421 (1908).

4. This, of course, brings up the theme of fighting an unjust battle for a just war. Brandeis and Goldmark obviously were setting the stage for protective labor laws for all workers.

5. Louis Brandeis & Josephine Goldmark, Brief for Defendant in Error, Muller v. Oregon, 208 U.S. 412 (1908), reprinted in AMERICAN LEGAL REALISM 238 (William W. Fisher, III et al. eds., 1993).

6. Muller v. Oregon, 208 U.S. at 419, 421.

7. 335 U.S. 464, 465–66 (1948).

8. Hoyt v. Florida, 368 U.S. 57 (1961).

9. 404 U.S. 71, 75 (1971).

10. 411 U.S. 677 (1973).

11. 429 U.S. 190 (1976).

12. 453 U.S. 57 (1981).

13. 450 U.S. 464, 471 (1981).

14. *Id.* at 494, 496 (Brennan, J., dissenting).

15. *Id.* at 499 (Stevens, J., dissenting).

16. 417 U.S. 484, 496 n.20 (1974).

17. 429 U.S. 125, 138 (1976).

18. 42 U.S.C. § 2000e(k) (1978).

19. Bray v. Alexandria Women's Health Clinic, 506 U.S. 263, 272 (1993).

20. 450 U.S. at 496 n.10.

21. Paula Abrams, *The Tradition of Reproduction*, 37 ARIZ. L. REV. 453, 496 (1995).

22. Tracy E. Higgins, *"By Reason of Their Sex": Feminism, Postmodernism, and Justice*, 80 CORNELL L. REV. 1536, 1553 (1995), citing Geduldig, 417 U.S. at 497 n.20.

23. Price Waterhouse v. Hopkins, 490 U.S. 228, 251 (1989). I argue though, in chapter 7, that the *Price Waterhouse* Court's reasoning did not go far enough to eradicate the most insidious and damaging stereotypes.

24. 477 U.S. 57, 68 (1986).

25. 458 U.S. 718, 730 (1982).

26. 441 U.S. 380 (1979).

27. 499 U.S. 187, 211 (1991).

28. Mary Becker, *Reproductive Hazards after* Johnson Controls, 31 Hous. L. Rev. 43, 53–54 (1994).

29. 433 U.S. 321, 335–36 (1977).

30. *See* Nadine Taub, *At the Intersection of Reproductive Freedom and Gender Equality: Problems in Addressing Reproductive Hazards in the Workplace*, 6 UCLA Women's L.J. 443, 446 (1996).

31. United States v. Virginia, 766 F. Supp. 1407, 1421–24 (W.D. Va. 1991).

32. United States v. Virginia, 976 F.2d 890 (4th Cir. 1992).

33. United States v. Virginia, 852 F. Supp. 471, 476 (W.D. Va. 1994).

34. United States v. Virginia, 116 S. Ct. 2264, 2284 (1996).

35. United States v. Virginia, 852 F. Supp. at 503.

36. *Id.* at 481.

37. United States v. Virginia, 44 F.3d 1229, 1234, 1239–41 (4th Cir. 1995).

38. United States v. Virginia, 116 S. Ct. at 2279.

39. *Id.* at 2284.

40. *Id.* at 2283, 2286.

41. United States v. Virginia, 766 F. Supp. at 1432, 1434.

42. *Id.* at 1434.

43. *Id.* at 1414.

44. United States v. Virginia, 44 F.3d at 1240.

45. United States v. Virginia, 766 F. Supp. at 1434.

46. United States v. Virginia, 116 S. Ct. at 2298.

47. Liz Mundy, *"It Couldn't Be the Same Thing as VMI,"* Wash. Post, Mar. 10, 1996, at 6.

48. United States v. Virginia, 44 F.3d at 1234.

49. An unpublished manuscript of a former VMI cadet suggests an entirely different etymological origin: that the word probably is derived from "decked" or "diked out," meaning "dressed." Michael A. Burke, *Cadet Slang at the Virginia Military Institute* 6 (VMI Archives 1981).

50. *Id.* at 1243 (Phillips, J., dissenting).

51. United States v. Virginia, 116 S. Ct. at 2308–09 (Scalia, J., dissenting).

52. *Id.* at 2276, 2268, 2280. In fairness, the Supreme Court did point out that "it is also probable that 'many men would not want to be educated in such an environment.'" *Id.* at 2280 (adopting Fourth Circuit Judge Diana Motz's observation, in her dissent from the Court of Appeals' denial of request for rehearing en banc).

53. United States Supreme Court Petitioner's Brief, United States v. Virginia, No. 94-1941 (filed Nov. 16, 1995), 1995 WL 703403 at 82 n.36.

54. Brown v. Board of Educ., 347 U.S. 483, 495 (1954).

55. *Id.* at 492, 494.

56. United States v. Virginia, 116 S. Ct. at 2276 n.7.

57. The social science evidence regarding advantages of single-sex schooling seems limited to benefits for girls, with little evidence that any benefits are empiri-

cally true for men; even those advantages for girls are modest. *See, e.g.,* Herbert W. Marsh, *Effects of Attending Single-Sex and Coeducational High Schools on Achievement, Attitudes, Behaviors, and Sex Differences,* 81 J. EDUC. PSYCHOL. 70, 71 (1989) ("Recent comparisons of achievement levels in single-sex and coed schools typically show that academic achievement is substantially higher in single-sex schools than in coed schools. Once preexisting characteristics such as intelligence, prior academic achievement, motivation, and social class are controlled, however, the differences tend to be much smaller or nonsignificant. The differences, therefore, are largely explicable in terms of the characteristics of students who attend single-sex and coed schools rather than the types of schools"). *But see* Valerie E. Lee & Anthony S. Bryk, *Effects of Single-Sex Secondary Schools on Student Achievement and Attitudes,* 78 J. EDUC. PSYCHOL. 381 (1986); Cornelius Riordan, *Public and Catholic Schooling: The Effects of Gender Context Policy,* 93 AM. J. EDUC. 518 (1985).

58. United States v. Virginia, 44 F.3d at 1237.

59. Lucinda Finley, *Sex-Blind, Separate but Equal, or Anti-Subordination? The Uneasy Legacy of* Plessy v. Ferguson *for Sex and Gender Discrimination,* 12 GA. ST. U. L. REV. 1089, 1103 (1996).

60. Faulkner v. Jones, 10 F.3d 226, 234 (4th Cir. 1993) (Hamilton, J., dissenting).

61. Valorie K. Vojdik, *At War: Narrative Tactics in the Citadel and VMI Litigation,* 19 HARV. WOMEN'S L.J. 1, 2 (1996), citing 766 F. Supp. at 1407, 1408.

62. VMI Defendants' Proposed Findings of Fact and Conclusions of Law (liability phase) (Apr. 26, 1991), at 115, cited in Supreme Court Petitioner's Brief, United States v. Virginia, No. 94-1941 (filed Nov. 16, 1995), 1995 WL 703403 at 18.

63. Reply Brief, United States v. Virginia, Nos. 94-1941, 94-2107 (filed Jan. 3, 1996), 1996 WL 2023 at 9.

64. United States v. Virginia, 766 F. Supp. at 1412. Judge Kiser discounted the evidence of several psychologists who testified for the government regarding the consensus of psychological research on sex differences in learning styles, particularly the evidence from noted psychologist Carol Nagy Jacklin that "the average differences between men and women are trivial compared to the very large individual differences within the group of men and within the group of women." Dianne Avery, *Institutional Myths, Historical Narratives, and Social Science Evidence: Reading the "Record" in the Virginia Military Institute Case,* 5 S. CAL. REV. L. & WOMEN'S STUD. 189, 306 (1996) (offering a thoughtful and detailed review of evidence in the VMI case).

65. United States v. Virginia, 44 F.3d at 1238.

66. Beth Willinger, *Single Gender Education and the Constitution,* 40 LOY. L. REV. 253, 268 (1994).

67. Amici Curiae Brief in Support of Petitioner by the American Association of University Professors et al. [hereinafter AAUP Brief], United States v. Virginia, No. 94-1941 (filed Nov. 16, 1995), 1995 WL 702833 at 60.

68. Valerie Lee et al., *Sexism in Single-Sex and Coeducational Independent Secondary School Classrooms*, 67 Soc. Educ. 97, 103–04 (1994).

69. Finley, *supra* note 59, at 1117.

70. Vojdik, *supra* note 61, at 5.

71. Sara L. Mandelbaum, *Single Gender Education and the Constitution*, 40 Loy. L. Rev. 253, 270 (1994).

72. *Compare* United States v. Virginia, 766 F. Supp. at 1411–12 *with* 766 F. Supp. at 1432–34.

73. Reply Brief, *supra* note 63, at 23.

74. Respondent's Brief, United States v. Virginia, No. 94-2107 (filed Dec. 15, 1995), 1995 WL 745010 at 52, 17.

75. AAUP Brief, *supra* note 67, at 53.

76. Christina Nifong, *Is the Once-Male Citadel Prepared for Co-ed 'Nobs'?*, Christian Sci. Monitor, Aug. 9, 1996, at 4. "Of those, 55 graduated from the Naval Academy, 62 from West Point, and 97 from the Air Force Academy." *Id.*

77. Stefani G. Kopenec, *Women Fight for All-Female College*, Det. News, Dec. 14, 1994, at A5.

78. David H. Hackworth, *Warrior Spirit Being Squelched in Politically Correct Military*, Ft. Lauderdale (Fla.) Sun-Sentinel, Feb. 13, 1997, at 23A.

79. Steve Goldstein, *Two Women Step Quietly into History of VMI*, Hous. Chron., Oct. 19, 1996, at 4.

80. *Civil Rights at the Citadel*, Wash. Times, Dec. 19, 1996, at A18.

81. Craig Whitlock, *The Citadel under Siege*, Raleigh News & Observer, Jan. 26, 1997, at A1.

82. Dan Fost, *Farewell to the Lodge*, 18 Am. Demographics, Jan. 1, 1996.

83. Michael M. Burns, *The Exclusion of Women from Influential Men's Clubs: The Inner Sanctum and the Myth of Full Equality*, 18 Harv. C.R.-C.L. L. Rev. 330 n.29 (1983).

84. Roberts v. United States Jaycees, 468 U.S. 609 (1984).

85. Rotary Int'l v. Rotary Club of Duarte, 481 U.S. 537, 549 (1987).

86. Michael Cordts, *Admit Women, Lions Clubs Locals Urged*, Chi. Sun-Times, May 13, 1987, at 20.

87. Lela Garlington, *After 127 Years, Elks Open Membership to Women*, Com. Appeal, Sept. 30, 1995, at B1 ("So far, the Chicago-based organization has spent more than $1 million fighting legal action by women who want to join the Elks in Michigan, Utah and Connecticut").

88. The organization is still listed as a "men's" group in the 1997 *Encyclopedia of Associations*.

89. Sara Rimer, *Asking, Not Demanding, to Be Elks*, N.Y. Times, Apr. 10, 1997, at A9.

90. *See* Sally Frank, *The Key to Unlocking the Clubhouse Door: The Application of*

Antidiscrimination Laws to Quasi-Private Clubs, 2 MICH. J. GENDER & L. 27, 60 (1994).

91. *See* Welsh v. Boy Scouts of America, 787 F. Supp. 1511 (N.D. Ill. 1992), *aff'd*, 993 F.2d 1267 (7th Cir. 1993) (atheist properly excluded because scouting group was not a public accommodation); Quinnipiac Council, Boy Scouts, Inc. v. Comm'n on Human Rights & Opportunities, 528 A.2d 352 (Conn. 1987) (denying woman ability to become scoutmaster did not violate state public accommodations law); Schwenk v. Boy Scouts of America, 551 P.2d 465, 474 (Or. 1976) (Boy Scouts not required to accept girl for membership). *But see* Curran v. Mount Diablo Council of the Boy Scouts, 195 Cal. Rptr. 325 (Ct. App. 1983) (exclusion of homosexual from membership on moral character grounds would violate Unruh Act).

92. Nancy S. Horton, *Traditional Single-Sex Fraternities on College Campuses: Will They Survive in the 1990s?*, 18 J.C. & U.L. 419, 482 n.30 (1992), quoting 120 CONG. REC. 39993 (1974) (statement of Sen. Bayh). *See* 20 U.S.C. § 1681(a) (6) (A-B) (1988).

93. *See, e.g.,* La Von Lanigan v. Bartlett, 46 F. Supp. 1388 (W.D. Mo. 1979). *See also* cases at notes 98–99 *infra*.

94. Tamimi v. Howard Johnson Co., 807 F.2d 1550 (11th Cir. 1987); Wislocki-Goin v. Mears, 831 F.2d 1374 (7th Cir. 1987); Craft v. Metromedia, Inc., 572 F. Supp. 868 (W.D. Mo. 1983), *modified*, 766 F.2d 1205 (8th Cir. 1985), *cert. denied*, 475 U.S. 1058 (1986).

95. *See, e.g.,* Lockhart v. Louisiana-Pacific Corp., 795 P.2d 602 (Or. Ct. App. 1990). *See generally* Katharine T. Bartlett, *Only Girls Wear Barrettes: Dress and Appearance Standards, Community Norms, and Workplace Equality*, 92 MICH. L. REV. 2541 (1994).

96. Bethanne Walz Mcnamara, Comment, *All Dressed Up with No Place to Go: Gender Bias in Oklahoma Federal Court Dress Codes*, 30 TULSA L.J. 395, 415 (1994).

97. Lynne D. Mapes-Riordan, *Sex Discrimination and Employer Weight and Appearance Standards*, EMP. REL. L.J., Mar. 22, 1991, at 496. A number of appellate courts have held that regulations of male hair length do not violate Title VII. *See, e.g.,* Tavora v. New York Mercantile Exch., 101 F.3d 907 (2d Cir. 1996); Barker v. Taft Broadcasting Co. (6th Cir. 1977); Earwood v. Continental Southeastern Lines, 539 F.2d 1349 (4th Cir. 1976); Knott v. Missouri Pacific R. R., 527 F.2d 1249 (8th Cir. 1975); Brown v. D.C. Transit System, Inc., 523 F.2d 725 (D.C. Cir. 1975); Willingham v. Macon Tel. Pub. Co., 507 F.2d 1084 (5th Cir. 1975); Baker v. California Land Title Co., 507 F.2d 895 (9th Cir. 1974), *cert. denied*, 422 U.S. 1046 (1975).

98. *See, e.g.,* Fountain v. Safeway Stores, Inc., 555 F.2d 753 (9th Cir. 1977) (holding that a store's policy requiring men to wear ties and women to wear skirts does not violate Title VII); Devine v. Lonschien, 621 F. Supp. 894 (S.D.N.Y. 1985) (holding that a judge may properly conclude that a male attorney is lacking appropriate

attire when he does not wear a necktie in the courtroom). *But see* Carroll v. Talman Sav. & Loan Ass'n of Chicago, 604 F.2d 1028, 1032 (7th Cir. 1979), *cert. denied*, 445 U.S. 929 (1980) (invalidating employer's requirement that female employees wear a uniform while male employees wear "customary business attire").

99. *See, e.g.,* Tavora v. New York Mercantile Exch., 101 F.3d 907 (2d Cir. 1996); Willingham v. Macon Tel. Pub. Co., 507 F.2d 1084 (5th Cir. 1975); EEOC v. Sage Realty Corp., 507 F. Supp. 599 (S.D.N.Y. 1981).

100. Mapes-Riordan, *supra* note 97, at 499.

101. Tyrone Beason, *Boys Skirt the Rules*, SEATTLE TIMES, Apr. 6, 1996, at A1; *Students Demand Skirt Equality*, SALT LAKE TRIB., Oct. 13, 1996, at C3.

102. *Students Demand Skirt Equality, supra* note 101, at C3.

103. Barber v. Colorado Indep. School Dist., 901 S.W.2d 447, 448 (Tex. 1995).

104. Hines v. Caston School Corp., 651 N.E.2d 330, 334 (Ind. Ct. App. 1995).

105. 655 F. Supp. 1353 (S.D. Ohio 1987).

106. Dana Wilkie, *Senators Act to Ban Sex Bias in Pricing*, SAN DIEGO UNION & TRIB., Sept. 7, 1995, at A1.

107. Stephanie Zimmerman, *Wallet vs. Purse: Men and Women Pay Varying Prices for the Same Things*, FT. LAUDERDALE (FLA.) SUN-SENTINEL, Feb. 23, 1995, at 1E.

108. Sandy Wells, *Gender Pricing Is Discriminatory*, CHARLESTON GAZETTE & DAILY MAIL, Apr. 14, 1995, at 1C.

109. *See* Dock Club, Inc. v. Illinois Liquor Control Comm'n, 428 N.E.2d 735, 738 (Ill. Ct. App. 1981). *See also* Tuchich v. Dearborn Indoor Racquet Club, 309 N.W.2d 615, 619 (Mich. Ct. App. 1981) (holding that a racquet club's "price differential is designed to encourage membership and make the club facilities more available to both sexes"); Magid v. Oak Park Racquet Club Assoc. Ltd., 269 N.W.2d 661, 663 (Mich. Ct. App. 1978) (upholding lower tennis club fee for women as not a "withholding, refusal or denial" of public accommodations); MacLean v. First N.W. Indus. of America, Inc., 635 P.2d 683, 687 (Wash. 1981) (holding that the male plaintiff himself benefited from ladies' night at the basketball game, since he purchased a half-price ticket for his wife, and finding that most fans approved of ladies' night).

110. City of Clearwater v. Studebaker's Dance Club, 516 So.2d 1106, 1108 (Fla. Dist. Ct. App. 1987).

111. *See* Ladd v. Iowa West Racing Ass'n, 438 N.W.2d 600, 602 (Iowa 1986) (determining that Ladies' Day free admission and discounted prices for women on food and beverages were prohibited by Iowa Civil Rights Act); Pennsylvania Liquor Control Bd. v. Dobrinoff, 471 A.2d 941, 943 (Pa. 1984) (holding that exempting women from cover charge on nights that "go go dancers" performed "may well have been intended for purposes other than a desire to oppress male customers (the trial court opinion suggests 'chivalry and courtesy to the fair sex')," but was nevertheless price discrimination based on sex). *But cf.* Koire v. Metro Car Wash, 707 P.2d 195,

201 (Cal. 1985) (ladies' day at car washes "reinforces harmful stereotypes" for both women and men).

112. *See* CAL. CIV. CODE § 51.6 (West 1996).

113. *See* Recent Litigation, *Civil Rights—Gender Discrimination—California Prohibits Gender-Based Pricing—Cal. Civ. Code § 51.6 (West. Supp. 1996)*, 109 HARV. L. REV. 1839, 1841 (1996).

114. *See* Peppin v. Woodside Delicatessen, 506 A.2d 263, 266 (Md. 1986) (finding a discriminatory effect on men from the requirement that they wear skirts or gowns to obtain price breaks).

NOTES TO CHAPTER 4

1. Martha Minow, *Surviving Victim Talk*, 40 UCLA L. REV. 1411, 1430- 31, 1444 (1993).

2. *See, e.g.*, Elizabeth A. Pendo, *Recognizing Violence against Women: Gender and the Hate Crimes Statistics Act*, 17 HARV. WOMEN'S L.J. 157, 164 (1994).

3. *See, e.g.*, James V. P. Check, *Hostility toward Women: Some Theoretical Considerations, in* VIOLENCE IN INTIMATE RELATIONSHIPS 29, 34 (Gordon W. Russell ed., 1988).

4. *See, e.g.*, GERDA SIANN, ACCOUNTING FOR AGGRESSION: PERSPECTIVES ON AGGRESSION AND VIOLENCE 16–17 (1985).

5. *See, e.g.*, State v. Rusk, 424 A.2d 720, 733 (Md. 1981) (Cole, J., dissenting) (arguing that a woman "must follow the natural instinct of every proud female to resist, by more than mere words, the violation of her person by a stranger or an unwelcomed friend").

6. Dorothy E. Roberts, *Deviance, Resistance, and Love*, 1994 UTAH L. REV. 179, 188.

7. Dianne Avery, *Gender Stereotypes, Picket Line Violence, and the "Law" of Strike Misconduct Cases*, 8 OHIO ST. J. ON DISP. RESOL. 251, 274 (1993).

8. 450 U.S. 464, 471 (1981).

9. Sylvia A. Law, *Rethinking Sex and the Constitution*, 132 U. PA. L. REV. 955, 1000 n.175 (1984).

10. 450 U.S. at 467.

11. Katharine T. Bartlett, *Feminist Legal Methods*, 103 HARV. L. REV. 829, 840 (1990).

12. "Men are three times as likely as women to be [homicide] victims." Bernie Zilbergeld, *Is Male Violence Inevitable?*, S.F. CHRON., June 23, 1991, at 6.

13. *See* Bennett Roth, *Most Women Know Their Attacker, Research Finds; Study Explores Crime Victims in U.S.*, HOUS. CHRON., Jan. 31, 1994, at A1.

14. *See, e.g.*, Wark v. Robbins, 458 F.2d 1295, 1298 (1st Cir. 1972) (holding that imposing a six- to twelve-year sentence on a male prisoner for escape while a similarly situated female prisoner who escaped would receive a maximum of eleven

months was justified by the different "risks of violence and danger to inmates, prison personnel, and the outside community"); United States v. Redondo-Lemos, 817 F. Supp. 812, 815 (D. Ariz. 1993) (finding an equal protection violation in sentencing from probation office statistics showing that male drug offenders were sentenced to thirty-six months while similarly situated female drug offenders were sentenced to an average of thirty-two months, and data that showed 11 percent of males and 35 percent of females received probation), *rev'd*, 27 F.3d 439 (9th Cir. 1994) (holding that the data relied on by the district court established disparate impact but not disparate treatment); U.S. SENTENCING COMM'N, SPECIAL REPORT TO THE CONGRESS: MANDATORY MINIMUM PENALTIES IN THE FEDERAL CRIMINAL JUSTICE SYSTEM 76 (1991) (finding that nationwide, 50.4 percent of women who committed crimes subject to mandatory minimum sentences received such a sentence while 61.5 percent of men did). *See also* Rodgers v. Ohio Parole Bd., No. 92AP-709, 1992 WL 341382 (Ohio Ct. App. Nov. 17, 1992); Charles J. Corley et al., *Sex and the Likelihood of Sanction*, 80 J. CRIM. L. & CRIMINOLOGY 540, 541 (1989); Michael E. Faulstich & John R. Moore, *The Insanity Plea: A Study of Societal Reactions*, 8 LAW & PSYCHOL. REV. 129, 132 (1984). *But see* Leslie G. Street, *Despair and Disparity in Florida's Prisons and Jails*, 18 FLA. ST. U. L. REV. 513, 520 (1991) ("Women are generally imprisoned for less serious offenses than men, but serve longer sentences for their lesser offenses"). Kit Kinports, *Evidence Engendered*, 1991 U. ILL. L. REV. 413, 421 (Women who "offend judicial expectations" of appropriate gender roles, such as women who commit crimes of violence, receive longer sentences than their male counterparts).

15. Harris v. Pulley, 692 F.2d 1189, 1198–99 (9th Cir. 1982), *rev'd*, 465 U.S. 37 (1984).

16. Victor L. Streib & Lynn Sametz, *Executing Female Juveniles*, 22 CONN. L. REV. 3, 4 (1989).

17. *See* American Academy of Family Physicians, *Review of Suicide in Patients with Major Depression*, 50 AM. J. PSYCHIATRY 1102 (1994).

18. Lucinda J. Peach, *Women at War: The Ethics of Women in Combat*, 15 HAMLINE J. PUB. L. & PUB. POL'Y 199, 208 (1994).

19. 291 F. Supp. 122 (S.D.N.Y. 1968).

20. *See, e.g.*, United States v. Yingling, 368 F. Supp. 379, 386 (W.D. Pa. 1973) (justifying selective service registration for males based only on "innate [physical] characteristics").

21. 453 U.S. 57 (1981).

22. *See* Alice S. Andre-Clark, Note, *Whither Statutory Rape Laws: Of Michael M., the Fourteenth Amendment, and Protecting Women from Sexual Aggression*, 65 S. CAL. L. REV. 1933, 1966 (1992).

23. *See* Peach, *supra* note 18, at 229.

24. *See supra* chapter 3.

25. Katherine M. Franke, *The Central Mistake of Sex Discrimination Law: The Disaggregation of Sex from Gender*, 144 U. PA. L. REV. 1, 86 (1995).

26. Selective Draft Law Cases, 245 U.S. 366, 368 (1918) ("The highest duty of the citizen is to bear arms at the call of the nation").

27. York v. Story, 324 F.2d 450, 455 (9th Cir. 1963).

28. On this issue, see the thoughtful concurrence and dissent by Judge Richard Posner in *Johnson v. Phelan*, 69 F.3d 144, 151 (7th Cir. 1995), *cert. denied*, 117 S. Ct. 506 (1996).

29. *See* Lee v. Downs, 641 F.2d 1117 (4th Cir. 1981); Forts v. Ward, 621 F.2d 1210 (7th Cir. 1980); Dawson v. Kendrick, 527 F. Supp. 1252, 1316–17 (S.D. W. Va. 1981).

30. 986 F.2d 1521, 1522–26 (9th Cir. 1993).

31. 779 F.2d 491, 492 (9th Cir. 1985).

32. *See* Tharp v. Iowa Dept. Corrections, 68 F.3d 223 (8th Cir. 1995); Torres v. Wisconsin Dept. Health & Soc. Servs., 859 F.2d 1523 (7th Cir. 1988).

33. *See, e.g.,* Madyun v. Franzen, 704 F.2d 954 (7th Cir. 1983) (dismissing free exercise and equal protection claims of an Islamic male prisoner who refused to submit to a frisk search by a female guard—even though the state had prison regulations that allowed only female guards to frisk female prisoners). *See also* Cookish v. Powell, 945 F.2d 441 (1st Cir. 1991) (prison officials' reasonable but mistaken belief that emergency existed justified a visual body cavity search of a male inmate in the presence of female guards); Michenfelder v. Sumner, 860 F.2d 328, 334 (9th Cir. 1988) ("assigned positions of female guards that require only infrequent and casual observation, or observation at distance, and that are reasonably related to prison needs are not so degrading as to warrant court interference"); Griffin v. Michigan Dept. Corrections, 654 F. Supp. 690 (E.D. Mich. 1982); Bagley v. Watson, 579 F. Supp. 1099 (D. Or. 1983). *But see contra* Canedy v. Boardman, 16 F.3d 183 (7th Cir. 1994); Fortner v. Thomas, 983 F.2d 1024, 1030 (11th Cir. 1993); Cornwell v. Dahlberg 963 F.2d 912 (6th Cir. 1992); Cumbey v. Meachum, 684 F.2d 712 (10th Cir. 1982).

34. 69 F.3d 144 (7th Cir. 1995), *cert. denied*, 117 S. Ct. 506 (1996).

35. Smith v. Fairman, 678 F.2d 52 (7th Cir. 1982); Bowling v. Enomoto, 514 F. Supp. 201 (N.D. Cal. 1981).

36. 109 F.3d 614, 624 (9th Cir. 1997).

37. Timm v. Gunter, 917 F.2d 1093, 1102 (8th Cir. 1990).

38. *Id.* at 1103.

39. Bill St. John, *Authors on Stage: William Styron on Styron; His Darkness and American Male Suicide*, ROCKY MTN. NEWS, May 1, 1994, at 74A (quoting William Styron).

40. Michael S. Kimmel, *Issues for Men in the 1990s*, 46 U. MIAMI L. REV. 671, 674 (1992).

41. For instance, the circuits split regarding whether male plaintiffs suing for sex discrimination, so-called reverse discrimination, are required to establish the additional element "that the defendant is the unusual employer who discriminates against the majority." *Compare* Lanphear v. Prokop, 703 F.2d 1311, 1315 (D.C. Cir. 1983) *and* Livingston v. Roadway Express, Inc., 802 F.2d 1250, 1251–52 (10th Cir. 1986) *with* Loeffler v. Carlin, 780 F.2d 1365, 1369 (8th Cir. 1985), *rev'd on other grounds sub nom.* Loeffler v. Frank, 486 U.S. 549 (1988).

42. *See* Martha Chamallas, *Writing about Sexual Harassment: A Guide to the Literature*, 4 UCLA Women's L.J. 37, 38 n.3 (1993).

43. Colleen O'Connor, *Films Distort Reality of Sexual Harassment*, Dallas Morning News, Jan. 5, 1995, at D2.

44. Daniel Seligman, *The Follies Come to Boston*, Fortune, Apr. 3, 1995, at 142.

45. 821 F. Supp. 225, 228, 230 (S.D.N.Y. 1993).

46. *See* David S. Hames, *An Actionable Condition of Work-Related Sexual Harassment*, 1992 Lab. L.J. 430, 430.

47. *See* Barbara A. Gutek, Sex and the Workplace: The Impact of Sexual Behavior and Harassment on Women, Men and Organizations 54 (1985) (noting that sexual harassment of men is "common" and estimating its incidence at perhaps up to 9 percent of the total cases occurring); Office of Merit Systems Reviews and Studies, U.S. Merit Systems Protection Board, Sexual Harassment in the Federal Workplace: Is It a Problem? 98 (1981) (results of an EEOC survey reported that "42% of all female federal employees but only 15% of male employees, reported being sexually harassed"); Bradley Golden, Note, Harris v. Forklift: *The Supreme Court Takes One Step Forward and Two Steps Back on the Issue of Hostile Work Environment Sexual Harassment*, 1994 Det. C.L. Rev. 1151, 1173 ("Although less common, the instances of female supervisors harassing male employees seem to increase with the number of female supervisors").

48. Catharine A. MacKinnon, Sexual Harassment of Working Women: A Case Study of Sex Discrimination 27 (1979). *See generally* Snider v. Consolidation Coal Co., 973 F.2d 555, 558 (7th Cir. 1992) (expert testimony that 95 percent of victims do not report sexual harassment "due to a fear of reprisal or loss of privacy"), *cert. denied*, 506 U.S. 1054 (1993).

49. Andrew Bolger, *Sexual Harassment of Men Highlighted*, Fin. Times, Mar. 3, 1995, at 11.

50. *See generally* Sarah A. DeCosse, *Simply Unbelievable: Reasonable Women and Hostile Environment Sexual Harassment*, 10 Law & Ineq. J. 285 (1992).

51. *See* Michael B. King, *Male Sexual Assault in the Community, in* Male Victims of Sexual Assault 1, 5–7 (Gillian C. Mezey & Michael B. King eds., 1992).

52. *See, e.g.*, Jane L. Dolkart, *Hostile Environment Harassment: Equality, Objectivity, and the Shaping of Legal Standards*, 43 Emory L.J. 151, 181 (1994).

53. *See, e.g.*, Hopkins v. Baltimore Gas & Elec. Co., 871 F. Supp. 822 (D. Md. 1994), *aff'd*, 70 Fair Empl. Prac. Cas. (BNA) 184 (4th Cir. 1996); Polly v. Houston

Lighting & Power Co., 803 F. Supp. 1 (S.D. Tex. 1992); Dillon v. Frank, 58 Fair Empl. Prac. Cas. (BNA) 90 (E.D. Mich. 1990), *aff'd*, 952 F.2d 403 (6th Cir. 1992).

54. Dillon v. Frank, 58 Fair Empl. Prac. Cas. (BNA) at 90.

55. 54 Fair Empl. Prac. Cas. (BNA) 81, 82 (D. Kan. 1990).

56. *See* Joyner v. AAA Cooper Transp., 597 F. Supp. 537 (M.D. Ala. 1983), *aff'd*, 749 F.2d 732 (11th Cir. 1984); Wright v. Methodist Youth Servs., Inc., 511 F. Supp. 307 (N.D. Ill. 1981); Mogilefsky v. Superior Court, 20 Cal. App. 4th 1409 (1993).

57. *See generally* Martha Chamallas, *Feminist Constructions of Objectivity: Multiple Perspectives in Sexual and Racial Harassment Litigation*, 1 Tex. J. Women & L. 95, 127 (1992).

58. *See, e.g.*, Williams v. District of Columbia, No. 94-02727 (JHG), 1996 WL 56100, at *7–8 (D.D.C Feb. 5, 1996) (listing cases). State statutes may provide a cause of action. *Compare* Lehmann v. Toys 'R' Us, Inc., 626 A.2d 445, 454 (N.J. 1993) (holding in dicta that "[t]he [New Jersey Law against Discrimination] protects both men and women and bars both heterosexual and homosexual harassment") *with* Hart v. Nat'l Mortgage & Land Co., 189 Cal. App. 3d 1420 (1987) (holding that California unfair employment practice statute did not apply to same-sex sexual harassment).

59. Oncale v. Sundowner Offshore Servs., Inc., 83 F.3d 118 (5th Cir. 1996), *cert. granted*, 65 USLW 3432 (U.S., June 9, 1997) (No. 96-568).

60. 803 F. Supp. 1, 4–5 (S.D. Tex. 1992).

61. 697 F. Supp. 1452, 1454 (N.D. Ill. 1988).

62. *Id.* at 1454, 1456.

63. *See, e.g.*, Garcia v. Elf Atochem N. Am., 28 F.3d 446 (5th Cir. 1994); Hopkins v. Baltimore Gas & Elec. Co., 871 F. Supp. 822 (D. Md. 1994), *aff'd*, 70 Fair Empl. Prac. Cas. (BNA) 184 (4th Cir. 1996); Vandeventer v. Wabash Nat'l Corp., 867 F. Supp. 790 (N.D. Ind. 1994).

64. Kathryn Abrams, *Title VII and the Complex Female Subject*, 92 Mich. L. Rev. 2479, 2515 (1994). Professor Abrams also notes that "courts are far more sympathetic to male sexual harassment claimants when they present the image of a normative, unambiguously male subject who receives unexpected sexual attention from another male in the workplace." *Id.*

65. 28 F.3d at 448.

66. *See, e.g.*, Cornwell v. Robinson, 23 F.3d 694, 698 (2d Cir. 1994) (holding that evidence of male coworkers grabbing their own crotches in plaintiff's presence, making sexual propositions, and touching plaintiff's chest constituted a cognizable Title VII claim); King v. Hillen, 21 F.3d 1572 (Fed. Cir. 1994) (holding that defendant's touching plaintiff's buttocks and thigh, looking at her in a sexually suggestive manner, and making remarks with sexual overtones amounted to potential sexual harassment).

67. 871 F. Supp. at 824–29.

68. *Id.* at 835.

69. *See, e.g.*, Harris v. Forklift Sys., Inc., 510 U.S. 17, 23 (1993); King v. Hillen, 21 F.3d at 1580.

70. 477 U.S. 57, 67 (1986).

71. *Cf.* Harris, 510 U.S. at 23 ("The effect on the employee's psychological well-being is, of course, relevant to determining whether the plaintiff actually found the environment abusive"); Yates v. Avco Corp., 819 F.2d 630, 637 (6th Cir. 1987) (noting the importance of evaluating alleged incidents of sexual harassment from the victim's perspective).

72. 867 F. Supp. 790, 798 (N.D. Ind. 1994) (emphasis added).

73. Goluszek v. Smith, 697 F. Supp. 1452, 1456 (N.D. Ill. 1988).

74. *See* Chiapuzio v. BLT Operating Corp., 826 F. Supp. 1334, 1337 (D. Wyo. 1993) ("the equal harassment of both genders does not escape the purview of Title VII"). *But see* Henson v. City of Dundee, 682 F.2d 897, 904 (11th Cir. 1982) (when a supervisor "makes sexual overtures to workers of both sexes . . . the sexual harassment would not be based upon sex because men and women are accorded like treatment").

75. *See, e.g.*, Burns v. McGregor Elec. Indus., Inc., 989 F.2d 959 (8th Cir. 1993) (finding that sexual advances of a single supervisor coupled with sexual innuendos and obscene name-calling constituted sexual harassment of a woman); Zabkowicz v. West Bend Co., 589 F. Supp. 780 (E.D. Wis. 1984) (holding that conduct consisting of offensive and abusive language, indecent exposure, and posted drawings depicting sex acts constituted sexual harassment).

76. *See* Vandeventer v. Wabash Nat'l Corp., No. 4:93 cv 46 AS, slip op. at 22 (N.D. Ind. Oct. 12, 1994) ("While this court will not argue with that assessment [that Vandeventer's affidavit is composed merely of vague conclusory statements with no supporting facts], it does not quite agree that this plaintiff has failed to make an issue of fact regarding incidents other than the two about which she complained").

77. *See, e.g.*, Lehmann v. Toys 'R' Us, Inc., 626 A.2d 445, 452 (N.J. 1993) (holding that if a plaintiff witnessed harassment of same-sex employees, this would support her perceptions of a sexually hostile work environment).

78. *See* Gillian K. Hadfield, *Households at Work: Beyond Labor Market Policies to Remedy the Gender Gap*, 82 GEO. L.J. 89 (1993).

79. David K. Haase, *Evaluating the Desirability of Federally Mandated Parental Leave*, 22 FAM. L.Q. 341, 360 (1988).

80. CATALYST, REPORT ON A NATIONAL STUDY OF PARENTAL LEAVES 65–66 (1986), *reprinted in* The Parental and Medical Leave Act of 1986: Joint Hearing on H.R. 4300 before the Subcomm. on Labor-Management Relations and the Subcomm. on Labor Standards of the House Comm. on Education & Labor, 99th Cong., 2d Sess. 151–228 (1986).

81. *See* Martin H. Malin, *Fathers and Parental Leave*, 72 TEX. L. REV. 1047, 1064–79 (1994).

82. *See, e.g.*, Ackerman v. Board of Educ., 372 F. Supp. 274 (S.D.N.Y. 1974); Danielson v. Board of Higher Educ., 358 F. Supp. 22 (S.D.N.Y. 1972).

83. 903 F.2d 243, 247–48 (3d Cir. 1990).

84. *See generally* Nancy D. Polikoff, *Why Are Mothers Losing: A Brief Analysis of Criteria Used in Child Custody Determinations*, 7 WOMEN'S RTS. L. REP. 235 (1982).

85. *See* Jamil S. Zainaldin, *The Emergence of a Modern American Family Law: Child Custody, Adoption, and the Courts, 1796–1851*, 73 Nw. U. L. REV. 1038, 1085 (1979).

86. *See* Elizabeth S. Scott, *Pluralism, Parental Preference, and Child Custody*, 80 CAL. L. REV. 615, 620 n.10 (1992).

87. *See, e.g.*, COLO. REV. STAT. § 14-10-123.5 (1987); OHIO REV. CODE ANN. § 3109.04 (Baldwin 1995); TEX. FAM. CODE ANN. § 14.021 (West 1993).

88. *See, e.g.*, TENN. CODE ANN. § 36-6-101(d) (1991); *see also* Judith Bond Jennison, *The Search for Equality in a Woman's World: Fathers' Rights to Child Custody*, 43 RUTGERS L. REV. 1141, 1149 (1991).

89. *See* Scott, *supra* note 86, at 622 n.20. *But see* Jana B. Singer & William L. Reynolds, *A Dissent on Joint Custody*, 47 MD. L. REV. 497 (1988).

90. Alan M. Levy, *Debunking Myths: The Indispensable Role of Fathers*, FAM. ADVOC., Winter 1993, at 30. *But see* Mary Becker, *Maternal Feelings: Myth, Taboo, and Child Custody*, 1 S. CAL. REV. L. & WOMEN'S STUD. 133, 193–96 (1992) (suggesting that, even under the primary caretaker standard, a strong judicial bias exists against mothers if the father does more child rearing than average, if the mother leaves the children for some reason, or if the mother has extramarital sex).

91. MARYLAND SPECIAL JOINT COMMISSION ON GENDER BIAS IN THE COURTS, REPORT OF THE MARYLAND SPECIAL JOINT COMMITTEE ON GENDER BIAS IN THE COURTS 27 (1989) (surveying judges); Leslie A. Cadwell, Note, *Gender Bias against Fathers in Custody? The Important Difference between Outcome and Process*, 18 VT. L. REV. 215, 249 (1993) (surveying lawyers).

92. *See* ELEANOR E. MACCOBY & ROBERT H. MNOOKIN, DIVIDING THE CHILD: SOCIAL AND LEGAL DILEMMAS OF CUSTODY 112 (1992); Stephen J. Bahr et al., *Trends in Child Custody Awards: Has the Removal of Maternal Preference Made a Difference?*, 28 FAM. L.Q. 247, 256 (1994) (while the mothers receiving sole custody in Utah decreased from "91 percent in 1970–74 to 70 percent in 1990–93," fathers were awarded sole custody 5 percent of the time during both those periods).

93. *See, e.g.*, Becker, *supra* note 90, at 182–83; Harriet Newman Cohen, *Finding Fairness in Financial Settlements*, FAM. ADVOC., Summer 1994, at 57, 59 (claiming statistics show that fathers may obtain custody in more than 50 percent of contested custody suits).

94. Bahr et al., *supra* note 92, at 257 (reporting on Utah cases between 1970 and 1993).

95. Maccoby & Mnookin, *supra* note 92, at 138.

96. "If only a small number of mothers and fathers litigate custody, the number of fathers and mothers who *win* these suits may be heavily influenced by which mothers and fathers go to court." Jennifer E. Horne, Note, *The Brady Bunch and Other Fictions: How Courts Decide Child Custody Disputes Involving Remarried Parents*, 45 STAN. L. REV. 2073, 2086 (1993) (emphasis added).

97. Robert H. Mnookin et al., *Private Ordering Revisited: What Custodial Arrangements Are Parents Negotiating?, in* DIVORCE REFORM AT THE CROSSROADS 37, 49 tbl. 2.3 (Stephen D. Sugarman & Herma H. Kay eds., 1990).

98. *See, e.g.*, Cadwell, *supra* note 91, at 244 (reporting the results of the Vermont Task Force on Gender Bias in the Legal System survey).

99. *See, e.g.*, BARBARA K. ROTHMAN, RECREATING MOTHERHOOD: IDEOLOGY AND TECHNOLOGY IN A PATRIARCHAL SOCIETY 244–55 (1989) (advocating that biological mothers should have the exclusive ability to make custody decisions for the first six weeks after a child is born); Martha A. Fineman, *The Neutered Mother*, 46 U. MIAMI L. REV. 653, 666–67 (1992) (suggesting that gender-neutral concepts may significantly harm mothers who have organized their lives around caregiving activities).

100. Becker, *supra* note 90, at 135, 137, 143–52.

101. *See, e.g.*, Martha Fineman, *Dominant Discourse, Professional Language, and Legal Change in Child Custody Decisionmaking*, 101 HARV. L. REV. 727 (1988).

NOTES TO CHAPTER 5

1. PETER HARRIS RESEARCH GROUP, INC., 1995 WOMEN'S EQUALITY POLL: A SURVEY OF THE ATTITUDES OF A CROSS-SECTION OF AMERICAN WOMEN AND MEN AND A CROSS-SECTION OF VOTERS IN CALIFORNIA ON AFFIRMATIVE ACTION, ABORTION, AND OTHER KEY ISSUES AFFECTING WOMEN AND MINORITIES 11 (1995).

2. *U.S. Women Are Conservative on Most Issues, Survey Shows*, WASH. TIMES, May 24, 1996, at A4.

3. Wendy Kaminer, *Feminism's Identity Crisis*, ATLANTIC, Oct. 1993, at 51. *See also* Elizabeth A. Cook, *Feminism and the Gender Gap: A Second Look*, 53 J. POL. 1111, 1113 (1991) ("Slightly more than a quarter of both men and women are classified as feminists, and slightly less than one-third of both sexes fall into the potential feminist category").

4. Judy Mann, *Attacking Their Own*, WASH. POST, June 28, 1995, at E15.

5. John R. O'Neill, *Ex-NOW Head Talks about Feminism*, INDIANAPOLIS STAR, June 11, 1995, at B01.

6. Susan Faludi, *"Feminism Is Not the Story of My Life": How Today's Feminist Elite Has Lost Touch with the Real Concerns of Women (Book Review)*, NATION, Jan. 8, 1996, at 25.

7. Rebecca Walker, *Changing the Face of Feminism*, ESSENCE, Jan. 1996, at 123.

8. Lisa Marie Hogeland, *Fear of Feminism*, Ms., Nov.–Dec. 1994, at 18.

9. *See, e.g.,* Richard Cohen, *The Wide Net of Sexual Harassment*, WASH. POST, June 15, 1993, at A21 ("In the lexicon of some radical feminists such as Andrea Dworkin, even willing sexual intercourse in marriage is a form of rape"); Lance Morrow, *Men: Are They Really That Bad?*, TIME, Feb. 14, 1994, at 58 ("Andrea Dworkin has simplified the discussion by asserting that every act of sex between a man and a woman, no matter what, is rape"); John A. Siliciano, *Fighting with Angry Women: A Response to Lasson*, 42 J. LEGAL EDUC. 461, 461 (1992) ("it is exceedingly unlikely that most men and women will stop enjoying consensual sex simply because Andrea Dworkin thinks it is indistinguishable from rape").

10. ANDREA DWORKIN, INTERCOURSE 122–23 (1987).

11. Howard Fineman, *Some Hard Right Turns for the GOP*, NEWSWEEK, June 20, 1994, at 38.

12. Karen M. Thomas, *It Takes a Proverb: Saying Has Gone from Humble Catch Phrase to Political Football*, DALLAS MORNING NEWS, Sept. 12, 1996, at 1C.

13. Joan C. Williams, *Gender Wars: Selfless Women in the Republic of Choice*, 66 N.Y.U. L. REV. 1559, 1586 (1991).

14. Mary Otto, *Phyllis Schlafly Still Blasting Liberals, Feminists at 70*, HOUS. CHRON., Aug. 7, 1994, at A4.

15. Karen De Witt, *Feminists Gather to Affirm Relevancy of Their Movement*, N.Y. TIMES, Feb. 3, 1996, at 9.

16. Tad Friend, *Yes, Feminist Women Who Like Sex*, ESQUIRE, Feb. 1994, at 48, 50.

17. Zia Jaffrey, *Is Feminism the New 'F' Word?*, SASSY, Aug. 1995, at 42.

18. Deborah L. Rhode, *The "No-Problem" Problem: Feminist Challenges and Cultural Change*, 100 YALE L.J. 1731, 1792 (1991).

19. CHRISTINA HOFF SOMMERS, WHO STOLE FEMINISM? HOW WOMEN HAVE BETRAYED WOMEN 17 (1994).

20. Patrice McDermott, *On Cultural Authority: Women's Studies, Feminist Politics, and the Popular Press*, 20 SIGNS 668, 671 (1995).

21. KATIE ROIPHE, THE MORNING AFTER: SEX, FEAR, AND FEMINISM ON CAMPUS 88–93 (1993).

22. CAMILLE PAGLIA, SEX, ART, AND AMERICAN CULTURE 53 (1992).

23. Elizabeth M. Schneider, *Feminism and the False Dichotomy of Victimization and Agency*, 38 N.Y. L. SCH. L. REV. 387, 389 (1993).

24. Kathryn Abrams, *Sex Wars Redux: Agency and Coercion in Feminist Legal Theory*, 95 COLUM. L. REV. 304, 355 (1995).

25. Deborah L. Rhode, *Media Images, Feminist Issues*, 20 SIGNS 685, 700 (1995).

26. *Id.* at 701.

27. 413 U.S. 15, 36 (1973).

28. Richard N. Ostling, *What Does God Really Think about Sex?*, TIME, June 4, 1991, at 48.

29. SUSAN FALUDI, BACKLASH: THE UNDECLARED WAR AGAINST AMERICAN WOMEN 75 (1991).

30. *Id.*

31. Barbara Ehrenreich et al., Re-Making Love: The Feminization of Sex 71 (1986).

32. Margaret Carlson, *Can Pro-Choicers Prevail?*, Time, Aug. 14, 1989, at 28.

33. Irving Kristol, *Countercultures*, Commentary, Dec. 1994, at 35.

34. U.S. Const., amend. XIV, sec. 2.

35. Joellen Lind, *Dominance and Democracy: The Legacy of Woman Suffrage for the Voting Right*, 5 UCLA Women's L.J. 103, 164 (1994).

36. Paula Giddings, When and Where I Enter: The Impact of Black Women on Race and Sex in America 126 (1984).

37. *Reminiscences by Frances D. Gage*, in 1 History of Women's Suffrage 1848–1861, at 115 (Elizabeth Cady Stanton et al. eds., reprint ed., 1985).

38. bell hooks, Ain't I a Woman: Black Women and Feminism 4 (1981).

39. *See* Carleton Mabee, Sojourner Truth: Slave, Prophet, Legend 182 (1993).

40. Eleanor Flexner, Century of Struggle: The Woman's Rights Movement in the United States 317 (rev. ed. 1975).

41. Barbara Holkert Andolsen, Daughters of Jefferson, Daughters of Bootblacks (1986); Anne Firor Scott, *Most Invisible of All: Black Women's Voluntary Associations*, 56 J. S. Hist. 3 (1990).

42. Lucretia P. Murphy, *Black Women: Organizing to Lift . . . to Climb . . . to Rise*, 4 Tex. J. Women & L. 267, 286 (1995).

43. Angela Harris, *Categorical Discourse and Dominance Theory*, 5 Berkeley Women's L.J. 181, 183 (1989–90).

44. bell hooks, Feminist Theory: From Margin to Center 1–2 (1984).

45. Audre Lorde, *An Open Letter to Mary Daly*, in This Bridge Called My Back: Writings by Radical Women of Color 94–95 (Gloria Anzaldúa & Cherríe Moraga eds., 1983).

46. Dorothy E. Roberts, *Punishing Drug Addicts Who Have Babies: Women of Color, Equality, and the Right of Privacy*, 104 Harv. L. Rev. 1419, 1441 (1991).

47. Robert S. Chang, *Toward an Asian American Legal Scholarship: Critical Race Theory, Post-Structuralism, and Narrative Space*, 81 Cal. L. Rev. 1243, 1258, 1261 (1993).

48. Charlotte Rutherford, *Reproductive Freedoms and African American Women*, 4 Yale J.L. & Feminism 255, 273–74 (1992).

49. Beverly Horsburgh, *Lifting the Veil of Secrecy: Domestic Violence in the Jewish Community*, 18 Harv. Women's L.J. 171 (1995).

50. Charles R. Lawrence, III, *Forward Ace, Multiculturalism, and the Jurisprudence of Transformation*, 47 Stan. L. Rev. 819 (1995).

51. Ruth Picardie, *Straight Sex: The Politics of Pleasure (Book Review)*, 7 New Statesman & Soc'y 39 (Sept. 23, 1994).

52. Andrew Koppelman, *Why Discrimination against Lesbians and Gay Men Is Sex Discrimination*, 69 N.Y.U. L. REV. 197, 236 (1994).

53. Adrienne Rich, *Compulsory Heterosexuality and Lesbian Existence*, 5 SIGNS 631, 638 (1980).

54. Kate Muir, *The Feminist Challenge*, TIMES (LONDON), May 6, 1995, Magazine, at 18.

55. Alice Echols, *Stonewall (Book Review)*, NATION, Aug. 23, 1993, at 215.

56. Radicalesbians, *The Woman Identified Woman*, in RADICAL FEMINISM 240 (Anne Koedt et al. eds., 1973).

57. Charlotte Bunch, *Lesbians in Revolt*, in FEMINIST FRAMEWORKS 165 (Alison M. Jaggar & Paula S. Rothenberg eds., 2d ed. 1984).

58. Patricia Cain, *Feminist Jurisprudence: Grounding the Theories*, 4 BERKELEY WOMEN'S L.J. 191, 214 (1990) ("Why is the lesbian so invisible in feminist legal theory?").

59. Mary Coombs, *Between Women/Between Men: The Significance for Lesbianism of Historical Understandings of Same-(Male) Sex Sexual Activities*, 8 YALE J. L. & HUMAN. 241, 259 (1996).

60. Radicalesbians, *supra* note 56, at 240.

61. *Redstockings Manifesto*, in SISTERHOOD IS POWERFUL 534 (Robin Morgan ed., 1970) (emphasis in original).

62. John Sweeney, *The A-Z of Conspiracy*, GUARDIAN, Feb. 12, 1995, at 12 (giving the theory a believability rating of seven on a scale of one to ten).

63. Yvonne Roberts, *Who Loves You Baby? Has Feminism Let Mothers Down?*, GUARDIAN, Oct. 9, 1995, at 6.

64. Dana Densmore, *Who Is Saying Men Are the Enemy*, THE FEMALE STATE 4 (April 1970), cited in GINETTE CASTRO, AMERICAN FEMINISM: A CONTEMPORARY HISTORY 72 (1990).

65. ANITA SHREVE, WOMEN TOGETHER, WOMEN ALONE: THE LEGACY OF THE CONSCIOUSNESS-RAISING MOVEMENT 6 (1989).

66. PAULA KAMEN, FEMINIST FATALE: VOICES FROM THE "TWENTYSOMETHING" GENERATION EXPLORE THE FUTURE OF THE WOMEN'S MOVEMENT 35 (1991).

67. ANGRY WOMEN 105 (Andrea Juno & V. Vale eds., 1991) (comments of Lydia Lunch).

68. Mary Joe Frug, *Sexual Equality and Sexual Difference in American Law*, 26 NEW ENG. L. REV. 665, 675–82 (1992).

69. Nina J. Easton, *"I'm Not a Feminist But . . ."; Can the Women's Movement March into the Mainstream?*, L.A. TIMES, Feb. 2, 1992, at 12.

70. John Leo, *Men as Beasts and Women as Victims*, CHARLESTON GAZETTE, Apr. 14, 1994, at 9A ("At anti-rape rallies, men were banned as oppressors and women began to tell colorful and ideological stories of rape as "white-male business as usual"); *Women's Rally Vows to "Take Back the Night,"* SEATTLE TIMES, Feb. 23, 1986,

at B2 ("Men were asked not to join the march. Instead, they were asked to attend a workshop sponsored by Men Against Rape").

71. Barbara Ehrenreich, *Feminism Confronts Bobbittry*, TIME, Jan. 24, 1994, at 74.

72. hooks, *supra* note 44, at 68–69.

73. *See* Kathleen Parker, *It's Time for Feminists to Champion Motherhood*, ORLANDO SENTINEL, June 19, 1996, at E1.

74. Nancy Gibbs, *The War against Feminism*, TIME, Mar. 9, 1992, at 50, 52.

75. Katha Pollitt, *Everything's Up to Date in North Dakota*, TIKKUN 57 (Jan.–Feb. 1990).

76. Lea Brilmayer, *Inclusive Feminism*, 38 N.Y. L. SCH. L. REV. 377, 385–86 (1993).

77. *See, e.g.*, Catharine A. MacKinnon, *Not a Moral Issue*, 2 YALE L. & POL'Y REV. 321, 325–26 (1984).

78. *See, e.g.*, Nadine Strossen, *A Feminist Critique of "The" Feminist Critique of Pornography*, 79 VA. L. REV. 1099 (1993).

79. *See* Leanne Katz, *Introduction: Women, Censorship, and "Pornography,"* 38 N.Y. L. SCH. L. REV. 9, 16–18 (1993).

80. Suzanne Fields, *Invasion of the Neoclassical Feminist Body Snatchers*, INSIGHT, June 5, 1995, at 40.

81. Geordie Greig, *Get Your Facts Straight, Sisters*, TIMES (LONDON), Aug. 14, 1994.

82. Susan Faludi, *Statistically Challenged*, NATION, Apr. 15, 1996, at 10.

83. Laura Berman, *Feminist Fatale*, DET. NEWS, Feb. 22, 1992, at 1C.

84. Helen Birch, *Unsisterly Conduct as Feminist Generations Fall Out*, INDEPENDENT, May 18, 1995, at 3.

85. Carole A. Stabile, *Postmodernism, Feminism, and Marx: Notes from the Abyss*, MONTHLY REV., July 1995, at 89.

86. Martha Minow, *Surviving Victim Talk*, 40 UCLA L. REV. 1411, 1413 (1993).

87. Martha Burk & Heidi Hartmann, *Beyond the Gender Gap: What Must the Women's Movement Do to Recover?*, NATION, June 10, 1996, at 20.

88. Verta Taylor, *The Future of Feminism: A Social Movement Analysis*, in FEMINIST FRONTIERS II: RETHINKING SEX, GENDER AND SOCIETY 473, 477–78 (Laurel Richardson & Verta Taylor eds., 1989).

89. Robert Putnam, *Bowling Alone: America's Declining Social Capital*, 6 J. DEMOCRACY 65 (Jan. 1995). *But see* Katha Pollitt, *For Whom the Ball Rolls*, NATION, Apr. 15, 1996, at 9 (suggesting that Putnam's examination of bowling leagues, the Elks, and the League of Women Voters focuses on groups that are historically on the wane, and concluding that "the whole theory is seriously out of touch with the complexities of contemporary life").

90. *See* Alan Bunce, *The Barn-Raising Spirit Still Thrives*, CHRISTIAN SCI. MONITOR, Apr. 26, 1996, at 10–11.

91. Joannie M. Schrof, *Feminism's Daughters: Their Agenda Is a Cultural Sea Change,* U.S. NEWS & WORLD REP., Sept. 27, 1993, at 70.

92. Janis Leibs Dworkis, *Mothers of a Movement: Feeling Alienated from '90s Women's Rights Groups, Veteran Feminists Are Reuniting and Remembering,* DALLAS MORNING NEWS, June 2, 1993, at 5C.

93. Carol Morell, *Riding the Third Wave: Feminism's New Generation Is Making Its Mark in NOW Chapters across the Country,* DALLAS MORNING NEWS, July 10, 1996, at 5C.

94. Jennifer Reid Maxcy Myhre, *One Bad Hair Day Too Many, or the Hairstory of an Androgynous Young Feminist, in* LISTEN UP: VOICES FROM THE NEXT FEMINIST GENERATION 132, 134 (Barbara Findlens ed., 1995).

95. Christine Doza, *Bloodlove, in* LISTEN UP, *supra* note 94, at 249, 251.

96. Gina Dent, *Missionary Position, in* TO BE REAL: TELLING THE TRUTH AND CHANGING THE FACE OF FEMINISM 61, 69 (Rebecca Walker ed., 1995).

97. Wendy Kaminer, *Feminism's Third Wave: What Do Young Women Want,* N.Y. TIMES, June 4, 1995, sec. 7, at 3.

98. Susan Alexander, *How the Next Generation Views Feminists,* CHI. TRIB., Dec. 17, 1995, at 9.

99. Shreve, *supra* note 65, at 226.

100. Claudia Wallis, *Onward, Women! The Superwoman Is Weary, the Young Are Complacent, but Feminism Is Not Dead, and Baby, There's Still a Long Way to Go,* TIME, Dec. 4, 1989, at 80.

101. Rene Sanchez, *Don't Know Much about History? Neither Do Most Students in U.S.* HOUS. CHRON., Nov. 2, 1995, at 9.

102. Ellen Goodman, *Would One Thousand Young American Women Rather Increase the Size of Their Income, Political Power, or Breasts?,* ESQUIRE, Feb. 1, 1994, at 65.

103. Easton, *supra* note 69, at 12.

104. Mike Kaszuba, *Feminists Seek Greater Appeal in the Suburbs,* STAR TRIB. (MINNEAPOLIS-ST. PAUL), Mar. 17, 1996, at 1B.

NOTES TO CHAPTER 6

1. *National Coalition of Free Men* (visited July 31, 1997) <http://www.ncfm.org/hist.htm>.

2. Melissa Fletcher Stoeltje, *Child Support: Fathers' Rights Advocates Dispute Stats, Urge Reforms,* HOUS. CHRON., Jan. 28, 1997, at 1.

3. Diane Mason, *National Men's Rights Group Has It All Wrong,* ST. PETERSBURG TIMES, June 15, 1990, at 1D.

4. David Behrens, *Real Men Don't Shirk Dad Role,* NEWSDAY, Nov. 30, 1994, at B3.

5. Tony Bozjak, *Today's Man Finds New Ways of Living, Loving,* S. F. CHRON., Aug. 15, 1989, at B3.

6. Michael S. Kimmel & Michael Kaufman, *Weekend Warriors: The New Men's Movement, in* THE POLITICS OF MANHOOD: PROFEMINIST MEN RESPOND TO THE MYTHOPOETIC MEN'S MOVEMENT 25 (Michael S. Kimmel ed., 1995).

7. ROBERT BLY, IRON JOHN: A BOOK ABOUT MEN x, 3 (1990).

8. Kimmel & Kaufman, *supra* note 6, at 25.

9. *Id.* at 27.

10. Brad Stetson, *The True Social Value of Promise Keepers*, SAN DIEGO UNION & TRIB., July 12, 1996, at B7.

11. John Leo, *If the Glove Won't Fit* . . . , U.S. NEWS & WORLD REP., Dec. 25, 1995, at 34 (emphasis added).

12. Scott Huler, *Closing the Gender Gap*, NEWS & OBSERVER (RALEIGH, N.C.), Dec. 8, 1992, at E1.

13. KENNETH CLATTERBAUGH, CONTEMPORARY PERSPECTIVES ON MASCULINITY: MEN, WOMEN, AND POLITICS IN MODERN SOCIETY 10 (2d ed. 1997). The background material for the next several paragraphs of this section comes in part from Clatterbaugh's excellent history. *Id.* at 41–44.

14. Carolyn Barta, *It's a Guy Thing: Men's Studies Examine What It Means to Be Male in a Changing World*, DALLAS MORNING NEWS, Apr. 24, 1997, at 1C.

15. *See, e.g.,* Jack Thomas, *The New Man: Finding Another Way to Be Male*, BOSTON GLOBE, Aug. 21, 1991.

16. Susan Riley, *Men's Movement Needed to Liberate Both Genders*, OTTAWA CITIZEN, Oct. 10, 1993, at A8.

17. Bly, *supra* note 7, at 2.

18. Eugene August, *Bringing Us Together*, M.E.N. (Nov. 1995) (visited June 9, 1997) <http://www.vix.com/menmag/august.html>.

19. JAMES DOYLE, SEX AND GENDER: THE HUMAN EXPERIENCE 341 (1985).

20. Steve Rabey, *Where Is the Christian Men's Movement Headed?*, CHRISTIANITY TODAY, Apr. 29, 1996, at 46, 47.

21. Stephen Goode, *Fathers Know Best*, INSIGHT, June 17, 1996, at 11.

22. Peter S. Canellos, *Groups Making Reform Next "Guy" Thing*, BOSTON GLOBE, Oct. 21, 1995, Metro, at 1 (quoting Rev. Tony Evans).

23. *Id.*

24. John D. Spalding, *Bonding in the Bleachers: A Visit to the Promise Keepers*, CHRISTIAN CENTURY, Mar. 6, 1966, at 260.

25. Mason, *supra* note 3, at 1D.

26. Ken Clatterbaugh, *Mythopoetic Foundations and New Age Patriarchy, in* THE POLITICS OF MANHOOD, *supra* note 6, at 50.

27. Melissa Fletcher Stoeltje, *Husbands, Fathers, Brothers, Keepers*, HOUS. CHRON., June 18, 1995, at 1.

28. Steve Arney, *Gary X Takes First Step on Million Man March*, PANTAGRAPH, Aug. 27, 1995, at A2.

29. STEPHEN WICKS, WARRIORS AND WILDMEN xii (1996).

30. Clatterbaugh, *supra* note 26, at 49.

31. Riley, *supra,* note 16.

32. Art Levine, *Masculinity's Champion,* U.S. NEWS & WORLD REP., Apr. 8, 1991, at 61.

33. ROBERT BLY, SELECTED POEMS 152 (1986), quoted in William S. Pollack, *No Man Is an Island: Toward a New Psychoanalytic Psychology of Men, in* A NEW PSYCHOLOGY OF MEN 54 (Ronald F. Levant & William S. Pollack eds., 1995).

34. K. D. O'Leary et al., *Prevalence and Stability of Physical Aggression between Spouses: A Longitudinal Analysis,* 57 J. CONSULTING & CLINICAL COUNSELING 263–68 (1989), quoted in David Gross, *Excerpts from Domestic Violence Research* (visited June 12, 1997) <http://www.vix.com/men/battery/studies/oleary-etal.html>.

35. LENORE WALKER, THE BATTERED WOMAN 60 (1979), *construed in* Melissa Hooper, *When Domestic Violence Diversion Is No Longer an Option: What to Do with the Female Offender,* 11 BERKELEY WOMEN'S L.J. 168, 175 n.24 (1996).

36. Joseph H. Pleck, *The Gender Role Strain Paradigm: An Update, in* A NEW PSYCHOLOGY OF MEN, *supra* note 33, at 20.

37. *Id.* at 18–21.

38. Stoeltje, *supra* note 27, at 1. Bill McCartney campaigned in favor of the Colorado anti–gay rights initiative that was struck down by the Supreme Court in *Romer v. Evans,* 116 S. Ct. 1620 (1996).

39. Richard Delgado & Jean Stefancic, *Minority Men, Misery, and the Marketplace of Ideas, in* CONSTRUCTING MASCULINITY (Maurice Berger et al. eds., 1995).

40. DEBORAH S. DAVID & ROBERT BRANNON, THE FORTY-NINE PERCENT MAJORITY: THE MALE SEX ROLE 49–232 (1976) (titles of chapter headings).

41. Gary R. Brooks & Louise B. Silverstein, *Understanding the Dark Side of Masculinity: An Interactive Systems Model, in* A NEW PSYCHOLOGY OF MEN, *supra* note 33, at 301.

42. *Id.* at 303.

43. *See* GAYLE KIMBALL, 50/50 PARENTING 9–12 (1988).

44. Brooks & Silverstein, *supra* note 41, at 288–91.

45. UNIFORM CRIME REPORTS FOR THE UNITED STATES 469, 484 (1995); *Violent Crime Grows Less Gender Specific,* ARIZ. REPUBLIC, Dec. 19, 1996, at A7.

46. Brooks & Silverstein, *supra* note 41, at 304.

47. Marion Crain, *Feminism, Labor, and Power,* 65 S. CAL. L. REV. 1819, 1854 n.165 (1992), citing Matt Moffett, *The Strong Women of a Mexican Town Crush Stereotypes,* WALL ST. J., Apr. 2, 1991, at A1.

48. Francisco Valdes, *Unpacking Hetero-Patriarchy: Tracing the Conflation of Sex, Gender and Sexual Orientation to Its Origins,* 8 YALE J.L. & HUMAN. 161, 211 (1996).

49. Barbara Demick, *Rural Albanian Woman Is the Man of the House,* TIMES UNION (ALBANY), July 21, 1996, at A2.

50. Martha L. Fineman, *Challenging Law, Establishing Differences: The Future of Feminist Legal Scholarship*, 42 FLA. L. REV. 25, 29 (1990).

51. Martha Minow, *Beyond Universality*, 1989 U. CHI. LEGAL F. 115, 116.

52. *See generally* Clare Dalton, *Where We Stand: Observations on the Situation of Feminist Legal Thought*, 3 BERKELEY WOMEN'S L.J. 1 (1987–88) (delineating historical stages of feminist theory). While there has been a historical progression through these stages of equal treatment theory, special treatment theory, dominance theory, and postmodern feminism, there currently exist proponents of each model. This classification comes with recognition that the categories are incomplete, overlapping, and populated with theorists who are not solidly unified.

53. Wendy W. Williams, *Equality's Riddle: Pregnancy and the Equal Treatment/Special Treatment Debate*, 13 N.Y.U. REV. L. & SOC. CHANGE 325, 329 (1984–85).

54. *See* Joan C. Williams, *Feminism and Post-Structuralism*, 88 MICH. L. REV. 1776, 1783 (1990).

55. *See, e.g.*, Mississippi Univ. for Women v. Hogan, 458 U.S. 718 (1982) (sustaining challenge of male plaintiffs that exclusion of men from state school's nursing program violates equal protection clause); Craig v. Boren, 429 U.S. 190 (1976) (rejecting an Oklahoma statute that set the minimum age for drinking 3.2 percent beer at eighteen for females and at twenty-one for males); Weinberger v. Weisenfeld, 420 U.S. 636 (1975) (holding unconstitutional a Social Security Act provision that granted survivor's benefits to a widow but not a widower); Frontiero v. Richardson, 411 U.S. 677 (1973) (striking a statute that required female service members to prove the dependency of their spouses while dependency was presumed for spouses of male service members).

56. *See* David Cole, *Strategies of Difference: Litigating for Women's Rights in a Man's World*, 2 LAW & INEQ. J. 33 (1984). It has been suggested that men were more likely to succeed as plaintiffs. *See* Christine Littleton, *Reconstructing Sexual Equality*, 75 CAL. L. REV. 1279, 1291 n.70 (1987).

57. Cole, *supra* note 56, at 54.

58. *Id.* at 57.

59. *See, e.g.*, Michael H. v. Gerald D., 491 U.S. 110 (1989) (rejecting biological and psychological father's claim of right to have a parent-child relationship with the child of a mother married to another man); Rostker v. Goldberg, 453 U.S. 57 (1981) (upholding male-only draft registration); Michael M. v. Superior Court of Sonoma County, 450 U.S. 464 (1981) (upholding statutory rape law applicable only to men).

60. *See, e.g.*, Robin West, *Jurisprudence and Gender*, 55 U. CHI. L. REV. 1 (1988).

61. *See, e.g.*, Nancy E. Dowd, *Maternity Leave: Taking Sex Differences into Account*, 54 FORDHAM L. REV. 699 (1986).

62. *See, e.g.*, Herma Hill Kay, *Equality and Difference: The Case of Pregnancy*, 1 BERKELEY WOMEN'S L.J. 1, 22 (1985). While Professor Kay is generally associated

with sameness feminism, she recognizes the need to make allowances for pregnancy and childbirth, a distinct area of biological differences.

63. *See generally* NEL NODDINGS, CARING: A FEMININE APPROACH TO ETHICS AND MORAL EDUCATION (1984).

64. *See* Stephen Ellmann, *The Ethic of Care as an Ethic for Lawyers*, 81 GEO. L.J. 2665, 2665–66 (1993). *See generally* CAROL GILLIGAN, IN A DIFFERENT VOICE: PSYCHOLOGICAL THEORY AND WOMEN'S DEVELOPMENT 17–23 (1982). Professor Gilligan might resist such a determinate reading of her works. *See* Affidavit of Carol Gilligan at 2–3, Johnson v. Jones, Civ. No. 2:92-1674-2 (D.S.C. filed Jan. 7, 1993), *cited in* Katherine M. Franke, *The Central Mistake of Sex Discrimination Law: The Disaggregation of Sex from Gender*, 144 U. PA. L. REV. 1, 83–85 (1995).

65. Gilligan, *supra* note 64; Leslie Bender, *From Gender Difference to Feminist Solidarity: Using Carol Gilligan and an Ethic of Care in Law*, 15 VT. L. REV. 1 (1990).

66. *See* Robin L. West, *The Difference in Women's Hedonic Lives: A Phenomenological Critique of Feminist Legal Theory*, 3 WIS. WOMEN'S L.J. 81 (1987).

67. *See generally* Carrie Menkel-Meadow, *Feminist Legal Theory, Critical Legal Studies, and Legal Education or "The Fem-Crits Go to Law School,"* 38 J. LEGAL EDUC. 61, 71–72 (1988).

68. *See, e.g.*, Kenneth L. Karst, *Woman's Constitution*, 1984 DUKE L.J. 447.

69. *See* Margaret Jane Radin, *Reply: Please Be Careful with Cultural Feminism*, 45 STAN. L. REV. 1567, 1568 (1993); West, *supra* note 60, at 3.

70. Robin West, *Economic Man and Literary Woman: One Contrast*, 39 MERCER L. REV. 867, 869 (1988).

71. Christine Littleton, *The Difference Method Makes*, 41 STAN. L. REV. 751, 784 n.72 (1989).

72. Susan M. Okin, *Thinking Like a Woman, in* THEORETICAL PERSPECTIVES ON SEXUAL DIFFERENCE 145, 152 (Deborah L. Rhode ed., 1990).

73. *See, e.g.*, Donna Haraway, *Situated Knowledges: The Science Question in Feminism and the Privilege of Partial Perspective*, 14 FEMINIST STUD. 575 (1988); Nancy C. M. Hartsock, *The Feminist Standpoint: Developing the Ground for a Specifically Feminist Historical Materialism, in* FEMINISM AND METHODOLOGY 157 (Sandra Harding ed., 1987).

74. *See* Knut H. Sørensen, *Towards a Feminized Technology? Gendered Values in the Construction of Technology*, 22 SOC. STUD. SCI. 5, 8–9 (1992).

75. *See, e.g.*, A. Yasmine Rassam, Note, *"Mother," "Parent," and Bias*, 69 IND. L.J. 1165, 1169 (1994) (arguing that a feminist approach "renders a more honest and fair decision-making process than do other legal methodologies").

76. *See, e.g.*, CATHARINE A. MACKINNON, FEMINISM UNMODIFIED 8 (1987).

77. *See generally* Ann C. Scales, *The Emergence of Feminist Jurisprudence: An Essay*, 95 YALE L.J. 1373 (1986).

78. *See, e.g.*, Catharine A. MacKinnon, *Not a Moral Issue*, 2 YALE L. & POL'Y REV. 321, 325 (1984).

79. West, *supra* note 60, at 13.

80. Andrew Ross, *Demonstrating Sexual Difference, in* MEN IN FEMINISM 47, 48–49 (Alice Jardine & Paul Smith eds., 1987) (referring to a syllogism constructed by some radical feminists: "Some men rape and kill women. All men are potential rapist-killers. Therefore, all women are potential victims").

81. I am deliberately engaging in hyperbole as a rhetorical device to make the point.

82. Robin West, *Feminism, Critical Social Theory and Law*, 1989 U. CHI. LEGAL F. 59, 63; *see also* Duncan Kennedy, *Sexual Abuse, Sexy Dressing and the Eroticization of Domination*, 26 NEW ENG. L. REV. 1309, 1311 (1992) (suggesting that all men derive incidental benefits from the phenomenon of rape).

83. ANDREA DWORKIN & CATHARINE A. MACKINNON, PORNOGRAPHY AND CIVIL RIGHTS: A NEW DAY FOR WOMEN'S EQUALITY 22–23 (1988).

84. Difference thus becomes not a binary phenomenon, but a multiply created, shifting set of phenomena. Mary Joe Frug, *Sexual Equality and Sexual Difference in American Law*, 26 NEW ENG. L. REV. 665, 674 (1992).

85. *See* Patricia A. Cain, *Feminism and the Limits of Equality*, 24 GA. L. REV. 803, 840 (1990).

86. *See, e.g.*, Marion Smiley, *Gender Justice without Foundations*, 89 MICH. L. REV. 1574, 1579 (1991).

87. *See, e.g.*, Angela P. Harris, *Race and Essentialism in Feminist Legal Theory*, 42 STAN. L. REV. 581 (1990).

88. *See* Mary Joe Frug, *A Postmodern Feminist Legal Manifesto (An Unfinished Draft)*, 105 HARV. L. REV. 1045, 1048 (1992).

89. *See* Michael M. v. Superior Court, 450 U.S. 464 (1981).

90. *See, e.g.*, Herma Hill Kay, *Models of Equality*, 1985 U. ILL. L. REV. 39, 70; Julie Novkov, Note, *A Deconstruction of (M)otherhood and a Reconstruction of Parenthood*, 19 N.Y.U. REV. L. & SOC. CHANGE 155, 174 (1992).

91. *See, e.g.*, POLITICS OF MANHOOD, *supra* note 6; DAVID H. J. MORGAN, DISCOVERING MEN 6–23 (1992).

92. Michael S. Kimmel, *Invisible Masculinity*, SOCIETY, Sept.–Oct. 1993, at 28.

93. *See* Mary Ann Case, *Disaggregating Gender from Sex and Sexual Orientation: The Effeminate Man in the Law and Feminist Jurisprudence*, 105 YALE L.J. 1, 33 (1995); Franke, *supra* note 64; Kenneth Karst, *The Pursuit of Manhood and the Desegregation of the Armed Forces*, 38 UCLA L. REV. 499 (1991).

94. Franke, *supra* note 64, at 3.

95. Karst, *supra* note 93, at 546, 534.

96. *See generally* Margaret Jane Radin, *The Pragmatist and the Feminist*, 63 S. CAL. L. REV. 1699 (1990).

NOTES TO CHAPTER 7

1. *See, e.g.*, PHYLLIS CHESLER, MOTHERS ON TRIAL: THE BATTLE FOR CHILDREN AND CUSTODY xiii (1986) ("The equal treatment of 'unequals' is unjust. The paternal demand for 'equal' custodial rights; the law that values legal paternity or male economic superiority over biological motherhood and/or maternal practice, degrades and violates both mothers and children").

2. Angela P. Harris, *Foreword: The Jurisprudence of Reconstruction*, 82 CAL. L. REV. 741, 768 (1994).

3. *See, e.g.*, R. W. Connell, *Men and the Women's Movement*, SOC. POL'Y, Summer 1993, at 72, 73 ("An academic man teaching a feminist course, for instance, may be seen as taking resources away from women").

4. Christine A. Littleton, *Does It Still Make Sense to Talk about "Women?"*, 1 UCLA WOMEN'S L.J. 15 (1991).

5. *Id.* at 32 n.78.

6. *See* 139 CONG. REC. S985-1003 (1993) (statement of Sen. Boxer) ("The [FMLA] does not just apply to women, but to men and women, to fathers, as well as to mothers, to sons as well as to daughters").

7. *See* Catharine A. MacKinnon, *Feminism, Marxism, Method, and the State: Toward Feminist Jurisprudence*, 8 SIGNS 635 (1983).

8. *See* Neil Netanel, *Copyright Alienability Restrictions and the Enhancement of Author Autonomy: A Normative Evaluation*, 24 RUTGERS L.J. 347, 418 (1993) (arguing that a class of people and even a whole society may suffer from "'false consciousness' . . . regarding its desires, values and general lifestyle").

9. *See, e.g.*, Jane L. Dolkart, *Hostile Environment Harassment: Equality, Objectivity, and the Shaping of Legal Standards*, 43 EMORY L.J. 151, 224–26 (1994).

10. *See, e.g.*, Sandra L. Bartky, *On Psychological Oppression*, in FEMININITY AND DOMINATION: STUDIES IN THE PHENOMENOLOGY OF OPPRESSION 23 (1990).

11. Barbara F. Reskin, *Bringing the Men Back In: Sex Differentiation and the Devaluation of Women's Work*, in THE SOCIAL CONSTRUCTION OF GENDER 141, 149 (Judith Lorber & Susan A. Farrell eds., 1991).

12. *But see* June Carbone & Margaret F. Brinig, *Rethinking Marriage: Feminist Ideology, Economic Change, and Divorce Reform*, 65 TUL. L. REV. 953 (1991); Martha Minow, *The Supreme Court 1986 Term—Foreword: Justice Engendered*, 101 HARV. L. REV. 10 (1987).

13. *See generally* MARY F. BELENKY et al., WOMEN'S WAYS OF KNOWING: THE DEVELOPMENT OF SELF, VOICE, AND MIND (1986); DEBORAH TANNEN, GENDER AND DISCOURSE (1994).

14. *See, e.g.*, SUSAN BROWNMILLER, AGAINST OUR WILL: MEN, WOMEN AND RAPE, 15 (1975) ("[Rape] is nothing more or less than a conscious process of intimidation by which *all men* keep *all women* in a state of fear") (emphasis in original); ANDREA DWORKIN, INTERCOURSE 63–67 (1987) (contrasting men's experience

of sex as subjects and women's experience of sex as objects); Lucinda M. Finley, *Breaking Women's Silence in Law: The Dilemma of the Gendered Nature of Legal Reasoning*, 64 NOTRE DAME L. REV. 886, 893 (1989) ("[L]egal language is a male language because it is principally informed by men's experiences. . . . Universal and objective thinking is male language because intellectually, economically, and politically privileged men have had the power to ignore other perspectives and thus to come to think of their situation as the norm, their reality as reality, and their views as objective"). *But see* Carrie Menkel-Meadow, *Feminization of the Legal Profession: The Comparative Sociology of Women Lawyers, in* 3 LAWYERS IN SOCIETY: COMPARATIVE THEORIES 196 (Richard L. Abel & Philip S. C. Lewis eds., 1989) (suggesting that gender differences within genders are far more significant than gender differences between genders).

15. *See, e.g.*, Charles R. Lawrence III, *If He Hollers Let Him Go: Regulating Racist Speech on Campus*, 1990 DUKE L.J. 431.

16. *See, e.g.*, William N. Eskridge, Jr., *Gaylegal Narratives*, 46 STAN. L. REV. 607 (1994); Samuel A. Marcosson, *The "Special Rights" Canard in the Debate over Lesbian and Gay Civil Rights*, 9 NOTRE DAME J.L. ETHICS & PUB. POL'Y 137 (1995).

17. *See* Leslie Bender, *Teaching Torts As If Gender Matters: Intentional Torts*, 2 VA. J. SOC. POL'Y & L. 115, 127–31 (1994); Emily F. Hartigan, *From Righteousness to Beauty: Reflections on Poethics and Justice as Translation*, 67 TUL. L. REV. 455, 480 (1992).

18. Mari J. Matsuda, *When the First Quail Calls: Multiple Consciousness as Jurisprudential Method*, 11 WOMEN'S RTS. L. REP. 7 (1989).

19. Isabel Marcus et al., *Feminist Discourse, Moral Values, and the Law: A Conversation*, 34 BUFF. L. REV. 11, 46–49 (1985).

20. *See generally* SUSAN FALUDI, BACKLASH: THE UNDECLARED WAR AGAINST AMERICAN WOMEN (1991).

21. Katharine T. Bartlett, *Feminist Legal Methods*, 103 HARV. L. REV. 829, 831 (1990).

22. Sally Jacobs, *The Put-Upon Privileged Ones: Feelings Wounded, White Men Complain Society Stereotypes Them as Boring Jerks*, BOSTON GLOBE, Nov. 22, 1992, at 1 (quoting civil rights activist Julian Bond).

23. Critical race theorists have employed consciousness-raising strategies, *see, e.g.*, Richard Delgado, *Storytelling for Oppositionists and Others: A Plea for Narrative*, 87 MICH. L. REV. 2411, 2411 (1989), as have gays and lesbians, *see, e.g.*, Patricia A. Cain, *Lesbian Perspective, Lesbian Experience, and the Risk of Essentialism*, 2 VA. J. SOC. POL'Y & L. 43, 67 (1994). One author has promoted "vicarious consciousness-raising" by adults on behalf of children. Barbara B. Woodhouse, *Hatching the Egg: A Child-Centered Perspective on Parents' Rights*, 14 CARDOZO L. REV. 1747, 1832 (1993). *See also* Carol Sanger, *The Reasonable Woman and the Ordinary Man*, 65 S. CAL. L. REV. 1411, 1417 (1992) (urging consciousness-raising to sensitize men to conduct that might be perceived as sexual harassment).

24. R. W. Connell, *Drumming Up the Wrong Tree*, 7 TIKKUN 31, 31 (Jan. 1992).

25. Philip Walzer, *Are We Not Men?*, VIRGINIAN PILOT, Nov. 28, 1994, at E1.

26. *See, e.g.*, ROBERT BLY, IRON JOHN: A BOOK ABOUT MEN (1990).

27. *See* Joyce Price, *Toppled by -Isms: White Males Say They're Now the Minority It's OK to Oppress*, WASH. TIMES, Mar. 31, 1993, at A1 ("Bill Spriggs, an economist with the Economic Policy Institute in Washington, says there is 'absolutely no academic evidence that supports the notion white men are losing ground'").

28. *See* ROBIN TOLMACH LAKOFF, TALKING POWER: THE POLITICS OF LANGUAGE IN OUR LIVES (1990); DEBORAH TANNEN, YOU JUST DON'T UNDERSTAND: WOMEN AND MEN IN CONVERSATION (1990).

29. *See, e.g.*, Kimberlé Crenshaw, *Demarginalizing the Intersection of Race and Sex: A Black Feminist Critique of Antidiscrimination Doctrine, Feminist Theory and Antiracist Politics*, 1989 U. CHI. LEGAL F. 139.

30. *See* ELIZABETH V. SPELMAN, INESSENTIAL WOMAN: PROBLEMS OF EXCLUSION IN FEMINIST THOUGHT (1988).

31. *See, e.g.*, Kevin Brown, *The Social Construction of a Rape Victim: Stories of African-American Males about the Rape of Desiree Washington*, 1992 U. ILL. L. REV. 997; Lawrence Vogelman, *The Big Black Man Syndrome: The Rodney King Trial and the Use of Racial Stereotypes in the Courtroom*, 20 FORDHAM URB. L.J. 571 (1993).

32. *See* Peter Kwan, *Beyond the Pale: Jeffrey Dahmer and the Effeminization of Gay Asian Men*, Speech Presented at the Crit Networks Conference on Critical Legal Studies (Mar. 11, 1995) (using the play M. BUTTERFLY, and Song's deception of M. Gallimard to which he was a willing participant, to demonstrate how perceptions of Asian women and men shape assumptions about their sexuality).

33. Peter B. Edelman, *The Next Century of Our Constitution: Rethinking Our Duty to the Poor*, 39 HASTINGS L.J. 1, 18 (1987).

34. *See generally* David K. Flaks, *Gay and Lesbian Families: Judicial Assumptions, Scientific Realities*, 3 WM. & MARY BILL RTS. J. 345 (1994); Nancy D. Polikoff, *This Child Does Have Two Mothers: Redefining Parenthood to Meet the Needs of Children in Lesbian-Mother and Other Nontraditional Families*, 78 GEO. L.J. 459 (1990).

35. *See* Jerome M. Culp, Jr., *Colorblind Remedies and the Intersectionality of Oppression: Policy Arguments Masquerading as Moral Claims*, 69 N.Y.U. L. REV. 162, 169 (1994).

36. Martin H. Malin, *Fathers and Parental Leave*, 72 TEX. L. REV. 1047, 1066 (1994).

37. *See, e.g.*, ANNE FAUSTO-STERLING, MYTHS OF GENDER: BIOLOGICAL THEORIES ABOUT WOMEN AND MEN (1985); CYNTHIA FUCHS-EPSTEIN, DECEPTIVE DISTINCTIONS: SEX, GENDER, AND THE SOCIAL ORDER (1988); SANDRA HARDING, THE SCIENCE QUESTION IN FEMINISM (1986); R. C. LEWONTIN, BIOLOGY AS IDEOLOGY: THE DOCTRINE OF DNA (1992). *But see* ROBERT POOL, EVE'S RIB: THE BIOLOGICAL ROOTS OF SEX DIFFERENCES (1994).

38. *See, e.g.*, ELIZABETH H. WOLGAST, EQUALITY AND THE RIGHTS OF WOMEN 14–15 (1980); Sylvia A. Law, *Rethinking Sex and the Constitution*, 132 U. PA. L. REV. 955, 966 (1984).

39. *See, e.g.*, LAURENCE H. TRIBE, AMERICAN CONSTITUTIONAL LAW 1578 (2d ed. 1988) (criticizing the distinction in *Geduldig v. Aiello* between pregnant and nonpregnant persons as "so artificial as to approach the farcical").

40. Joan C. Williams, *Feminism and Post-Structuralism*, 88 MICH. L. REV. 1776, 1784–85 (1990); Joan C. Williams, *Deconstructing Gender*, 87 MICH. L. REV. 797 (1989).

41. *See supra* chapter 2.

42. Tribe, *supra* note 39, at 1571.

43. *See* Christine A. Littleton, *Equality and Feminist Legal Theory*, 48 U. PITT. L. REV. 1043, 1051 (1987) ("The category is social, not biological").

44. *See, e.g.*, Leslie Bender, *Sex Discrimination or Gender Inequality*, 57 FORDHAM L. REV. 941, 946 (1989).

45. Sandra Harding, *Introduction* to FEMINISM AND METHODOLOGY 1, 8 (Sandra Harding ed., 1987).

46. 479 U.S. 272 (1987). In *Cal Fed*, the Court reasoned that the goals of the Pregnancy Discrimination Act to provide equal employment opportunities to pregnant women justified the preferential treatment. *Id.* at 286–87. The literature on the issues involved in the *Cal Fed* debate is vast. *See, e.g.*, Wendy S. Strimling, *The Constitutionality of State Laws Providing Employment Leave for Pregnancy: Rethinking Geduldig after* Cal Fed, 77 CAL. L. REV. 171 (1989); Wendy W. Williams, *Equality's Riddle: Pregnancy and the Equal Treatment/Special Treatment Debate*, 13 N.Y.U. REV. L. & SOC. CHANGE 325 (1984–85). Feminists were sharply divided over whether to argue in favor of the equal or special treatment models.

47. 453 U.S. 57 (1981).

48. 450 U.S. 464 (1981).

49. United States v. Virginia, 766 F. Supp. 1407, 1421 (W.D. Va. 1991) (the attributes of which include "[p]hysical rigor, mental stress, absolute equality of treatment, absence of privacy, minute regulation of behavior, and indoctrination of desirable values").

50. Brief for Appellee at 20, United States v. Virginia, 976 F.2d 890 (4th Cir. 1992) (No. 91-1690), cited in Brian Scott Yablonski, *Marching to the Beat of a Different Drummer: The Case of the Virginia Military Institute*, 47 U. MIAMI L. REV. 1449, 1468 (1993).

51. United States v. Virginia, 976 F.2d 890, 899 (4th Cir. 1992), *cert. denied*, 113 S. Ct. 2431 (1993).

52. *See* United States v. Virginia, 766 F. Supp. at 1434–35.

53. *Id.* at 1412–13.

54. *See* United States v. Virginia, 976 F.2d at 899; United States v. Virginia, 44 F.3d 1229, 1238–39 (4th Cir. 1995), *cert. granted*, 116 S. Ct. 281 (1995).

55. For a more complete discussion of *United States v. Virginia*, see chapter 3.

56. *See* Faulkner v. Jones, 51 F.3d 440 (4th Cir. 1995), *cert. dismissed*, 116 S. Ct. 331 (1995), *and cert. denied*, 116 S. Ct. 352 (1995); United States v. Virginia, 976 F.2d 890 (4th Cir. 1992), *cert. denied*, 113 S. Ct. 2431 (1993).

57. *See* Carrie Menkel-Meadow, *Feminist Legal Theory, Critical Legal Studies, and Legal Education or "The Fem-Crits Go to Law School,"* 38 J. LEGAL EDUC. 61, 76 (1988).

58. *See, e.g.*, DEBORAH MEIER, THE POWER OF THEIR IDEAS: LESSONS FOR AMERICA FROM A SMALL SCHOOL IN HARLEM (1995); JOHN N. THOMPSON, THE CO-EVOLUTIONARY PROCESS (1994).

59. *See generally* Martha Minow, *Choices and Constraints: For Justice Thurgood Marshall*, 80 GEO. L.J. 2093, 2104 (1992); Vicki Schultz, *Telling Stories about Women and Work: Judicial Interpretations of Sex Segregation in the Workplace in Title VII Cases Raising the Lack of Interest Argument*, 103 HARV. L. REV. 1749, 1757 (1990).

60. Maxine N. Eichner, Note, *Getting Women Work That Isn't Women's Work: Challenging Gender Biases in the Workplace under Title VII*, 97 YALE L.J. 1397, 1397 (1988).

61. *See* Donald R. McCreary, *The Male Role and Avoiding Femininity*, 31 SEX ROLES 517 (1994).

62. *See, e.g.*, Diaz v. Pan Am. World Airways, 442 F.2d 385 (5th Cir.) (holding that hiring only females as flight attendants is not justified by customer preferences for being served by women), *cert. denied*, 404 U.S. 950 (1971).

63. *See, e.g.*, Gerdom v. Continental Airlines, Inc., 692 F.2d 602 (9th Cir. 1982) (holding that airline's strict weight requirements for flight hostesses was discriminatory), *cert. denied*, 460 U.S. 1074 (1982).

64. Deborah L. Rhode, *Perspectives on Professional Women*, 40 STAN. L. REV. 1163, 1188 (1988).

65. *See, e.g.*, Loeffler v. Frank, 486 U.S. 549 (1988); Mississippi Univ. for Women v. Hogan, 458 U.S. 718 (1982).

66. *See, e.g.*, Craft v. Metromedia, Inc., 766 F.2d 1205 (8th Cir. 1985), *cert. denied*, 475 U.S. 1058 (1986).

67. 490 U.S. 228 (1989).

68. Hopkins v. Price Waterhouse, 618 F. Supp. 1109, 1113, 1116–17 (D.D.C. 1985), *aff'd in part and rev'd in part*, 825 F.2d 458, *rev'd*, 490 U.S. 228 (1989).

69. *Id.; cf.* Craft v. Metromedia, Inc., 572 F. Supp. 868, 878 (W.D. Mo. 1983), *aff'd in part and rev'd in part*, 766 F.2d 1205, 1211 (8th Cir. 1985), *cert. denied*, 475 U.S. 1058 (1986) (co-anchor of nightly news was given makeup and wardrobe counseling, and was effectively demoted to general reporting because the broadcast company allegedly considered her "too old, too unattractive, and not deferential enough to men"; the court of appeals upheld the district court's determination that appearance standards were not based on stereotypical images of women).

70. 490 U.S. at 250.

71. I am indebted to Sam Marcosson for this example.

72. *See, e.g.*, Watson v. Fort Worth Bank & Trust, 487 U.S. 977, 999 (1988).

73. *See, e.g.*, Smith v. Liberty Mut. Co., 569 F.2d 325 (5th Cir. 1978) (holding that an employer's refusal to hire an effeminate male did not constitute a Title VII violation).

74. 490 U.S. at 256.

75. Kari Aamot-Snapp, Note, *Putting Teeth into Minnesota's Employment Discrimination Law: A Legislative Proposal Defining Gender Stereotyping*, 79 MINN. L. REV. 211, 235 n.119 (1994).

76. *See* J. Cindy Eson, *In Praise of Macho Women: Price Waterhouse v. Hopkins*, 46 U. MIAMI L. REV. 835, 850 (1992).

77. *See* Anthony S. Winer, *Hate Crimes, Homosexuals, and the Constitution*, 29 HARV. C.R.-C.L. L. REV. 387 (1994); *see also* Judith H. Stiehm, *Managing the Military's Homosexual Exclusion Policy: Text and Subtext*, 46 U. MIAMI L. REV. 685, 688–89 (1992) ("[E]ffeminate men were either not inducted or forced to fail basic [military] training").

78. 608 F.2d 327 (9th Cir. 1979).

79. *Id.* at 332.

80. 740 F.2d 686 (9th Cir.), *cert. denied*, 469 U.S. 1036 (1984).

81. *Id.* at 709 (emphasis added).

82. While the *Spaulding* court ultimately rejected the comparable worth theory advanced by the female nurse plaintiffs, *id.* at 705–06, the court denied the male nurse plaintiff the opportunity to have the substance of his claim reviewed. *Id.* at 709.

83. *See* Nancy Levit, *Defining Cutting Edge Scholarship: Feminism and Criteria of Rationality*, 61 CHI.-KENT L. REV. 947 (1996) (discussing the principles of the scientific method—openness, testability, cumulative, comprehensive, and converging evidence, simplicity—as criteria of rationality).

84. *See, e.g.*, JAMES BOHMAN, NEW PHILOSOPHY OF SOCIAL SCIENCE: PROBLEMS OF INDETERMINACY (1991); STEPHEN H. KELLERT, IN THE WAKE OF CHAOS: UNPREDICTABLE ORDER IN DYNAMICAL SYSTEMS (1993); BART KOSKO, FUZZY THINKING: THE NEW SCIENCE OF FUZZY LOGIC (1993).

85. *See* WILLIAM HARE, IN DEFENCE OF OPEN-MINDEDNESS (1985); MICHAEL ROOT, PHILOSOPHY OF SOCIAL SCIENCE: THE METHODS, IDEALS, AND POLITICS OF SOCIAL INQUIRY (1993).

86. *See* CULTURAL PLURALISM AND MORAL KNOWLEDGE (Ellen F. Paul et al. eds., 1994); ROBERT C. ELLICKSON, ORDER WITHOUT LAW: HOW NEIGHBORS SETTLE DISPUTES (1991); JAMES A. MONTMARQUET, EPISTEMIC VIRTUE AND DOXASTIC RESPONSIBILITY (1993); MARION SMILEY, MORAL RESPONSIBILITY AND THE BOUNDARIES OF COMMUNITY: POWER AND ACCOUNTABILITY FROM A PRAGMATIC POINT OF VIEW (1992).

87. Christine Jolls, *The Rule of Law and Economics in Feminist Legal Theory*, Presented at the AALS Annual Meeting (Jan. 5, 1996) (arguing that feminist theory could bring a more behavioral approach to law and economics that would inform economic conceptions of value and individual preferences by importing distributional objectives—such as improving the situations of women—as measures of efficiency).

88. Jane E. Larson, *The World and Other Things*, Presented at the AALS Annual Meeting (Jan. 5, 1996) (suggesting that the important questions for the future of feminist theory are tied to broader humanist inquiries, such as questions of human nature, public good, or appropriate relations between individuals and the state).

89. The dangers of exalting "group thought" can be seen in varied examples throughout history in claims of absolute epistemological privilege based on social class, city, state, race or "blood," ethnicity, nationality, and ideology. *See, e.g.*, BARROWS DUNHAM, HEROES AND HERETICS: A POLITICAL HISTORY OF WESTERN THOUGHT (1964). This is not to discount different perceptions based on some of those same categories.

90. *See* Kathryn Abrams, *Hearing the Call of Stories*, 79 CAL. L. REV. 971, 976, 983–84, 1004, 1016, 1028 (1991).

91. *See* PAUL HELM, BELIEF POLICIES (1994); Joan W. Scott, *The Evidence of Experience, in* QUESTIONS OF EVIDENCE 363–87 (James Chandler et al. eds., 1994).

NOTES TO CHAPTER 8

1. Charles Paul Freud, *Rhetorical Questions: The Power of, and behind, a Name*, WASH. POST, Feb. 7, 1989, at A23.

2. Martha Minow, *The Supreme Court, 1986 Term—Foreword: Justice Engendered*, 101 HARV. L. REV. 10, 61 (1987).

3. Francisco Valdes, *Queers, Sissies, Dykes, and Tomboys: Deconstructing the Conflation of "Sex," "Gender," and "Sexual Orientation" in Euro-American Law and Society*, 83 CAL. L. REV. 1, 377 n.1231 (1995).

4. Dianne Aprile, *Feminism Is New "F-Word,"* GANNETT NEWS SERV., Dec. 29, 1992.

5. Lea Brilmayer, *Inclusive Feminism*, 38 N.Y. L. SCH. L. REV. 377, 386 (1993).

6. *See generally* ELIZABETH V. SPELMAN, INESSENTIAL WOMAN: PROBLEMS OF EXCLUSION IN FEMINIST THOUGHT (1988); Carrie Menkel-Meadow, *Excluded Voices: New Voices in the Legal Profession Making New Voices in the Law*, 42 U. MIAMI L. REV. 29 (1987).

7. RICHARD DELGADO, THE RODRIGO CHRONICLES: CONVERSATIONS ABOUT AMERICA AND RACE 118–19 (1995).

8. Linda J. Lacey, *Mimicking the Words, but Missing the Message: The Misuse of Cultural Feminist Themes in Religion and Family Law Jurisprudence*, 35 B.C. L. REV. 1, 48 (1993).

9. CATHARINE A. MacKINNON, TOWARD A FEMINIST THEORY OF THE STATE 224 (1989).

10. A NEW PSYCHOLOGY OF MEN 1 (Ronald F. Levant & William S. Pollack eds., 1995).

11. Harry Brod, *The Case for Men's Studies,* in THE MAKING OF MASCULINITIES: THE NEW MEN'S STUDIES 40 (Harry Brod ed., 1987).

12. *See* JACK GREENBERG, CRUSADERS IN THE COURTS: HOW A DEDICATED BAND OF LAWYERS FOUGHT FOR THE CIVIL RIGHTS REVOLUTION (1994). *But see* DERRICK BELL, AND WE ARE NOT SAVED: THE ELUSIVE QUEST FOR RACIAL JUSTICE 60–74 (1987) (arguing that civil rights reforms generally promote majoritarian interests). The reverse is also probably true: civil rights progress has essentially stalled because of white resistance.

13. Michael Shiffman, *The Men's Movement: An Exploratory Empirical Investigation,* in CHANGING MEN: NEW DIRECTIONS IN RESEARCH ON MEN AND MASCULINITY 295, 295 (Michael S. Kimmel ed., 1987).

14. Carrie Menkel-Meadow, *Portia Redux: Another Look at Gender, Feminism, and Legal Ethics,* 2 VA. J. SOC. POL'Y & L. 75, 113–14 (1994).

15. *See* BARBARA EHRENREICH, THE HEARTS OF MEN: AMERICAN DREAMS AND THE FLIGHT FROM COMMITMENT (1983).

16. "The history of antisexist men is an essential part of the history of feminism. In the nineteenth century, for example, many men supported feminist demands; many of them were also active as abolitionists; William Lloyd Garrison, Frederick Douglass, Thomas Wentworth Higginson, Parker Pillsbury, and Samuel Joseph May. Some supportive husbands of suffrage leaders, such as Henry Blackwell, husband of Lucy Stone, and James Mott, husband of Lucretia Mott, were activists for women's rights in their own right as well. The history of profeminist men includes not only support of women but also men's relationships reconstructed to feminist or humanitarian standards, rather than patriarchal 'male bonding.'" Brod, *supra* note 11, at 49.

17. *See generally* ANTIFEMINISM IN AMERICAN THOUGHT: AN ANNOTATED BIBLIOGRAPHY (Cynthia D. Kinnard ed., 1986); Michael S. Kimmel, *Men's Responses to Feminism at the Turn of the Century,* 1 GENDER & SOC'Y 261 (1987).

18. *See* Note, *White Knight,* 108 HARV. L. REV. 959, 963 n.21 (1995).

19. *See, e.g.,* NANCY CHODOROW, THE REPRODUCTION OF MOTHERING: PSYCHOANALYSIS AND THE SOCIOLOGY OF GENDER (1978); Janet S. Chafetz & Anthony G. Dworkin, *In the Face of Threat: Organized Antifeminism in Comparative Perspective,* 1 GENDER & SOC'Y 33 (1987); Jerome L. Himmelstein, *The Social Basis of Antifeminism: Religious Networks and Culture,* 25 J. SCI. STUDY RELIGION 1 (1986); Josefina Figueira-McDonough, *Gender, Race, and Class: Differences in Levels of Feminist Orientation,* 21 J. APPLIED BEHAV. SCI. 121 (1985); Patricia Gurin, *Women's Gender Consciousness,* 49 PUB. OPINION Q. 143 (1985); Eric Plutzer, *Work Life, Fam-*

ily Life, and Women's Support of Feminism, 53 Am. Soc. Rev. 640 (1988); Sara Ruddick, *Maternal Thinking*, 6 Feminist Stud. 342 (1980); Arland Thornton et al., *Causes and Consequences of Sex-Role Attitudes and Attitude Change*, 48 Am. Soc. Rev. 211 (1983); William J. Goode, *Why Men Resist*, 27 Dissent 181 (1980).

20. Ethel Klein, Gender Politics: From Consciousness to Mass Politics 96–97 (1984).

21. *See* Debra Kalmuss et al., *Feminist and Sympathetic Feminist Consciousness*, 11 Eur. J. Soc. Psychol. 131, 136 (1981).

22. Joseph Tamney et al., *Personal Experience, Ideology and Support for Feminism*, 25 Soc. Focus 203 (1992).

23. *Id.* at 212. On the one hand, the direct effect of class on feminism, as well as the indirect effect through the relation between class and belief in economic restructuring, means that class is negatively related to feminism. On the other hand, the indirect effect of class because of the relationship of class to financial dissatisfaction means that social class is positively related to feminism. The latter relationship suggests that some men feel financially secure and thus are not threatened by a nondiscriminatory job market. *Id.* at 214.

24. While a small number of men in the legal academy are writing about feminism, *see, e.g.*, Roy L. Brooks, *Feminist Jurisdiction: Toward an Understanding of Feminist Procedure*, 43 U. Kan. L. Rev. 317 (1995); Stephen Ellmann, *The Ethic of Care as an Ethic for Lawyers*, 81 Geo. L.J. 2665 (1993); Dennis Patterson, *Postmodernism/Feminism/Law*, 77 Cornell L. Rev. 254 (1992); Robert R. M. Verchick, *In a Greener Voice: Feminist Theory and Environmental Justice*, 19 Harv. Women's L.J. 23 (1996), the field is composed predominantly of female writers.

25. *See, e.g.*, Against the Tide: Pro-Feminist Men in the United States, 1776–1990: A Documentary History (Michael S. Kimmel & Thomas E. Mosmiller eds., 1992).

26. Michael S. Kimmel, *Invisible Masculinity*, Society, Sept.–Oct. 1993, at 30.

27. Neil Thompson, *Men and Anti-Sexism*, 25 Brit. J. Social Work 459, 462 (1995).

28. Paul Lichterman, *Making a Politics of Masculinity*, 11 Comp. Soc. Res. 185, 187 (1989).

29. *See, e.g.*, June Carbone & Margaret F. Brinig, *Rethinking Marriage: Feminist Ideology, Economic Change, and Divorce Reform*, 65 Tul. L. Rev. 953, 1007–08 (1991) (arguing for the separation of marital roles and child rearing and the substitution of a child-centered approach).

30. Shannon Brownlee & Matthew Miller, *Lies Parents Tell Themselves about Why They Work*, U.S. News & World Rep., May 12, 1997, at 5; Laura Shapiro, *The Myth of Quality Time*, Newsweek, May 12, 1997, at 62.

31. Jane Meyer & Jill Abramson, Strange Justice: The Selling of Clarence Thomas (1994).

32. *See supra* chapter 3.

33. Brief for the Amici Curiae Women Who Have Had Abortions and Friends of Amici Curiae in Support of Appellees, Webster v. Reproductive Health Servs., 492 U.S. 490 (1989) (No. 88-605); Brief of Amici Curiae National Abortion Rights Action League et al., Thornburgh v. American College of Obstetricians & Gynecologists, 476 U.S. 747 (1985) (Nos. 84-495 & 84-1379).

34. Sarah Burns, *Notes from the Field: A Reply to Professor Colker*, 13 HARV. WOMEN'S L.J. 189, 197 (1990).

35. Robin L. West, *The Constitution of Reasons*, 92 MICH. L. REV. 1409, 1436 (1994).

36. *See* Marvin Lazerson & Ursula Wagener, *Missed Opportunities: Lessons from the Title IX Case at Brown*, CHANGE, July 17, 1996, at 46.

37. *Id.*

38. Cohen v. Brown Univ., 879 F. Supp. 185, 211 (D.R.I. 1995).

39. 101 F.3d 155 (1st Cir. 1996), *cert. denied*, 117 S. Ct. 1469 (1997).

40. *NCAA Title IX: A Local Analysis*, WASH. POST, Apr. 27, 1997, at D6.

41. Doug Bedell, *Women Make Small Gains*, DALLAS MORNING NEWS, Apr. 29, 1997, at 1B.

42. Michael Dobie, *Title IX: No Easy Answer*, NEWSDAY, Apr. 27, 1997, at B12.

43. Kevin B. Blackistone, *Courts Right Wrong of Gender Inequality*, DALLAS MORNING NEWS, Apr. 22, 1997, at 1B.

44. Jennifer Steinhauer, *Daughters Visit Work in Growing Numbers, but Backlash Builds*, N.Y. TIMES, Apr. 28, 1995, at A14.

45. Christina Hoff Sommers, *A Holiday Based on Ms. Information*, WALL ST. J., Apr. 10, 1995, at A20.

46. MARTHA MINOW, MAKING ALL THE DIFFERENCE: INCLUSION, EXCLUSION, AND AMERICAN LAW 3 (1990).

47. City of Cleburne v. Cleburne Living Ctr., Inc., 473 U.S. 432, 468–69 (1985) (Marshall, J., concurring in the judgment in part and dissenting in part).

48. Joseph H. Pleck, *The Theory of Male Sex-Role Identity: Its Rise and Fall, 1936 to the Present, in* THE MAKING OF MASCULINITIES, *supra* note 11, at 19.

49. AMERICAN PSYCHIATRIC ASSOCIATION, DIAGNOSTIC AND STATISTICAL MANUAL OF MENTAL DISORDERS 532 (4th ed. 1994), cited in Sonia Renee Martin, Note, *A Child's Right to Be Gay: Addressing the Emotional Maltreatment of Queer Youth*, 48 HASTINGS L.J. 167, 187 (1996).

50. *See, e.g.*, PHYLLIS BURKE, GENDER SHOCK: EXPLODING THE MYTHS OF MALE AND FEMALE 60–66 (1996); Valdes, *supra* note 3, at 85.

51. Pleck, *supra* note 48, at 37.

52. Deborrah E. S. Frable, *Gender, Racial, Ethnic, Sexual, and Class Identities*, 48 ANN. REV. PSYCHOL. 139 (Jan. 1, 1997).

53. *See* Frances Cerra Whitelsey, *SHOP! Information Services* (visited June 19, 1997) <http://www.sis.org/docs/hotoff.html>.

54. *See, e.g.,* DONALD G. MATHEWS & JANE S. DE HART, SEX, GENDER, AND THE POLITICS OF ERA: A STATE AND THE NATION 138–40 (1990) (describing resistance of military personnel to the Equal Rights Amendment); Sylvia A. Law, *Homosexuality and the Social Meaning of Gender*, 1988 WIS. L. REV. 187, 216 (discussing religiously based opposition to feminism).

55. Minow, *supra* note 2, at 68.

56. Charles R. Lawrence III, *The Id, the Ego, and Equal Protection: Reckoning with Unconscious Racism*, 39 STAN. L. REV. 317 (1987).

57. For example, the choice of terms like "domestic violence" (implicitly a private affair) or "spousal battery" (a real crime deserving of prosecution) may affect public responses.

Index

About the Author

Nancy Levit is a professor at the University of Missouri-Kansas City School of Law where she has taught Constitutional Law, Criminal Law, Gender and Justice, Jurisprudence, and Torts. She is coauthor of *Jurisprudence: Contemporary Readings, Problems, and Narratives.*